PHP AND MY-SQL A FULL BASICS & ADVANCED

BY ROBERT PETERSON

CONTENTS
PHP

MYSQL

3

iv

PHP Introduction

• PHP is a recursive acronym for "PHP: Hypertext Preprocessor" – It is a widely-used open source general-purpose scripting language that is especially suted for web development and can be embedded into HTML.

• > PHP is a server-side scripting language

• > PHP scripts are executed on the server

• > PHP supports many databases (MySQL, Informix, Oracle, Sybase, Solid, PostgreSQL, Generic ODBC, etc.)

• > PHP is open source software

• > PHP is free to download and use

- > PHP runs on different platforms (Windows, Linux, Unix, etc.)
- > PHP is compatible with almost all servers used today (Apache, IIS, etc.)
- > PHP is FREE to download from the official PHP resource: www.php.net
- > PHP is easy to learn and runs efficiently on the server side

- Some info on MySQL which we will cover in the next workshop...

- > MySQL is a database server

- > MySQL is ideal for both small and large applications
- > MySQL supports standard SQL

- > MySQL compiles on a number of platforms

- > MySQL is free to download and use

- Instead of lots of commands to output HTML (as seen in C or Perl), PHP pages contain HTML with embedded code that does "something" (like in the next slide, it outputs "Hi, I'm a PHP script!").

- The PHP code is enclosed in special start and end processing instructions <?php and ?> that allow you to jump into and out of "PHP mode."

```
<!DOCTYPE HTML PUBLIC "-//W3C//DTD HTML 4.01 Transitional//EN"
    "http://www.w3.org/TR/html4/loose.dtd">
<html>
    <head>
        <title>Example</title>
    </head>
    <body>

        <?php
            echo "Hi, I'm a PHP script!";
        ?>

    </body>
</html>
```

P code is executed on the server, generating HTML which is then sent to the client. The client would receive the results of running that script, but would not know what the underlying code was.

A visual, if you please...

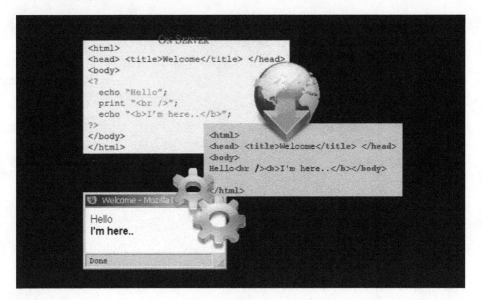

```
<html>
 <head>
  <title>PHP Test</title>
 </head>
 <body>
 <?php echo '<p>Hello World</p>'; ?>
 </body>
</html>
```

• Above is the PHP source code.

• It renders as HTML that looks like this:

```
<html>
 <head>
  <title>PHP Test</title>
 </head>
 <body>
 <p>Hello World</p>
 </body>
</html>
```

PHP Hello World

- This program is extremely simple and you really did not need to use PHP to create a page like this. All it does is display: Hello World using the PHP echo() statement.

- Think of this as a normal HTML file which happens to have a set of special tags available to you that do a lot of interesting things.

}In PHP, we use // to make
• single-line comment or /* and */ to make a large comment block.

```
<html>
<body>

<?php
//This is a comment

/*
This is
a comment
block
*/
?>

</body>
</html>
```

PHP Variables

}> Variables are used for storing values, like text strings, numbers or arrays.
}> When a variable is declared, it can be used over and over again in your script.
}> All variables in PHP start with a $ sign symbol. }> The correct way of declaring a variable in PHP:

```
$var_name = value;
```

PHP Variables

```php
<?php
$txt="Hello World!";
$x=16;
?>
```

}> In PHP, a variable does not need to be declared before adding a value to it.

}> In the example above, you see that you do not have to tell PHP which data type the variable is. }> PHP automatically converts the variable to the correct data type, depending on its value.

PHP Variables

• > A variable name must start with a letter or an underscore "_" – not a number
• > A variable name can only contain alpha-numeric characters, underscores (a-z, A-Z, 0-9, and _)
• > A variable name should not contain spaces. If a variable name is more than one word, it should be separated with an underscore ($my_string) or with capitalization ($myString)

• > The concatenation operator (.) is used to put two string values together.
• > To concatenate two string variables together, use the concatenation operator:

```php
<?php
$txt1="Hello World!";
$txt2="What a nice day!";
echo $txt1 . " " . $txt2;
?>
```

PHP Concatenation

• The output of the code on the last slide will be:

```
Hello World! What a nice day!
```

• If we look at the code you see that we used the concatenation operator two times. This is because we had to insert a third string (a space character), to separate the two strings.

• Operators are used to operate on values.
There are four classifications of operators:

- > Arithmetic
- > Assignment
- > Comparison
- > Logical

Arithmetic Operators

Operator	Description	Example	Result
+	Addition	x=2 x+2	4
-	Subtraction	x=2 5-x	3
*	Multiplication	x=4 x*5	20
/	Division	15/5 5/2	3 2.5
%	Modulus (division remainder)	5%2 10%8 10%2	1 2 0
++	Increment	x=5 x++	x=6
--	Decrement	x=5 x--	x=4

Assignment Operators

Operator	Example	Is The Same As
=	x=y	x=y
+=	x+=y	x=x+y
-=	x-=y	x=x-y
*=	x*=y	x=x*y
/=	x/=y	x=x/y
.=	x.=y	x=x.y
%=	x%=y	x=x%y

Comparison Operators

Operator	Description	Example
==	is equal to	5==8 returns false
!=	is not equal	5!=8 returns true
<>	is not equal	5<>8 returns true
>	is greater than	5>8 returns false
<	is less than	5<8 returns true
>=	is greater than or equal to	5>=8 returns false
<=	is less than or equal to	5<=8 returns true

Logical Operators

Operator	Description	Example
&&	and	x=6 y=3 (x < 10 && y > 1) returns true
||	or	x=6 y=3 (x==5 || y==5) returns false
!	not	x=6 y=3 !(x==y) returns true

PHP Conditional Statements

}> Very often when you write code, you want to perform different actions for different decisions. }> You can use conditional statements in your code to do this.
}> In PHP we have the following conditional statements...

PHP Conditional Statements

}> If statement - use this statement to execute some code only if a specified condition is true }> If...else statement - use this statement to execute some code if a condition is true and another code if the condition is false
}> If...elself....else statement - use this
statement to select one of several blocks of code to be executed
}> switch statement - use this statement to select one of many blocks of code to be executed

PHP Conditional Statements

• The following example will output "Have a nice weekend!" if the current day is Friday:

```php
<html>
<body>

<?php
$d=date("D");
if ($d=="Fri") echo "Have a nice weekend!";
?>

</body>
</html>
```

PHP Conditional Statements

}Use the **if....else** statement to execute some code if
a condition is true and another code if a condition is false.

```
<html>
<body>

<?php
$d=date("D");
if ($d=="Fri")
   echo "Have a nice weekend!";
else
   echo "Have a nice day!";
?>

</body>
</html>
```

• If more than one line should be executed if a condition is true/false, the lines should be enclosed within curly braces { }

```
<html>
<body>

<?php
$d=date("D");
if ($d=="Fri")
  {
  echo "Hello!<br />";
  echo "Have a nice weekend!";
  echo "See you on Monday!";
  }
?>

</body>
</html>
```

]The following example will output "Have a nice weekend!" if the current day is Friday, and "Have a nice Sunday!" if the current day is Sunday. Otherwise it will output "Have a nice day!":

```
<html>
<body>

<?php
$d=date("D");
if ($d=="Fri")
  echo "Have a nice weekend!";
elseif ($d=="Sun")
  echo "Have a nice Sunday!";
else
  echo "Have a nice day!";
?>

</body>
</html>
```

}Use the switch statement to select one of many blocks of code to be executed.

```
switch (n)
{
case label1:
  code to be executed if n=label1;
  break;
case label2:
  code to be executed if n=label2;
  break;
default:
  code to be executed if n is different from both label1 and label2;
}
```

PHP Conditional Statements

}For switches, first we have a single expression n (most often a variable), that is evaluated once.

}The value of the expression is then compared with the values for each case in the structure. If there is a match, the block of code associated with that case is executed.

}Use break to prevent the code from running into the next case automatically. The default statement is used if no match is found.

```
<html>
<body>

<?php
switch ($x)
{
case 1:
  echo "Number 1";
  break;
case 2:
  echo "Number 2";
  break;
case 3:
  echo "Number 3";
  break;
default:
  echo "No number between 1 and 3";
}
?>

</body>
</html>
```

PHP Arrays

• > An array variable is a storage area holding a number or text. The problem is, a variable will hold only one value.
• > An array is a special variable, which can store multiple values in one single variable.

PHP Arrays

• If you have a list of items (a list of car names, for example), storing the cars in single variables could look like this:

```
$cars1="Saab";
$cars2="Volvo";
$cars3="BMW";
```

PHP Arrays

• > However, what if you want to loop through the cars and find a specific one? And what if you had not 3 cars, but 300?

• > The best solution here is to use an array.

• > An array can hold all your variable values under a single name. And you can access the values by referring to the array name.

• > Each element in the array has its own index so that it can be easily accessed.

- In PHP, there are three kind of arrays:

- > Numeric array - An array with a numeric index
- > Associative array - An array where each ID key is associated with a value
- > Multidimensional array - An array containing one or more arrays

• > A numeric array stores each array element with a numeric index.
• > There are two methods to create a numeric array.

PHP Numeric Arrays

• In the following example the index is automatically assigned (the index starts at 0):

```
$cars=array("Saab","Volvo","BMW","Toyota");
```

• In the following example we assign the index manually:

```
$cars[0]="Saab";
$cars[1]="Volvo";
$cars[2]="BMW";
$cars[3]="Toyota";
```

PHP Numeric Arrays

• In the following example you access the variable values by referring to the array name and index:

```php
<?php
$cars[0]="Saab";
$cars[1]="Volvo";
$cars[2]="BMW";
$cars[3]="Toyota";
echo $cars[0] . " and " . $cars[1] . " are Swedish cars.";
?>
```

• The code above will output:

```
Saab and Volvo are Swedish cars.
```

• > With an associative array, each ID key is associated with a value.
• > When storing data about specific named values, a numerical array is not always the best way to do it.
• > With associative arrays we can use the values as keys and assign values to them.

PHP Associative Arrays

• In this example we use an array to assign ages to the different persons:

```php
$ages = array("Peter"=>32, "Quagmire"=>30, "Joe"=>34);
```

• This example is the same as the one above, but shows a different way of creating the array:

```php
$ages['Peter'] = "32";
$ages['Quagmire'] = "30";
$ages['Joe'] = "34";
```

The ID keys can be used in a script:

```php
<?php
$ages['Peter'] = "32";
$ages['Quagmire'] = "30";
$ages['Joe'] = "34";

echo "Peter is " . $ages['Peter'] . " years old.";
?>
```

The code above will output:

```
Peter is 32 years old.
```

PHP Multidimensional Arrays

- In a multidimensional array, each element in the main array can also be an array.

- And each element in the sub-array can be an array, and so on.

In this example we create a multidimensional array, with automatically assigned ID keys:

```
$families = array
  (
  "Griffin"=>array
  (
  "Peter",
  "Lois",
  "Megan"
  ),
  "Quagmire"=>array
  (
  "Glenn"
  ),
  "Brown"=>array
  (
  "Cleveland",
  "Loretta",
  "Junior"
  )
  );
```

The array above would look like this if written to the output:

```
Array
(
[Griffin] => Array
   (
   [0] => Peter
   [1] => Lois
   [2] => Megan
   )
[Quagmire] => Array
   (
   [0] => Glenn
   )
[Brown] => Array
   (
   [0] => Cleveland
   [1] => Loretta
   [2] => Junior
   )
)
```

Lets try displaying a single value from the array above:

```php
echo "Is " . $families['Griffin'][2] .
" a part of the Griffin family?";
```

The code above will output:

```
Is Megan a part of the Griffin family?
```

PHP Loops

• > Often when you write code, you want the same block of code to run over and over again in a row. Instead of adding several almost equal lines in a script we can use loops to perform a task like this.

• > In PHP, we have the following looping statements:

- > while - loops through a block of code while a specified condition is true
- > do...while - loops through a block of code once, and then repeats the loop as long as a specified condition is true
- > for - loops through a block of code a specified number of times
- > foreach - loops through a block of code for each element in an array

The while loop executes a block of code while a condition is true. The example below defines a loop that starts with i=1. The loop will continue to run as long as i is less than, or equal to 5. i will increase by 1 each time the loop runs:

```
<html>
<body>

<?php
$i=1;
while($i<=5)
  {
  echo "The number is " . $i . "<br />";
  $i++;
  }
?>

</body>
</html>
```

Output:

```
The number is 1
The number is 2
The number is 3
The number is 4
The number is 5
```

PHP Loops – Do ... While

• The do...while statement will always execute the block of code once, it will then check the condition, and repeat the loop while the condition is true.

• The next example defines a loop that starts with i=1. It will then increment i with 1, and write some output. Then the condition is checked, and the loop will continue to run as long as i is less than, or equal to 5:

```
<html>
<body>

<?php
$i=1;
do
  {
  $i++;
  echo "The number is " . $i . "<br />";
  }
while ($i<=5);
?>

</body>
</html>
```

Output:

```
The number is 2
The number is 3
The number is 4
The number is 5
The number is 6
```

The for loop is used when you know in advance how many times the script should run.

Syntax

```
for (init; condition; increment)
  {
  code to be executed;
  }
```

PHP Loops - For

]Parameters:
}> Init: Mostly used to set a counter (but can be any code to be executed once at the beginning of the loop)
}> condition: Evaluated for each loop iteration. If it evaluates to TRUE, the loop continues. If it evaluates to FALSE, the loop ends.
}> Increment: Mostly used to increment a counter (but can be any code to be executed at the end of the loop)

PHP Loops - For

• The example below defines a loop that starts with i=1. The loop will continue to run as long as i is less than, or equal to 5. i will increase by 1 each time the loop runs:

```
<html>
<body>

<?php
for ($i=1; $i<=5; $i++)
  {
  echo "The number is " . $i . "<br />";
  }
?>

</body>
</html>
```

Output:

```
The number is 1
The number is 2
The number is 3
The number is 4
The number is 5
```

```
foreach ($array as $value)
    {
    code to be executed;
    }
```

}For every loop iteration, the value of the current array element is assigned to $value (and the array pointer is moved by one) - so on the next loop iteration, you'll be looking at the next array value.

PHP Loops - Foreach

• The following example demonstrates a loop that will print the values of the given array:

```php
<html>
<body>

<?php
$x=array("one","two","three");
foreach ($x as $value)
    {
    echo $value . "<br />";
    }
?>

</body>
</html>
```

• Winner of the most impressive slide award

Output:

```
one
two
three
```

• > We will now explore how to create your own functions.
• > To keep the script from being executed when the page loads, you can put it into a function.
• > A function will be executed by a call to the function.
• > You may call a function from anywhere within a page.

PHP Functions

}A function will be executed by a call to the function.

```
function functionName()
{
code to be executed;
}
```

}> Give the function a name that reflects what the function does
}> The function name can start with a letter or underscore (not a number)

PHP Functions

}A simple function that writes a name when it is called:

```php
<html>
<body>

<?php
function writeName()
{
echo "Kai Jim Refsnes";
}

echo "My name is ";
writeName();
?>

</body>
</html>
```

- Adding parameters...
- > To add more functionality to a function, we can add parameters. A parameter is just like a variable.
- > Parameters are specified after the function name, inside the parentheses.

The following example will write different first names, but equal last name:

```
<html>
<body>

<?php
function writeName($fname)
{
echo $fname . " Refsnes.<br />";
}

echo "My name is ";
writeName("Kai Jim");
echo "My sister's name is ";
writeName("Hege");
echo "My brother's name is ";
writeName("Stale");
?>

</body>
</html>
```

Output:

```
My name is Kai Jim Refsnes.
My sister's name is Hege Refsnes.
My brother's name is Stale Refsnes.
```

```
<html>
<body>

<?php
function writeName($fname,$punctuation)
{
echo $fname . " Refsnes" . $punctuation . "<br />";
}

echo "My name is ";
writeName("Kai Jim",".");
echo "My sister's name is ";
writeName("Hege","!");
echo "My brother's name is ";
writeName("Ståle","?");
?>

</body>
</html>
```

This example adds different punctuation.

Output:

```
My name is Kai Jim Refsnes.
My sister's name is Hege Refsnes!
My brother's name is Ståle Refsnes?
```

• > The built-in $_GET function is used to collect values from a form sent with method="get".
• > Information sent from a form with the GET method is visible to everyone (it will be displayed in the browser's address bar) and has limits on the amount of information to send (max. 100 characters).

```
<form action="welcome.php" method="get">
Name: <input type="text" name="fname" />
Age: <input type="text" name="age" />
<input type="submit" />
</form>
```

```
http://www.w3schools.com/welcome.php?fname=Peter&age=37
```

Notice how the URL carries the information after the file name.

```
Welcome <?php echo $_GET["fname"]; ?>.<br />
You are <?php echo $_GET["age"]; ?> years old!
```

}The "welcome.php" file can now use the $_GET function to collect form data (the names of the form fields will automatically be the keys in the $_GET array)

```
Welcome <?php echo $_GET["fname"]; ?>.<br />
You are <?php echo $_GET["age"]; ?> years old!
```

Chapter 1. Introduction

Table of Contents

What is PHP?

PHP (recursive acronym for "PHP: Hypertext Preprocessor") is a widely-used Open Source general-purpose scripting lan-guage that is especially suited for Web development and can be embedded into HTML.

Simple answer, but what does that mean? An example:

Example 1.1. An introductory example

```html
<html>
    <head>
        <title>Example</title>
    </head>
    <body>

        <?php
        echo "Hi, I'm a PHP script!";
        ?>

    </body>
</html>
```

Notice how this is different from a script written in other languages like Perl or C – instead of writing a program with lots of commands to output HTML, you write an HTML script with some embedded code to do something (in this case, output some text). The PHP code is enclosed in special start and end tags that allow you to jump into and out of "PHP mode".

What distinguishes PHP from something like client-side JavaScript is that the code is executed on the server. If you were to have a script similar to the above on your server, the client would receive the results of running that script, with no way of determining what the underlying code may be. You can even configure your web server to process all your HTML files with PHP, and then there's really no way that users can tell what you have up your sleeve.

The best things in using PHP are that it is extremely simple for a newcomer, but offers many advanced features for a profes-sional programmer. Don't be afraid reading the long list of PHP's features. You can jump in, in a short time, and start writ-ing simple scripts in a few hours.

Although PHP's development is focused on server-side scripting, you can do much more with it. Read on, and see more in the What can PHP do? section.

What can PHP do?

Anything. PHP is mainly focused on server-side scripting, so you can do anything any other CGI program can do, such as collect form data, generate dynamic page content, or send and receive cookies. But PHP can do much more.

2

There are three main fields where PHP scripts are used.

- Server-side scripting. This is the most traditional and main target field for PHP. You need three things to make this work. The PHP parser (CGI or server module), a webserver and a web browser. You need to run the webserver, with a connected PHP installation. You can access the PHP program output with a web browser, viewing the PHP page through the server. See the installation instructions section for more information.

- Command line scripting. You can make a PHP script to run it without any server or browser. You only need the PHP parser to use it this way. This type of usage is ideal for scripts regularly executed using cron (on *nix or Linux) or Task Scheduler (on Windows). These scripts can also be used for simple text processing tasks. See the section about Com-mand line usage of PHP for more information.

- Writing client-side GUI applications. PHP is probably not the very best language to write windowing applications, but if you know PHP very well, and would like to use some advanced PHP features in your client-side applications you can also use PHP-GTK to write such programs. You also have the ability to write cross-platform applications this way. PHP-GTK is an extension to PHP, not available in the main distribution. If you are interested in PHP-GTK, visit its own web-site [http://gtk.php.net/].

PHP can be used on all major operating systems, including Linux, many Unix variants (including HP-UX, Solaris and OpenBSD), Microsoft Windows, Mac OS X, RISC OS, and probably others. PHP has also support for most of the web serv-ers today. This includes Apache, Microsoft Internet Information Server, Personal Web Server, Netscape and iPlanet servers, Oreilly Website Pro server, Caudium, Xitami, OmniHTTPd, and many others. For the majority of the servers PHP has a module, for the others supporting the CGI standard, PHP can work as a CGI processor.

So with PHP, you have the freedom of choosing an operating system and a web server. Furthermore, you also have the choice of using procedural programming or object oriented programming, or a mixture of them. Although not every stand-ard OOP feature is realized in the current version of PHP, many code libraries and large applications (including the PEAR library) are written only using OOP code.

With PHP you are not limited to output HTML. PHP's abilities includes outputting images, PDF files and even Flash movies (using libswf and Ming) generated on the fly. You can also output easily any text, such as XHTML and any other XML file. PHP can autogenerate these files, and save them in the file system, instead of printing it out, forming a server-side cache for your dynamic content.

One of the strongest and most significant feature in PHP is its support for a wide range of databases. Writing a database-en-abled web page is incredibly simple. The following databases are currently supported:

Adabas D	Ingres	Oracle(OCI7and OCI8)
dBase	InterBase	Ovrimos
Empress	FrontBase	PostgreSQL
FilePro (read-only)	mSQL	Solid
Hyperwave	Direct MS-SQL	Sybase
IBM DB2	MySQL	Velocis
Informix	ODBC	Unix dbm

We also have a DBX database abstraction extension allowing you to transparently use any database supported by that exten-sion. Additionally PHP supports ODBC, the Open Database Connection standard, so you can connect to any other database supporting this world standard.

PHP also has support for talking to other services using protocols such as LDAP, IMAP, SNMP, NNTP, POP3, HTTP, COM (on Windows) and countless others. You can also open raw network sockets and interact using any other protocol. PHP has support for the WDDX complex data exchange between virtually all Web programming languages. Talking about interconnection, PHP has support for instantiation of Java objects and using them transparently as PHP objects. You can also use our CORBA extension to access remote objects.

PHP has extremely useful text processing features, from the POSIX Extended or Perl regular expressions to parsing XML

documents. For parsing and accessing XML documents, we support the SAX and DOM standards. You can use our XSLT extension to transform XML documents.

While using PHP in the ecommerce field, you'll find the Cybercash payment, CyberMUT, VeriSign Payflow Pro and CCVS functions useful for your online payment programs.

At last but not least, we have many other interesting extensions, the mnoGoSearch search engine functions, the IRC Gate-way functions, many compression utilities (gzip, bz2), calendar conversion, translation...

As you can see this page is not enough to list all the features and benefits PHP can offer. Read on in the sections about in-stalling PHP, and see the function reference part for explanation of the extensions mentioned here.

Chapter 2. A simple tutorial

Table of Contents

Here we would like to show the very basics of PHP in a short simple tutorial. This text only deals with dynamic webpage creation with PHP, though PHP is not only capable of creating webpages. See the section titled What can PHP do for more information.

PHP-enabled web pages are treated just like regular HTML pages and you can create and edit them the same way you nor-mally create regular HTML pages.

What do I need?

In this tutorial we assume that your server has support for PHP activated and that all files ending in .php are handled by PHP. On most servers this is the default extension for PHP files, but ask your server administrator to be sure. If your server supports PHP then you don't need to do anything. Just create your .php files and put them in your web directory and the server will magically parse them for you. There is no need to compile anything nor do you need to install any extra tools. Think of these PHP-enabled files as simple HTML files with a whole new family of magical tags that let you do all sorts of things. Most web hosts offer PHP support but if your host doesn't consider reading the PHP Links [http:/ / www.php.net/ links.php] section for resources on finding PHP enabled web hosts.

Let's say you want to save precious bandwidth and develop locally. In this case, you'll want to install a web server, such as Apache, and of course PHP [http://www.php.net/downloads.php]. You'll most likely want to install a database as well, such as MySQL [http://www.mysql.com/documentation/]. You can install these individually or a simpler way is to locate a pre-configured package [http://www.hotscripts.com/PHP/Software_and_Servers/Installation_Kits/] that automatically installs all of these with just a few mouse clicks. It's easy to setup a web server with PHP support on any operating system, including Linux and Windows. In linux, you may find rpmfind [http://www.rpmfind.net/] helpful for locating RPMs.

Your first PHP-enabled page

Create a file named hello.php and put it in your web servers root directory (DOCUMENT_ROOT) with the following content:

Example 2.1. Our first PHP script: hello.php

```
<html>
 <head>
  <title>PHP Test</title>
 </head>
 <body>
 <?php echo "<p>Hello World</p>"; ?>
 </body>
</html>
```

5

Use your browser to access the file with your web access URL, ending with the "/hello.php" file reference. When develop-ing locally this url will be something like http://localhost/hello.php or http://127.0.0.1/hello.php but this depends on the web servers configuration. Although this is outside the scope of this tutorial, see also the DocumentRoot and ServerName directives in your web servers configuration file. (on Apache this is httpd.conf). If everything is setup correctly, this file will be parsed by PHP and the following output will make it to your browser:

```
<html>
  <head>
   <title>PHP Test</title>
  </head>
  <body>
  <p>Hello World</p>
  </body>
</html>
```

Note that this is not like a CGI script. The file does not need to be executable or special in any way. Think of it as a normal HTML file which happens to have a set of special tags available to you that do a lot of interesting things.

This program is extremely simple and you really didn't need to use PHP to create a page like this. All it does is display:
Hello World using the PHP **echo()** statement.

If you tried this example and it didn't output anything, or it prompted for download, or you see the whole file as text, chances are that the server you are on does not have PHP enabled. Ask your administrator to enable it for you using the In-stallation chapter of the manual. If you're developing locally, also read the installation chapter to make sure everything is configured properly. If problems continue to persist, don't hesitate to use one of the many PHP support [http://www.php.net/ support.php] options.

The point of the example is to show the special PHP tag format. In this example we used <?php to indicate the start of a PHP tag. Then we put the PHP statement and left PHP mode by adding the closing tag, ?>. You may jump in and out of PHP mode in an HTML file like this all you want. For more details, read the manual section on basic PHP syntax.

A Note on Text Editors: There are many text editors and Integrated Development Environments (IDEs) that you can use to create, edit and manage PHP files. A partial list of these tools is maintained at PHP Editor's List [http:// phpeditors.dancinghippo.com/]. If you wish to recommend an editor, please visit the above page and ask the page maintainer to add the editor to the list. Having an editor with syntax highlighting can be helpful.

A Note on Word Processors: Word processors such as StarOffice Writer, Microsoft Word and Abiword are not good choices for editing PHP files. If you wish to use one for this test script, you must ensure that you save the file as PLAIN TEXT or PHP will not be able to read and execute the script.

A Note on Windows Notepad: If you are writing your PHP scripts using Windows Notepad, you will need to en-sure that your files are saved with the .php extension. (Notepad adds a .txt extension to files automatically unless you take one of the following steps to prevent it.) When you save the file and are prompted to provide a name for the file, place the filename in quotes (i.e. "hello.php"). Alternately, you can click on the 'Text Documents' drop-down menu in the save dialog box and change the setting to "All Files". You can then enter your filename without quotes.

Now that you've successfully created a simple PHP script that works, it's time to create the most famous PHP script! Make a call to the **phpinfo()** function and you'll see a lot of useful information about your system and setup such as available Pre-defined Variables, loaded PHP modules, and configuration settings. Take some time and review this important information.

Something Useful

Let's do something a bit more useful now. We are going to check what sort of browser the person viewing the page is using. In order to do that we check the user agent string that the browser sends as part of its HTTP request. This information is stored in a variable. Variables always start with a dollar-sign in PHP. The variable we are interested in right now is

---

$_SERVER["HTTP_USER_AGENT"].

PHP Autoglobals Note: $_SERVER is a special reserved PHP variable that contains all web server information. It's known as an Autoglobal (or Superglobal). See the related manual page on Autoglobals for more information. These special variables were introduced in PHP 4.1.0 [http:/ / www.php.net/ release_4_1_0.php]. Before this time, we used the older $HTTP_*_VARS arrays instead, such as $HTTP_SERVER_VARS. Although deprecated, these older variables still exist. (See also the note on old code.)

To display this variable, we can simply do:

Example 2.2. Printing a variable (Array element)

```php
<?php echo $_SERVER["HTTP_USER_AGENT"]; ?>
```

A sample output of this script may be:

Mozilla/4.0 (compatible; MSIE 5.01; Windows NT 5.0)

There are many types of variables available in PHP. In the above example we printed an Array element. Arrays can be very useful.

$_SERVER is just one variable that's automatically made available to you by PHP. A list can be seen in the Reserved Vari-ables section of the manual or you can get a complete list of them by creating a file that looks like this:

Example 2.3. Show all predefined variables with phpinfo()

```php
<?php phpinfo(); ?>
```

If you load up this file in your browser you will see a page full of information about PHP along with a list of all the vari-ables available to you.

You can put multiple PHP statements inside a PHP tag and create little blocks of code that do more than just a single echo.
For example, if we wanted to check for Internet Explorer we could do something like this:

Example 2.4. Example using control structures and functions

```php
<?php
if (strstr($_SERVER["HTTP_USER_AGENT"], "MSIE")) { echo "You
        are using Internet Explorer<br />";
}
?>
```

A sample output of this script may be:

You are using Internet Explorer

Here we introduce a couple of new concepts. We have an if statement. If you are familiar with the basic syntax used by the C language this should look logical to you. If you don't know enough C or some other language where the syntax used above is used, you should probably pick up any introductory PHP book and read the first couple of chapters, or read the Language Reference part of the manual. You can find a list of PHP books at http://www.php.net/books.php.

The second concept we introduced was the **strstr()** function call. **strstr()** is a function built into PHP which searches a string for another string. In this case we are looking for "MSIE" inside $_SERVER["HTTP_USER_AGENT"]. If the string is found, the function returns TRUE and if it isn't, it returns FALSE. If it returns TRUE, the if statement evaluates to TRUE and the code within its {braces} is executed. Otherwise, it's not. Feel free to create similar examples, with if, else, and other functions such as **strtoupper()** and **strlen()**. Each related manual page contains examples too. If you're unsure how to use functions, you'll want to read both the manual page on how to read a function definition and the section about PHP func-tions.

We can take this a step further and show how you can jump in and out of PHP mode even in the middle of a PHP block:

Example 2.5. Mixing both HTML and PHP modes

```
<?php
if (strstr($_SERVER["HTTP_USER_AGENT"], "MSIE")) { ?>
<h3>strstr must have returned true</h3>
<center><b>You are using Internet Explorer</b></center> <?php
} else { ?>
<h3>strstr must have returned false</h3>
<center><b>You are not using Internet Explorer</b></center> <?php
}
?>
```

A sample output of this script may be:

```
<h3>strstr must have returned true</h3>
<center><b>You are using Internet Explorer</b></center>
```

Instead of using a PHP echo statement to output something, we jumped out of PHP mode and just sent straight HTML. The important and powerful point to note here is that the logical flow of the script remains intact. Only one of the HTML blocks will end up getting sent to the viewer depending on if **strstr()** returned TRUE or FALSE In other words, if the string MSIE was found or not.

Dealing with Forms

One of the most powerful features of PHP is the way it handles HTML forms. The basic concept that is important to under-stand is that any form element in a form will automatically be available to your PHP scripts. Please read the manual section on Variables from outside of PHP for more information and examples on using forms with PHP. Here's an example HTML form:

Example 2.6. A simple HTML form

```
<form action="action.php" method="POST">
 Your name: <input type="text" name="name" />
 Your age: <input type="text" name="age" />
 <input type="submit">
</form>
```

There is nothing special about this form. It is a straight HTML form with no special tags of any kind. When the user fills in this form and hits the submit button, the action.php page is called. In this file you would have something like this:

8

Example 2.7. Printing data from our form

Hi <?php echo $_POST["name"]; ?>.
You are <?php echo $_POST["age"]; ?> years old.

A sample output of this script may be:

Hi Joe.
You are 22 years old.

It should be obvious what this does. There is nothing more to it. The $_POST["name"] and $_POST["age"] variables are automatically set for you by PHP. Earlier we used the $_SERVER autoglobal, now above we just introduced the $_POST autoglobal which contains all POST data. Notice how the *method* of our form is POST. If we used the method *GET* then our form information would live in the $_GET autoglobal instead. You may also use the $_REQUEST autoglobal if you don't care the source of your request data. It contains a mix of GET, POST, COOKIE and FILE data. See also the **im-port_request_variables()** function.

Using old code with new versions of PHP

Now that PHP has grown to be a popular scripting language, there are more resources out there that have listings of code you can reuse in your own scripts. For the most part the developers of the PHP language have tried to be backwards compat-ible, so a script written for an older version should run (ideally) without changes in a newer version of PHP, in practice some changes will usually be needed.

Two of the most important recent changes that affect old code are:

*   The deprecation of the old $HTTP_*_VARS arrays (which need to be indicated as global when used inside a function or method). The following autoglobal arrays were introduced in PHP 4.1.0 [http://www.php.net/release_4_1_0.php]. They are: $_GET, $_POST, $_COOKIE, $_SERVER, $_ENV, $_REQUEST, and $_SESSION. The older $HTTP_*_VARS arrays, such as $HTTP_POST_VARS, still exist and have since PHP 3.

*   External variables are no longer registered in the global scope by default. In other words, as of PHP 4.2.0 [http:/ / www.php.net/release_4_2_0.php] the PHP directive register_globals is *off* by default in php.ini. The preferred method of accessing these values is via the autoglobal arrays mentioned above. Older scripts, books, and tutorials may rely on this directive being on. If on, for example, one could use $id from the URL ht-tp://www.example.com/foo.php?id=42. Whether on or off, $_GET['id'] is available.

For more details on these changes, see the section on predefined variables and links therein.

What's next?

With what you know now you should be able to understand most of the manual and also the various example scripts avail-able in the example archives. You can also find other examples on the php.net websites in the links section: http:/ / www.php.net/links.php.

To view various slide presentations that show more of what PHP can do, see the PHP Conference Material Sites: http:/ / conf.php.net/and http://talks.php.net/

9

Chapter 3. Installation

Table of Contents

General Installation Considerations

Before installing first, you need to know what do you want to use PHP for. There are three main fields you can use PHP, as described in the What can PHP do? section:

- Server-side scripting

- Command line scripting

- Client-side GUI applications

For the first and most common form, you need three things: PHP itself, a web server and a web browser. You probably already have a web browser, and depending on your operating system setup, you may also have a web server (eg. Apache on Linux or IIS on Windows). You may also rent webspace at a company. This way, you don't need to set up anything on your own, only write your PHP scripts, upload it to the server you rent, and see the results in your browser.

While setting up the server and PHP on your own, you have two choices for the method of connecting PHP to the server. For many servers PHP has a direct module interface (also called SAPI). These servers include Apache, Microsoft Internet Information Server, Netscape and iPlanet servers. Many other servers have support for ISAPI, the Microsoft module inter-face (OmniHTTPd for example). If PHP has no module support for your web server, you can always use it as a CGI pro-cessor. This means you set up your server to use the command line executable of PHP (php.exe on Windows) to process all PHP file requests on the server.

10

If you are also interested to use PHP for command line scripting (eg. write scripts autogenerating some images for you off-line, or processing text files depending on some arguments you pass to them), you always need the command line execut-able. For more information, read the section about writing command line PHP applications. In this case, you need no server and no browser.

With PHP you can also write client side GUI applications using the PHP-GTK extension. This is a completely different ap-proach than writing web pages, as you do not output any HTML, but manage windows and objects within them. For more information about PHP-GTK, please visit the site dedicated to this extension [http://gtk.php.net/]. PHP-GTK is not included in the official PHP distribution.

From now on, this section deals with setting up PHP for web servers on Unix and Windows with server module interfaces and CGI executables.

Downloading PHP, the source code, and binary distributions for Windows can be found at http://www.php.net/. We recom-mend you to choose a mirror [http://www.php.net/mirrors.php] nearest to you for downloading the distributions.

Unix/HP-UX installs

This section contains notes and hints specific to installing PHP on HP-UX systems.

Example 3.1. Installation Instructions for HP-UX 10

From: paul_mckay@clearwater-it.co.uk
04-Jan-2001 09:49
(These tips are for PHP 4.0.4 and Apache v1.3.9)

So you want to install PHP and Apache on a HP-UX 10.20 box?

• You need gzip, download a binary distribution from
http://hpux.connect.org.uk/ftp/hpux/Gnu/gzip-1.2.4a/gzip-1.2.4a-sd-10.20.depot.Z
uncompress the file and install using swinstall

• You need gcc, download a binary distribution from
http://gatekeep.cs.utah.edu/ftp/hpux/Gnu/gcc-2.95.2/gcc-2.95.2-sd-10.20.depot.gz gunzip
this file and install gcc using swinstall.

• You need the GNU binutils, you can download a binary distribution from
http://hpux.connect.org.uk/ftp/hpux/Gnu/binutils-2.9.1/binutils-2.9.1-sd-10.20.depot.gz gunzip and
install using swinstall.

• You now need bison, you can download a binary distribution from
http://hpux.connect.org.uk/ftp/hpux/Gnu/bison-1.28/bison-1.28-sd-10.20.depot.gz install as
above.

• You now need flex, you need to download the source from one of the
http://www.gnu.org mirrors. It is in the non-gnu directory of the ftp site. Download the file,
gunzip, then tar -xvf it. Go into the newly created flex directory and do a ./configure, then a
make, and then a make install

If you have errors here, it's probably because gcc etc. are not in your PATH so add
them to your PATH.

Right, now into the hard stuff.

• Download the PHP and apache sources.

• gunzip and tar -xvf them.

We need to hack a couple of files so that they can compile ok.

>>> Firstly the configure file needs to be hacked because it seems to lose track of
the fact that you are a hpux machine, there will be a
better way of doing this but a cheap and cheerful hack is to put
  lt_target=hpux10.20

85

11

- Next, the Apache GuessOS file needs to be hacked. Under apache_1.3.9/src/helpers change line 89 from
    "echo "hp${HPUXMACH}-hpux${HPUXVER}"; exit 0"
to:
    "echo "hp${HPUXMACH}-hp-hpux${HPUXVER}"; exit 0"

- You cannot install PHP as a shared object under HP-UX so you must compile it as a static, just follow the instructions at the Apache page.

- PHP and apache should have compiled OK, but Apache won't start. you need to create a new user for Apache, eg www, or apache. You then change lines 252 and 253 of the conf/httpd.conf in Apache so that instead of
    User nobody
    Group nogroup
you have something like
    User www
    Group sys

This is because you can't run Apache as nobody under hp-ux.
Apache and PHP should then work.

Hope this helps somebody,
Paul Mckay.

Unix/Linux installs

This section contains notes and hints specific to installing PHP on Linux distributions.

Using Packages

Many Linux distributions have some sort of package installation system, such as RPM. This can assist in setting up a stand-ard configuration, but if you need to have a different set of features (such as a secure server, or a different database driver), you may need to build PHP and/or your webserver. If you are unfamiliar with building and compiling your own software, it is worth checking to see whether somebody has already built a packaged version of PHP with the features you need.

Unix/Mac OS X installs

This section contains notes and hints specific to installing PHP on Mac OS X Server.

Using Packages

There are a few pre-packaged and pre-compiled versions of PHP for Mac OS X. This can help in setting up a standard con-figuration, but if you need to have a different set of features (such as a secure server, or a different database driver), you may need to build PHP and/or your web server yourself. If you are unfamiliar with building and compiling your own soft-ware, it's worth checking whether somebody has already built a packaged version of PHP with the features you need.

Compiling for OS X server

There are two slightly different versions of Mac OS X, client and server. The following is for OS X Server.

Example 3.2. Mac OS X server install

- Get the latest distributions of Apache and PHP
- Untar them, and run the configure program on Apache like so.
    ./configure –exec-prefix=/usr \ –
    localstatedir=/var \

12

```
   –mandir=/usr/share/man \
   –libexecdir=/System/Library/Apache/Modules \
   –iconsdir=/System/Library/Apache/Icons \
   –includedir=/System/Library/Frameworks/Apache.framework/Versions/1.3/Headers \
   –enable-shared=max \
   –enable-module=most \
   –target=apache
```

- You may also want to add this line: setenv
  OPTIM=–O2
  If you want the compiler to do some optimization.

- Next, go to the PHP 4 source directory and configure it.
  ./configure –prefix=/usr \ –
  sysconfdir=/etc \ –localstatedir=/var
  \ –mandir=/usr/share/man \ –with-
  xml \ –with-
  apache=/src/apache_1.3.12

  If you have any other additions (MySQL, GD, etc.), be sure to add them here.
  For the –with-apache string, put in the path to your apache source directory,
  for example "/src/apache_1.3.12".
- make
- make install
  This will add a directory to your Apache source directory under
  src/modules/php4.

- Now, reconfigure Apache to build in PHP 4.
  ./configure –exec-prefix=/usr \ –localstatedir=/var \ –
  mandir=/usr/share/man \ –
  libexecdir=/System/Library/Apache/Modules \ –
  iconsdir=/System/Library/Apache/Icons \
  –includedir=/System/Library/Frameworks/Apache.framework/Versions/1.3/Headers \ –
  enable-shared=max \
  –enable-module=most \ –
  target=apache \
  –activate-module=src/modules/php4/libphp4.a

  You may get a message telling you that libmodphp4.a is out of date. If so, go to
  the src/modules/php4 directory inside your apache source directory and run this
  command:

  ranlib libmodphp4.a

  Then go back to the root of the apache source directory and run the above
  configure command again. That'll bring the link table up to date.

- make

- make install

- copy and rename the php.ini-dist file to your "bin" directory from your PHP 4 source
  directory:
  cp php.ini-dist /usr/local/bin/php.ini

  or (if your don't have a local directory) cp php.ini-

  dist /usr/bin/php.ini

Compiling for MacOS X client

Those tips are graciously provided by Marc Liyanage [http://www.entropy.ch/software/macosx/].

The PHP module for the Apache web server included in Mac OS X. This version includes support for the MySQL
and Post-

greSQL databases.

NOTE: Be careful when you do this, you could screw up your Apache web server!

Do this to install:

- 1. Open a terminal window

- 2. Type "wget http://www.diax.ch/users/liyanage/software/macosx/libphp4.so.gz", wait for download to finish

- 3. Type "gunzip libphp4.so.gz"

- 4. Type "sudo apxs -i -a -n php4 libphp4.so"

Now type "sudo open -a TextEdit /etc/httpd/httpd.conf" TextEdit will open with the web server configuration file. Locate these two lines towards the end of the file: (Use the Find command)

```
#AddType application/x-httpd-php .php
   #AddType application/x-httpd-php-source .phps
```

Remove the two hash marks (#), then save the file and quit TextEdit.

Finally, type "sudo apachectl graceful" to restart the web server.

PHP should now be up and running. You can test it by dropping a file into your "Sites" folder which is called "test.php". In-to that file, write this line: "<?php phpinfo() ?>".

Now open up 127.0.0.1/~your_username/test.php in your web browser. You should see a status table with informa-tion about the PHP module.

Unix/OpenBSD installs

This section contains notes and hints specific to installing PHP on OpenBSD 3.2 [http://www.openbsd.org/].

Using Binary Packages

Using binary packages to install PHP on OpenBSD is the recommended and simplest method. The core package has been separated from the various modules, and each can be installed and removed independently from the others. The files you need can be found on your OpenBSD CD or on the FTP site.

The main package you need to install is php4-core-4.2.3.tgz, which contains the basic engine (plus gettext and iconv). Next, take a look at the module packages, such as php4-mysql-4.2.3.tgz or php4-imap-4.2.3.tgz. You need to use the **phpxs** command to activate and deactivate these modules in your php.ini.

Example 3.3. OpenBSD Package Install Example

```
>>>     pkg_add php4-core-4.2.3.tgz
>>>     /usr/local/sbin/phpxs -s
>>>     cp /usr/local/share/doc/php4/php.ini-recommended /var/www/conf/php.ini
  (add in mysql)
>>>     pkg_add php4-mysql-4.2.3.tgz
>>>     /usr/local/sbin/phpxs -a
  mysql (add in imap)
>>>     pkg_add php4-imap-4.2.3.tgz
>>>     /usr/local/sbin/phpxs -a
  imap (remove mysql as a test)
>>>     pkg_delete php4-mysql-4.2.3
>>>     /usr/local/sbin/phpxs -r
  mysql (install the PEAR libraries)
```

14

```
# pkg_add php4-pear-4.2.3.tgz
```

Read the packages(7) [http://www.openbsd.org/cgi-bin/man.cgi?query=packages] manual page for more information about binary packages on OpenBSD.

Using Ports

You can also compile up PHP from source using the ports tree [http://www.openbsd.org/ports.html]. However, this is only recommended for users familiar with OpenBSD. The PHP4 port is split into three sub-directories: core, extensions and pear. The extensions directory generates sub-packages for all of the supported PHP modules. If you find you do not want to create some of these modules, use the **no_*** FLAVOR. For example, to skip building the imap module, set the FLAVOR to **no_imap**.

Older Releases

Older releases of OpenBSD used the FLAVORS system to compile up a statically linked PHP. Since it is hard to generate binary packages using this method, it is now deprecated. You can still use the old stable ports trees if you wish, but they are unsupported by the OpenBSD team. If you have any comments about this, the current maintainer for the port is Anil Madhavapeddy [mailto:avsm@openbsd.org].

Unix/Solaris installs

This section contains notes and hints specific to installing PHP on Solaris systems.

Required software

Solaris installs often lack C compilers and their related tools. The required software is as follows:

>>>   gcc (recommended, other C compilers may work)

>>>   make

>>>   flex

>>>   bison

>>>   m4

>>>   autoconf

>>>   automake

>>>   perl

>>>   gzip

>>>   tar

>>>   GNU sed

In addition, you will need to install (and possibly compile) any additional software specific to your configuration, such as Oracle or MySQL.

15

Using Packages

You can simplify the Solaris install process by using pkgadd to install most of your needed components.

Installation on UNIX systems

This section will guide you through the general configuration and installation of PHP on Unix systems. Be sure to investig-ate any sections specific to your platform or web server before you begin the process.

Prerequisite knowledge and software:

>>> Basic UNIX skills (being able to operate "make" and a C compiler, if compiling)

>>> An ANSI C compiler (if compiling)

>>> flex (for compiling)

>>> bison (for compiling)

>>> A web server

>>> Any module specific components (such as gd, pdf libs, etc.)

There are several ways to install PHP for the Unix platform, either with a compile and configure process, or through various pre-packaged methods. This documentation is mainly focused around the process of compiling and configuring PHP.

The initial PHP setup and configuration process is controlled by the use of the commandline options of the configure script. This page outlines the usage of the most common options, but there are many others to play with. Check out the Complete list of configure options for an exhaustive rundown. There are several ways to install PHP:

• As an Apache module

• As an fhttpd module

• For use with AOLServer, NSAPI, phttpd, Pi3Web, Roxen, thttpd, or Zeus.

• As a CGI executable

Apache Module Quick Reference

PHP can be compiled in a number of different ways, but one of the most popular is as an Apache module. The following is a quick installation overview.

Example 3.4. Quick Installation Instructions for PHP 4 (Apache Module Version)

```
•   gunzip apache_1.3.x.tar.gz
•   tar xvf apache_1.3.x.tar
•   gunzip php-x.x.x.tar.gz
•   tar xvf php-x.x.x.tar
•   cd apache_1.3.x
6.  ./configure –prefix=/www
•   cd ../php-x.x.x
8.  ./configure –with-mysql –with-apache=../apache_1.3.x –enable-track-vars
•   make
•   make install
```

16

11. cd ../apache_1.3.x
12. ./configure –activate-module=src/modules/php4/libphp4.a
- make
- make install
- cd ../php-x.x.x
- cp php.ini-dist /usr/local/lib/php.ini
- Edit your httpd.conf or srm.conf file and add: AddType
  application/x-httpd-php .php

- Use your normal procedure for restarting the Apache server. (You must stop and
  restart the server, not just cause the server to reload by use a HUP or USR1 signal.)

Building

When PHP is configured, you are ready to build the CGI executable. The command **make** should take care of this. If it fails and you can't figure out why, see the Problems section.

Installation on Windows systems

This section applies to Windows 98/Me and Windows NT/2000/XP. PHP will not work on 16 bit platforms such as Win-dows 3.1 and sometimes we refer to the supported Windows platforms as Win32. Windows 95 is no longer supported as of PHP 4.3.0.

There are two main ways to install PHP for Windows: either manually or by using the InstallShield installer.

If you have Microsoft Visual Studio, you can also build PHP from the original source code.

Once you have PHP installed on your Windows system, you may also want to load various extensions for added functional-ity.

Windows InstallShield

The Windows PHP installer is available from the downloads page at http:/ / www.php.net/ downloads.php. This installs the *CGI version* of PHP and, for IIS, PWS, and Xitami, configures the web server as well.

> **Note:** While the InstallShield installer is an easy way to make PHP work, it is restricted in many aspects, as auto-matic setup of extensions for example is not supported. The whole set of supported extensions is only available by downloading the zip binary distribution.

Install your selected HTTP server on your system and make sure that it works.

Run the executable installer and follow the instructions provided by the installation wizard. Two types of installation are supported - standard, which provides sensible defaults for all the settings it can, and advanced, which asks questions as it goes along.

The installation wizard gathers enough information to set up the php.ini file and configure the web server to use PHP. For IIS and also PWS on NT Workstation, a list of all the nodes on the server with script map settings is displayed, and you can choose those nodes to which you wish to add the PHP script mappings.

Once the installation has completed the installer will inform you if you need to restart your system, restart the server, or just start using PHP.

Warning

Be aware, that this setup of PHP is not secure. If you would like to have a secure PHP setup, you'd better go on the

17

manual way, and set every option carefully. This automatically working setup gives you an instantly working PHP installation, but it is not meant to be used on online servers.

Manual Installation Steps

This install guide will help you manually install and configure PHP on your Windows webserver. The original version of this guide was compiled by Bob Silva [mailto:bob_silva@mail.umesd.k12.or.us], and can be found at http:/ / www.umesd.k12.or.us/php/win32install.html. You need to download the zip binary distribution from the downloads page at http://www.php.net/downloads.php.

PHP 4 for Windows comes in three flavours - a CGI executable (php.exe), a CLI executable (sapi/php.exe) and some other
SAPI modules:

php4apache.dll - Apache 1.3.x module
php4apache2.dll - Apache 2.0.x module
php4isapi.dll - ISAPI Module for ISAPI compliant webservers like IIS 4.0/PWS 4.0 or newer.
php4nsapi.dll - Netscape/iPlanet module

The latter form is new to PHP 4, and provides significantly improved performance and some new functionality. The CLI version is designed to use PHP for command line scripting. More information about CLI is available in the chapter about us-ing PHP from the command line

Warning

The SAPI modules have been significantly improved in the 4.1 release, however, you may find that you encounter possible server errors or other server modules such as ASP failing, in older systems.

DCOM and MDAC requirements: If you choose one of the SAPI modules and use *Windows 95*, be sure to download and install the DCOM update from the Microsoft DCOM pages [http:/ / download.microsoft.com/ ms-download/dcom/95/x86/en/dcom95.exe]. If you use Microsoft *Windows 9x/NT4* download the latest version of the Microsoft Data Access Components (MDAC) for your platform. MDAC is available at http://www.microsoft.com/ data/.

The following steps should be performed on all installations before any server specific instructions.

*   Extract the distribution file to a directory of your choice, c:\ is a good start. The zip package expands to a foldername like php-4.3.1-Win32 which is assumed to be renamed to php. For the sake of convinience and to be version inde-pendant the following steps assume your extracted version of PHP lives in c:\php. You might choose any other loca-tion but you probably do not want to use a path in which spaces are included (for example: c:\program files\php is not a good idea). Some web servers will crash if you do. The struture of your directory you extracted the zip file will look like:

```
c:\php
   |
   +-cli
   |   |
   |   |-php.exe            - CLI executable - ONLY for commandline scripting
   |
   +-dlls                   - support dlls for extensions -> windows system directory
   |   |
   |   |-expat.dll
   |   |
   |   |-fdftk.dll
   |   |
   |   |-...
   |
   +--extensions            - extension dlls for PHP
   |   |
   |   |-php_bz2.dll
```

```
| |
| |-php_cpdf.dll
| |
| |-..
|
+-mibs                    - support files for SNMP
|
+-openssl                 - support files for Openssl
|
+-pdf-related             - support files for PDF
|
+-sapi                    - SAPI dlls
| |
| |-php4apache.dll
| |
| |-php4apache2.dll
| |
| |-php4isapi.dll
| |
| |-..
|
|-install.txt
|
|-..
|
|-php.exe                 - CGI executable
|
|-..
|
|-php.ini-dist
|
|-php.ini-recommended
|
|-php4ts.dll              - main dll -> windows system directory
|
|-...
```

The CGI binary - C:/php/php.exe -, the CLI binary - c:\php\cli\php.exe -, and the SAPI modules - c:\php\sapi*.dll - rely on the main dll c:\php\php4ts.dll. You have to make sure, that this dll can be found by your PHP installation. The search order for this dll is as follows:

The same directory from where php.exe is called. In case you use a SAPI module the same directory from where your webserver loads the dll (e.g. php4apache.dll).
Any directory in your Windows PATH environment variable.

* The best bet is to make php4ts.dll available, regardless which interface (CGI or SAPI module) you plan to use. To do so, you have to copy this dll to a directory on your Windows path. The best place is your windows system directory:

c:\windows\system for Windows 9x/ME
c:\winnt\system32 for Windows NT/2000 or c:\winnt40\system32 for NT/2000
server c:\windows\system32 for Windows XP

If you plan to use a SAPI module from c:\php\sapi and do not like to copy dlls to your Windows system directory, you have the alternative choice to simply copy php4ts.dll to the sapi folder of your extracted zip package, c:\php\sapi.

- The next step is to set up a valid configuration file for PHP, php.ini. There are two ini files distributed in the zip file, php.ini-dist and php.ini-recommended. We advise you to use php.ini-recommended, because we optimized the default settings in this file for performance, and security. Read this well documented file carefully and in addition study the ini settings and set every element manually yourself. If you would like to achieve the best security, then this is the way for you, although PHP works fine with these default ini files. Copy your choosen ini-file to a directory where PHP is able to find and rename it to php.ini. By default PHP searchs php.ini in your Windows directory:

19

On Windows 9x/ME/XP copy your choosen ini file to your %WINDIR%, which is typically c:\windows.
On Windows NT/2000 copy your choosen ini file to your %WINDIR% or %SYSTEMROOT%, which is typically c:\winnt or c:\winnt40 for NT/2000 servers.

- If you're using NTFS on Windows NT, 2000 or XP, make sure that the user running the webserver has read permissions to your php.ini (e.g. make it readable by Everyone).

The following steps are optional.

- Edit your new php.ini file. If you plan to use OmniHTTPd, do not follow the next step. Set the doc_root to point to your webservers document_root. For example:

  doc_root = c:\inetpub   // for IIS/PWS

  doc_root = c:\apache\htdocs // for Apache

- Choose which extensions you would like to load when PHP starts. See the section about Windows extensions, about how to set up one, and what is already built in. Note that on a new installation it is advisable to first get PHP working and tested without any extensions before enabling them in php.ini.

- OnPWSandIIS,youcansetthebrowscapconfigurationsettingtopointto:
  c:\windows\system\inetsrv\browscap.inionWindows9x/Me,
  c:\winnt\system32\inetsrv\browscap.ini on NT/2000, and c:\windows\system32\inetsrv\browscap.ini on XP.

Following this instructions you are done with the basic steps to setup PHP on Windows. The next step is to choose a web-server and enable it to run PHP. Installation instructions for the following webservers are available:

- .. the Windows server family, Personal Web server (PWS) 3 and 4 or newer; Internet Information Server (IIS) 3 and 4 or newer.

- .. the Apache servers Apache 1.3.x, and Apache 2.x.

- .. the Netscape/iPlanet servers.

- .. the OmniHTTPd server.

- .. the Oreilly Website Pro server.

- .. the Sambar server.

- .. the Xitami server.

Building from source

Before getting started, it is worthwhile answering the question: "Why is building on Windows so hard?" Two reasons come to mind:

- Windows does not (yet) enjoy a large community of developers who are willing to freely share their source. As a direct result, the necessary investment in infrastructure required to support such development hasn't been made. By and large, what is available has been made possible by the porting of necessary utilities from Unix. Don't be surprised if some of this heritage shows through from time to time.

20

- Pretty much all of the instructions that follow are of the "set and forget" variety. So sit back and try follow the instruc-tions below as faithfully as you can.

Requirements

To compile and build PHP you need a Microsoft Development Environment. Microsoft Visuaul C++ 6.0 is recommended. To extract the downloaded files you need a extraction utilitiy (e.g.: Winzip). If you don't already have an unzip utility, you can get a free version from InfoZip [http://www.info-zip.org/pub/infozip/].

Before you get started, you have to download...

- ..the win32 buildtools from the PHP site at http://www.php.net/extra/win32build.zip.

- ..the source code for the DNS name resolver used by PHP from http://www.php.net/extra/bindlib_w32.zip. This is a re-placement for the resolv.lib library included in win32build.zip.

- If you plan to compile PHP as a Apache module you will also need the Apache sources [http://www.apache.org/dist/ht-tpd/].

Finally, you are going to need the source to PHP 4 itself. You can get the latest development version using anonymous CVS [http:/ / www.php.net/ anoncvs.php], a snapshot [http:/ / snaps.php.net/] or the most recent released source [http:/ / www.php.net/downloads.php] tarball.

Putting it all together

After downloading the required packages you have to extract them in a proper place.

- Create a working directory where all files end up after extracting, e.g: c:\work.

- Create the directory win32build under your working directory (c:\work) and unzip win32build.zip into it.

- Create the directory bindlib_w32 under your working directory (c:\work) and unzip bindlib_w32.zip into it.

- Extract the downloaded PHP source code into your working directory (c:\work).

Following this steps your directory structure looks like this:

```
+-c:\work
  |
  +-bindlib_w32
  |   |
  |   +-arpa
  |   |
  |   +-conf
  |   |
  |   +-...
  |   |
  +-php-4.x.x
  |   |
  |   +-build
  |   |
  |   +-...
  |   |
  |   +-win32
  |   |
  |   +-...
  |   |
  +-win32build
  |   |
```

21

```
|   |   +–bin
|   |   |
|   |   +–include
|   |   |
|   |   +–lib
```

Create the directories c:\usr\local\lib. Copy bison.simple from c:\work\win32build\bin to c:\usr\local\lib.

> **Note:** Cygwin [http://sources.redhat.com/cygwin/] **users** may omit the last step. A properly installed Cygwin envir-onment provides the mandatory files bison.simple and bison.exe.

Configure MVC ++

The next step is to configure MVC ++ to prepare for compiling. Launch Microsoft Visual C++, and from the menu select Tools => Options. In the dialog, select the directories tab. Sequentially change the dropdown to Executables, Includes, and Library files. Your entries should look like this:

- Executable files: c:\work\win32build\bin, Cygwin users: cygwin\bin

- Include files: c:\work\win32build\include

- Library files: c:\work\win32build\lib

Build resolv.lib

You must build the resolv.lib library. Decide whether you want to have debug symbols available (bindlib - Win32 De-bug) or not (bindlib - Win32 Release). Build the appropriate configuration:

- For GUI users, launch VC++, and then select File => Open Workspace, navigate to c:\work\bindlib_w32 and select bindlib.dsw. Then select Build=>Set Active Configuration and select the desired configuration. Finally select Build=>Rebuild All.

- For command line users, make sure that you either have the C++ environment variables registered, or have run **vcvars.bat**, and then execute one of the following commands:

  msdev bindlib.dsp /MAKE "bindlib - Win32 Debug"

  msdev bindlib.dsp /MAKE "bindlib - Win32 Release"

At this point, you should have a usable resolv.lib in either your c:\work\bindlib_w32\Debug or Release subdir-ectories. Copy this file into your c:\work\win32build\lib directory over the file by the same name found in there.

Compiling

The best way to get started is to build the CGI version.

- For GUI users, launch VC++, and then select File => Open Workspace and select c:\work\php-4.x.x\win32\php4ts.dsw . Then select Build=>Set Active Configuration and select the desired configuration, either php4ts - Win32 Debug_TS or php4ts - Win32 Release_TS. Finally select Build=>Rebuild All.

- For command line users, make sure that you either have the C++ environment variables registered, or have run

22

vcvars.bat, and then execute one of the following commands from the c:\work\php-4.x.x\win32 directory:

>>> **msdev php4ts.dsp /MAKE "php4ts - Win32 Debug_TS"**

>>> **msdev php4ts.dsp /MAKE "php4ts - Win32 Release_TS"**

>>> At this point, you should have a usable php.exe in either your c:\work\php-4.x.x.\Debug_TS or Release_TS subdirectories.

It is possible to do minor customization to the build process by editing the main/config.win32.h file. For example you can change the builtin extensions, the location of php.ini and

Next you may want to build the CLI version which is designed to use PHP from the command line. The steps are the same as for building the CGI version, except you have to select the php4ts_cli - Win32 Debug_TS or php4ts_cli - Win32 Release_TS project file. After a succcessfull compiling run you will find the php.exe in either the directory Re-lease_TS\cli\ or Debug_TS\cli\.

Note: If you want to use PEAR and the comfortable command line installer, the CLI-SAPI is mandatory. For more information about PEAR and the installer read the documantation at the PEAR [http://pear.php.net/manual/] web-site.

In order to build the SAPI module (php4isapi.dll) for integrating PHP with Microsoft IIS, set your active configuration to php4isapi-whatever-config and build the desired dll.

Installation of Windows extensions

After installing PHP and a webserver on Windows, you will probably want to install some extensions for added functional-ity. You can choose which extensions you would like to load when PHP starts by modifying your php.ini. You can also load a module dynamically in your script using **dl()**.

The DLLs for PHP extensions are prefixed with 'php_' in PHP 4 (and 'php3_' in PHP 3). This prevents confusion between PHP extensions and their supporting libraries.

Note: In PHP 4.3.1 BCMath, Calendar, COM, Ctype, FTP, MySQL, ODBC, Overload, PCRE, Session, Tokenizer, WDDX, XML and Zlib support is *built in*. You don't need to load any additional extensions in order to use these functions. See your distributions README.txt or install.txt or this table for a list of built in modules.

Edit your php.ini file:

- You will need to change the extension_dir setting to point to the directory where your extensions lives, or where you have placed your php_*.dll files. Please do not forget the last backslash. For example:

  extension_dir = c:/php/extensions/

- Enable the extension(s) in php.ini you want to use by uncommenting the extension=php_*.dll lines in php.ini. This is done by deleting the leading ; form the extension you want to load.

Example 3.5. Enable Bzip2 extension for PHP-Windows

```
>>> change the following line from ...
;extension=php_bz2.dll

>>> ... to
extension=php_bz2.dll
```

23

>>> Some of the extensions need extra DLLs to work. Couple of them can be found in the distribution package, in the c:\php\dlls\ folder but some, for example Oracle (php_oci8.dll) require DLLs which are not bundled with the distribution package. Copy the bundled DLLs from c:\php\dlls folder to your Windows PATH, safe places are:

c:\windows\system for Windows
9x/Me c:\winnt\system32 for
Windows NT/2000
c:\windows\system32 for Windows
XP

If you have them already installed on your system, overwrite them only if something doesn't work correctly (Before overwriting them, it is a good idea to make a backup of them, or move them to another folder - just in case something goes wrong).

The following table describes some of the extensions available and required additional dlls.

Table 3.1. PHP Extensions

Extension	Description	Notes
php_bz2.dll	bzip2 compression functions	None
php_calendar.dll	Calendar conversion functions	Built in since PHP 4.0.3
php_cpdf.dll	ClibPDF functions	None
php_crack.dll	Crack functions	None
php3_crypt.dll	Crypt functions	unknown
php_ctype.dll	ctype family functions	Built in since PHP 4.3.0
php_curl.dll	CURL, Client URL library functions	Requires: libeay32.dll, ssleay32.dll (bundled)
php_cybercash.dll	Cybercash payment functions	PHP <= 4.2.0
php_db.dll	DBM functions	Deprecated. Use DBA instead (php_dba.dll)
php_dba.dll	DBA: DataBase (dbm-style) Abstrac-tion layer functions	None
php_dbase.dll	dBase functions	None
php3_dbm.dll	Berkeley DB2 library	unknown
php_dbx.dll	dbx functions	
php_domxml.dll	DOM XML functions	PHP <= 4.2.0 requires: libxml2.dll (bundled) PHP >= 4.3.0 requires:

		iconv.dll (bundled)
php_dotnet.dll	.NET functions	PHP <= 4.1.1
php_exif.dll	Read EXIF headers from JPEG	None
php_fbsql.dll	FrontBase functions	PHP <= 4.2.0
php_fdf.dll	FDF: Forms Data Format functions.	Requires: fdftk.dll (bundled)
php_filepro.dll	filePro functions	Read-only access
php_ftp.dll	FTP functions	Built-in since PHP 4.0.3
php_gd.dll	GD library image functions	Removed in PHP 4.3.2. Also note that truecolor functions are not available in GD1, instead, use php_gd2.dll.
php_gd2.dll	GD library image functions	GD2
php_gettext.dll	Gettext functions	PHP <= 4.2.0 requires gnu_gettext.dll (bundled), PHP >= 4.2.3 requires libintl-1.dll

24

Extension	Description	Notes
		(bundled).
php_hyperwave.dll	HyperWave functions	None
php_iconv.dll	ICONV characterset conversion	Requires: iconv-1.3.dll (bundled), PHP >=4.2.1 iconv.dll
php_ifx.dll	Informix functions	Requires: Informix libraries
php_iisfunc.dll	IIS management functions	None
php_imap.dll	IMAP POP3 and NNTP functions	PHP 3: php3_imap4r1.dll
php_ingres.dll	Ingres II functions	Requires: Ingres II libraries
php_interbase.dll	InterBase functions	Requires: gds32.dll (bundled)
php_java.dll	Java functions	PHP <= 4.0.6 requires: jvm.dll (bundled)
php_ldap.dll	LDAP functions	PHP <= 4.2.0 requires libsasl.dll (bundled), PHP >= 4.3.0 requires libeay32.dll, ssleay32.dll (bundled)
php_mbstring.dll	Multi-Byte String functions	None
php_mcrypt.dll	Mcrypt Encryption functions	Requires: libmcrypt.dll
php_mhash.dll	Mhash functions	PHP >= 4.3.0 requires: libmhash.dll (bundled)
php_mime_magic.dll	Mimetype functions	Requires: magic.mime (bundled)
php_ming.dll	Ming functions for Flash	None
php_msql.dll	mSQL functions	Requires: msql.dll (bundled)
php3_msql1.dll	mSQL 1 client	unknown
php3_msql2.dll	mSQL 2 client	unknown
php_mssql.dll	MSSQL functions	Requires: ntwdblib.dll (bundled)
php3_mysql.dll	MySQL functions	Built-in in PHP 4
php3_nsmail.dll	Netscape mail functions	unknown
php3_oci73.dll	Oracle functions	unknown
php_oci8.dll	Oracle 8 functions	Requires: Oracle 8.1+ client libraries
php_openssl.dll	OpenSSL functions	Requires: libeay32.dll (bundled)
php_oracle.dll	Oracle functions	Requires: Oracle 7 client libraries

php_overload.dll	Object overloading functions	Built in since PHP 4.3.0
php_pdf.dll	PDF functions	None
php_pgsql.dll	PostgreSQL functions	None
php_printer.dll	Printer functions	None
php_shmop.dll	Shared Memory functions	None
php_snmp.dll	SNMP get and walk functions	NT only!
php_sockets.dll	Socket functions	None
php_sybase_ct.dll	Sybase functions	Requires: Sybase client libraries
php_tokenizer.dll	Tokenizer functions	Built in since PHP 4.3.0
php_w32api.dll	W32api functions	None
php_xmlrpc.dll	XML-RPC functions	PHP >= 4.2.1 requires: iconv.dll (bundled)

25

Extension	Description	Notes
php_xslt.dll	XSLT functions	PHP <= 4.2.0 requires sablot.dll, expat.dll (bundled). PHP >= 4.2.1 requires sablot.dll, expat.dll, iconv.dll (bundled).
php_yaz.dll	YAZ functions	Requires: yaz.dll (bundled)
php_zib.dll	Zip File functions	Read only access
php_zlib.dll	ZLib compression functions	Built in since PHP 4.3.0

Servers-CGI/Commandline

The default is to build PHP as a CGI program. This creates a commandline interpreter, which can be used for CGI pro-cessing, or for non-web-related PHP scripting. If you are running a web server PHP has module support for, you should generally go for that solution for performance reasons. However, the CGI version enables Apache users to run different PHP-enabled pages under different user-ids. Please make sure you read through the Security chapter if you are going to run PHP as a CGI.

As of PHP 4.3.0, some important additions have happened to PHP. A new SAPI named CLI also exists and it has the same name as the CGI binary. What is installed at {PREFIX}/bin/php depends on your configure line and this is described in detail in the manual section named . For further details please read that section of the manual.

Testing

If you have built PHP as a CGI program, you may test your build by typing **make test**. It is always a good idea to test your build. This way you may catch a problem with PHP on your platform early instead of having to struggle with it later.

Benchmarking

If you have built PHP 3 as a CGI program, you may benchmark your build by typing **make bench**. Note that if safe mode is on by default, the benchmark may not be able to finish if it takes longer then the 30 seconds allowed. This is because the **set_time_limit()** can not be used in safe mode. Use the max_execution_time configuration setting to control this time for your own scripts. **make bench** ignores the configuration file.

Note: **make bench** is only available for PHP 3.

Using Variables

Some server supplied enviroment variables are not defined in the current CGI/1.1 specification [http:/ / hoo-hoo.ncsa.uiuc.edu/cgi/env.html]. Only the following variables are defined there; everything else should be treated as 'vendor extensions': AUTH_TYPE, CONTENT_LENGTH, CONTENT_TYPE, GATEWAY_INTERFACE, PATH_INFO,
PATH_TRANSLATED, QUERY_STRING, REMOTE_ADDR, REMOTE_HOST, REMOTE_IDENT, REMOTE_USER, REQUEST_METHOD, SCRIPT_NAME, SERVER_NAME, SERVER_PORT, SERVER_PROTOCOL and SERV-ER_SOFTWARE

Servers-Apache

This section contains notes and hints specific to Apache installs of PHP, both for Unix and Windows versions. We also have instructions and notes for Apache 2 on a separate page.

Details of Installing PHP with Apache on Unix

You can select arguments to add to the **configure** on line 10 below from the Complete list of configure options. The version numbers have been omitted here, to ensure the instructions are not incorrect. You will need to replace the 'xxx' here with the correct values from your files.

Example 3.6. Installation Instructions (Apache Shared Module Version) for PHP 4

- gunzip apache_xxx.tar.gz
- tar -xvf apache_xxx.tar
- gunzip php-xxx.tar.gz
- tar -xvf php-xxx.tar
- cd apache_xxx
6. ./configure –prefix=/www –enable-module=so
- make
- make install
- cd ../php-xxx
10. ./configure –with-mysql –with-apxs=/www/bin/apxs
- make
- make install

If you decide to change your configure options after installation you only need to repeat the last three steps. You only need to restart apache for the new module to take effect. A recompile of Apache is not needed.

13. cp php.ini-dist /usr/local/lib/php.ini

You can edit your .ini file to set PHP options. If you prefer this file in another location, use –with-config-file-path=/path in step 10.

>>> Edit your httpd.conf or srm.conf file and check that these lines are present and not commented out:

AddType application/x-httpd-php .php

LoadModule php4_module   libexec/libphp4.so

You can choose any extension you wish here. .php is simply the one we suggest. You can even include .html, and .php3 can be added for backwards compatibility.

The path on the right hand side of the LoadModule statement must point to the path of the PHP module on your system. The above statement is correct for the steps shown above.

>>> Use your normal procedure for starting the Apache server. (You must stop and restart the server, not just cause the server to reload by use a HUP or USR1 signal.)

Depending on your Apache install and Unix variant, there are many possible ways to stop and restart the server. Below are some typical lines used in restarting the server, for different apache/unix installations. You should replace /path/to/ with the path to these applications on your systems.

\# Several Linux and SysV variants:
/etc/rc.d/init.d/httpd restart

\# Using apachectl scripts:
/path/to/apachectl stop
/path/to/apachectl start

\# httpdctl and httpsdctl (Using OpenSSL), similar to apachectl:
/path/to/httpsdctl stop
/path/to/httpsdctl start

\# Using mod_ssl, or another SSL server, you may want to manually

27

stop and start:
/path/to/apachectl stop
/path/to/apachectl startssl

The locations of the apachectl and http(s)dctl binaries often vary. If your system has locate or whereis or which com-mands, these can assist you in finding your server control programs.

Different examples of compiling PHP for apache are as follows:

./configure –with-apxs –with-pgsql

This will create a libphp4.so shared library that is loaded into Apache using a LoadModule line in Apache's httpd.conf file. The PostgreSQL support is embedded into this libphp4.so library.

./configure –with-apxs –with-pgsql=shared

This will create a libphp4.so shared library for Apache, but it will also create a pgsql.so shared library that is loaded into PHP either by using the extension directive in php.ini file or by loading it explicitly in a script using the **dl()** function.

./configure –with-apache=/path/to/apache_source –with-pgsql

This will create a libmodphp4.a library, a mod_php4.c and some accompanying files and copy this into the src/ modules/php4 directory in the Apache source tree. Then you compile Apache using - -activate-module=src/modules/php4/libphp4.a and the Apache build system will create libphp4.a and link it statically into the httpd binary. The PostgreSQL support is included directly into this httpd binary, so the final result here is a single httpd binary that includes all of Apache and all of PHP.

./configure –with-apache=/path/to/apache_source –with-pgsql=shared

Same as before, except instead of including PostgreSQL support directly into the final httpd you will get a pgsql.so shared library that you can load into PHP from either the php.ini file or directly using **dl()**.

When choosing to build PHP in different ways, you should consider the advantages and drawbacks of each method. Build-ing as a shared object will mean that you can compile apache separately, and don't have to recompile everything as you add to, or change, PHP. Building PHP into apache (static method) means that PHP will load and run faster. For more informa-tion, see the Apache webpage on DSO support [http://httpd.apache.org/docs/dso.html].

Note: Apache's default httpd.conf currently ships with a section that looks like this:

User nobody
Group "#-1"

Unless you change that to "Group nogroup" or something like that ("Group daemon" is also very common) PHP will not be able to open files.

Note: Make sure you specify the installed version of apxs when using –with-apxs=/path/to/apxs. You must NOT use the apxs version that is in the apache sources but the one that is actually installed on your system.

Installing PHP on Windows with Apache 1.3.x

There are two ways to set up PHP to work with Apache 1.3.x on Windows. One is to use the CGI binary (php.exe), the other is to use the Apache module DLL. In either case you need to stop the Apache server, and edit your httpd.conf to config-ure Apache to work with PHP.

It is worth noting here that now the SAPI module has been made more stable under windows, we recommend it's use above

---

28

the CGI binary, since it is more transparent and secure.

Although there can be a few variations of configuring PHP under Apache, these are simple enough to be used by the new-comer. Please consult the Apache Docs for further configuration directives.

If you unziped the PHP package to c:\php\ as described in the Manual Installation Steps section, you need to insert these lines to your Apache configuration file to set up the CGI binary:

- ScriptAlias /php/ "c:/php/"

- AddType application/x-httpd-php .php .phtml

- Action application/x-httpd-php "/php/php.exe"

Note that the second line in the list above can be found in the actual versions of httpd.conf, but it is commented out. Re-member also to substitute the c:/php/ for your actual path to PHP.

Warning

By using the CGI setup, your server is open to several possible attacks. Please read our CGI security section to learn how to defend yourself from attacks.

If you would like to use PHP as a module in Apache, be sure to copy php4ts.dll to the windows/system (for Windows 9x/Me), winnt/system32 (for Windows NT/2000) or windows/system32 (for Windows XP) directory, overwriting any older file. Then you should add the following lines to your Apache httpd.conf file:

- Open httpd.conf with your favorite editor and locate the LoadModule directive and add the following line *at the end* of the list: LoadModule php4_module c:/php/sapi/php4apache.dll

- You may find after using the windows installer for Apache that you need to define the AddModule directive for mod_php4.c. This is especially important if the ClearModuleList directive is defined, which you will find by scrolling down a few lines. You will see a list of AddModule entries, add the following line *at the end* of the list:
AddModule mod_php4.c

- Search for a phrase similar to # AddType allows you to tweak mime.types. You will see some AddType entries, add the following line *at the end* of the list: AddType application/x-httpd-php .php. You can choose any extension you want to parse through PHP here. .php is simply the one we suggest. You can even include .html, and
.php3 can be added for backwards compatibility.

After changing the configuration file, remember to restart the server, for example, **NET STOP APACHE** followed by **NET START APACHE**, if you run Apache as a Windows Service, or use your regular shortcuts.

There are two ways you can use the source code highlighting feature, however their ability to work depends on your install-ation. If you have configured Apache to use PHP as an SAPI module, then by adding the following line to your ht-tpd.conf (at the same place you inserted AddType application/x-httpd-php .php, see above) you can use this fea-ture: AddType application/x-httpd-php-source .phps.

If you chose to configure Apache to use PHP as a CGI binary, you will need to use the **show_source() function. To do this simply create a PHP script file and add this code: <?php show_source ("original_php_script.php"); ?>. Substi-tute original_php_script.php with the name of the file you wish to show the source of.**

Note: On Win-Apache all backslashes in a path statement such as "c:\directory\file.ext", must be converted to for-ward slashes, as "c:/directory/file.ext".

Servers-Apache 2.0

29

This section contains notes and hints specific to Apache 2.0 installs of PHP, both for Unix and Windows versions.

Warning

Do not use Apache 2.0 and PHP in a production environment neither on Unix nor on Windows.

You are highly encouraged to take a look at the Apache Documentation [http://httpd.apache.org/docs-2.0/] to get a basic un-derstanding of the Apache 2.0 Server.

PHP and Apache 2.0 compatibility notes

The following versions of PHP are known to work with the most recent version of Apache 2.0:

- PHP 4.3.0 or later available at http://www.php.net/downloads.php.
- the latest stable development version. Get the source code http:/ / snaps.php.net/ php4-latest.tar.gz or download binaries for windows http://snaps.php.net/win32/php4-win32-latest.zip.
- a prerelease version downloadable from http://qa.php.net/.
- you have always the option to obtain PHP through anonymous CVS [http://www.php.net/anoncvs.php].

These versions of PHP are compatible to Apache 2.0.40 and later.

Note: Apache 2.0 SAPI-support started with PHP 4.2.0. PHP 4.2.3 works with Apache 2.0.39, don't use any other version of Apache with PHP 4.2.3. However, the recommended setup is to use PHP 4.3.0 or later with the most re-cent version of Apache2.

All mentioned versions of PHP will work still with Apache 1.3.x.

PHP and Apache 2 on Linux

Download the most recent version of Apache 2.0 [http://www.apache.org/] and a fitting PHP version from the above men-tioned places. This quick guide covers only the basics to get started with Apache 2.0 and PHP. For more information read the Apache Documentation [http://httpd.apache.org/docs-2.0/]. The version numbers have been omitted here, to ensure the instructions are not incorrect. You will need to replace the 'NN' here with the correct values from your files.

Example 3.7. Installation Instructions (Apache 2 Shared Module Version)

```
>>> gzip -d httpd-2_0_NN.tar.gz
>>> tar xvf httpd-2_0_NN.tar
>>> gunzip php-NN.tar.gz
>>> tar -xvf php-NN.tar
>>> cd httpd-2_0_NN
6.    ./configure --enable-so
2.    make
3.    make install

      Now you have Apache 2.0.NN available under /usr/local/apache2, configured with
      loadable module support and the standard MPM prefork. To test the installation
      use your normal procedure for starting
      the Apache server, e.g.:
      /usr/local/apache2/bin/apachectl start
      and stop the server to go on with the configuration for PHP:
      /usr/local/apache2/bin/apachectl stop.

4.    cd ../php4-NN
10.   ./configure --with-apxs2=/usr/local/apache2/bin/apxs
2.    make
3.    make install
4.    cp php.ini-dist /usr/local/lib/php.ini

      Edit your php.ini file to set PHP options. If you prefer
      this file in another location, use
```

–with-config-file-path=/path in step 10.

2. Edit your httpd.conf file and check that these lines are present:

    LoadModule php4_module modules/libphp4.so
    AddType application/x-httpd-php .php

    You can choose any extension you wish here. .php is simply the one we suggest.

    The path on the right hand side of the LoadModule statement must point to the path of the PHP module on your system. The above statement is correct for the steps shown above.

*   Use your normal procedure for starting the Apache server, e.g.:
    /usr/local/apache2/bin/apachectl start

Following the steps above you will have a running Apache 2.0 with support for PHP as SAPI module. Of course there are many more configuration options available for both, Apache and PHP. For more information use ./configure –help in the corresponding source tree. In case you wish to build a multithreaded version of Apache 2.0 you must overwrite the standard MPM-Module prefork either with worker or perchild. To do so append to your configure line in step 6 above either the option –with-mpm=worker or –with-mpm=perchild. Take care about the consequences and understand what you are doing. For more information read the Apache documentation about the MPM-Modules [http:/ / httpd.apache.org/ docs-2.0/ mpm.html].

Note: To build a multithreaded version of Apache your system must support threads. This also implies to build PHP with experimental Zend Thread Safety (ZTS). Therefore not all extensions might be available. The recommen-ded setup is to build Apache with the standard prefork MPM-Module.

PHP and Apache 2.0 on Windows

Consider to read the Windows specific notes [http://httpd.apache.org/docs-2.0/platform/windows.html] for Apache 2.0.

Warning

Apache 2.0 is designed to run on Windows NT 4.0, Windows 2000 or Windows XP. At this time, support for Win-dows 9x is incomplete. Apache 2.0 is not expected to work on those platforms at this time.

Download the most recent version of Apache 2.0 [http://www.apache.org/] and a fitting PHP version from the above men-tioned places. Follow the Manual Installation Steps and come back to go on with the integration of PHP and Apache.

There are two ways to set up PHP to work with Apache 2.0 on Windows. One is to use the CGI binary the other is to use the Apache module DLL. In either case you need to stop the Apache server, and edit your httpd.conf to configure Apache to work with PHP.

You need to insert these three lines to your Apache httpd.conf configuration file to set up the *CGI binary*:

Example 3.8. PHP and Apache 2.0 as CGI

```
ScriptAlias /php/ "c:/php/"
AddType application/x-httpd-php .php
Action application/x-httpd-php "/php/php.exe"
```

If you would like to use PHP as a module in Apache 2.0, be sure to move php4ts.dll to winnt/system32 (for Windows NT/2000) or windows/system32 (for Windows XP), overwriting any older file. You need to insert these two lines to your Apache httpd.conf configuration file to set up the *PHP-Module* for Apache 2.0:

31

Example 3.9. PHP and Apache 2.0 as Module

```
LoadModule php4_module "c:/php/sapi/php4apache2.dll"
AddType application/x-httpd-php .php
```

> **Note:** Remember to substitute the c:/php/ for your actual path to PHP in the above examples. Take care to use php4apache2.dll in your LoadModule directive and *not*php4apche.dll. The latter one is designd to run with Apache 1.3.x.

Warning

Don't mix up your installation with dll files from *different PHP versions* . You have the only choice to use the dll's and extensions that ship with your downloaded PHP version.

Servers-Caudium

PHP 4 can be built as a Pike module for the Caudium webserver [http://caudium.net/]. Note that this is not supported with PHP 3. Follow the simple instructions below to install PHP 4 for Caudium.

Example 3.10. Caudium Installation Instructions

>>> Make sure you have Caudium installed prior to attempting to install PHP
   4. For PHP 4 to work correctly, you will need Pike 7.0.268 or newer. For
   the sake of this example we assume that Caudium is installed in
   /opt/caudium/server/.
>>> Change directory to php-x.y.z (where x.y.z is the version number).
>>> ./configure –with-caudium=/opt/caudium/server
* make
* make install
* Restart Caudium if it's currently running.
* Log into the graphical configuration interface and go to the virtual
   server where you want to add PHP 4 support.
* Click Add Module and locate and then add the PHP 4 Script Support module.
* If the documentation says that the 'PHP 4 interpreter isn't available', make
   sure that you restarted the server. If you did check
   /opt/caudium/logs/debug/default.1 for any errors related to
   <filename>PHP4.so</filename>. Also make sure that
   <filename>caudium/server/lib/[pike-version]/PHP4.so</filename> is
   present.
* Configure the PHP Script Support module if needed.

You can of course compile your Caudium module with support for the various extensions available in PHP 4. See the com-plete list of configure options for an exhaustive rundown.

> **Note:** When compiling PHP 4 with MySQL support you must make sure that the normal MySQL client code is used. Otherwise there might be conflicts if your Pike already has MySQL support. You do this by specifying a MySQL install directory the –with-mysql option.

Servers-fhttpd

To build PHP as an fhttpd module, answer "yes" to "Build as an fhttpd module?" (the –with-fhttpd=*DIR* option to config-ure) and specify the fhttpd source base directory. The default directory is /usr/local/src/fhttpd. If you are running fhttpd, building PHP as a module will give better performance, more control and remote execution capability.

> **Note:** Support for fhttpd is no longer available as of PHP 4.3.0.

32

Servers-IIS/PWS

This section contains notes and hints specific to IIS (Microsoft Internet Information Server). Installing PHP for PWS/IIS 3, PWS 4 or newer and IIS 4 or newer versions.

Important for CGI users: Read the faq on cgi.force_redirect for important details. This directive needs to be set to 0.

Windows and PWS/IIS 3

The recommended method for configuring these servers is to use the REG file included with the distribution (pws-php4cgi.reg). You may want to edit this file and make sure the extensions and PHP install directories match your con-figuration. Or you can follow the steps below to do it manually.

Warning

These steps involve working directly with the Windows registry. One error here can leave your system in an un-stable state. We highly recommend that you back up your registry first. The PHP Development team will not be held responsible if you damage your registry.

>>> Run Regedit.

>>> Navigate to: HKEY_LOCAL_MACHINE /System /CurrentControlSet /Services /W3Svc /Parameters / ScriptMap.

>>> On the edit menu select: New->String Value.

>>> Type in the extension you wish to use for your php scripts. For example .php

>>> Double click on the new string value and enter the path to php.exe in the value data field. ex: c:\php\php.exe.

>>> Repeat these steps for each extension you wish to associate with PHP scripts.

The following steps do not affect the web server installation and only apply if you want your php scripts to be executed when they are run from the command line (ex. run c:\myscripts\test.php) or by double clicking on them in a direct-ory viewer window. You may wish to skip these steps as you might prefer the PHP files to load into a text editor when you double click on them.

- Navigate to: HKEY_CLASSES_ROOT
- On the edit menu select: New->Key.
- Name the key to the extension you setup in the previous section. ex: .php
- Highlight the new key and in the right side pane, double click the "default value" and enter phpfile.
- Repeat the last step for each extension you set up in the previous section.
- Now create another New->Key under HKEY_CLASSES_ROOT and name it phpfile.
- Highlight the new key phpfile and in the right side pane, double click the "default value" and enter PHP Script.
- Right click on the phpfile key and select New->Key, name it Shell.

33

>>> Right click on the Shell key and select New->Key, name it open.

>>> Right click on the open key and select New->Key, name it command.

>>> Highlight the new key command and in the right side pane, double click the "default value" and enter the path to php.exe. ex: c:\php\php.exe -q %1. (don't forget the %1).

>>> Exit Regedit.

>>> If using PWS on Windows, reboot to reload the registry.

PWS and IIS 3 users now have a fully operational system. IIS 3 users can use a nifty tool [http://www.genusa.com/iis/iis-cfg.html] from Steven Genusa to configure their script maps.

Windows and PWS 4 or newer

When installing PHP on Windows with PWS 4 or newer version, you have two options. One to set up the PHP CGI binary, the other is to use the ISAPI module DLL.

If you choose the CGI binary, do the following:

* Edit the enclosed pws-php4cgi.reg file (look into the SAPI dir) to reflect the location of your php.exe. Backslashes shouldbeescaped,forexample:
[HKEY_LOCAL_MACHINE\SYSTEM\CurrentControlSet\Services\w3svc\parameters\Script   Map] ".php"="c:\\php\\php.exe" Now merge this registery file into your system; you may do this by double-clicking it.

* In the PWS Manager, right click on a given directory you want to add PHP support to, and select Properties. Check the 'Execute' checkbox, and confirm.

If you choose the ISAPI module, do the following:

>>> Edit the enclosed pws-php4isapi.reg file (look into the SAPI dir) to reflect the location of your php4isapi.dll.
Backslasheshouldbeescaped,forexample:
[HKEY_LOCAL_MACHINE\SYSTEM\CurrentControlSet\Services\w3svc\parameters\Script   Map] ".php"="c:\\php\\sapi\\php4isapi.dll" Now merge this registery file into your system; you may do this by double-clicking it.

>>> In the PWS Manager, right click on a given directory you want to add PHP support to, and select Properties. Check the 'Execute' checkbox, and confirm.

Windows NT/2000/XP and IIS 4 or newer

To install PHP on an NT/2000/XP Server running IIS 4 or newer, follow these instructions. You have two options to set up PHP, using the CGI binary (php.exe) or with the ISAPI module.

In either case, you need to start the Microsoft Management Console (may appear as 'Internet Services Manager', either in your Windows NT 4.0 Option Pack branch or the Control Panel=>Administrative Tools under Windows 2000/XP). Then right click on your Web server node (this will most probably appear as 'Default Web Server'), and select 'Properties'.

If you want to use the CGI binary, do the following:

* Under 'Home Directory', 'Virtual Directory', or 'Directory', click on the 'Configuration' button, and then enter the App

## 34

Mappings tab.

>>>   Click Add, and in the Executable box, type: c:\php\php.exe (assuming that you have unziped PHP in c:\php\).

>>>   In the Extension box, type the file name extension you want associated with PHP scripts. Leave 'Method exclusions' blank, and check the Script engine checkbox. You may also like to check the 'check that file exists' box - for a small per-formance penalty, IIS (or PWS) will check that the script file exists and sort out authentication before firing up php. This means that you will get sensible 404 style error messages instead of cgi errors complaining that php did not output any data.

You must start over from the previous step for each extension you want associated with PHP scripts. .php and .phtml are common, although .php3 may be required for legacy applications.

>>>   Set up the appropriate security. (This is done in Internet Service Manager), and if your NT Server uses NTFS file sys-tem, add execute rights for I_USR_ to the directory that contains php.exe.

To use the ISAPI module, do the following:

- If you don't want to perform HTTP Authentication using PHP, you can (and should) skip this step. Under ISAPI Filters, add a new ISAPI filter. Use PHP as the filter name, and supply a path to the php4isapi.dll.

- Under 'Home Directory', click on the 'Configuration' button. Add a new entry to the Application Mappings. Use the path to the php4isapi.dll as the Executable, supply .php as the extension, leave Method exclusions blank, and check the Script engine checkbox.

- Stop IIS completely (NET STOP iisadmin)

- Start IIS again (NET START w3svc)

Servers-Netscape and iPlanet

This section contains notes and hints specific to Netscape and iPlanet installs of PHP, both for Sun Solaris and Windows versions.

You can find more information about setting up PHP for the Netscape Enterprise Server here: http://benoit.noss.free.fr/php/ install-php4.html

Installing PHP with Netscape on Sun Solaris

To build PHP with NES or iPlanet web servers, enter the proper install directory for the –with-nsapi = *DIR* option. The default directory is usually /opt/netscape/suitespot/. Please also read / php-xxx-version/sapi/nsapi/nsapi-readme.txt.

Example 3.11. Installation Example for Netscape Enterprise on Solaris

Instructions for Sun Solaris 2.6 with Netscape Enterprise Server 3.6 From: bhager@invacare.com

>>>   Install the following packages from www.sunfreeware.com or another download site:

```
flex-2_5_4a-sol26-sparc-local
gcc-2_95_2-sol26-sparc-local
gzip-1.2.4-sol26-sparc-local
perl-5_005_03-sol26-sparc-local
```

35

```
bison-1_25-sol26-sparc-local
make-3_76_1-sol26-sparc-local
m4-1_4-sol26-sparc-local
autoconf-2.13
automake-1.4
mysql-3.23.24-beta (if you want mysql support)
tar-1.13 (GNU tar)
```

- Make sure your path includes the proper directories
  PATH=.:/usr/local/bin:/usr/sbin:/usr/bin:/usr/ccs/bin export
  PATH

- gunzip php-x.x.x.tar.gz (if you have a .gz dist, otherwise go to 4)
- tar xvf php-x.x.x.tar
- cd ./php-x.x.x

- For the following step, make sure /opt/netscape/suitespot/ is where your
  netscape server is installed. Otherwise, change to correct path:
  /configure –with-mysql=/usr/local/mysql –with-nsapi=/opt/netscape/suitespot/ –enable-track-vars
- make
- make install

After performing the base install and reading the appropriate readme file, you may need to performs some additional config-uration steps.

Firstly you may need to add some paths to the **LD_LIBRARY_PATH** environment for Netscape to find all the shared libs. This can best done in the start script for your Netscape server. Windows users can probably skip this step. The start script is often located in: /path/to/server/https-servername/start

You may also need to edit the configuration files that are located in:/path/to/server/https-servername/config/.

Example 3.12. Configuration Example for Netscape Enterprise

Configuration Instructions for Netscape Enterprise Server From:
bhager@invacare.com

- Add the following line to mime.types:
  type=magnus-internal/x-httpd-php exts=php

- Add the following to obj.conf, shlib will vary depending on your OS, for
  unix it will be something like
  /opt/netscape/suitespot/bin/libphp4.so.

  You should place the following lines after mime types init.
  Init fn="load-modules" funcs="php4_init,php4_close,php4_execute,php4_auth_trans" shlib="/php4/nsapi Init
  fn=php4_init errorString="Failed to initialize PHP!"

  <object name="default">
  .
  .
  .
  .#NOTE this next line should happen after all 'ObjectType' and before all 'AddLog' lines Service
  fn="php4_execute" type="magnus-internal/x-httpd-php" .
  .
  </Object>

  <Object name="x-httpd-php">
  ObjectType fn="force-type" type="magnus-internal/x-httpd-php"
  Service fn=php4_execute
  </Object>

Authentication configuration

PHP authentication cannot be used with any other authentication. ALL AUTHENTICATION IS

36

PASSED TO YOUR PHP SCRIPT. To configure PHP Authentication for the entire server, add the following line:

```
<Object name="default">
AuthTrans fn=php4_auth_trans
.
.
.
.
</Object>
```

To use PHP Authentication on a single directory, add the following:

```
<Object ppath="d:\path\to\authenticated\dir\*">
AuthTrans fn=php4_auth_trans
</Object>
```

If you are running Netscape Enterprise 4.x, then you should use the following:

Example 3.13. Configuration Example for Netscape Enterprise 4.x

Place these lines after the mime types init, and everything else is similar to the example configuration above.
From: Graeme Hoose (GraemeHoose@BrightStation.com)

Init fn="load-modules" shlib="/path/to/server4/bin/libphp4.so" funcs="php4_init,php4_close,php4_execute Init fn="php4_init" LateInit="yes"

Installing PHP with Netscape on Windows

To Install PHP as CGI (for Netscape Enterprise Server, iPlanet, perhaps Fastrack), do the following:

>>>   Copy php4ts.dll to your systemroot (the directory where you installed windows)

>>>   Make a file association from the command line. Type the following two lines:

```
assoc .php=PHPScript
ftype PHPScript=c:\php\php.exe %1 %*
```

>>>   In the Netscape Enterprise Administration Server create a dummy shellcgi directory and remove it just after (this step creates 5 important lines in obj.conf and allow the web server to handle shellcgi scripts).

>>>   In the Netscape Enterprise Administration Server create a new mime type (Category: type, Content-Type: magnus-in-ternal/shellcgi, File Suffix:php).

>>>   Do it for each web server instance you want php to run

More details about setting up PHP as a CGI executable can be found here: http://benoit.noss.free.fr/php/install-php.html

To Install PHP as NSAPI (for Netscape Enterprise Server, iPlanet, perhaps Fastrack, do the following:

>>>   Copy php4ts.dll to your systemroot (the directory where you installed windows)

>>>   Make a file association from the command line. Type the

following two lines: assoc .php=PHPScript

37

```
ftype PHPScript=c:\php\php.exe %1 %*
```

\# In the Netscape Enterprise Administration Server create a new mime type (Category: type, Content-Type: magnus-in-ternal/x-httpd-php, File Suffix:php).

\# Stop your web service and edit obj.conf. At the end of the Init section, place these two lines (necessarily after mime type init!):

```
Init fn="load-modules" funcs="php4_init,php4_close,php4_execute,php4_auth_trans" shlib="c:/php/sapi/ Init fn="php4_init" errorString="Failed to initialise PHP!"
```

\# In The < Object name="default" > section, place this line necessarily after all 'ObjectType' and before all 'AddLog' lines:

```
Service fn="php4_execute" type="magnus-internal/x-httpd-php"
```

\# At the end of the file, create a new object called x-httpd-php, by inserting these lines:

```
<Object name="x-httpd-php">
ObjectType fn="force-type" type="magnus-internal/x-httpd-php" Service
fn=php4_execute
</Object>
```

\# Restart your web service and apply changes

\# Do it for each web server instance you want PHP to run

More details about setting up PHP as an NSAPI filter can be found here: http://benoit.noss.free.fr/php/install-php4.html

Servers-OmniHTTPd Server

This section contains notes and hints specific to OmniHTTPd.

OmniHTTPd 2.0b1 and up for Windows

You need to complete the following steps to make PHP work with OmniHTTPd. This is a CGI executable setup. SAPI is supported by OmniHTTPd, but some tests have shown that it is not so stable to use PHP as an ISAPI module.

> **Important for CGI users:** Read the faq on cgi.force_redirect for important details. This directive needs to be set to 0.

- Step 1: Install OmniHTTPd server.
- Step 2: Right click on the blue OmniHTTPd icon in the system tray and select Properties
- Step 3: Click on Web Server Global Settings
- Step 4: On the 'External' tab, enter: virtual = .php | actual = c:\path-to-php-dir\php.exe, and use the Add button.
- Step 5: On the Mime tab, enter: virtual = wwwserver/stdcgi | actual = .php, and use the Add button.

38

- Step 6: Click OK

Repeat steps 2 - 6 for each extension you want to associate with PHP.

> **Note:** Some OmniHTTPd packages come with built in PHP support. You can choose at setup time to do a custom setup, and uncheck the PHP component. We recommend you to use the latest PHP binaries. Some OmniHTTPd servers come with PHP 4 beta distributions, so you should choose not to set up the built in support, but install your own. If the server is already on your machine, use the Replace button in Step 4 and 5 to set the new, correct in-formation.

Servers-Oreilly Website Pro

This section contains notes and hints specific to Oreilly Website Pro.

Oreilly Website Pro 2.5 and up for Windows

This list describes how to set up the PHP CGI binary or the ISAPI module to work with Oreilly Website Pro on Windows.

- Edit the Server Properties and select the tab "Mapping".

- From the List select "Associations" and enter the desired extension (.php) and the path to the CGI exe (ex. c:\php\php.exe) or the ISAPI DLL file (ex. c:\php\sapi\php4isapi.dll).

- Select "Content Types" add the same extension (.php) and enter the content type. If you choose the CGI executable file, enter 'wwwserver/shellcgi', if you choose the ISAPI module, enter 'wwwserver/isapi' (both without quotes).

Servers-Sambar

This section contains notes and hints specific to the Sambar server for Windows.

Sambar Windows

This list describes how to set up the ISAPI module to work with the Sambar server on Windows.

- Find the file called mappings.ini (in the config directory) in the Sambar isntall directory.

- Open mappings.ini and add the following line under [ISAPI]:

    *.php = c:\php\php4isapi.dll

    (This line assumes that PHP was installed in c:\php.)

- Now restart the Sambar server for the changes to take effect.

Servers-Xitami

This section contains notes and hints specific to Xitami.

39

Xitami for Windows

This list describes how to set up the PHP CGI binary to work with Xitami on Windows.

> **Important for CGI users:** Read the faq on cgi.force_redirect for important details. This directive needs to be set to 0.

- Make sure the webserver is running, and point your browser to xitamis admin console (usually http://127.0.0.1/admin), and click on Configuration.

- Navigate to the Filters, and put the extension which PHP should parse (i.e. .php) into the field File extensions (.xxx).

- In Filter command or script put the path and name of your php executable i.e. c:\php\php.exe.

- Press the 'Save' icon.

- Restart the server to reflect changes.

Servers-Other web servers

PHP can be built to support a large number of web servers. Please see Server-related options for a full list of server-related configure options. The PHP CGI binaries are compatible with almost all webservers supporting the CGI standard.

Problems?

Read the FAQ

Some problems are more common than others. The most common ones are listed in the PHP FAQ, part of this manual.

Other problems

If you are still stuck, someone on the PHP installation mailing list may be able to help you. You should check out the archive first, in case someone already answered someone else who had the same problem as you. The archives are available from the support page on http://www.php.net/. To subscribe to the PHP installation mailing list, send an empty mail to php-install-subscribe@lists.php.net [mailto:php-install-subscribe@lists.php.net]. The mailing list address is php-in-stall@lists.php.net.

If you want to get help on the mailing list, please try to be precise and give the necessary details about your environment (which operating system, what PHP version, what web server, if you are running PHP as CGI or a server module, safe mode, etc...), and preferably enough code to make others able to reproduce and test your problem.

Bug reports

If you think you have found a bug in PHP, please report it. The PHP developers probably don't know about it, and unless you report it, chances are it won't be fixed. You can report bugs using the bug-tracking system at http://bugs.php.net/. Please do not send bug reports in mailing list or personal letters. The bug system is also suitable to submit feature requests.

Read the How to report a bug [http://bugs.php.net/how-to-report.php] document before submitting any bug reports!

Miscellaneous configure options

40

Below is a partial list of configure options used by the PHP configure scripts when compiling in Unix-like environments. Most configure options are listed in their appropriate locations and not here. For a complete up-to-date list of configure op-tions, run ./**configure –help** in your PHP source directory after running **autoconf** (see also the Installation chapter). You may also be interested in reading the GNU configure [http://www.airs.com/ian/configure/] documentation for information on additional **configure** options such as –prefix=PREFIX.

> **Note:** These are only used at compile time. If you want to alter PHP's runtime configuration, please see the chapter on Configuration.

* Graphics

* Miscellaneous

* PHP Behaviour

* Server

Configure Options in PHP 4

> **Note:** These options are only used in PHP 4 as of PHP 4.1.0. Some are available in older versions of PHP 4, some even in PHP 3, some only in PHP 4.1.0. If you want to compile an older version, some options will probably not be available.

Graphics options

–with-imagick
The imagick extension has been moved to PECL in PEAR and can be found here [http://pear.php.net/imagick]. Install instructions for PHP 4 can be found on the PEAR site.

Simply doing –with-imagick is only supported in PHP 3 unless you follow the instructions found on the PEAR site.

Misc options

–enable-debug
Compile with debugging symbols.

–with-layout=TYPE
Sets how installed files will be laid out. Type is one of PHP (default) or GNU.

–with-pear=DIR
Install PEAR in DIR (default PREFIX/lib/php).

–without-pear
Do not install PEAR.

–enable-sigchild
Enable PHP's own SIGCHLD handler.

–disable-rpath
Disable passing additional runtime library search paths.

–enable-libgcc
Enable explicitly linking against libgcc.

41

–enable-php-streams
  Include experimental php streams. Do not use unless you are testing the code!

–with-zlib-dir=<DIR>
  Define the location of zlib install directory.

–enable-trans-sid
  Enable transparent session id propagation. Only valid for PHP 4.1.2 or less. From PHP 4.2.0, trans-sid feature is always compiled.

–with-tsrm-pthreads
  Use POSIX threads (default).

–enable-shared[=PKGS]
  Build shared libraries [default=yes].

–enable-static[=PKGS]
  Build static libraries [default=yes].

–enable-fast-install[=PKGS]
  Optimize for fast installation [default=yes].

–with-gnu-ld
  Assume the C compiler uses GNU ld [default=no].

–disable-libtool-lock
  Avoid locking (might break parallel builds).

–with-pic
  Try to use only PIC/non-PIC objects [default=use both].

–enable-memory-limit
  Compile with memory limit support.

–disable-url-fopen-wrapper
  Disable the URL-aware fopen wrapper that allows accessing files via HTTP or FTP.

–enable-versioning
  Export only required symbols. See INSTALL for more information.

–with-imsp[=DIR]
  Include IMSp support (DIR is IMSP's include dir and libimsp.a dir). PHP 3 only!

–with-mck[=DIR]
  Include Cybercash MCK support. DIR is the cybercash mck build directory, defaults to /usr/src/mck-3.2.0.3-linux for help look in extra/cyberlib. PHP 3 only!

–with-mod-dav=DIR
  Include DAV support through Apache's mod_dav, DIR is mod_dav's installation directory (Apache module version only!) PHP 3 only!

–enable-debugger
  Compile with remote debugging functions. PHP 3 only!

–enable-versioning
  Take advantage of versioning and scoping provided by Solaris 2.x and Linux. PHP 3 only!

PHP options

42

–enable-maintainer-mode
　　Enable make rules and dependencies not useful (and sometimes confusing) to the casual installer.

–with-config-file-path=PATH
　　Sets the path in which to look for php.ini, defaults to PREFIX/lib.

–enable-safe-mode
　　Enable safe mode by default.

–with-exec-dir[=DIR]
　　Only allow executables in DIR when in safe mode defaults to /usr/local/php/bin.

–enable-magic-quotes
　　Enable magic quotes by default.

–disable-short-tags
　　Disable the short-form <? start tag by default.

Server options

–with-aolserver=DIR
　　Specify path to the installed AOLserver.

–with-apxs[=FILE]
　　Build shared Apache module. FILE is the optional pathname to the Apache apxs tool; defaults to apxs. Make sure you specify the version of apxs that is actually installed on your system and NOT the one that is in the apache source tarball.

–with-apache[=DIR]
　　Build Apache module. DIR is the top-level Apache build directory, defaults to /usr/local/apache.

–with-mod_charset
　　Enable transfer tables for mod_charset (Rus Apache).

–with-apxs2[=FILE]
　　Build shared Apache 2.0 module. FILE is the optional pathname to the Apache apxs tool; defaults to apxs.

–with-caudium=DIR
　　Build PHP as a Pike module for use with Caudium. DIR is the Caudium server dir, with the default value /usr/local/caudium/server.

–disable-cli
　　Disable building the CLI version of PHP (this forces –without-pear). Available with PHP 4.3.0.

–enable-embed[=TYPE]
　　Enable building of the embedded SAPI library. TYPE is either shared or static, which defaults to shared. Avail-able with PHP 4.3.0.

–with-fhttpd[=DIR]
　　Build fhttpd module. DIR is the fhttpd sources directory, defaults to /usr/local/src/fhttpd. No longer available as of PHP 4.3.0.

–with-isapi=DIR
　　Build PHP as an ISAPI module for use with Zeus.

–with-nsapi=DIR
　　Specify path to the installed Netscape Server.

43

–with-phttpd=DIR
  No information yet.

–with-pi3web=DIR
  Build PHP as a module for use with Pi3Web.

–with-roxen=DIR
  Build PHP as a Pike module. DIR is the base Roxen directory, normally /usr/local/roxen/server.

–enable-roxen-zts
  Build the Roxen module using Zend Thread Safety.

–with-servlet[=DIR]
  Include servlet support. DIR is the base install directory for the JSDK. This SAPI requires the java extension must be built as a shared dl.

–with-thttpd=SRCDIR
  Build PHP as thttpd module.

–with-tux=MODULEDIR
  Build PHP as a TUX module (Linux only).

–with-webjames=SRCDIR
  Build PHP as a WebJames module (RISC OS only)

–disable-cgi
  Disable building CGI version of PHP. Available with PHP 4.3.0.

–enable-force-cgi-redirect
  Enable the security check for internal server redirects. You should use this if you are running the CGI version with Apache.

–enable-discard-path
  If this is enabled, the PHP CGI binary can safely be placed outside of the web tree and people will not be able to cir-cumvent .htaccess security.

–with-fastcgi
  Build PHP as FastCGI application. No longer available as of PHP 4.3.0.

–enable-fastcgi
  If this is enabled, the CGI module will be built with support for FastCGI also. Available since PHP 4.3.0

–disable-path-info-check
  If this is disabled, paths such as /info.php/test?a=b will fail to work. Available since PHP 4.3.0

44

Chapter 4. Configuration

Table of Contents

The configuration file

The configuration file (called php3.ini in PHP 3.0, and simply php.ini as of PHP 4.0) is read when PHP starts up. For the server module versions of PHP, this happens only once when the web server is started. For the CGI and CLI version, it happens on every invocation.

The default location of php.ini is a compile time option (see the FAQ entry), but can be changed for the CGI and CLI ver-sion with the -c command line switch, see the chapter about using PHP from the command line. You can also use the envir-onment variable PHPRC for an additional path to search for a php.ini file.

> **Note:** The Apache web server changes the directory to root at startup causing PHP to attempt to read php.ini from the root filesystem if it exists.

Not every PHP directive is documented below. For a list of all directives, please read your well commented php.ini file.
You may want to view the latest php.ini here [http://cvs.php.net/co.php/php4/php.ini-dist] from CVS.

> **Note:** The default value for the PHP directive register_globals changed from *on* to *off* in PHP 4.2.0 [http:/ / www.php.net/release_4_2_0.php].

Example 4.1. php.ini example

```
; any text on a line after an unquoted semicolon (;) is ignored
[php] ; section markers (text within square brackets) are also ignored
>>>      Boolean values can be set to either:
>>>   true, on, yes
>>>   or false, off, no, none
register_globals = off
magic_quotes_gpc = yes

• you can enclose strings in double-quotes
include_path = ".:/usr/local/lib/php"

• backslashes are treated the same as any other character
include_path = ".;c:\php\lib"
```

How to change configuration settings

Running PHP as Apache module

When using PHP as an Apache module, you can also change the configuration settings using directives in Apache configur-ation files (e.g. httpd.conf) and .htaccess files (You will need "AllowOverride Options" or "AllowOverride All" priv-ileges)

45

With PHP 4.0, there are several Apache directives that allow you to change the PHP configuration from within the Apache configuration files. For a listing of which directives are PHP_INI_ALL, PHP_INI_PERDIR, or PHP_INI_SYSTEM, have a look at the table found within the **Ini_set()** documentation.

Note: With PHP 3.0, there are Apache directives that correspond to each configuration setting in the php3.ini name, except the name is prefixed by "php3_".

php_value *name value*
    Sets the value of the specified directive. Can be used only with PHP_INI_ALL and PHP_INI_PERDIR type directives.
    To clear a previously set value use none as the value.

    php_value auto_prepend_file none

Note: Don't use php_value to set boolean values. php_flag (see below) should be used instead.

php_flag *name on|off*
    Used to set a Boolean configuration directive. Can be used only with PHP_INI_ALL and PHP_INI_PERDIR type direct-ives.

php_admin_value *name value*
    Sets the value of the specified directive. This can NOT be used in .htaccess files. Any directive type set with php_admin_value can not be overridden by .htaccess or virtualhost directives. To clear a previously set value use none as the value.

    php_admin_value open_basedir none

php_admin_flag *name on|off*
    Used to set a Boolean configuration directive. This can NOT be used in .htaccess files. Any directive type set with php_admin_flag can not be overridden by .htaccess or virtualhost directives.

Example 4.2. Apache configuration example

```
<IfModule mod_php4.c>
    php_value include_path ".:/usr/local/lib/php"
    php_admin_flag safe_mode on
</IfModule>
<IfModule mod_php3.c>
    php3_include_path ".:/usr/local/lib/php"
    php3_safe_mode on
</IfModule>
```

Note: PHP constants do not exist outside of PHP. For example, in httpd.conf you can not use PHP constants such as E_ALL or E_NOTICE to set the error_reporting directive as they will have no meaning and will evaluate to 0. Use the associated bitmask values instead. These constants can be used in php.ini

Other interfaces to PHP

Regardless of the interface to PHP you can change certain values at runtime of your scripts through **Ini_set()**. The following table provides an overview at which level a directive can be set/changed.

Table 4.1. Definition of PHP_INI_* constants

Constant	Value	Meaning
PHP_INI_USER	1	Entry can be set in user scripts
PHP_INI_PERDIR	2	Entry can be set in php.ini, .htaccess or httpd.conf
PHP_INI_SYSTEM	4	Entry can be set in php.ini or httpd.conf
PHP_INI_ALL	7	Entry can be set anywhere

You can view the settings of the configuration values in the output of **phpinfo()**. You can also access the values of individual configuration directives using **ini_get()** or **get_cfg_var()**.

Miscellaneous configuration directives

This is not a complete list of PHP directives. Directives are listed in their appropriate locations so for example information on session directives is located in the sessions chapter.

Httpd Options

Table 4.2. Httpd Options

Name	Default	Changeable
async_send	"0"	PHP_INI_ALL

Language Options

Table 4.3. Language and Misc Configuration Options

Name	Default	Changeable
short_open_tag	On	PHP_INI_SYSTEM|PHP_INI_PERDIR
asp_tags	Off	PHP_INI_SYSTEM|PHP_INI_PERDIR
precision	"14"	PHP_INI_ALL
y2k_compliance	Off	PHP_INI_ALL
allow_call_time_pass_reference	On	PHP_INI_SYSTEM|PHP_INI_PERDIR
expose_php	On	PHP_INI_SYSTEM

Here's a short explanation of the configuration directives.

short_open_tag boolean

Tells whether the short form (**<? ?>**) of PHP's open tag should be allowed. If you want to use PHP in combination with XML, you can disable this option in order to use **<?xml ?>** inline. Otherwise, you can print it with PHP, for example: **<?php echo '<?xml version="1.0"; ?>**. Also if disabled, you must use the long form of the PHP open tag (**<?php ?>**).

Note: This directive also affects the shorthand **<?=**, which is identical to **<? echo**. Use of this shortcut requires short_open_tag to be on.

47

asp_tags boolean

Enables the use of ASP-like <% %> tags in addition to the usual <?php ?> tags. This includes the variable-value print-ing shorthand of <%= $value %>. For more information, see Escaping from HTML.

Note: Support for ASP-style tags was added in 3.0.4.

precision integer

The number of significant digits displayed in floating point numbers.

y2k_compliance boolean

Enforce year 2000 compliance (will cause problems with non-compliant browsers)

allow_call_time_pass_reference boolean

Whether to enable the ability to force arguments to be passed by reference at function call time. This method is deprec-ated and is likely to be unsupported in future versions of PHP/Zend. The encouraged method of specifying which argu-ments should be passed by reference is in the function declaration. You're encouraged to try and turn this option Off and make sure your scripts work properly with it in order to ensure they will work with future versions of the language (you will receive a warning each time you use this feature, and the argument will be passed by value instead of by refer-ence).

See also References Explained.

expose_php boolean

Decides whether PHP may expose the fact that it is installed on the server (e.g. by adding its signature to the Web serv-er header). It is no security threat in any way, but it makes it possible to determine whether you use PHP on your server or not.

Resource Limits

Table 4.4. Resource Limits

Name	Default	Changeable
memory_limit	"8M"	PHP_INI_ALL

Here's a short explanation of the configuration directives.

memory_limit integer

This sets the maximum amount of memory in bytes that a script is allowed to allocate. This helps prevent poorly written scripts for eating up all available memory on a server. In order to use this directive you must have enabled it at compile time. So, your configure line would have included: --enable-memory-limit. Note that you have to set it to -1 if you don't want any limit for your memory.

See also: max_execution_time.

Data Handling

Table 4.5. Data Handling Configuration Options

Name	Default	Changeable
track-vars	"On"	PHP_INI_??

Name	Default	Changeable
arg_separator.output	"&"	PHP_INI_ALL
arg_separator.input	"&"	PHP_INI_SYSTEM | PHP_INI_PERDIR
variables_order	"EGPCS"	PHP_INI_ALL
register_globals	"Off"	PHP_INI_PERDIR | PHP_INI_SYSTEM
register_argc_argv	"On"	PHP_INI_PERDIR | PHP_INI_SYSTEM
post_max_size	"8M"	PHP_INI_SYSTEM | PHP_INI_PERDIR
gpc_order	"GPC"	PHP_INI_ALL
auto_prepend_file	""	PHP_INI_SYSTEM | PHP_INI_PERDIR
auto_append_file	""	PHP_INI_SYSTEM | PHP_INI_PERDIR
default_mimetype	"text/html"	PHP_INI_ALL
default_charset	"iso-8859-1"	PHP_INI_ALL
always_populate_raw_post_data	"0"	PHP_INI_SYSTEM | PHP_INI_PERDIR
allow_webdav_methods	"0"	PHP_INI_SYSTEM | PHP_INI_PERDIR

Here's a short explanation of the configuration directives.

track_vars boolean
> If enabled, then Environment, GET, POST, Cookie, and Server variables can be found in the global associative arrays $_ENV, $_GET, $_POST, $_COOKIE, and $_SERVER.

> Note that as of PHP 4.0.3, track_vars is always turned on.

arg_separator.output string
> The separator used in PHP generated URLs to separate arguments.

arg_separator.input string
> List of separator(s) used by PHP to parse input URLs into variables.

> **Note:** Every character in this directive is considered as separator!

variables_order string
> Set the order of the EGPCS (Environment, GET, POST, Cookie, Server) variable parsing. The default setting of this directive is "EGPCS". Setting this to "GP", for example, will cause PHP to completely ignore environment variables, cookies and server variables, and to overwrite any GET method variables with POST-method variables of the same name.

> See also register_globals.

register_globals boolean

Tells whether or not to register the EGPCS (Environment, GET, POST, Cookie, Server) variables as global variables. For example; if register_globals = on, the url http://www.example.com/test.php?id=3 will produce $id. Or, $DOCUMENT_ROOT from $_SERVER['DOCUMENT_ROOT']. You may want to turn this off if you don't want to clutter your scripts' global scope with user data. As of PHP 4.2.0 [http:/ / www.php.net/ release_4_2_0.php], this directive de-faults to *off*. It's preferred to go through PHP Predefined Variables instead, such as the superglobals: $_ENV, $_GET, $_POST, $_COOKIE, and $_SERVER. Please read the security chapter on Using register_globals for related information.

Please note that register_globals cannot be set at runtime (**ini_set()**). **Although, you can use .htaccess if your host allows it as described above. An example .htaccess entry: php_flag register_globals on.**

Note: register_globals is affected by the variables_order directive.

49

register_argc_argv boolean
Tells PHP whether to declare the argv & argc variables (that would contain the GET information).

See also command line. Also, this directive became available in PHP 4.0.0 and was always "on" before that.

post_max_size integer
Sets max size of post data allowed. This setting also affects file upload. To upload large files, this value must be larger than upload_max_filesize.

If memory limit is enabled by your configure script, memory_limit also affects file uploading. Generally speaking, memory_limit should be larger than *post_max_size*.

gpc_order string
Set the order of GET/POST/COOKIE variable parsing. The default setting of this directive is "GPC". Setting this to "GP", for example, will cause PHP to completely ignore cookies and to overwrite any GET method variables with POST-method variables of the same name.

Note: This option is not available in PHP 4. Use variables_order instead.

auto_prepend_file string
Specifies the name of a file that is automatically parsed before the main file. The file is included as if it was called with the **include()** function, so include_path is used.

The special value none disables auto-prepending.

auto_append_file string
Specifies the name of a file that is automatically parsed after the main file. The file is included as if it was called with the **include()** function, so include_path is used.

The special value none disables auto-appending.

Note: If the script is terminated with **exit()**, auto-append will *not* occur.

default_mimetype string

default_charset string
As of 4.0b4, PHP always outputs a character encoding by default in the Content-type: header. To disable sending of the charset, simply set it to be empty.

always_populate_raw_post_data boolean
Always populate the $HTTP_RAW_POST_DATA variable.

allow_webdav_methods boolean
Allow handling of WebDAV http requests within PHP scripts (eg. PROPFIND, PROPPATCH, MOVE, COPY, etc..) If you want to get the post data of those requests, you have to set always_populate_raw_post_data as well.

See also: magic_quotes_gpc, magic-quotes-runtime, and magic_quotes_sybase.

Paths and Directories

Table 4.6. Paths and Directories Configuration Options

Name	Default	Changeable
include_path	PHP_INCLUDE_PATH	PHP_INI_ALL
doc_root	PHP_INCLUDE_PATH	PHP_INI_SYSTEM

| user_dir | NULL | PHP_INI_SYSTEM |

50

Name	Default	Changeable
extension_dir	PHP_EXTENSION_DIR	PHP_INI_SYSTEM
cgi.force_redirect	"1"	PHP_INI_SYSTEM
cgi.redirect_status_env	""	PHP_INI_SYSTEM
fastcgi.impersonate	"0"	PHP_INI_SYSTEM

Here's a short explanation of the configuration directives.

include_path string

Specifies a list of directories where the **require()**, **include()** and **fopen_with_path()** functions look for files. The format is like the system's PATH environment variable: a list of directories separated with a colon in UNIX or semicolon in Windows.

Example 4.3. UNIX include_path

include_path=".:/php/includes"

Example 4.4. Windows include_path

include_path=".;c:\php\includes"

Using a . in the include path allows for relative includes as it means the current directory.

doc_root string

PHP's "root directory" on the server. Only used if non-empty. If PHP is configured with safe mode, no files outside this directory are served. If PHP was not compiled with FORCE_REDIRECT, you SHOULD set doc_root if you are run-ning php as a CGI under any web server (other than IIS) The alternative is to use the cgi.force_redirect configuration below.

user_dir string

The base name of the directory used on a user's home directory for PHP files, for example public_html.

extension_dir string

In what directory PHP should look for dynamically loadable extensions. See also: enable_dl, and **dl()**.

extension string

Which dynamically loadable extensions to load when PHP starts up.

cgi.force_redirect boolean

cgi.force_redirect is necessary to provide security running PHP as a CGI under most web servers. Left undefined, PHP turns this on by default. You can turn it off *AT YOUR OWN RISK*.

Note: Windows Users: You CAN safely turn this off for IIS, in fact, you MUST. To get OmniHTTPD or Xitami to work you MUST turn it off.

cgi.redirect_status_env string

If cgi.force_redirect is turned on, and you are not running under Apache or Netscape (iPlanet) web servers, you MAY need to set an environment variable name that PHP will look for to know it is OK to continue execution.

## 51

Note: Setting this variable MAY cause security issues, KNOW WHAT YOU ARE DOING FIRST.

fastcgi.impersonate string
  FastCGI under IIS (on WINNT based OS) supports the ability to impersonate security tokens of the calling client. This allows IIS to define the security context that the request runs under. mod_fastcgi under Apache does not currently sup-port this feature (03/17/2002) Set to 1 if running under IIS. Default is zero.

File Uploads

Table 4.7. File Uploads Configuration Options

Name	Default	Changeable
file_uploads	"1"	PHP_INI_SYSTEM
upload_tmp_dir	NULL	PHP_INI_SYSTEM
upload_max_filesize	"2M"	PHP_INI_SYSTEM | PHP_INI_PERDIR

Here's a short explanation of the configuration directives.

file_uploads boolean
  Whether or not to allow HTTP file uploads. See also the upload_max_filesize, upload_tmp_dir, and post_max_size dir-ectives.

upload_tmp_dir string
  The temporary directory used for storing files when doing file upload. Must be writable by whatever user PHP is run-ning as. If not specified PHP will use the system's default.

upload_max_filesize integer
  The maximum size of an uploaded file.

General SQL

Table 4.8. General SQL Configuration Options

Name	Default	Changeable
sql.safe_mode	"0"	PHP_INI_SYSTEM

Here's a short explanation of the configuration directives.

sql.safe_mode boolean

Debugger Configuration Directives

debugger.host string
  DNS name or IP address of host used by the debugger.

debugger.port string
Port number used by the debugger.

debugger.enabled boolean
Whether the debugger is enabled.

Chapter 5. Security

Table of Contents

PHP is a powerful language and the interpreter, whether included in a web server as a module or executed as a separate CGI binary, is able to access files, execute commands and open network connections on the server. These properties make any-thing run on a web server insecure by default. PHP is designed specifically to be a more secure language for writing CGI programs than Perl or C, and with correct selection of compile-time and runtime configuration options, and proper coding practices, it can give you exactly the combination of freedom and security you need.

As there are many different ways of utilizing PHP, there are many configuration options controlling its behaviour. A large selection of options guarantees you can use PHP for a lot of purposes, but it also means there are combinations of these op-tions and server configurations that result in an insecure setup.

The configuration flexibility of PHP is equally rivalled by the code flexibility. PHP can be used to build complete server ap-plications, with all the power of a shell user, or it can be used for simple server-side includes with little risk in a tightly con-trolled environment. How you build that environment, and how secure it is, is largely up to the PHP developer.

This chapter starts with some general security advice, explains the different configuration option combinations and the situ-ations they can be safely used, and describes different considerations in coding for different levels of security.

General considerations

A completely secure system is a virtual impossibility, so an approach often used in the security profession is one of balan-cing risk and usability. If every variable submitted by a user required two forms of biometric validation (such as a retinal scan and a fingerprint), you would have an extremely high level of accountability. It would also take half an hour to fill out a fairly complex form, which would tend to encourage users to find ways of bypassing the security.

The best security is often inobtrusive enough to suit the requirements without the user being prevented from accomplishing their work, or over-burdening the code author with excessive complexity. Indeed, some security attacks are merely exploits of this kind of overly built security, which tends to erode over time.

A phrase worth remembering: A system is only as good as the weakest link in a chain. If all transactions are heavily logged based on time, location, transaction type, etc. but the user is only verified based on a single cookie, the validity of tying the users to the transaction log is severely weakened.

When testing, keep in mind that you will not be able to test all possibilities for even the simplest of pages. The input you may expect will be completely unrelated to the input given by a disgruntled employee, a cracker with months of time on their hands, or a housecat walking across the keyboard. This is why it's best to look at the code from a logical perspective, to discern where unexpected data can be introduced, and then follow how it is modified, reduced, or amplified.

## 54

The Internet is filled with people trying to make a name for themselves by breaking your code, crashing your site, posting inappropriate content, and otherwise making your day interesting. It doesn't matter if you have a small or large site, you are a target by simply being online, by having a server that can be connected to. Many cracking programs do not discern by size, they simply trawl massive IP blocks looking for victims. Try not to become one.

Installed as CGI binary

Possible attacks

Using PHP as a CGI binary is an option for setups that for some reason do not wish to integrate PHP as a module into server software (like Apache), or will use PHP with different kinds of CGI wrappers to create safe chroot and setuid environments for scripts. This setup usually involves installing executable PHP binary to the web server cgi-bin directory. CERT advisory CA-96.11 [http://www.cert.org/advisories/CA-96.11.interpreters_in_cgi_bin_dir.html] recommends against placing any in-terpreters into cgi-bin. Even if the PHP binary can be used as a standalone interpreter, PHP is designed to prevent the at-tacks this setup makes possible:

>>>   Accessing system files: http://my.host/cgi-bin/php?/etc/passwd

The query information in a url after the question mark (?) is passed as command line arguments to the interpreter by the CGI interface. Usually interpreters open and execute the file specified as the first argument on the command line.

When invoked as a CGI binary, PHP refuses to interpret the command line arguments.

>>>   Accessing any web document on server: http://my.host/cgi-bin/php/secret/doc.html

The path information part of the url after the PHP binary name, /secret/doc.html is conventionally used to specify the name of the file to be opened and interpreted by the CGI program. Usually some web server configuration directives (Apache: Action) are used to redirect requests to documents like http://my.host/secret/script.php to the PHP interpreter. With this setup, the web server first checks the access permissions to the directory /secret, and after that creates the redirected request http://my.host/cgi-bin/php/secret/script.php. Unfortunately, if the request is originally given in this form, no access checks are made by web server for file /secret/script.php, but only for the /cgi-bin/php file. This way any user able to access /cgi-bin/php is able to access any protected document on the web server.

In PHP, compile-time configuration option –enable-force-cgi-redirect and runtime configuration directives doc_root and user_dir can be used to prevent this attack, if the server document tree has any directories with access restrictions. See below for full the explanation of the different combinations.

Case 1: only public files served

If your server does not have any content that is not restricted by password or ip based access control, there is no need for these configuration options. If your web server does not allow you to do redirects, or the server does not have a way to com-municate to the PHP binary that the request is a safely redirected request, you can specify the option - -enable-force-cgi-redirect to the configure script. You still have to make sure your PHP scripts do not rely on one or another way of calling the script, neither by directly http://my.host/cgi-bin/php/dir/script.php nor by redirection ht-tp://my.host/dir/script.php.

Redirection can be configured in Apache by using AddHandler and Action directives (see below).

Case 2: using –enable-force-cgi-redirect

This compile-time option prevents anyone from calling PHP directly with a url like ht-tp://my.host/cgi-bin/php/secretdir/script.php. Instead, PHP will only parse in this mode if it has gone

55

through a web server redirect rule.

Usually the redirection in the Apache configuration is done with the following directives:

```
Action php-script /cgi-bin/php
AddHandler php-script .php
```

This option has only been tested with the Apache web server, and relies on Apache to set the non-standard CGI environment variable REDIRECT_STATUS on redirected requests. If your web server does not support any way of telling if the request is direct or redirected, you cannot use this option and you must use one of the other ways of running the CGI version docu-mented here.

Case 3: setting doc_root or user_dir

To include active content, like scripts and executables, in the web server document directories is sometimes consider an in-secure practice. If, because of some configuration mistake, the scripts are not executed but displayed as regular HTML doc-uments, this may result in leakage of intellectual property or security information like passwords. Therefore many sysad-mins will prefer setting up another directory structure for scripts that are accessible only through the PHP CGI, and there-fore always interpreted and not displayed as such.

Also if the method for making sure the requests are not redirected, as described in the previous section, is not available, it is necessary to set up a script doc_root that is different from web document root.

You can set the PHP script document root by the configuration directive doc_root in the configuration file, or you can set the environment variable PHP_DOCUMENT_ROOT. If it is set, the CGI version of PHP will always construct the file name to open with this *doc_root* and the path information in the request, so you can be sure no script is executed outside this direct-ory (except for *user_dir* below).

Another option usable here is user_dir. When user_dir is unset, only thing controlling the opened file name is *doc_root*. Opening an url like http://my.host/~user/doc.php does not result in opening a file under users home directory, but a file called ~user/doc.php under doc_root (yes, a directory name starting with a tilde [~]).

If user_dir is set to for example public_php, a request like http://my.host/~user/doc.php will open a file called doc.php under the directory named public_php under the home directory of the user. If the home of the user is /home/user, the file executed is /home/user/public_php/doc.php.

user_dir expansion happens regardless of the *doc_root* setting, so you can control the document root and user directory ac-cess separately.

Case 4: PHP parser outside of web tree

A very secure option is to put the PHP parser binary somewhere outside of the web tree of files. In /usr/local/bin, for example. The only real downside to this option is that you will now have to put a line similar to:

```
#!/usr/local/bin/php
```

as the first line of any file containing PHP tags. You will also need to make the file executable. That is, treat it exactly as you would treat any other CGI script written in Perl or sh or any other common scripting language which uses the #! shell-escape mechanism for launching itself.

To get PHP to handle PATH_INFO and PATH_TRANSLATED information correctly with this setup, the php parser should be compiled with the —enable-discard-path configure option.

Installed as an Apache module

When PHP is used as an Apache module it inherits Apache's user permissions (typically those of the "nobody" user). This has several impacts on security and authorization. For example, if you are using PHP to access a database, unless that data-

---

56

base has built-in access control, you will have to make the database accessable to the "nobody" user. This means a malicious script could access and modify the database, even without a username and password. It's entirely possible that a web spider could stumble across a database administrator's web page, and drop all of your databases. You can protect against this with Apache authorization, or you can design your own access model using LDAP, .htaccess files, etc. and include that code as part of your PHP scripts.

Often, once security is established to the point where the PHP user (in this case, the apache user) has very little risk attached to it, it is discovered that PHP is now prevented from writing any files to user directories. Or perhaps it has been prevented from accessing or changing databases. It has equally been secured from writing good and bad files, or entering good and bad database transactions.

A frequent security mistake made at this point is to allow apache root permissions, or to escalate apache's abilitites in some other way.

Escalating the Apache user's permissions to root is extremely dangerous and may compromise the entire system, so sudo'ing, chroot'ing, or otherwise running as root should not be considered by those who are not security professionals.

There are some simpler solutions. By using open_basedir you can control and restrict what directories are allowed to be used for PHP. You can also set up apache-only areas, to restrict all web based activity to non-user, or non-system, files.

Filesystem Security

PHP is subject to the security built into most server systems with respect to permissions on a file and directory basis. This allows you to control which files in the filesystem may be read. Care should be taken with any files which are world read-able to ensure that they are safe for reading by all users who have access to that filesystem.

Since PHP was designed to allow user level access to the filesystem, it's entirely possible to write a PHP script that will al-low you to read system files such as /etc/passwd, modify your ethernet connections, send massive printer jobs out, etc. This has some obvious implications, in that you need to ensure that the files that you read from and write to are the appropriate ones.

Consider the following script, where a user indicates that they'd like to delete a file in their home directory. This assumes a situation where a PHP web interface is regularly used for file management, so the Apache user is allowed to delete files in the user home directories.

Example 5.1. Poor variable checking leads to....

```
<?php
>>>    remove a file from the user's home directory
$username = $_POST['user_submitted_name'];
$homedir = "/home/$username"; $file_to_delete =
"$userfile";
unlink ("$homedir/$userfile");
echo "$file_to_delete has been deleted!"; ?>
```

Since the username is postable from a user form, they can submit a username and file belonging to someone else, and delete files. In this case, you'd want to use some other form of authentication. Consider what could happen if the variables submit-ted were "../etc/" and "passwd". The code would then effectively read:

Example 5.2. ... A filesystem attack

```
<?php
>>>    removes a file from anywhere on the hard drive that
>>>    the PHP user has access to. If PHP has root access:
$username = "../etc/";
$homedir  =  "/home/../etc/";
$file_to_delete = "passwd";
```

```
unlink ("/home/../etc/passwd");
echo "/home/../etc/passwd has been deleted!";
?>
```

There are two important measures you should take to prevent these issues.

>>>   Only allow limited permissions to the PHP web user binary.

>>>   Check all variables which are submitted.

Here is an improved script:

Example 5.3. More secure file name checking

```
<?php
#   removes a file from the hard drive that
#   the PHP user has access to.
$username = $_SERVER['REMOTE_USER']; // using an authentication mechanisim

$homedir = "/home/$username";

$file_to_delete = basename("$userfile"); // strip paths unlink
($homedir/$file_to_delete);

$fp = fopen("/home/logging/filedelete.log","+a"); //log the deletion $logstring =
"$username $homedir $file_to_delete"; fputs ($fp, $logstring);
fclose($fp);

echo "$file_to_delete has been deleted!";
?>
```

However, even this is not without it's flaws. If your authentication system allowed users to create their own user logins, and a user chose the login "../etc/", the system is once again exposed. For this reason, you may prefer to write a more custom-ized check:

Example 5.4. More secure file name checking

```
<?php
$username = $_SERVER['REMOTE_USER']; // using an authentication mechanisim
$homedir = "/home/$username";

if (!ereg('^[^./][^/]*$', $userfile))
     die('bad filename'); //die, do not process

if (!ereg('^[^./][^/]*$', $username))
     die('bad username'); //die, do not process
//etc...
?>
```

Depending on your operating system, there are a wide variety of files which you should be concerned about, including device entries (/dev/ or COM1), configuration files (/etc/ files and the .ini files), well known file storage areas (/home/, My Documents), etc. For this reason, it's usually easier to create a policy where you forbid everything except for what you ex-plicitly allow.

Database Security

Nowadays, databases are cardinal components of any web based application by enabling websites to provide varying dy-

namic content. Since very sensitive or secret informations can be stored in such database, you should strongly consider to protect them somehow.

To retrieve or to store any information you need to connect to the database, send a legitimate query, fetch the result, and close the connecion. Nowadays, the commonly used query language in this interaction is the Structured Query Language (SQL). See how an attacker can tamper with an SQL query.

As you can realize, PHP cannot protect your database by itself. The following sections aim to be an introduction into the very basics of how to access and manipulate databases within PHP scripts.

Keep in mind this simple rule: defence in depth. In the more place you take the more action to increase the protection of your database, the less probability of that an attacker succeeds, and exposes or abuse any stored secret information. Good design of the database schema and the application deals with your greatest fears.

Designing Databases

The first step is always to create the database, unless you want to use an existing third party's one. When a database is cre-ated, it is assigned to an owner, who executed the creation statement. Usually, only the owner (or a superuser) can do any-thing with the objects in that database, and in order to allow other users to use it, privileges must be granted.

Applications should never connect to the database as its owner or a superuser, because these users can execute any query at will, for example, modifying the schema (e.g. dropping tables) or deleting its entire content.

You may create different database users for every aspect of your application with very limited rights to database objects. The most required privileges should be granted only, and avoid that the same user can interact with the database in different use cases. This means that if intruders gain access to your database using one of these credentials, they can only effect as many changes as your application can.

You are encouraged not to implement all the business logic in the web application (i.e. your script), instead to do it in the database schema using views, triggers or rules. If the system evolves, new ports will be intended to open to the database, and you have to reimplement the logic in each separate database client. Over and above, triggers can be used to transpar-ently and automatically handle fields, which often provides insight when debugging problems with your application or tra-cing back transactions.

Connecting to Database

You may want to estabilish the connections over SSL to encrypt client/server communications for increased security, or you can use ssh to encrypt the network connection between clients and the database server. If either of them is done, then monit-oring your traffic and gaining informations in this way will be a hard work.

Encrypted Storage Model

SSL/SSH protects data travelling from the client to the server, SSL/SSH does not protect the persistent data stored in a data-base. SSL is an on-the-wire protocol.

Once an attacker gains access to your database directly (bypassing the webserver), the stored sensitive data may be exposed or misused, unless the information is protected by the database itself. Encrypting the data is a good way to mitigate this threat, but very few databases offer this type of data encryption.

The easiest way to work around this problem is to first create your own encryption package, and then use it from within your PHP scripts. PHP can assist you in this case with its several extensions, such as Mcrypt and Mhash, covering a wide variety of encryption algorithms. The script encrypts the data be stored first, and decrypts it when retrieving. See the refer-ences for further examples how encryption works.

In case of truly hidden data, if its raw representation is not needed (i.e. not be displayed), hashing may be also taken into consideration. The well-known example for the hashing is storing the MD5 hash of a password in a database, instead of the password itself. See also **crypt()** and **md5()**.

Example 5.5. Using hashed password field

```
// storing password hash
$query      = sprintf("INSERT INTO users(name,pwd) VALUES('%s','%s');",
                addslashes($username), md5($password));
$result = pg_exec($connection, $query);

// querying if user submitted the right password
$query = sprintf("SELECT 1 FROM users WHERE name='%s' AND pwd='%s';",
                addslashes($username), md5($password));
$result = pg_exec($connection, $query);

if (pg_numrows($result) > 0) {
    echo "Welcome, $username!";
}
else {
    echo "Authentication failed for $username.";
}
```

SQL Injection

Many web developers are unaware of how SQL queries can be tampered with, and assume that an SQL query is a trusted command. It means that SQL queries are able to circumvent access controls, thereby bypassing standard authentication and authorization checks, and sometimes SQL queries even may allow access to host operating system level commands.

Direct SQL Command Injection is a technique where an attacker creates or alters existing SQL commands to expose hidden data, or to override valuable ones, or even to execute dangerous system level commands on the database host. This is ac-complished by the application taking user input and combining it with static parameters to build a SQL query. The follow-ing examples are based on true stories, unfortunately.

Owing to the lack of input validation and connecting to the database on behalf of a superuser or the one who can create users, the attacker may create a superuser in your database.

Example 5.6. Splitting the result set into pages ... and making superusers (PostgreSQL and MySQL)

```
$offset = argv[0]; // beware, no input validation!
$query = "SELECT id, name FROM products ORDER BY name LIMIT 20 OFFSET $offset;"; // with
PostgreSQL
$result = pg_exec($conn, $query);
// with MySQL
$result = mysql_query($query);
```

Normal users click on the 'next', 'prev' links where the $offset is encoded into the URL. The script expects that the incom-ing $offset is decimal number. However, someone tries to break in with appending **urlencode()**'d form of the following to the URL

```
>>>    in case of PostgreSQL
0;
insert into pg_shadow(usename,usesysid,usesuper,usecatupd,passwd) select
    'crack', usesysid, 't','t','crack'
    from pg_shadow where usename='postgres';
_

>>>    in case of MySQL
0;
UPDATE user SET Password=PASSWORD('crack') WHERE user='root';
FLUSH PRIVILEGES;
```

If it happened, then the script would present a superuser access to him. Note that 0; is to supply a valid offset to the original

---

60

query and to terminate it.

Note: It is common technique to force the SQL parser to ignore the rest of the query written by the developer with

- which is the comment sign in SQL.

A feasible way to gain passwords is to circumvent your search result pages. What the attacker needs only is to try if there is any submitted variable used in SQL statement which is not handled properly. These filters can be set commonly in a preced-ing form to customize WHERE, ORDER BY, LIMIT and OFFSET clauses in SELECT statements. If your database supports the UNION construct, the attacker may try to append an entire query to the original one to list passwords from an arbitrary ta-ble. Using encrypted password fields is strongly encouraged.

Example 5.7. Listing out articles ... and some passwords (any database server)

```
$query = "SELECT id, name, inserted, size FROM products
              WHERE size = '$size'
              ORDER BY $order LIMIT $limit, $offset;";
$result = odbc_exec($conn, $query);
```

The static part of the query can be combined with another SELECT statement which reveals all passwords:

```
union select '1', concat(uname||'-'||passwd) as name, '1971-01-01', '0' from usertable;
```

If this query (playing with the ' and –) were assigned to one of the variables used in $query, the query beast awakened.

SQL UPDATEs are also subject to attacking your database. These queries are also threatened by chopping and appending an entirely new query to it. But the attacker might fiddle with the SET clause. In this case some schema information must be possessed to manipulate the query successfully. This can be acquired by examing the form variable names, or just simply brute forcing. There are not so many naming convention for fields storing passwords or usernames.

Example 5.8. From resetting a password ... to gaining more privileges (any database server)

```
$query = "UPDATE usertable SET pwd='$pwd' WHERE uid='$uid';";
```

But a malicious user sumbits the value ' or uid like'%admin%'; – to $uid to change the admin's password, or simply sets $pwd to "hehehe', admin='yes', trusted=100 " (with a trailing space) to gain more privileges. Then, the query will be twisted:

```
// $uid == ' or uid like'%admin%'; –
$query = "UPDATE usertable SET pwd='...' WHERE uid='' or uid like '%admin%'; –'";

// $pwd == "hehehe', admin='yes', trusted=100 "
$query = "UPDATE usertable SET pwd='hehehe', admin='yes', trusted=100 WHERE ...;"
```

A frightening example how operating system level commands can be accessed on some database hosts.

Example 5.9. Attacking the database host's operating system (MSSQL Server)

```
$query = "SELECT * FROM products WHERE id LIKE '%$prod%'";
$result = mssql_query($query);
```

If attacker submits the value a%' exec master..xp_cmdshell 'net user test testpass /ADD' – to $prod, then the $query will be:

```
$query = "SELECT * FROM products
              WHERE id LIKE '%a%'
```

```
                    exec master..xp_cmdshell 'net user test testpass /ADD'–"; $result =
mssql_query($query);
```

61

MSSQL Server executes the SQL statements in the batch including a command to add a new user to the local accounts data-base. If this application were running as sa and the MSSQLSERVER service is running with sufficient privileges, the at-tacker would now have an account with which to access this machine.

Note: Some of the examples above is tied to a specific database server. This does not mean that a similar attack is impossible against other products. Your database server may be so vulnerable in other manner.

Avoiding techniques

You may plead that the attacker must possess a piece of information about the database schema in most examples. You are right, but you never know when and how it can be taken out, and if it happens, your database may be exposed. If you are us-ing an open source, or publicly available database handling package, which may belong to a content management system or forum, the intruders easily produce a copy of a piece of your code. It may be also a security risk if it is a poorly designed one.

These attacks are mainly based on exploiting the code not being written with security in mind. Never trust on any kind of in-put, especially which comes from the client side, even though it comes from a select box, a hidden input field or a cookie. The first example shows that such a blameless query can cause disasters.

>>>   Never connect to the database as a superuser or as the database owner. Use always customized users with very limited privileges.

>>>   Check if the given input has the expected data type. PHP has a wide range of input validating functions, from the simplest ones found in Variable Functions and in Character Type Functions (e.g. **is_numeric(), ctype_digit()** respect-ively) onwards the **Perl compatible Regular Expressions support.**

>>>   If the application waits for numerical input, consider to verify data with **is_numeric(), or silently change its type using settype()**, or use its numeric representation by **sprintf().**

Example 5.10. A more secure way to compose a query for paging

```
settype($offset, 'integer');
$query = "SELECT id, name FROM products ORDER BY name LIMIT 20 OFFSET $offset;";

// please note %d in the format string, using %s would be meaningless
$query = sprintf("SELECT id, name FROM products ORDER BY name LIMIT 20 OFFSET %d;", $offset);
```

>>>   Quote each non numeric user input which is passed to the database with **addslashes()** or **addcslashes()**. See the first ex-ample. As the examples shows, quotes burnt into the static part of the query is not enough, and can be easily hacked.

>>>   Do not print out any database specific information, especially about the schema, by fair means or foul. See also Error Reporting and Error Handling and Logging Functions.

>>>   You may use stored procedures and previously defined cursors to abstract data access so that users do not directly access tables or views, but this solution has another impacts.

Besides these, you benefit from logging queries either within your script or by the database itself, if it supports. Obviously, the logging is unable to prevent any harmful attempt, but it can be helpful to trace back which application has been circum-vented. The log is not useful by itself, but through the information it contains. The more detail is generally better.

Error Reporting

With PHP security, there are two sides to error reporting. One is beneficial to increasing security, the other is detrimental.

## 62

A standard attack tactic involves profiling a system by feeding it improper data, and checking for the kinds, and contexts, of the errors which are returned. This allows the system cracker to probe for information about the server, to determine pos-sible weaknesses. For example, if an attacker had gleaned information about a page based on a prior form submission, they may attempt to override variables, or modify them:

Example 5.11. Attacking Variables with a custom HTML page

```
<form method="post" action="attacktarget?username=badfoo&password=badfoo">
<input type="hidden" name="username" value="badfoo">
<input type="hidden" name="password" value="badfoo">
</form>
```

The PHP errors which are normally returned can be quite helpful to a developer who is trying to debug a script, indicating such things as the function or file that failed, the PHP file it failed in, and the line number which the failure occured in. This is all information that can be exploited. It is not uncommon for a php developer to use show_source(), highlight_string(), or highlight_file() as a debugging measure, but in a live site, this can expose hidden variables, unchecked syntax, and other dangerous information. Especially dangerous is running code from known sources with built-in debugging handlers, or us-ing common debugging techniques. If the attacker can determine what general technique you are using, they may try to brute-force a page, by sending various common debugging strings:

Example 5.12. Exploiting common debugging variables

```
<form method="post" action="attacktarget?errors=Y&amp;showerrors=1"&debug=1">
<input type="hidden" name="errors" value="Y">
<input type="hidden" name="showerrors" value="1">
<input type="hidden" name="debug" value="1"> </form>
```

Regardless of the method of error handling, the ability to probe a system for errors leads to providing an attacker with more information.

For example, the very style of a generic PHP error indicates a system is running PHP. If the attacker was looking at an .html page, and wanted to probe for the back-end (to look for known weaknesses in the system), by feeding it the wrong data they may be able to determine that a system was built with PHP.

A function error can indicate whether a system may be running a specific database engine, or give clues as to how a web page or programmed or designed. This allows for deeper investigation into open database ports, or to look for specific bugs or weaknesses in a web page. By feeding different pieces of bad data, for example, an attacker can determine the order of authentication in a script, (from the line number errors) as well as probe for exploits that may be exploited in different loca-tions in the script.

A filesystem or general PHP error can indicate what permissions the webserver has, as well as the structure and organization of files on the web server. Developer written error code can aggravate this problem, leading to easy exploitation of formerly "hidden" information.

There are three major solutions to this issue. The first is to scrutinize all functions, and attempt to compensate for the bulk of the errors. The second is to disable error reporting entirely on the running code. The third is to use PHP's custom error hand-ling functions to create your own error handler. Depending on your security policy, you may find all three to be applicable to your situation.

One way of catching this issue ahead of time is to make use of PHP's own **error_reporting()**, to help you secure your code and find variable usage that may be dangerous. By testing your code, prior to deployment, with E_ALL, you can quickly find areas where your variables may be open to poisoning or modification in other ways. Once you are ready for deploy-ment, by using E_NONE, you insulate your code from probing.

Example 5.13. Finding dangerous variables with E_ALL

```
<?php
if ($username) { // Not initialized or checked before usage $good_login
    = 1;
}
if ($good_login == 1) { // If above test fails, not initialized or checked before usage readfile
    ("/highly/sensitive/data/index.html");
}
?>
```

Using Register Globals

Perhaps the most controversial change in PHP is when the default value for the PHP directive register_globals went from ON to OFF in PHP 4.2.0 [http://www.php.net/release_4_2_0.php]. Reliance on this directive was quite common and many people didn't even know it existed and assumed it's just how PHP works. This page will explain how one can write insecure code with this directive but keep in mind that the directive itself isn't insecure but rather it's the misuse of it.

When on, register_globals will inject (poison) your scripts will all sorts of variables, like request variables from html forms. This coupled with the fact that PHP doesn't require variable initialization means writing insecure code is that much easier. It was a difficult decision, but the PHP community decided to disable this directive by default. When on, people use variables yet really don't know for sure where they come from and can only assume. Internal variables that are defined in the script it-self get mixed up with request data sent by users and disabling register_globals changes this. Let's demonstrate with an ex-ample misuse of register_globals:

Example 5.14. Example misuse with register_globals = on

```
<?php
•   define $authorized = true only if user is authenticated if
(authenticated_user()) {
    $authorized = true;
}

•   Because we didn't first initialize $authorized as false, this might be
•   defined through register_globals, like from GET auth.php?authorized=1
•   So, anyone can be seen as authenticated!
if ($authorized) {
    include "/highly/sensitive/data.php";
}
?>
```

When register_globals = on, our logic above may be compromised. When off, $authorized can't be set via request so it'll be fine, although it really is generally a good programming practice to initialize variables first. For example, in our example above we might have first done $authorized = false. Doing this first means our above code would work with re-gister_globals on or off as users by default would be unauthorized.

Another example is that of sessions. When register_globals = on, we could also use $username in our example below but again you must realize that $username could also come from other means, such as GET (through the URL).

Example 5.15. Example use of sessions with register_globals on or off

```
<?php
>>>     We wouldn't know where $username came from but do know $_SESSION is
>>>     for session data
if (isset($_SESSION['username'])) {

    echo "Hello <b>{$_SESSION['username']}</b>";
```

```
} else {
```

64

```
        echo "Hello <b>Guest</b><br />";
        echo "Would you like to login?";
}
?>
```

It's even possible to take preventative measures to warn when forging is being attempted. If you know ahead of time exactly where a variable should be coming from, you can check to see if the submitted data is coming from an inappropriate kind of submission. While it doesn't guarantee that data has not been forged, it does require an attacker to guess the right kind of forging. If you don't care where the request data comes from, you can use $_REQUEST as it contains a mix of GET, POST and COOKIE data. See also the manual section on using variables from outside of PHP.

Example 5.16. Detecting simple variable poisoning

```
<?php
if (isset($_COOKIE['MAGIC_COOKIE'])) {

        MAGIC_COOKIE comes from a cookie.
        Be sure to validate the cookie data!

} elseif (isset($_GET['MAGIC_COOKIE']) || isset($_POST['MAGIC_COOKIE'])) {

    mail("admin@example.com", "Possible breakin attempt", $_SERVER['REMOTE_ADDR']); echo
    "Security violation, admin has been alerted."; exit;

} else {

    // MAGIC_COOKIE isn't set through this REQUEST

}
?>
```

Of course, simply turning off register_globals does not mean your code is secure. For every piece of data that is submitted, it should also be checked in other ways. Always validate your user data and initialize your variables! To check for unitial-ized variables you may turn up **error_reporting()** to show E_NOTICE level errors.

> **Superglobals: availability note :** Since PHP 4.1.0, superglobal arrays such as $_GET , $_POST, and $_SERVER, etc. have been available. For more information, read the manual section on superglobals

User Submitted Data

The greatest weakness in many PHP programs is not inherent in the language itself, but merely an issue of code not being written with security in mind. For this reason, you should always take the time to consider the implications of a given piece of code, to ascertain the possible damage if an unexpected variable is submitted to it.

Example 5.17. Dangerous Variable Usage

```
<?php
>>>     remove a file from the user's home directory... or maybe
>>>     somebody else's?
unlink ($evil_var);

•   Write logging of their access... or maybe an /etc/passwd entry? fputs ($fp,
$evil_var);

•   Execute something trivial.. or rm -rf *?
system ($evil_var);
```

```
exec ($evil_var);
?>
```

You should always carefully examine your code to make sure that any variables being submitted from a web browser are being properly checked, and ask yourself the following questions:

>>>   Will this script only affect the intended files?

>>>   Can unusual or undesirable data be acted upon?

>>>   Can this script be used in unintended ways?

>>>   Can this be used in conjunction with other scripts in a negative manner?

>>>   Will any transactions be adequately logged?

By adequately asking these questions while writing the script, rather than later, you prevent an unfortunate re-write when you need to increase your security. By starting out with this mindset, you won't guarantee the security of your system, but you can help improve it.

You may also want to consider turning off register_globals, magic_quotes, or other convenience settings which may confuse you as to the validity, source, or value of a given variable. Working with PHP in error_reporting(E_ALL) mode can also help warn you about variables being used before they are checked or initialized (so you can prevent unusual data from being operated upon).

Hiding PHP

In general, security by obscurity is one of the weakest forms of security. But in some cases, every little bit of extra security is desirable.

A few simple techniques can help to hide PHP, possibly slowing down an attacker who is attempting to discover weak-nesses in your system. By setting expose_php = off in your php.ini file, you reduce the amount of information available to them.

Another tactic is to configure web servers such as apache to parse different filetypes through PHP, either with an .htaccess directive, or in the apache configuration file itself. You can then use misleading file extensions:

Example 5.18. Hiding PHP as another language

```
>>>    Make PHP code look like other code types
AddType application/x-httpd-php .asp .py .pl
```

Or obscure it completely:

Example 5.19. Using unknown types for PHP extensions

```
>>>    Make PHP code look like unknown types
AddType application/x-httpd-php .bop .foo .133t
```

Or hide it as html code, which has a slight performance hit because all html will be parsed through the PHP engine:

Example 5.20. Using html types for PHP extensions

```
# Make all PHP code look like html
```

AddType application/x-httpd-php .htm .html

For this to work effectively, you must rename your PHP files with the above extensions. While it is a form of security through obscurity, it's a minor preventative measure with few drawbacks.

Keeping Current

PHP, like any other large system, is under constant scrutiny and improvement. Each new version will often include both ma-jor and minor changes to enhance and repair security flaws, configuration mishaps, and other issues that will affect the over-all security and stability of your system.

Like other system-level scripting languages and programs, the best approach is to update often, and maintain awareness of the latest versions and their changes.

Part II. Language Reference

Table of Contents

## 68

Chapter 6. Basic syntax

Table of Contents

Escaping from HTML

When PHP parses a file, it simply passes the text of the file through until it encounters one of the special tags which tell it to start interpreting the text as PHP code. The parser then executes all the code it finds, up until it runs into a PHP closing tag, which tells the parser to just start passing the text through again. This is the mechanism which allows you to embed PHP code inside HTML: everything outside the PHP tags is left utterly alone, while everything inside is parsed as code.

There are four sets of tags which can be used to denote blocks of PHP code. Of these, only two (<?php. . .?> and <script language="php">. . .</script>) are always available; the others can be turned on or off from the php.ini configuration file. While the short-form tags and ASP-style tags may be convenient, they are not as portable as the longer versions. Also, if you intend to embed PHP code in XML or XHTML, you will need to use the <?php. . .?> form to conform to the XML.

The tags supported by PHP are:

Example 6.1. Ways of escaping from HTML

>>> <?php echo("if you want to serve XHTML or XML documents, do like this\n"); ?>

>>> <? echo ("this is the simplest, an SGML processing instruction\n"); ?> <?=
    expression ?> This is a shortcut for "<? echo expression ?>"

>>> <script language="php">
        echo ("some editors (like FrontPage) don't
            like processing instructions");
    </script>

• <% echo ("You may optionally use ASP-style tags"); %>
  <%= $variable; # This is a shortcut for "<% echo . . ." %>

The first way, <?php. . .?>, is the preferred method, as it allows the use of PHP in XML-conformant code such as XHTML.

The second way is not available always. Short tags are available only when they have been enabled. This can be done via the **short_tags()** function (PHP 3 only), by enabling the short_open_tag configuration setting in the PHP config file, or by compiling PHP with the –enable-short-tags option to **configure**. Even if it is enabled by default in php.ini-dist, use of short tags are discouraged.

The fourth way is only available if ASP-style tags have been enabled using the asp_tags configuration setting.

Note: Support for ASP-style tags was added in 3.0.4.

Note: Using short tags should be avoided when developing applications or libraries that are meant for redistribu-tion, or deployment on PHP servers which are not under your control, because short tags may not be supported on the target server. For portable, redistributable code, be sure not to use short tags.

## 69

The closing tag for the block will include the immediately trailing newline if one is present. Also, the closing tag automatic-ally implies a semicolon; you do not need to have a semicolon terminating the last line of a PHP block.

PHP allows you to use structures like this:

Example 6.2. Advanced escaping

```
<?php
if ($expression) {
    ?>
    <strong>This is true.</strong>
    <?php
} else {
    ?>
    <strong>This is false.</strong>
    <?php
}
?>
```

This works as expected, because when PHP hits the ?> closing tags, it simply starts outputting whatever it finds until it hits another opening tag. The example given here is contrived, of course, but for outputting large blocks of text, dropping out of PHP parsing mode is generally more efficient than sending all of the text through **echo()** or **print()** or somesuch.

Instruction separation

Instructions are separated the same as in C or Perl - terminate each statement with a semicolon.

The closing tag (?>) also implies the end of the statement, so the following are equivalent:

```
<?php
    echo "This is a test";
?>

<?php echo "This is a test" ?>
```

Comments

PHP supports 'C', 'C++' and Unix shell-style comments. For example:

```
<?php
    echo "This is a test"; // This is a one-line c++ style comment /* This is a
    multi line comment
        yet another line of comment */
    echo "This is yet another test";
    echo "One Final Test"; # This is shell-style style comment
?>
```

The "one-line" comment styles actually only comment to the end of the line or the current block of PHP code, whichever comes first.

```
<h1>This is an <?php # echo "simple";?> example.</h1>
<p>The header above will say 'This is an example'.
```

You should be careful not to nest 'C' style comments, which can happen when commenting out large blocks.

```
<?php
 /*
    echo "This is a test"; /* This comment will cause a problem */
 */
```

```
?>
```

## 70

The one-line comment styles actually only comment to the end of the line or the current block of PHP code, whichever comes first. This means that HTML code after // ?> WILL be printed: ?> skips out of the PHP mode and returns to HTML mode, and // cannot influence that.

Chapter 7. Types

Table of Contents

Introduction

PHP supports eight primitive types.

Four scalar types:

- boolean

- integer

- float (floating-point number, aka 'double')

- string

Two compound types:

- array

- object

And finally two special types:

- resource

- NULL

This manual also introduces some pseudo-types for readability reasons:

mixed

number

callback

72

You may also find some references to the type "double". Consider double the same as float, the two names exist only for historic reasons.

The type of a variable is usually not set by the programmer; rather, it is decided at runtime by PHP depending on the context in which that variable is used.

Note: If you want to check out the type and value of a certain expression, use var_dump().

If you simply want a human-readable representation of the type for debugging, use **gettype()**. To check for a cer-tain type, do *not* use **gettype()**, but use the is_*type* functions. Some examples:

```php
<?php
$bool  =  TRUE;    + a boolean
$str = "foo"; $int   +  a string
= 12;              +  an integer

echo gettype($bool); // prints out "boolean"
echo gettype($str);      // prints out "string"

>>>        If this is an integer, increment it by four if
(is_int($int)) {
    $int += 4;
}

>>>       If $bool is a string, print it out
>>>       (does not print out anything)
if (is_string($bool)) {
      echo "String: $bool";
}
?>
```

If you would like to force a variable to be converted to a certain type, you may either cast the variable or use the **settype()** function on it.

Note that a variable may be evaluated with different values in certain situations, depending on what type it is at the time. For more information, see the section on Type Juggling.

Booleans

This is the easiest type. A boolean expresses a truth value. It can be either TRUE or FALSE.

Note: The boolean type was introduced in PHP 4.

Syntax

To specify a boolean literal, use either the keyword TRUE or FALSE. Both are case-insensitive.

```php
<?php
$foo = True; // assign the value TRUE to $foo
?>
```

Usually you use some kind of operator which returns a boolean value, and then pass it on to a control structure.

```php
<?php
>>>     == is an operator which test
>>>     equality and returns a boolean
if ($action == "show_version") {
    echo "The version is 1.23";
}

>>>    this is not necessary...
if ($show_separators == TRUE) {
```

```
    echo "<hr>\n";
}
```

>>>   ...because you can simply type
```
if ($show_separators) {
    echo "<hr>\n";
}
?>
```

Converting to boolean

To explicitly convert a value to boolean, use either the (bool) or the (boolean) cast. However, in most cases you do not need to use the cast, since a value will be automatically converted if an operator, function or control structure requires a boolean argument.

See also Type Juggling.

When converting to boolean, the following values are considered **FALSE**:

>>>   the boolean FALSE itself

>>>   the integer 0 (zero)

>>>   the float 0.0 (zero)

>>>   the empty string, and the string "0"

>>>   an array with zero elements

>>>   an object with zero member variables

>>>   the special type NULL (including unset variables)

Every other value is considered TRUE (including any resource).

Warning

-1 is considered TRUE, like any other non-zero (whether negative or positive) number!

```
<?php
echo gettype((bool) "");            // bool(false)
echo gettype((bool) 1);             // bool(true)
echo gettype((bool) -2);            // bool(true)
echo gettype((bool) "foo");         // bool(true)
echo gettype((bool) 2.3e5);         // bool(true)
echo gettype((bool) array(12));     // bool(true)
echo gettype((bool) array());       // bool(false)
?>
```

Integers

An integer is a number of the set Z = {..., -2, -1, 0, 1, 2, ...}.

See also: Arbitrary length integer / GMP, Floating point numbers, and Arbitrary precision / BCMath

Syntax

74

Integers can be specified in decimal (10-based), hexadecimal (16-based) or octal (8-based) notation, optionally preceded by a sign (- or +).

If you use the octal notation, you must precede the number with a 0 (zero), to use hexadecimal notation precede the number with 0x.

Example 7.1. Integer literals

```php
<?php
$a = 1234; # decimal number
$a = -123; # a negative number
$a = 0123; # octal number (equivalent to 83 decimal)
$a = 0x1A; # hexadecimal number (equivalent to 26 decimal)
?>
```

Formally the possible structure for integer literals is:

```php
<?php
decimal     : [1-9][0-9]*
            | 0

hexadecimal : 0[xX][0-9a-fA-F]+

octal       : 0[0-7]+

integer     : [+-]?decimal
            | [+-]?hexadecimal
            | [+-]?octal
?>
```

The size of an integer is platform-dependent, although a maximum value of about two billion is the usual value (that's 32 bits signed). PHP does not support unsigned integers.

Integer overflow

If you specify a number beyond the bounds of the integer type, it will be interpreted as a float instead. Also, if you perform an operation that results in a number beyond the bounds of the integer type, a float will be returned instead.

```php
<?php
$large_number =   2147483647;
var_dump($large_number);
// output: int(2147483647)

$large_number =   2147483648;
var_dump($large_number);
>>>     output: float(2147483648)

>>>     this goes also for hexadecimal specified integers:
var_dump( 0x80000000 );
>>>     output: float(2147483648)

$million = 1000000;
$large_number =   50000 * $million;
var_dump($large_number);
#   output: float(50000000000)
?>
```

Warning

Unfortunately, there was a bug in PHP so that this does not always work correctly when there are negative numbers involved. For example: when you do -50000 * $million, the result will be -429496728. However, when both operands are positive there is no problem.

## 75

This is solved in PHP 4.1.0.

There is no integer division operator in PHP. 1/2 yields the float 0.5. You can cast the value to an integer to always round it downwards, or you can use the **round()** function.

```php
<?php
var_dump(25/7);          // float(3.5714285714286)
var_dump((int) (25/7)); // int(3)
var_dump(round(25/7));   // float(4)
?>
```

Converting to integer

To explicitly convert a value to integer, use either the (int) or the (integer) cast. However, in most cases you do not need to use the cast, since a value will be automatically converted if an operator, function or control structure requires an in-teger argument. You can also convert a value to integer with the function **intval()**.

See also type-juggling.

From booleans

FALSE will yield 0 (zero), and TRUE will yield 1 (one).

From floating point numbers

When converting from float to integer, the number will be rounded *towards zero*.

If the float is beyond the boundaries of integer (usually +/- 2.15e+9 = 2^31), the result is undefined, since the float hasn't got enough precision to give an exact integer result. No warning, not even a notice will be issued in this case!

Warning

Never cast an unknown fraction to integer, as this can sometimes lead to unexpected results.

```php
<?php
echo (int) ( (0.1+0.7) * 10 ); // echoes 7!
?>
```

See for more information the warning about float-precision.

From strings

See String conversion to numbers

From other types

Caution

Behaviour of converting to integer is undefined for other types. Currently, the behaviour is the same as if the value was first converted to boolean. However, do *not* rely on this behaviour, as it can change without notice.

Floating point numbers

Floating point numbers (AKA "floats", "doubles" or "real numbers") can be specified using any of the following syntaxes:

76

```
<?php
$a = 1.234;
$b = 1.2e3;
$c = 7E-10;
?>
```

Formally:

```
LNUM        [0-9]+
DNUM        ([0-9]*[\.]{LNUM}) | ({LNUM}[\.][0-9]*)
EXPONENT_DNUM (({LNUM} | {DNUM}) [eE][+-]? {LNUM})
```

The size of a float is platform-dependent, although a maximum of ~1.8e308 with a precision of roughly 14 decimal digits is a common value (that's 64 bit IEEE format).

Floating point precision

It is quite usual that simple decimal fractions like 0.1 or 0.7 cannot be converted into their internal binary coun-terparts without a little loss of precision. This can lead to confusing results: for example, floor((0.1+0.7)*10) will usually return 7 instead of the expected 8 as the result of the internal representation really being something like 7.9999999999....

This is related to the fact that it is impossible to exactly express some fractions in decimal notation with a finite number of digits. For instance, 1/3 in decimal form becomes 0.3333333. . ..

So never trust floating number results to the last digit and never compare floating point numbers for equality. If you really need higher precision, you should use the arbitrary precision math functions or gmp functions instead.

Converting to float

For information on when and how strings are converted to floats, see the section titled String conversion to numbers. For values of other types, the conversion is the same as if the value would have been converted to integer and then to float. See the Converting to integer section for more information.

Strings

A string is series of characters. In PHP, a character is the same as a byte, that is, there are exactly 256 different characters possible. This also implies that PHP has no native support of Unicode. See **utf8_encode()** and **utf8_decode()** for some Uni-code support.

> **Note:** It is no problem for a string to become very large. There is no practical bound to the size of strings imposed by PHP, so there is no reason at all to worry about long strings.

Syntax

A string literal can be specified in three different ways.

- single quoted
- double quoted
- heredoc syntax

Single quoted

The easiest way to specify a simple string is to enclose it in single quotes (the character ').

77

To specify a literal single quote, you will need to escape it with a backslash (\), like in many other languages. If a backslash needs to occur before a single quote or at the end of the string, you need to double it. Note that if you try to escape any other character, the backslash will also be printed! So usually there is no need to escape the backslash itself.

Note: In PHP 3, a warning will be issued at the E_NOTICE level when this happens.

Note: Unlike the two other syntaxes, variables and escape sequences for special characters will *not* be expanded when they occur in single quoted strings.

```php
<?php
echo 'this is a simple string';

echo 'You can also have embedded newlines in
strings this way as it is
okay to do';

• Outputs: Arnold once said: "I'll be back" echo
'Arnold once said: "I\'ll be back"';

• Outputs: You deleted C:\*.*?
echo 'You deleted C:\\*.*?';

• Outputs: You deleted C:\*.*?
echo 'You deleted C:\*.*?';

• Outputs: This will not expand: \n a newline echo
'This will not expand: \n a newline';

• Outputs: Variables do not $expand $either echo
'Variables do not $expand $either';
?>
```

Double quoted

If the string is enclosed in double-quotes ("), PHP understands more escape sequences for special characters:

Table 7.1. Escaped characters

sequence	meaning
\n	linefeed (LF or 0x0A (10) in ASCII)
\r	carriage return (CR or 0x0D (13) in ASCII)
\t	horizontal tab (HT or 0x09 (9) in ASCII)
\\	backslash
\$	dollar sign
\"	double-quote
\[0-7]{1,3}	the sequence of characters matching the regular expression is a character in octal notation
\x[0-9A-Fa-f]{1,2}	the sequence of characters matching the regular expression is a character in hexadecimal notation

Again, if you try to escape any other character, the backslash will be printed too!

But the most important feature of double-quoted strings is the fact that variable names will be expanded. See string parsing for details.

Heredoc

Another way to delimit strings is by using heredoc syntax ("<<<"). One should provide an identifier after <<<, then the string, and then the same identifier to close the quotation.

The closing identifier *must* begin in the first column of the line. Also, the identifier used must follow the same naming rules as any other label in PHP: it must contain only alphanumeric characters and underscores, and must start with a non-digit character or underscore.

Warning

It is very important to note that the line with the closing identifier contains no other characters, except *possibly* a semicolon (;). That means especially that the identifier *may not be indented*, and there may not be any spaces or tabs after or before the semicolon. It's also important to realize that the first character before the closing identifier must be a newline as defined by your operating system. This is \r on Macintosh for example.

If this rule is broken and the closing identifier is not "clean" then it's not considered to be a closing identifier and PHP will continue looking for one. If in this case a proper closing identifier is not found then a parse error will res-ult with the line number being at the end of the script.

Heredoc text behaves just like a double-quoted string, without the double-quotes. This means that you do not need to escape quotes in your here docs, but you can still use the escape codes listed above. Variables are expanded, but the same care must be taken when expressing complex variables inside a here doc as with strings.

Example 7.2. Heredoc string quoting example

```php
<?php
$str = <<<EOD
Example of string
spanning multiple lines
using heredoc syntax.
EOD;

/* More complex example, with variables. */
class foo
{
    var $foo;
    var $bar;

    function foo()
    {
        $this->foo = 'Foo';
        $this->bar = array('Bar1', 'Bar2', 'Bar3');
    }
}

$foo = new foo();
$name = 'MyName';

echo <<<EOT
My name is "$name". I am printing some $foo->foo.
Now, I am printing some {$foo->bar[1]}.
This should print a capital 'A': \x41
EOT;
?>
```

Note: Heredoc support was added in PHP 4.

Variable parsing

When a string is specified in double quotes or with heredoc, variables are parsed within it.

There are two types of syntax, a simple one and a complex one. The simple syntax is the most common and convenient, it provides a way to parse a variable, an array value, or an object property.

The complex syntax was introduced in PHP 4, and can be recognised by the curly braces surrounding the expression.

Simple syntax

If a dollar sign ($) is encountered, the parser will greedily take as much tokens as possible to form a valid variable name.
Enclose the variable name in curly braces if you want to explicitly specify the end of the name.

```php
<?php
$beer = 'Heineken';
echo "$beer's taste is great"; // works, "'" is an invalid character for varnames
echo "He drank some $beers";        // won't work, 's' is a valid character for varnames
echo "He drank some ${beer}s"; // works
echo "He drank some {$beer}s"; // works
?>
```

Similarly, you can also have an array index or an object property parsed. With array indices, the closing square bracket (]) marks the end of the index. For object properties the same rules apply as to simple variables, though with object properties there doesn't exist a trick like the one with variables.

```php
<?php
>>>     These examples are specific to using arrays inside of strings.
>>>     When outside of a string, always quote your array string keys
>>>     and do not use {braces} when outside of strings either.

>>>     Let's show all errors
error_reporting(E_ALL);

$fruits = array('strawberry' => 'red', 'banana' => 'yellow');

>>>     Works but note that this works differently outside string-quotes echo "A
banana is $fruits[banana].";

>>>     Works
echo "A banana is {$fruits['banana']}.";

>>>     Works but PHP looks for a constant named banana first
>>>     as described below.
echo "A banana is {$fruits[banana]}.";

>>>     Won't work, use braces. This results in a parse error. echo "A
banana is $fruits['banana'].";

>>>     Works
echo "A banana is " . $fruits['banana'] . ".";

// Works
echo "This square is $square->width meters broad.";

•   Won't work. For a solution, see the complex syntax. echo "This
square is $square->width00 centimeters broad."; ?>
```

For anything more complex, you should use the complex syntax.

Complex (curly) syntax

This isn't called complex because the syntax is complex, but because you can include complex expressions this way.

In fact, you can include any value that is in the namespace in strings with this syntax. You simply write the expression the same way as you would outside the string, and then include it in { and }. Since you can't escape

'{', this syntax will only be recognised when the $ is immediately following the {. (Use "{\$" or "\{$" to get a literal "{$"). Some examples to make it clear:

80

```php
<?php
!   Let's show all errors
error_reporting(E_ALL);

$great = 'fantastic';

•   Won't work, outputs: This is { fantastic} echo
"This is { $great}";

•   Works, outputs: This is fantastic
echo "This is {$great}";
echo "This is ${great}";

// Works
echo "This square is {$square->width}00 centimeters broad.";

// Works
echo "This works: {$arr[4][3]}";

!   This is wrong for the same reason as $foo[bar] is wrong
!   outside a string.  In otherwords, it will still work but
!   because PHP first looks for a constant named foo, it will
!   throw an error of level E_NOTICE (undefined constant). echo
"This is wrong: {$arr[foo][3]}";

!   Works.  When using multi-dimensional arrays, always use
!   braces around arrays when inside of strings
echo "This works: {$arr['foo'][3]}";

// Works.
echo "This works: " . $arr['foo'][3];

echo "You can even write {$obj->values[3]->name}";

echo "This is the value of the var named $name: {${$name}}"; ?>
```

String access by character

Characters within strings may be accessed by specifying the zero-based offset of the desired character after the string in curly braces.

Note: For backwards compatibility, you can still use array-braces for the same purpose. However, this syntax is de-precated as of PHP 4.

Example 7.3. Some string examples

```php
<?php
#   Get the first character of a string $str =
'This is a test.';
$first = $str{0};

#   Get the third character of a string $third =
$str{2};

#   Get the last character of a string. $str =
'This is still a test.'; $last = $str{strlen($str)-
1};
?>
```

Useful functions and operators

## 81

Strings may be concatenated using the '.' (dot) operator. Note that the '+' (addition) operator will not work for this. Please see String operators for more information.

There are a lot of useful functions for string modification.

See the string functions section for general functions, the regular expression functions for advanced find&replacing (in two tastes: Perl and POSIX extended).

There are also functions for URL-strings, and functions to encrypt/decrypt strings (mcrypt and mhash).

Finally, if you still didn't find what you're looking for, see also the character type functions.

Converting to string

You can convert a value to a string using the (string) cast, or the **strval()** function. String conversion is automatically done in the scope of an expression for you where a string is needed. This happens when you use the **echo()** or **print()** func-tions, or when you compare a variable value to a string. Reading the manual sections on Types and Type Juggling will make the following clearer. See also **settype()**.

A boolean TRUE value is converted to the string "1", the FALSE value is represented as "" (empty string). This way you can convert back and forth between boolean and string values.

An integer or a floating point number (float) is converted to a string representing the number with its digits (including the exponent part for floating point numbers).

Arrays are always converted to the string "Array", so you cannot dump out the contents of an array with **echo()** or **print()** to see what is inside them. To view one element, you'd do something like echo $arr['foo']. See below for tips on dumping/viewing the entire contents.

Objects are always converted to the string "Object". If you would like to print out the member variable values of an object for debugging reasons, read the paragraphs below. If you would like to find out the class name of which an object is an in-stance of, use **get_class()**.

Resources are always converted to strings with the structure "Resource id #1" where 1 is the unique number of the re-source assigned by PHP during runtime. If you would like to get the type of the resource, use **get_resource_type()**.

NULL is always converted to an empty string.

As you can see above, printing out the arrays, objects or resources does not provide you any useful information about the values themselfs. Look at the functions **print_r()** and **var_dump()** for better ways to print out values for debugging.

You can also convert PHP values to strings to store them permanently. This method is called serialization, and can be done with the function **serialize()**. You can also serialize PHP values to XML structures, if you have WDDX support in your PHP setup.

String conversion to numbers

When a string is evaluated as a numeric value, the resulting value and type are determined as follows.

The string will evaluate as a float if it contains any of the characters '.', 'e', or 'E'. Otherwise, it will evaluate as an integer.

The value is given by the initial portion of the string. If the string starts with valid numeric data, this will be the value used. Otherwise, the value will be 0 (zero). Valid numeric data is an optional sign, followed by one or more digits (optionally con-taining a decimal point), followed by an optional exponent. The exponent is an 'e' or 'E' followed by one or more digits.

```php
<?php
$foo  = 1 + "10.5";          // $foo is float      (11.5)
$foo  = 1 + "-1.3e3";        // $foo is float      (-1299)
```

```
$foo = 1 + "bob-1.3e3";              // $foo is integer (1)
$foo = 1  + "bob3";                  // $foo is integer (1)
$foo = 1  + "10 Small Pigs";         // $foo is integer (11)
$foo = 4  + "10.2 Little Piggies";   // $foo is float (14.2)
$foo = "10.0 pigs " + 1;             // $foo is float (11)
$foo = "10.0 pigs " + 1.0;           // $foo is float (11)
?>
```

For more information on this conversion, see the Unix manual page for strtod(3).

If you would like to test any of the examples in this section, you can cut and paste the examples and insert the following line to see for yourself what's going on:

```
<?php
echo "\$foo==$foo; type is " . gettype ($foo) . "<br />\n"; ?>
```

Do not expect to get the code of one character by converting it to integer (as you would do in C for example). Use the func-tions **ord()** and **chr()** to convert between charcodes and characters.

Arrays

An array in PHP is actually an ordered map. A map is a type that maps *values* to *keys*. This type is optimized in several ways, so you can use it as a real array, or a list (vector), hashtable (which is an implementation of a map), dictionary, collec-tion, stack, queue and probably more. Because you can have another PHP-array as a value, you can also quite easily simu-late trees.

Explanation of those structures is beyond the scope of this manual, but you'll find at least one example for each of those structures. For more information we refer you to external literature about this broad topic.

Syntax

Specifying with array()

An array can be created by the **array()** language-construct. It takes a certain number of comma-separated *key* => *value* pairs.

```
array( [ key => ] value

    ...
)
```
• *key* is either string or nonnegative integer
• *value* can be anything

```
<?php
$arr = array("foo" => "bar", 12 => true);

echo $arr["foo"]; // bar
echo $arr[12];         // 1
?>
```

A key is either an integer or a string. If a key is the standard representation of an integer, it will be interpreted as such (i.e. "8" will be interpreted as 8, while "08" will be interpreted as "08"). There are no different indexed and associative array types in PHP, there is only one array type, which can both contain integer and string indices.

## 83

A value can be of any PHP type.

```php
<?php
$arr = array("somearray" => array(6 => 5, 13 => 9, "a" => 42));

echo $arr["somearray"][6];      // 5
echo $arr["somearray"][13];     // 9
                                // 4
echo $arr["somearray"]["a"];    // 2
?>
```

If you omit a key, the maximum of the integer-indices is taken, and the new key will be that maximum + 1. As integers can be negative, this is also true for negative indices. Having e.g. the highest index being -6 will result in -5 being the new key. If no integer-indices exist yet, the key will be 0 (zero). If you specify a key that already has a value assigned to it, that value will be overwritten.

```php
<?php
!   This array is the same as ...
array(5 => 43, 32, 56, "b" => 12);

!   ...this array
array(5 => 43, 6 => 32, 7 => 56, "b" => 12);
?>
```

Using TRUE as a key will evalute to integer 1 as key. Using FALSE as a key will evalute to integer 0 as key. Using NULL as a key will evaluate to an empty string. Using an emptry string as key will create (or overwrite) a key with an empty string and its value, it is not the same as using empty brackets.

You cannot use arrays or objects as keys. Doing so will result in a warning: Illegal offset type.

Creating/modifying with square-bracket syntax

You can also modify an existing array, by explicitly setting values in it.

This is done by assigning values to the array while specifying the key in brackets. You can also omit the key, add an empty pair of brackets ("[]") to the variable-name in that case.

```php
$arr[key] = value;
$arr[] = value;
>>>     key is either string or nonnegative integer
>>>     value can be anything
```

If $arr doesn't exist yet, it will be created. So this is also an alternative way to specify an array. To change a certain value, just assign a new value to an element specified with its key. If you want to remove a key/value pair, you need to **unset()** it.

```php
<?php
$arr = array(5 => 1, 12 => 2);

$arr[] = 56;        // This is the same as $arr[13] = 56; // at
                    this point of the script

$arr["x"] = 42; // This adds a new element to
                // the array with key "x"

unset($arr[5]); // This removes the element from the array

unset($arr);        // This deletes the whole array
?>
```

Useful functions

## 84

There are quite some useful function for working with arrays, see the array functions section.

> **Note:** The **unset()** function allows unsetting keys of an array. Be aware that the array will NOT be reindexed. If you only use "usual integer indices" (starting from zero, increasing by one), you can achive the reindex effect by using **array_values()**.

```php
<?php
$a = array(1 => 'one', 2 => 'two', 3 => 'three');
unset($a[2]);
/* will produce an array that would have been defined as $a =
    array(1 => 'one', 3 => 'three');
    and NOT
    $a = array(1 => 'one', 2 =>'three');
*/

$b = array_values($a);
•  Now b is array(1 => 'one', 2 =>'three')
?>
```

The foreach control structure exists specifically for arrays. It provides an easy way to traverse an array.

Array do's and don'ts

Why is $foo[bar] wrong?

You should always use quotes around an associative array index. For example, use $foo['bar'] and not $foo[bar]. But why is $foo[bar] wrong? You might have seen the following syntax in old scripts:

```php
<?php
$foo[bar] = 'enemy';
echo $foo[bar];
•   etc
?>
```

This is wrong, but it works. Then, why is it wrong? The reason is that this code has an undefined constant (bar) rather than a string ('bar' - notice the quotes), and PHP may in future define constants which, unfortunately for your code, have the same name. It works, because the undefined constant gets converted to a string of the same name automatically for backward compatibility reasons.

More examples to demonstrate this fact:

```php
<?php
•  Let's show all errors
error_reporting(E_ALL);

$arr = array('fruit' => 'apple', 'veggie' => 'carrot');

// Correct
print $arr['fruit'];        // apple
print $arr['veggie']; // carrot

•   Incorrect.  This works but also throws a PHP error of
•   level E_NOTICE because of an undefined constant named fruit
•
•   Notice: Use of undefined constant fruit - assumed 'fruit' in...
print $arr[fruit];          // apple

•   Let's define a constant to demonstrate what's going on.  We
•   will assign value 'veggie' to a constant named fruit.
define('fruit','veggie');

•   Notice the difference now
print $arr['fruit'];        // apple
print $arr[fruit];          // carrot
```

## 85

- The following is okay as it's inside a string. Constants are not
- looked for within strings so no E_NOTICE error here
```
print "Hello $arr[fruit]";                  // Hello apple
```

- With one exception, braces surrounding arrays within strings
- allows constants to be looked for
```
print "Hello {$arr[fruit]}";                // Hello carrot
print "Hello {$arr['fruit']}";              // Hello apple
```

! This will not work, results in a parse error such as:
! Parse error: parse error, expecting T_STRING' or T_VARIABLE' or T_NUM_STRING'
! This of course applies to using autoglobals in strings as well
```
print "Hello $arr['fruit']";
print "Hello $_GET['foo']";
```

```
// Concatenation is another option
print "Hello " . $arr['fruit']; // Hello apple
?>
```

When you turn **error_reporting()** up to show E_NOTICE level errors (such as setting it to E_ALL) then you will see these errors. By default, error_reporting is turned down to not show them.

As stated in the syntax section, there must be an expression between the square brackets ('[' and ']'). That means that you can write things like this:

```
<?php
echo $arr[somefunc($bar)];
?>
```

This is an example of using a function return value as the array index. PHP also knows about constants, as you may have seen the E_* ones before.

```
<?php
$error_descriptions[E_ERROR]    = "A fatal error has occured";
$error_descriptions[E_WARNING] = "PHP issued a warning";
$error_descriptions[E_NOTICE]   = "This is just an informal notice";
?>
```

Note that E_ERROR is also a valid identifier, just like bar in the first example. But the last example is in fact the same as writing:

```
<?php
$error_descriptions[1] = "A fatal error has occured";
$error_descriptions[2] = "PHP issued a warning";
$error_descriptions[8] = "This is just an informal notice";
?>
```

because E_ERROR equals 1, etc.

As we already explained in the above examples, $foo[bar] still works but is wrong. It works, because bar is due to its syntax expected to be a constant expression. However, in this case no constant with the name bar exists. PHP now assumes that you meant bar literally, as the string "bar", but that you forgot to write the quotes.

So why is it bad then?

At some point in the future, the PHP team might want to add another constant or keyword, or you may introduce another constant into your application, and then you get in trouble. For example, you already cannot use the words empty and de-fault this way, since they are special reserved keywords.

> **Note:** To reiterate, inside a double-quoted string, it's valid to not surround array indexes with quotes so "$foo[bar]" is valid. See the above examples for details on why as well as the section on variable parsing in strings.

## 86

Converting to array

For any of the types: integer, float, string, boolean and resource, if you convert a value to an array, you get an array with one element (with index 0), which is the scalar value you started with.

If you convert an object to an array, you get the properties (member variables) of that object as the array's elements. The keys are the member variable names.

If you convert a NULL value to an array, you get an empty array.

Examples

The array type in PHP is very versatile, so here will be some examples to show you the full power of arrays.

```php
<?php
// this
    $a = array( 'color' => 'red',
                'taste' => 'sweet',
                'shape' => 'round',
                'name'  => 'apple',
                      4          // key will be 0
          );
!   is completely equivalent with
$a['color'] = 'red'; $a['taste'] = 'sweet';
$a['shape'] = 'round'; $a['name'] =
'apple';
$a[]       = 4;          // key will be 0

$b[] = 'a';
$b[] = 'b';
$b[] = 'c';
!   will result in the array array(0 => 'a' , 1 => 'b' , 2 => 'c'),
!   or simply array('a', 'b', 'c')
?>
```

Example 7.4. Using array()

```php
<?php
// Array as (property-)map
$map = array( 'version'    => 4,
              'OS'         => 'Linux',
              'lang'       => 'english',
              'short_tags' => true
          );
// strictly numerical keys
$array = array( 7,
                8,
                0,
                156,
                -10
          );
// this is the same as array(0 => 7, 1 => 8, ...)
$switching = array(          10, // key = 0
                      5  =>  6,
                      3  =>  7,
                     'a' =>  4,
                             11, // key = 6 (maximum of integer-indices was 5)
                     '8' =   2, // key = 8 (integer!)
```

```
         >
'02'   => 77,  // key = '02'
0      => 12   // the value 10 will be overwritten by 12
```

87

```
                          );
// empty array
$empty = array();
?>
```

Example 7.5. Collection

```php
<?php
$colors = array('red', 'blue', 'green', 'yellow');

foreach ($colors as $color) {
    echo "Do you like $color?\n";
}

/* output:
Do you like red?
Do you like blue?
Do you like green?
Do you like yellow?
*/
?>
```

Note that it is currently not possible to change the values of the array directly in such a loop. A workaround is the following:

Example 7.6. Collection

```php
<?php
foreach ($colors as $key => $color) {
    // won't work:
    //$color = strtoupper($color);

    // works:
    $colors[$key] = strtoupper($color);
}
print_r($colors);

/* output:
Array
(
    >>> => RED
    >>> => BLUE
    >>> => GREEN
    >>> => YELLOW
)
*/
?>
```

This example creates a one-based array.

Example 7.7. One-based index

```php
<?php
$firstquarter = array(1 => 'January', 'February', 'March');
print_r($firstquarter);

/* output:
```

```
Array
(
    [1] => 'January'
```

```
>>> => 'February'
>>> => 'March'
)
*/
```

Example 7.8. Filling an array

```
•   fill an array with all items from a directory $handle =
opendir('.');
while ($file = readdir($handle)) { $files[]
    = $file;
}
closedir($handle); ?>
```

Arrays are ordered. You can also change the order using various sorting-functions. See the array functions section for more information. You can count the number of items in an array using the **count()** function.

Example 7.9. Sorting array

```
<?php
sort($files);
print_r($files);
?>
```

Because the value of an array can be everything, it can also be another array. This way you can make recursive and multi-dimensional arrays.

Example 7.10. Recursive and multi-dimensional arrays

```
<?php
$fruits = array ( "fruits"         => array ( "a" => "orange",
                                              "b" => "banana",
                                              "c" => "apple"
                                            ),
                  "numbers" => array ( 1,
                                       2,
                                       3,
                                       4,
                                       5,
                                       6,
                                     ),
                  "holes"    => array (        "first",
                                        5 => "second",
                                             "third"
                                      )
                );
// Some examples to address values in the array above
echo $fruits["holes"][5];         // prints "second"
echo $fruits["fruits"]["a"]; // prints "orange"
unset($fruits["holes"][0]);       // remove "first"

!   Create a new multi-dimensional array
$juices["apple"]["green"] = "good";
?>
```

You should be aware, that array assignment always involves value copying. You need to use the reference operator to copy

---

89

an array by reference.

```php
<?php
$arr1 = array(2, 3);
$arr2 = $arr1;
$arr2[] = 4; // $arr2 is changed,
             // $arr1 is still array(2,3)

$arr3 = &$arr1;
$arr3[] = 4; // now $arr1 and $arr3 are the same ?>
```

Objects

Object Initialization

To initialize an object, you use the new statement to instantiate the object to a variable.

```php
<?php
class foo
{
    function do_foo()
    {
        echo "Doing foo.";
    }
}

$bar = new foo;
$bar->do_foo();
?>
```

For a full discussion, please read the section Classes and Objects.

Converting to object

If an object is converted to an object, it is not modified. If a value of any other type is converted to an object, a new instance of the stdClass built in class is created. If the value was null, the new instance will be empty. For any other value, a mem-ber variable named scalar will contain the value.

```php
<?php
$obj = (object) 'ciao';
echo $obj->scalar;      // outputs 'ciao'
?>
```

Resource

A resource is a special variable, holding a reference to an external resource. Resources are created and used by special func-tions. See the appendix for a listing of all these functions and the corresponding resource types.

Note: The resource type was introduced in PHP 4

Converting to resource

As resource types hold special handlers to opened files, database connections, image canvas areas and the like, you cannot convert any value to a resource.

90

Freeing resources

Due to the reference-counting system introduced with PHP4's Zend-engine, it is automatically detected when a resource is no longer referred to (just like Java). When this is the case, all resources that were in use for this resource are made free by the garbage collector. For this reason, it is rarely ever necessary to free the memory manually by using some free_result function.

> **Note:** Persistent database links are special, they are *not* destroyed by the garbage collector. See also the section about persistent connections.

NULL

The special NULL value represents that a variable has no value. NULL is the only possible value of type NULL.

> **Note:** The null type was introduced in PHP 4

A variable is considered to be NULL if

! it has been assigned the constant NULL.

! it has not been set to any value yet.

! it has been **unset()**.

Syntax

There is only one value of type NULL, and that is the case-insensitive keyword NULL.

```php
<?php
$var = NULL;

?>
```

See also **is_null()** and **unset()**.

Pseudo-types used in this documentation

mixed

mixed indicates that a parameter may accept multiple (but not necesseraly all) types.

gettype() for example will accept all PHP types, while **str_replace()** will accept strings and arrays.

number

number indicates that a parameter can be either integer or float.

callback

Some functions like **call_user_function()** or **usort()** accept user defined callback functions as a parameter. Callback func-tions can not only be simple functions but also object methods including static class methods.

91

A PHP function is simply passed by its name as a string. You can pass any builtin or user defined function with the excep-tion of **array()**, **echo()**, **empty()**, **eval()**, **exit()**, **isset()**, **list()**, **print()** and **unset()**.

A method of an instantiated object is passed as an array containing an object as the element with index 0 and a method name as the element with index 1.

Static class methods can also be passed without instantiating an object of that class by passing the class name instead of an object as the element with index 0.

Example 7.11. Callback function examples

```php
<?php

>>>     simple callback
example function foobar() {
    echo "hello world!";
}
call_user_function("foobar");

>>>     method callback
examples class foo {
    function bar() { echo
      "hello world!";
    }
}

$foo = new foo;

call_user_function(array($foo, "bar")); // object method call

call_user_function(array("foo", "bar")); // static class method call

?>
```

Type Juggling

PHP does not require (or support) explicit type definition in variable declaration; a variable's type is determined by the con-text in which that variable is used. That is to say, if you assign a string value to variable $var, $var becomes a string. If you then assign an integer value to $var, it becomes an integer.

An example of PHP's automatic type conversion is the addition operator '+'. If any of the operands is a float, then all oper-ands are evaluated as floats, and the result will be a float. Otherwise, the operands will be interpreted as integers, and the result will also be an integer. Note that this does NOT change the types of the operands themselves; the only change is in how the operands are evaluated.

```php
<?php
$foo = "0"; // $foo is string (ASCII 48)
$foo += 2; // $foo is now an integer (2)
$foo = $foo + 1.3; // $foo is now      a float    (3.3)
$foo = 5   + "10 Little Piggies";   // $foo is    integer (15)
$foo = 5   + "10 Small Pigs";       // $foo is integer (15)
?>
```

If the last two examples above seem odd, see String conversion to numbers.

If you wish to force a variable to be evaluated as a certain type, see the section on Type casting. If you wish to change the type of a variable, see **settype()**.

## 92

If you would like to test any of the examples in this section, you can use the **var_dump()** function.

Note: The behaviour of an automatic conversion to array is currently undefined.

```php
<?php
$a = "1";          // $a is a string
$a[0]  = "f";      // What about string offsets? What happens?
?>
```

Since PHP (for historical reasons) supports indexing into strings via offsets using the same syntax as array index-ing, the example above leads to a problem: should $a become an array with its first element being "f", or should "f" become the first character of the string $a?

The current versions of PHP interpret the second assignment as a string offset identification, so $a becomes "f", the result of this automatic conversion however should be considered undefined. PHP 4 introduced the new curly bracket syntax to access characters in string, use this syntax instead of the one presented above:

```php
<?php
$a    = "abc"; // $a is a string
$a{1} = "f";       // $a is now "afc"
?>
```

See the section titled String access by character for more informaton.

Type Casting

Type casting in PHP works much as it does in C: the name of the desired type is written in parentheses before the variable which is to be cast.

```php
<?php
$foo = 10;      // $foo is an integer
$bar = (boolean) $foo;      // $bar is a boolean
?>
```

The casts allowed are:

- (int), (integer) - cast to integer

- (bool), (boolean) - cast to boolean

- (float), (double), (real) - cast to float

- (string) - cast to string

- (array) - cast to array

- (object) - cast to object

Note that tabs and spaces are allowed inside the parentheses, so the following are functionally equivalent:

```php
<?php
$foo = (int) $bar;
$foo = ( int ) $bar;
?>
```

Note: Instead of casting a variable to string, you can also enclose the variable in double quotes.

```
<?php
$foo =  10;                 // $foo is an integer
$str  = "$foo";             // $str  is a string
$fst  =        (string) $foo; // $fst   is also a string

•   This prints out that "they are the same" if ($fst
=== $str) {
        echo "they are the same";
}
?>
```

It may not be obvious exactly what will happen when casting between certain types. For more info, see these sections:

- Converting to boolean

- Converting to integer

- Converting to float

- Converting to string

- Converting to array

- Converting to object

- Converting to resource

Chapter 8. Variables

Table of Contents

Basics

Variables in PHP are represented by a dollar sign followed by the name of the variable. The variable name is case-sensitive.

Variable names follow the same rules as other labels in PHP. A valid variable name starts with a letter or underscore, fol-lowed by any number of letters, numbers, or underscores. As a regular expression, it would be expressed thus: '[a-zA-Z_\x7f-\xff][a-zA-Z0-9_\x7f-\xff]*'

Note: For our purposes here, a letter is a-z, A-Z, and the ASCII characters from 127 through 255 (0x7f-0xff).

```php
<?php
$var = "Bob"; $Var =
"Joe"; echo "$var,
$Var";

$4site = 'not yet';
$_4site = 'not yet';
$täyte = 'mansikka'; ?>
```

- outputs "Bob, Joe"

- invalid; starts with a number
- valid; starts with an underscore
- valid; 'ä' is ASCII 228.

In PHP 3, variables are always assigned by value. That is to say, when you assign an expression to a variable, the entire value of the original expression is copied into the destination variable. This means, for instance, that after assigning one variable's value to another, changing one of those variables will have no effect on the other. For more information on this kind of assignment, see the chapter on Expressions.

PHP 4 offers another way to assign values to variables: assign by reference. This means that the new variable simply refer-ences (in other words, "becomes an alias for" or "points to") the original variable. Changes to the new variable affect the ori-ginal, and vice versa. This also means that no copying is performed; thus, the assignment happens more quickly. However, any speedup will likely be noticed only in tight loops or when assigning large arrays or objects.

To assign by reference, simply prepend an ampersand (&) to the beginning of the variable which is being assigned (the source variable). For instance, the following code snippet outputs 'My name is Bob' twice:

```php
<?php
$foo = 'Bob';            // Assign the value 'Bob' to $foo
$bar = &$foo;            // Reference $foo via $bar.
$bar = "My name is $bar";  // Alter $bar...
echo $bar;
echo $foo;               // $foo is altered too.
?>
```

One important thing to note is that only named variables may be assigned by reference.

```
<?php
$foo = 25;
$bar = &$foo;          // This is a valid assignment.
$bar = &(24 * 7);      // Invalid; references an unnamed expression.

function test()
{
    return 25;
}

$bar = &test();        // Invalid.
?>
```

Predefined variables

PHP provides a large number of predefined variables to any script which it runs. Many of these variables, however, cannot be fully documented as they are dependent upon which server is running, the version and setup of the server, and other factors. Some of these variables will not be available when PHP is run on the command line. For a listing of these variables, please see the section on Reserved Predefined Variables.

Warning

In PHP 4.2.0 and later, the default value for the PHP directive register_globals is *off*. This is a major change in PHP. Having register_globals *off* affects the set of predefined variables available in the global scope. For example, to get DOCUMENT_ROOT you'll use $_SERVER['DOCUMENT_ROOT'] instead of $DOCUMENT_ROOT, or $_GET['id'] from the URL http://www.example.com/test.php?id=3 instead of $id, or $_ENV['HOME'] instead of $HOME.

For related information on this change, read the configuration entry for register_globals, the security chapter on Using Register Globals , as well as the PHP 4.1.0 [http:/ / www.php.net/ release_4_1_0.php] and 4.2.0 [http:/ / www.php.net/release_4_2_0.php] Release Announcements.

Using the available PHP Reserved Predefined Variables, like the superglobal arrays, is preferred.

From version 4.1.0 onward, PHP provides an additional set of predefined arrays containing variables from the web server (if applicable), the environment, and user input. These new arrays are rather special in that they are automatically global–i.e., automatically available in every scope. For this reason, they are often known as 'autoglobals' or 'superglobals'. (There is no mechanism in PHP for user-defined superglobals.) The superglobals are listed below; however, for a listing of their contents and further discussion on PHP predefined variables and their natures, please see the section Reserved Predefined Variables. Also, you'll notice how the older predefined variables ($HTTP_*_VARS) still exist.

Variable variables: Superglobals cannot be used as variable variables.

If certain variables in variables_order are not set, their appropriate PHP predefined arrays are also left empty.

PHP Superglobals

$GLOBALS
  Contains a reference to every variable which is currently available within the global scope of the script. The keys of this array are the names of the global variables. $GLOBALS has existed since PHP 3.

$_SERVER
  Variables set by the web server or otherwise directly related to the execution environment of the current script. Analog-ous to the old $HTTP_SERVER_VARS array (which is still available, but deprecated).

$_GET
  Variables provided to the script via HTTP GET. Analogous to the old $HTTP_GET_VARS array (which is still available, but deprecated).

## 96

$_POST
> Variables provided to the script via HTTP POST. Analogous to the old $HTTP_POST_VARS array (which is still avail-able, but deprecated).

$_COOKIE
> Variables provided to the script via HTTP cookies. Analogous to the old $HTTP_COOKIE_VARS array (which is still available, but deprecated).

$_FILES
> Variables provided to the script via HTTP post file uploads. Analogous to the old $HTTP_POST_FILES array (which is still available, but deprecated). See POST method uploads for more information.

$_ENV
> Variables provided to the script via the environment. Analogous to the old $HTTP_ENV_VARS array (which is still avail-able, but deprecated).

$_REQUEST
> Variables provided to the script via any user input mechanism, and which therefore cannot be trusted. The presence and order of variable inclusion in this array is defined according to the variables_order configuration directive. This array has no direct analogue in versions of PHP prior to 4.1.0. See also **import_request_variables()**.
>
> **Note:** When running on the command line , this will *not* include the argv and argc entries; these are present in the $_SERVER array.

$_SESSION
> Variables which are currently registered to a script's session. Analogous to the old $HTTP_SESSION_VARS array (which is still available, but deprecated). See the Session handling functions section for more information.

Variable scope

The scope of a variable is the context within which it is defined. For the most part all PHP variables only have a single scope. This single scope spans included and required files as well. For example:

```php
<?php
$a = 1;
include "b.inc";
?>
```

Here the $a variable will be available within the included b.inc script. However, within user-defined functions a local function scope is introduced. Any variable used inside a function is by default limited to the local function scope. For ex-ample:

```php
<?php
$a = 1; /* global scope */

function Test()
{
    echo $a; /* reference to local scope variable */
}

Test();
?>
```

This script will not produce any output because the echo statement refers to a local version of the $a variable, and it has not been assigned a value within this scope. You may notice that this is a little bit different from the C language in that global variables in C are automatically available to functions unless specifically overridden by a local definition. This can cause some problems in that people may inadvertently change a global variable. In PHP global variables must be declared global inside a function if they are going to be used in that function. An example:

```php
<?php
$a = 1;
$b = 2;

function Sum()
{
    global $a, $b;

    $b = $a + $b;
}

Sum();
echo $b;
?>
```

The above script will output "3". By declaring $a and $b global within the function, all references to either variable will refer to the global version. There is no limit to the number of global variables that can be manipulated by a function.

A second way to access variables from the global scope is to use the special PHP-defined $GLOBALS array. The previous example can be rewritten as:

```php
<?php
$a = 1;
$b = 2;

function Sum()
{
    $GLOBALS["b"] = $GLOBALS["a"] + $GLOBALS["b"];
}

Sum();
echo $b;
?>
```

The $GLOBALS array is an associative array with the name of the global variable being the key and the contents of that vari-able being the value of the array element. Notice how $GLOBALS exists in any scope, this is because $GLOBALS is a super-global. Here's an example demonstrating the power of superglobals:

```php
<?php
function test_global()
{
    !    Most predefined variables aren't "super" and require
    !    'global' to be available to the functions local scope. global
    $HTTP_POST_VARS;

    print $HTTP_POST_VARS['name'];

    •    Superglobals are available in any scope and do
    •    not require 'global'.  Superglobals are available
    •    as of PHP 4.1.0
    print $_POST['name'];
}
?>
```

Another important feature of variable scoping is the *static* variable. A static variable exists only in a local function scope, but it does not lose its value when program execution leaves this scope. Consider the following example:

```php
<?php
function Test ()
{
```

```
    $a = 0;
    echo $a;
    $a++;
}
```

```
?>
```

This function is quite useless since every time it is called it sets $a to 0 and prints "0". The $a++ which increments the vari-able serves no purpose since as soon as the function exits the $a variable disappears. To make a useful counting function which will not lose track of the current count, the $a variable is declared static:

```php
<?php
function Test()
{
    static $a = 0;
    echo $a;
    $a++;
}
?>
```

Now, every time the Test() function is called it will print the value of $a and increment it.

Static variables also provide one way to deal with recursive functions. A recursive function is one which calls itself. Care must be taken when writing a recursive function because it is possible to make it recurse indefinitely. You must make sure you have an adequate way of terminating the recursion. The following simple function recursively counts to 10, using the static variable $count to know when to stop:

```php
<?php
function Test()
{
    static $count = 0;

    $count++;
    echo $count;
    if ($count < 10) {
        Test ();
    }
    $count-;
}
?>
```

The Zend Engine 1, driving PHP4, implements the static and global modifier for variables in terms of references. For example, a true global variable imported inside a function scope with the global statement actually creates a reference to the global variable. This can lead to unexpected behaviour which the following example addresses:

```php
<?php
function test_global_ref() {
    global $obj;
    $obj = &new stdclass;
}

function test_global_noref() {
    global $obj;
    $obj = new stdclass;
}

test_global_ref();
var_dump($obj);
test_global_noref();
var_dump($obj);
?>
```

Executing this example will result in the following output:

```
NULL
```

```
object(stdClass)(0) {
}
```

A similar behaviour applies to the static statement. References are not stored statically:

```php
<?php
function &get_instance_ref() {
    static $obj;

    echo "Static object: ";
    var_dump($obj);
    if (!isset($obj)) {
        •   Assign a reference to the static variable $obj =
            &new stdclass;
    }
    $obj->property++;
    return $obj;
}

function &get_instance_noref() {
    static $obj;

    echo "Static object: ";
    var_dump($obj);
    if (!isset($obj)) {
        •   Assign the object to the static variable $obj =
            new stdclass;
    }
    $obj->property++;
    return $obj;
}

$obj1 = get_instance_ref();
$still_obj1 = get_instance_ref();
echo "\n";
$obj2 = get_instance_noref();
$still_obj2 = get_instance_noref();
?>
```

Executing this example will result in the following output:

```
Static object: NULL
Static object: NULL

Static object: NULL
Static object: object(stdClass)(1) {
  ["property"]=>
  int(1)
}
```

This example demonstrates that when assigning a reference to a static variable, it's not *remembered* when you call the &get_instance_ref() function a second time.

Variable variables

Sometimes it is convenient to be able to have variable variable names. That is, a variable name which can be set and used dynamically. A normal variable is set with a statement such as:

```php
<?php
$a = "hello";
?>
```

A variable variable takes the value of a variable and treats that as the name of a variable. In the above example, *hello*, can be used as the name of a variable by using two dollar signs. i.e.

```php
<?php
```

```
$$a = "world";
```

100

```
?>
```

At this point two variables have been defined and stored in the PHP symbol tree: $a with contents "hello" and $hello with contents "world". Therefore, this statement:

```php
<?php
echo "$a ${$a}";
?>
```

produces the exact same output as:

```php
<?php
echo "$a $hello";
?>
```

i.e. they both produce: hello world.

In order to use variable variables with arrays, you have to resolve an ambiguity problem. That is, if you write $$a[1] then the parser needs to know if you meant to use $a[1] as a variable, or if you wanted $$a as the variable and then the [1] in-dex from that variable. The syntax for resolving this ambiguity is: ${$a[1]} for the first case and ${$a}[1] for the second.

Warning

Please note that variable variables cannot be used with PHP's Superglobal arrays. This means you cannot do things like ${$_GET}. If you are looking for a way to handle availability of superglobals and the old HTTP_*_VARS, you might want to try referencing them.

Variables from outside PHP

HTML Forms (GET and POST)

When a form is submitted to a PHP script, the information from that form is automatically made available to the script.
There are many ways to access this information, for example:

Example 8.1. A simple HTML form

```
<form action="foo.php" method="post">
    Name:  <input type="text" name="username"><br>
    Email: <input type="text" name="email"><br>
    <input type="submit" name="submit" value="Submit me!">
</form>
```

Depending on your particular setup and personal preferences, there are many ways to access data from your HTML forms.
Some examples are:

Example 8.2. Accessing data from a simple POST HTML form

```php
<?php
```
• Available since PHP 4.1.0

```
print $_POST['username']; print
$_REQUEST['username'];
```

```
import_request_variables('p', 'p_');
print $p_username;
```

- Available since PHP 3.

```
print $HTTP_POST_VARS['username'];
```

- Available if the PHP directive register_globals = on. As of
- PHP 4.2.0 the default value of register_globals = off.
- Using/relying on this method is not preferred.

```
    print $username;
?>
```

Using a GET form is similar except you'll use the appropriate GET predefined variable instead. GET also applies to the
QUERY_STRING (the information after the '?' in an URL). So, for example, http://www.example.com/test.php?id=3 contains GET data which is accessible with $_GET['id']. See also $_REQUEST and import_request_variables().

Note: Superglobal arrays, like $_POST and $_GET, became available in PHP 4.1.0

As shown, before PHP 4.2.0 the default value for register_globals was *on*. And, in PHP 3 it was always on. The PHP com-munity is encouraging all to not rely on this directive as it's preferred to assume it's *off* and code accordingly.

Note: The magic_quotes_gpc configuration directive affects Get, Post and Cookie values. If turned on, value (It's "PHP!") will automagically become (It\'s \"PHP!\"). Escaping is needed for DB insertion. See also **addslashes()**, **stripslashes()** and magic_quotes_sybase.

PHP also understands arrays in the context of form variables (see the related faq). You may, for example, group related vari-ables together, or use this feature to retrieve values from a multiple select input. For example, let's post a form to itself and upon submission display the data:

Example 8.3. More complex form variables

```php
<?php
if ($HTTP_POST_VARS['action'] == 'submitted') { print
    '<pre>';

    print_r($HTTP_POST_VARS);
    print '<a href="'. $HTTP_SERVER_VARS['PHP_SELF'] .'">Please try again</a>';

    print '</pre>';
} else { ?>
<form action="<?php echo $HTTP_SERVER_VARS['PHP_SELF']; ?>" method="post">
    Name: <input type="text" name="personal[name]"><br>
    Email: <input type="text" name="personal[email]"><br>
    Beer: <br>
    <select multiple name="beer[]">
        <option value="warthog">Warthog</option>
        <option value="guinness">Guinness</option>
        <option value="stuttgarter">Stuttgarter Schwabenbräu</option>
    </select><br>
    <input type="hidden" name="action" value="submitted"> <input
    type="submit" name="submit" value="submit me!">
</form>
<?php
}
?>
```

227

## 102

In PHP 3, the array form variable usage is limited to single-dimensional arrays. In PHP 4, no such restriction applies.

IMAGE SUBMIT variable names

When submitting a form, it is possible to use an image instead of the standard submit button with a tag like:

```
<input type="image" src="image.gif" name="sub">
```

When the user clicks somewhere on the image, the accompanying form will be transmitted to the server with two additional variables, sub_x and sub_y. These contain the coordinates of the user click within the image. The experienced may note that the actual variable names sent by the browser contains a period rather than an underscore, but PHP converts the period to an underscore automatically.

HTTP Cookies

PHP transparently supports HTTP cookies as defined by Netscape's Spec [http:/ / www.netscape.com/ newsref/ std/ cook-ie_spec.html]. Cookies are a mechanism for storing data in the remote browser and thus tracking or identifying return users. You can set cookies using the **setcookie()** function. Cookies are part of the HTTP header, so the SetCookie function must be called before any output is sent to the browser. This is the same restriction as for the **header()** function. Cookie data is then available in the appropriate cookie data arrays, such as $_COOKIE, $HTTP_COOKIE_VARS as well as in $_REQUEST. See the **setcookie()** manual page for more details and examples.

If you wish to assign multiple values to a single cookie variable, you may assign it as an array. For example:

```php
<?php
    setcookie("MyCookie[foo]",    "Testing    1",    time()+3600);
    setcookie("MyCookie[bar]", "Testing 2", time()+3600);
?>
```

That will create two seperate cookies although MyCookie will now be a single array in your script. If you want to set just one cookie with multiple values, consider using **serialize()** or **explode()** on the value first.

Note that a cookie will replace a previous cookie by the same name in your browser unless the path or domain is different.
So, for a shopping cart application you may want to keep a counter and pass this along. i.e.

Example 8.4. A setcookie() example

```php
<?php
$count++;
setcookie("count", $count, time()+3600);
setcookie("Cart[$count]", $item, time()+3600);
?>
```

Dots in incoming variable names

Typically, PHP does not alter the names of variables when they are passed into a script. However, it should be noted that the dot (period, full stop) is not a valid character in a PHP variable name. For the reason, look at it:

```php
<?php
$varname.ext;    /* invalid variable name */
?>
```

Now, what the parser sees is a variable named $varname, followed by the string concatenation operator, followed by the barestring (i.e. unquoted string which doesn't match any known key or reserved words) 'ext'. Obviously, this doesn't have the intended result.

## 103

For this reason, it is important to note that PHP will automatically replace any dots in incoming variable names with under-scores.

Determining variable types

Because PHP determines the types of variables and converts them (generally) as needed, it is not always obvious what type a given variable is at any one time. PHP includes several functions which find out what type a variable is, such as: **gettype()**, **is_array()**, **is_float()**, **is_int()**, **is_object()**, and **is_string()**. See also the chapter on Types.

Chapter 9. Constants

Table of Contents

A constant is an identifier (name) for a simple value. As the name suggests, that value cannot change during the execution of the script (except for magic constants, which aren't actually constants). A constant is case-sensitive by default. By con-vention, constant identifiers are always uppercase.

The name of a constant follows the same rules as any label in PHP. A valid constant name starts with a letter or underscore, followed by any number of letters, numbers, or underscores. As a regular expression, it would be expressed thusly:
[a-zA-Z_\x7f-\xff][a-zA-Z0-9_\x7f-\xff]*

> Note: For our purposes here, a letter is a-z, A-Z, and the ASCII characters from 127 through 255 (0x7f-0xff).

Like superglobals, the scope of a constant is global. You can access constants anywhere in your script without regard to scope. For more information on scope, read the manual section on variable scope.

Syntax

You can define a constant by using the **define()**-function. Once a constant is defined, it can never be changed or undefined.

Only scalar data (boolean, integer, float and string) can be contained in constants.

You can get the value of a constant by simply specifying its name. Unlike with variables, you should *not* prepend a constant with a $. You can also use the function **constant()** to read a constant's value if you wish to obtain the constant's name dy-namically. Use **get_defined_constants()** to get a list of all defined constants.

> Note: Constants and (global) variables are in a different namespace. This implies that for example TRUE and $TRUE are generally different.

If you use an undefined constant, PHP assumes that you mean the name of the constant itself. A notice will be issued when this happens. Use the **defined()**-function if you want to know if a constant is set.

These are the differences between constants and variables:

- Constants do not have a dollar sign ($) before them;

- Constants may only be defined using the **define()** function, not by simple assignment;

- Constants may be defined and accessed anywhere without regard to variable scoping rules;

- Constants may not be redefined or undefined once they have been set; and

- Constants may only evaluate to scalar values.

Example 9.1. Defining Constants

105

```php
<?php
define("CONSTANT", "Hello world.");
echo CONSTANT; // outputs "Hello world."
echo Constant; // outputs "Constant" and issues a notice.
?>
```

Predefined constants

PHP provides a large number of predefined constants to any script which it runs. Many of these constants, however, are cre-ated by various extensions, and will only be present when those extensions are available, either via dynamic loading or be-cause they have been compiled in.

There are four magical constants that change depending on where they are used. For example, the value of __LINE__ de-pends on the line that it's used on in your script. These special constants are case-insensitive and are as follows:

Table 9.1. A few "magical" PHP constants

Name	Description
__LINE__	The current line number of the file.
__FILE__	The full path and filename of the file.
__FUNCTION__	The function name. (This was added in PHP 4.3.0.)
__CLASS__	The class name. (This was added in PHP 4.3.0.)
__METHOD__	The class method name. (This was added in PHP 5.0.0)

A list of predefined constants is available in the reserved predefined constants section.

Chapter 10. Expressions

Expressions are the most important building stones of PHP. In PHP, almost anything you write is an expression. The simplest yet most accurate way to define an expression is "anything that has a value".

The most basic forms of expressions are constants and variables. When you type "$a = 5", you're assigning '5' into $a. '5', obviously, has the value 5, or in other words '5' is an expression with the value of 5 (in this case, '5' is an integer constant).

After this assignment, you'd expect $a's value to be 5 as well, so if you wrote $b = $a, you'd expect it to behave just as if you wrote $b = 5. In other words, $a is an expression with the value of 5 as well. If everything works right, this is exactly what will happen.

Slightly more complex examples for expressions are functions. For instance, consider the following function:

```
function foo ()
{
    return 5;
}
```

Assuming you're familiar with the concept of functions (if you're not, take a look at the chapter about functions), you'd as-sume that typing $c = foo() is essentially just like writing $c = 5, and you're right. Functions are expressions with the value of their return value. Since foo() returns 5, the value of the expression 'foo()' is 5. Usually functions don't just return a static value but compute something.

Of course, values in PHP don't have to be integers, and very often they aren't. PHP supports three scalar value types: integer values, floating point values and string values (scalar values are values that you can't 'break' into smaller pieces, unlike ar-rays, for instance). PHP also supports two composite (non-scalar) types: arrays and objects. Each of these value types can be assigned into variables or returned from functions.

So far, users of PHP/FI 2 shouldn't feel any change. However, PHP takes expressions much further, in the same way many other languages do. PHP is an expression-oriented language, in the sense that almost everything is an expression. Consider the example we've already dealt with, '$a = 5'. It's easy to see that there are two values involved here, the value of the in-teger constant '5', and the value of $a which is being updated to 5 as well. But the truth is that there's one additional value involved here, and that's the value of the assignment itself. The assignment itself evaluates to the assigned value, in this case
• In practice, it means that '$a = 5', regardless of what it does, is an expression with the value 5. Thus, writing something like '$b = ($a = 5)' is like writing '$a = 5; $b = 5;' (a semicolon marks the end of a statement). Since assignments are parsed in a right to left order, you can also write '$b = $a = 5'.

Another good example of expression orientation is pre- and post-increment and decrement. Users of PHP/FI 2 and many other languages may be familiar with the notation of variable++ and variable–. These are increment and decrement operat-ors. In PHP/FI 2, the statement '$a++' has no value (is not an expression), and thus you can't assign it or use it in any way. PHP enhances the increment/decrement capabilities by making these expressions as well, like in C. In PHP, like in C, there are two types of increment - pre-increment and post-increment. Both pre-increment and post-increment essentially incre-ment the variable, and the effect on the variable is idential. The difference is with the value of the increment expression. Pre-increment, which is written '++$variable', evaluates to the incremented value (PHP increments the variable before read-ing its value, thus the name 'pre-increment'). Post-increment, which is written '$variable++' evaluates to the original value of $variable, before it was incremented (PHP increments the variable after reading its value, thus the name 'post-increment').

A very common type of expressions are comparison expressions. These expressions evaluate to either 0 or 1, meaning FALSE or TRUE (respectively). PHP supports > (bigger than), >= (bigger than or equal to), == (equal), != (not equal), < (smaller than) and <= (smaller than or equal to). These expressions are most commonly used inside conditional execution, such as if statements.

The last example of expressions we'll deal with here is combined operator-assignment expressions. You already know that if you want to increment $a by 1, you can simply write '$a++' or '++$a'. But what if you want to add more than one to it, for instance 3? You could write '$a++' multiple times, but this is obviously not a

235

very efficient or comfortable way. A much more common practice is to write '$a = $a + 3'. '$a + 3' evaluates to the value of $a plus 3, and is assigned back into $a, which results in incrementing $a by 3. In PHP, as in several other languages like C, you can write this in a shorter way, which with time would become clearer and quicker to understand as well. Adding 3 to the current value of $a can be written '$a += 3'. This means exactly "take the value of $a, add 3 to it, and assign it back into $a". In addition to being shorter and clearer, this also results in faster execution. The value of '$a += 3', like the value of a regular assignment, is the assigned value. Notice that it is NOT 3, but the combined value of $a plus 3 (this is the value that's assigned into $a). Any two-place operator can be used in this operator-assignment mode, for example '$a -= 5' (subtract 5 from the value of $a), '$b *= 7' (multiply the value of $b by 7), etc.

There is one more expression that may seem odd if you haven't seen it in other languages, the ternary conditional operator:

$first ? $second : $third

If the value of the first subexpression is TRUE (non-zero), then the second subexpression is evaluated, and that is the result of the conditional expression. Otherwise, the third subexpression is evaluated, and that is the value.

The following example should help you understand pre- and post-increment and expressions in general a bit better:

```
function double($i)
{
    return $i*2;
}
$b = $a = 5;          /* assign   the value five into the variable $a and $b */
$c = $a++;            /* post-increment, assign original value of $a
                         (5) to   $c */
$e = $d = ++$b;       /* pre-increment, assign the incremented value of
                         $b (6)   to $d and $e */

/* at this point, both $d and       $e are equal to 6 */

$f = double($d++);    /* assign   twice the value of $d <emphasis>before</emphasis>
                         the increment, 2*6 = 12 to $f */
$g = double(++$e);    /* assign   twice the value of $e <emphasis>after</emphasis>
                         the increment, 2*7 = 14 to $g */
$h = $g += 10;        /* first,       $g is incremented by 10 and ends with the
                         value of 24. the value of the assignment (24) is
                         then assigned into $h, and $h ends with the value
                         of 24 as well. */
```

In the beginning of the chapter we said that we'll be describing the various statement types, and as promised, expressions can be statements. However, not every expression is a statement. In this case, a statement has the form of 'expr' ';' that is, an expression followed by a semicolon. In '$b=$a=5;', $a=5 is a valid expression, but it's not a statement by itself. '$b=$a=5;' however is a valid statement.

One last thing worth mentioning is the truth value of expressions. In many events, mainly in conditional execution and loops, you're not interested in the specific value of the expression, but only care about whether it means TRUE or FALSE. The constants TRUE and FALSE (case-insensitive) are the two possible boolean values. When necessary, an expression is automatically converted to boolean. See the section about type-casting for details about how.

PHP provides a full and powerful implementation of expressions, and documenting it entirely goes beyond the scope of this manual. The above examples should give you a good idea about what expressions are and how you can construct useful ex-pressions. Throughout the rest of this manual we'll write *expr* to indicate any valid PHP expression.

Chapter 11. Operators

Table of Contents

Operator Precedence

The precedence of an operator specifies how "tightly" it binds two expressions together. For example, in the expression 1 +
* * 3, the answer is 16 and not 18 because the multiplication ("*") operator has a higher precedence than the addition ("+") operator. Parentheses may be used to force precedence, if necessary. For instance: (1 + 5) * 3 evaluates to 18.

The following table lists the precedence of operators with the lowest-precedence operators listed first.

Table 11.1. Operator Precedence

Associativity	Operators
left	,
left	or
left	xor
left	and
right	print
left	= += -= *= /= .= %= &= |= ^= <<= >>=
left	? :
left	||
left	&&
left	|
left	^
left	&
non-associative	== != === !==

239

non-associative	< <= > >=
left	<< >>
left	+ - .
left	* / %

Associativity	Operators
right	! ~ ++ -- (int) (float) (string) (array) (object) @
right	[
non-associative	new

Note: Although ! has a higher precedence than =, PHP will still allow expressions similar to the following: if (!$a = foo()), in which case the output from foo() is put into $a.

Arithmetic Operators

Remember basic arithmetic from school? These work just like those.

Table 11.2. Arithmetic Operators

Example	Name	Result
$a + $b	Addition	Sum of $a and $b.
$a - $b	Subtraction	Difference of $a and $b.
$a * $b	Multiplication	Product of $a and $b.
$a / $b	Division	Quotient of $a and $b.
$a % $b	Modulus	Remainder of $a divided by $b.

The division operator ("/") returns a float value anytime, even if the two operands are integers (or strings that get converted to integers).

See also the manual page on Math functions.

Assignment Operators

The basic assignment operator is "=". Your first inclination might be to think of this as "equal to". Don't. It really means that the the left operand gets set to the value of the expression on the rights (that is, "gets set to").

The value of an assignment expression is the value assigned. That is, the value of "$a = 3" is 3. This allows you to do some tricky things:

$a = ($b = 4) + 5; // $a is equal to 9 now, and $b has been set to 4.

In addition to the basic assignment operator, there are "combined operators" for all of the binary arithmetic and string oper-ators that allow you to use a value in an expression and then set its value to the result of that expression. For example:

```
$a = 3;
$a += 5; // sets $a to 8, as if we had said: $a = $a + 5; $b = "Hello
";
$b .= "There!"; // sets $b to "Hello There!", just like $b = $b . "There!";
```

Note that the assignment copies the original variable to the new one (assignment by value), so changes to one will not affect the other. This may also have relevance if you need to copy something like a large array inside a tight loop. PHP 4 supports assignment by reference, using the $var = &$othervar; syntax, but this is not possible in PHP 3. 'Assignment by refer-ence' means that both variables end up pointing at the same data, and nothing is copied anywhere. To learn more about ref-erences, please read References explained.

Bitwise Operators

Bitwise operators allow you to turn specific bits within an integer on or off. If both the left- and right-hand parameters are strings, the bitwise operator will operate on the characters in this string.

```php
<?php
    echo 12 ^ 9; // Outputs '5'

    echo "12" ^ "9"; // Outputs the Backspace character (ascii 8)
            // ('1' (ascii 49)) ^ ('9' (ascii 57)) = #8

        echo "hallo" ^ "hello"; // Outputs the ascii values #0 #4 #0 #0 #0
            // 'a' ^ 'e' = #4
?>
```

Table 11.3. Bitwise Operators

Example	Name	Result
$a & $b	And	Bits that are set in both $a and $b are set.
$a | $b	Or	Bits that are set in either $a or $b are set.
$a ^ $b	Xor	Bits that are set in $a or $b but not both are set.
~ $a	Not	Bits that are set in $a are not set, and vice versa.
$a << $b	Shift left	Shift the bits of $a $b steps to the left (each step means "multiply by two")
$a >> $b	Shift right	Shift the bits of $a $b steps to the right (each step means "divide by two")

Comparison Operators

Comparison operators, as their name implies, allow you to compare two values.

Table 11.4. Comparison Operators

Example	Name	Result
$a == $b	Equal	TRUE if $a is equal to $b.
$a === $b	Identical	TRUE if $a is equal to $b, and they are of the same type. (PHP 4 only)
$a != $b	Not equal	TRUE if $a is not equal to $b.

$a <> $b	Not equal	TRUE if $a is not equal to $b.
$a !== $b	Not identical	TRUE if $a is not equal to $b, or they are not of the same type. (PHP 4 only)
$a < $b	Less than	TRUE if $a is strictly less than $b.
$a > $b	Greater than	TRUE if $a is strictly greater than $b.
$a <= $b	Less than or equal to	TRUE if $a is less than or equal to $b.
$a >= $b	Greater than or equal to	TRUE if $a is greater than or equal to $b.

Another conditional operator is the "?:" (or ternary) operator, which operates as in C and many other languages.

```php
<?php
// Example usage for: Ternary Operator
$action = (empty($_POST['action'])) ? 'default' : $_POST['action'];

• The above is identical to this if/else statement if
(empty($_POST['action'])) {
    $action = 'default'; }
else {
    $action = $_POST['action'];
}
?>
```

The expression (expr1) ? (expr2) : (expr3) evaluates to *expr2* if *expr1* evaluates to TRUE, and *expr3* if *expr1* evaluates to FALSE.

See also **strcasecmp()**, **strcmp()**, and the manual section on Types.

Error Control Operators

PHP supports one error control operator: the at sign (@). When prepended to an expression in PHP, any error messages that might be generated by that expression will be ignored.

If the track_errors feature is enabled, any error message generated by the expression will be saved in the variable $php_errormsg. This variable will be overwritten on each error, so check early if you want to use it.

```php
<?php
/* Intentional file error */
$my_file = @file ('non_existent_file') or
    die ("Failed opening file: error was '$php_errormsg'");

• this works for any expression, not just functions: $value =
@$cache[$key];
• will not issue a notice if the index $key doesn't exist.

?>
```

Note: The @-operator works only on expressions. A simple rule of thumb is: if you can take the value of something, you can prepend the @ operator to it. For instance, you can prepend it to variables, function and **in-clude()** calls, constants, and so forth. You cannot prepend it to function or class definitions, or conditional struc-tures such as if and foreach, and so forth.

See also **error_reporting()** and the manual section for Error Handling and Logging functions.

Note: The "@" error-control operator prefix will not disable messages that are the result of parse errors.

Warning

Currently the "@" error-control operator prefix will even disable error reporting for critical errors that will termin-ate script execution. Among other things, this means that if you use "@" to suppress errors from a certain function and either it isn't available or has been mistyped, the script will die right there with no indication as to why.

Execution Operators

PHP supports one execution operator: backticks (``). Note that these are not single-quotes! PHP will attempt to execute the contents of the backticks as a shell command; the output will be returned (i.e., it won't simply be dumped to output; it can be assigned to a variable). Use of the backtick operator is identical to **shell_exec()**.

```php
$output = `ls -al`;
echo "<pre>$output</pre>";
```

112

Note: The backtick operator is disabled when safe mode is enabled or shell_exec() is disabled.

See also the manual section on Program Execution functions, **popen()** proc_**open()**, and Using PHP from the commandline.

Incrementing/Decrementing Operators

PHP supports C-style pre- and post-increment and decrement operators.

Table 11.5. Increment/decrement Operators

Example	Name	Effect
++$a	Pre-increment	Increments $a by one, then returns $a.
$a++	Post-increment	Returns $a, then increments $a by one.
–$a	Pre-decrement	Decrements $a by one, then returns $a.
$a–	Post-decrement	Returns $a, then decrements $a by one.

Here's a simple example script:

```php
<?php
echo "<h3>Postincrement</h3>";
$a = 5;
echo "Should be 5: " . $a++ . "<br />\n";
echo "Should be 6: " . $a . "<br />\n";

echo "<h3>Preincrement</h3>";
$a = 5;
echo "Should be 6: " . ++$a . "<br />\n";
echo "Should be 6: " . $a . "<br />\n";

echo "<h3>Postdecrement</h3>";
$a = 5;
echo "Should be 5: " . $a-- . "<br />\n";
echo "Should be 4: " . $a . "<br />\n";

echo "<h3>Predecrement</h3>";
$a = 5;
echo "Should be 4: " . --$a . "<br />\n";
echo "Should be 4: " . $a . "<br />\n";
?>
```

PHP follows Perl's convention when dealing with arithmetic operations on character variables and not C's. For example, in Perl 'Z'+1 turns into 'AA', while in C 'Z'+1 turns into '[' (ord('Z') == 90, ord('[') == 91). Note that character variables can be incremented but not decremented.

Example 11.1. Arithmetic Operations on Character Variables

```php
<?php
$i = 'W';
for($n=0; $n<6; $n++)
   echo ++$i . "\n";
```

```
/*
Produces the output similar to the following:

X
Y
Z
AA
AB
AC
```

113

```
*/
?>
```

Logical Operators

Table 11.6. Logical Operators

Example	Name	Result
$a and $b	And	TRUE if both $a and $b are TRUE.
$a or $b	Or	TRUE if either $a or $b is TRUE.
$a xor $b	Xor	TRUE if either $a or $b is TRUE, but not both.
! $a	Not	TRUE if $a is not TRUE.
$a && $b	And	TRUE if both $a and $b are TRUE.
$a || $b	Or	TRUE if either $a or $b is TRUE.

The reason for the two different variations of "and" and "or" operators is that they operate at different precedences. (See Op-erator Precedence.)

String Operators

There are two string operators. The first is the concatenation operator ('.'), which returns the concatenation of its right and left arguments. The second is the concatenating assignment operator ('.='), which appends the argument on the right side to the argument on the left side. Please read Assignment Operators for more information.

```
$a = "Hello    ";
$b = $a . "World!"; // now    $b contains  "Hello World!"

$a = "Hello    ";
$a .= "World!";      // now  $a contains   "Hello World!"
```

See also the manual sections on the String type and String functions.

Array Operators

The only array operator in PHP is the + operator. It appends the right handed array to the left handed, whereas duplicated keys are NOT overwritten.

```
$a = array("a" => "apple", "b" => "banana");
$b = array("a" =>"pear", "b" => "strawberry", "c" => "cherry");

$c = $a + $b;

var_dump($c);
```

When executed, this script will print the following:

```
array(3) {
```

```
["a"]=>
string(5) "apple"
["b"]=>
```

114

```
  string(6) "banana"
  ["c"]=>
  string(6) "cherry"
}
```

See also the manual sections on the Array type and Array functions.

Chapter 12. Control Structures

Table of Contents

Any PHP script is built out of a series of statements. A statement can be an assignment, a function call, a loop, a conditional statement of even a statement that does nothing (an empty statement). Statements usually end with a semicolon. In addition, statements can be grouped into a statement-group by encapsulating a group of statements with curly braces. A statement-group is a statement by itself as well. The various statement types are described in this chapter.

If

The if construct is one of the most important features of many languages, PHP included. It allows for conditional execution of code fragments. PHP features an if structure that is similar to that of C:

```
if (expr)
    statement
```

As described in the section about expressions, *expr* is evaluated to its Boolean value. If *expr* evaluates to TRUE, PHP will execute *statement*, and if it evaluates to FALSE - it'll ignore it. More information about what values evaluate to FALSE can be found in the 'Converting to boolean' section.

The following example would display a is bigger than b if $a is bigger than $b:

```
if ($a > $b)
    print "a is bigger than b";
```

Often you'd want to have more than one statement to be executed conditionally. Of course, there's no need to wrap each statement with an if clause. Instead, you can group several statements into a statement group. For example, this code would display a is bigger than b if $a is bigger than $b, and would then assign the value of $a into $b:

```
if ($a > $b) {
    print "a is bigger than b";
    $b = $a;
}
```

116

If statements can be nested indefinitely within other if statements, which provides you with complete flexibility for condi-tional execution of the various parts of your program.

else

Often you'd want to execute a statement if a certain condition is met, and a different statement if the condition is not met. This is what else is for. else extends an if statement to execute a statement in case the expression in the if statement evaluates to FALSE. For example, the following code would display a is bigger than b if $a is bigger than $b, and a is NOT bigger than b otherwise:

```
if ($a > $b)     {
      print "a    is bigger than b";
} else {
      print "a    is NOT bigger than b";
}
```

The else statement is only executed if the if expression evaluated to FALSE, and if there were any elseif expressions - only if they evaluated to FALSE as well (see elseif).

elseif

elseif, as its name suggests, is a combination of if and else. Like else, it extends an if statement to execute a different statement in case the original if expression evaluates to FALSE. However, unlike else, it will execute that alternative ex-pression only if the elseif conditional expression evaluates to TRUE. For example, the following code would display a is bigger than b, a equal to b or a is smaller than b:

```
    if ($a > $b) {
        print "a is bigger than b";
    } elseif ($a == $b) {
        print "a is equal to b";
} else {
        print "a is smaller than b";
}
```

There may be several elseifs within the same if statement. The first elseif expression (if any) that evaluates to TRUE would be executed. In PHP, you can also write 'else if' (in two words) and the behavior would be identical to the one of 'el-seif' (in a single word). The syntactic meaning is slightly different (if you're familiar with C, this is the same behavior) but the bottom line is that both would result in exactly the same behavior.

The elseif statement is only executed if the preceding if expression and any preceding elseif expressions evaluated to FALSE, and the current elseif expression evaluated to TRUE.

Alternative syntax for control structures

PHP offers an alternative syntax for some of its control structures; namely, if, while, for, foreach, and switch. In each case, the basic form of the alternate syntax is to change the opening brace to a colon (:) and the closing brace to endif;, endwhile;, endfor;, endforeach;, or endswitch;, respectively.

```
<?php if ($a == 5): ?>
A is equal to 5
<?php endif; ?>
```

In the above example, the HTML block "A is equal to 5" is nested within an if statement written in the alternative syntax.
The HTML block would be displayed only if $a is equal to 5.

The alternative syntax applies to else and elseif as well. The following is an if structure with elseif and else in the alternative format:

117

```
if ($a ==    5):
    print    "a equals 5";
    print    "...";
elseif ($a == 6):
    print    "a equals 6";
    print    "!!!";
else:
    print    "a is neither 5 nor 6";
endif;
```

See also while, for, and if for further examples.

while

while loops are the simplest type of loop in PHP. They behave just like their C counterparts. The basic form of a while statement is:

while (expr) statement

The meaning of a while statement is simple. It tells PHP to execute the nested statement(s) repeatedly, as long as the while expression evaluates to TRUE. The value of the expression is checked each time at the beginning of the loop, so even if this value changes during the execution of the nested statement(s), execution will not stop until the end of the iteration (each time PHP runs the statements in the loop is one iteration). Sometimes, if the while expression evaluates to FALSE from the very beginning, the nested statement(s) won't even be run once.

Like with the if statement, you can group multiple statements within the same while loop by surrounding a group of state-ments with curly braces, or by using the alternate syntax:

while (expr): statement ... endwhile;

The following examples are identical, and both print numbers from 1 to 10:

```
/* example 1 */

$i = 1;
while ($i <= 10) {
    print $i++;      /* the printed value would be
                        $i before the increment
                        (post-increment) */

}

/* example 2 */

$i = 1;
while ($i <= 10):
    print $i;
    $i++;
endwhile;
```

do..while

do..while loops are very similar to while loops, except the truth expression is checked at the end of each iteration instead of in the beginning. The main difference from regular while loops is that the first iteration of a do..while loop is guaran-teed to run (the truth expression is only checked at the end of the iteration), whereas it's may not necessarily run with a regu-lar while loop (the truth expression is checked at the beginning of each iteration, if it evaluates to FALSE right from the be-ginning, the loop execution would end immediately).

There is just one syntax for do..while loops:

118

```
$i = 0;
do {
    print $i;
  } while ($i>0);
```

The above loop would run one time exactly, since after the first iteration, when truth expression is checked, it evaluates to FALSE ($i is not bigger than 0) and the loop execution ends.

Advanced C users may be familiar with a different usage of the do..while loop, to allow stopping execution in the middle of code blocks, by encapsulating them with do..while(0), and using the break statement. The following code fragment demonstrates this:

```
do {
    if ($i < 5) {
        print "i is not big enough";
        break;
    }
    $i *= $factor;
    if ($i < $minimum_limit) {
        break;
    }
    print "i is ok";

    ...process i...

} while(0);
```

Don't worry if you don't understand this right away or at all. You can code scripts and even powerful scripts without using this 'feature'.

for

for loops are the most complex loops in PHP. They behave like their C counterparts. The syntax of a for loop is:

```
for (expr1; expr2; expr3) statement
```

The first expression (*expr1*) is evaluated (executed) once unconditionally at the beginning of the loop.

In the beginning of each iteration, *expr2* is evaluated. If it evaluates to TRUE, the loop continues and the nested statement(s) are executed. If it evaluates to FALSE, the execution of the loop ends.

At the end of each iteration, *expr3* is evaluated (executed).

Each of the expressions can be empty. *expr2* being empty means the loop should be run indefinitely (PHP implicitly con-siders it as TRUE, like C). This may not be as useless as you might think, since often you'd want to end the loop using a con-ditional break statement instead of using the for truth expression.

Consider the following examples. All of them display numbers from 1 to 10:

```
/* example 1 */

for ($i = 1; $i <= 10; $i++) {
    print $i;
}

/* example 2 */

    for ($i = 1;;$i++) {
        if ($i > 10) {
            break;
        }
    print $i;
```

```
}
/* example 3 */

$i = 1;
for (;;) {
        if ($i > 10) {
            break;
        }
        print $i;
        $i++;
}
/* example 4 */

for ($i = 1; $i <= 10; print $i, $i++);
```

Of course, the first example appears to be the nicest one (or perhaps the fourth), but you may find that being able to use empty expressions in for loops comes in handy in many occasions.

PHP also supports the alternate "colon syntax" for for loops.

```
for (expr1; expr2; expr3): statement; ...; endfor;
```

Other languages have a foreach statement to traverse an array or hash. PHP 3 has no such construct; PHP 4 does (see foreach). In PHP 3, you can combine while with the list() and each() functions to achieve the same effect. See the docu-mentation for these functions for an example.

foreach

PHP 4 (not PHP 3) includes a foreach construct, much like Perl and some other languages. This simply gives an easy way to iterate over arrays. foreach works only on arrays, and will issue an error when you try to use it on a variable with a dif-ferent data type or an uninitialized variables. There are two syntaxes; the second is a minor but useful extension of the first:

```
foreach(array_expression as $value) statement
foreach(array_expression as $key => $value) statement
```

The first form loops over the array given by array_expression. On each loop, the value of the current element is as-signed to $value and the internal array pointer is advanced by one (so on the next loop, you'll be looking at the next ele-ment).

The second form does the same thing, except that the current element's key will be assigned to the variable $key on each loop.

> **Note:** When foreach first starts executing, the internal array pointer is automatically reset to the first element of the array. This means that you do not need to call reset() before a foreach loop.

> **Note:** Also note that foreach operates on a copy of the specified array, not the array itself, therefore the array pointer is not modified as with the each() construct and changes to the array element returned are not reflected in the original array. However, the internal pointer of the original array *is* advanced with the processing of the array. Assuming the foreach loop runs to completion, the array's internal pointer will be at the end of the array.

> **Note:** foreach does not support the ability to suppress error messages using '@'.

You may have noticed that the following are functionally identical:

```
$arr = array("one", "two", "three");
reset ($arr);
```

```php
while (list(, $value) = each ($arr)) {
    echo "Value: $value<br>\n";
}

foreach ($arr as $value) {
    echo "Value: $value<br>\n";
}
```

The following are also functionally identical:

```php
reset ($arr);
        while (list($key, $value) = each ($arr)) {
        echo "Key: $key; Value: $value<br>\n";
}

foreach ($arr as $key => $value) {
    echo "Key: $key; Value: $value<br>\n";
}
```

Some more examples to demonstrate usages:

```php
/* foreach example 1: value only */

$a = array (1, 2, 3, 17);

foreach ($a as $v) {
    print "Current value of \$a: $v.\n";
}

/* foreach example 2: value (with key printed for illustration) */

$a = array (1, 2, 3, 17);

$i = 0; /* for illustrative purposes only */

foreach($a as $v) {
    print "\$a[$i] => $v.\n";
    $i++;
}

/* foreach example 3: key and value */

$a = array (
    "one" => 1,
    "two" => 2,
    "three" => 3,
    "seventeen" => 17
);

foreach($a as $k => $v) {
    print "\$a[$k] => $v.\n";
}

/* foreach example 4: multi-dimensional arrays */

$a[0][0] = "a";
$a[0][1] = "b";
$a[1][0] = "y";
$a[1][1] = "z";

foreach($a as $v1) {
    foreach ($v1 as $v2) {
        print "$v2\n";
    }
}

/* foreach example 5: dynamic arrays */
```

```
foreach(array(1, 2, 3, 4, 5) as $v) {
    print "$v\n";
```

121

```
}
```

break

break ends execution of the current for, foreach while, do..while or switch structure.

break accepts an optional numeric argument which tells it how many nested enclosing structures are to be broken out of.

```
$arr = array ('one', 'two', 'three', 'four', 'stop', 'five');
while (list (, $val) = each ($arr)) {
    if ($val == 'stop') {
        break;        /* You could also write 'break 1;' here. */
    }
    echo "$val<br>\n";
}

/* Using the optional argument. */

$i = 0;
while (++$i) {
    switch ($i) {
    case 5:
        echo "At 5<br>\n";
        break 1;     /* Exit only the switch. */
    case 10:
        echo "At 10; quitting<br>\n";
        break 2; /* Exit the switch and the while. */ default:
        break;
    }
}
```

continue

continue is used within looping structures to skip the rest of the current loop iteration and continue execution at the begin-ning of the next iteration.

Note: Note that in PHP the switch statement is considered a looping structure for the purposes of continue.

continue accepts an optional numeric argument which tells it how many levels of enclosing loops it should skip to the end of.

```
while (list ($key, $value) = each ($arr)) {
    if (!($key % 2)) { // skip odd members
        continue;
    }
    do_something_odd ($value);
}

$i = 0;
while ($i++ < 5) {
    echo "Outer<br>\n";
    while (1) {
        echo "  Middle<br>\n";
        while (1) {
            echo "  Inner<br>\n";
            continue 3;
        }
        echo "This never gets output.<br>\n";
    }
    echo "Neither does this.<br>\n";
```

}

switch

The switch statement is similar to a series of IF statements on the same expression. In many occasions, you may want to compare the same variable (or expression) with many different values, and execute a different piece of code depending on which value it equals to. This is exactly what the switch statement is for.

Note: Note that unlike some other languages, the continue statement applies to switch and acts similar to break. If you have a switch inside a loop and wish to continue to the next iteration of the outer loop, use continue 2.

The following two examples are two different ways to write the same thing, one using a series of if statements, and the oth-er using the switch statement:

```
if ($i == 0) {
    print "i equals 0";
} elseif ($i == 1) { print "i
    equals 1";
} elseif ($i == 2) { print "i
    equals 2";
}

switch ($i) {
    case 0:
        print "i equals 0";
        break;
    case 1:
        print "i equals 1";
        break;
    case 2:
        print "i equals 2";
        break;
}
```

It is important to understand how the switch statement is executed in order to avoid mistakes. The switch statement ex-ecutes line by line (actually, statement by statement). In the beginning, no code is executed. Only when a case statement is found with a value that matches the value of the switch expression does PHP begin to execute the statements. PHP contin-ues to execute the statements until the end of the switch block, or the first time it sees a break statement. If you don't write a break statement at the end of a case's statement list, PHP will go on executing the statements of the following case. For example:

```
switch ($i) {
    case 0:
        print "i equals 0";
    case 1:
        print "i equals 1";
    case 2:
        print "i equals 2";
}
```

Here, if $i is equal to 0, PHP would execute all of the print statements! If $i is equal to 1, PHP would execute the last two print statements. You would get the expected behavior ('i equals 2' would be displayed) only if $i is equal to 2. Thus, it is important not to forget break statements (even though you may want to avoid supplying them on purpose under certain cir-cumstances).

In a switch statement, the condition is evaluated only once and the result is compared to each case statement. In an el-seif statement, the condition is evaluated again. If your condition is more complicated than a simple compare and/or is in a tight loop, a switch may be faster.

The statement list for a case can also be empty, which simply passes control into the statement list for the next case.

```
switch ($i) {
    case 0:
    case 1:
    case 2:
        print "i is less than 3 but not negative";
        break;
    case 3:
        print "i is 3";
}
```

A special case is the default case. This case matches anything that wasn't matched by the other cases, and should be the last case statement. For example:

```
switch ($i) {
    case 0:
        print "i equals 0";
        break;
    case 1:
        print "i equals 1";
        break;
    case 2:
        print "i equals 2";
        break;
    default:
        print "i is not equal to 0, 1 or 2";
}
```

The case expression may be any expression that evaluates to a simple type, that is, integer or floating-point numbers and strings. Arrays or objects cannot be used here unless they are dereferenced to a simple type.

The alternative syntax for control structures is supported with switches. For more information, see Alternative syntax for control structures .

```
switch ($i):
    case 0:
        print "i equals 0";
        break;
    case 1:
        print "i equals 1";
        break;
    case 2:
        print "i equals 2";
        break;
    default:
        print "i is not equal to 0, 1 or 2";
endswitch;
```

declare

The declare construct is used to set execution directives for a block of code. The syntax of declare is similar to the syn-tax of other flow control constructs:

declare (directive) statement

The directive section allows the behavior of the declare block to be set. Currently only one directive is recognized: the ticks directive. (See below for more information on the ticks directive)

The statement part of the declare block will be executed – how it is executed and what side effects occur during execu-tion may depend on the directive set in the directive block.

Ticks

## 124

A tick is an event that occurs for every N low-level statements executed by the parser within the declare block. The value for N is specified using ticks=N within the declare blocks's directive section.

The event(s) that occur on each tick are specified using the **register_tick_function()**. See the example below for more de-tails. Note that more than one event can occur for each tick.

Example 12.1. Profile a section of PHP code

```
<?php
•  A function that records the time when it is called function
profile ($dump = FALSE)
{
    static $profile;

    Return the times stored in profile, then erase it if ($dump)
    {
        $temp   =  $profile;
        unset     ($profile);
        return ($temp);
    }

    $profile[] = microtime ();
}
// Set up a tick handler
register_tick_function("profile");

•  Initialize the function before the declare block profile ();

•  Run a block of code, throw a tick every 2nd statement declare
(ticks=2) {
    for ($x = 1; $x < 50; ++$x) {
        echo similar_text (md5($x), md5($x*$x)), "<br />;";
    }
}
•  Display the data stored in the profiler
print_r (profile (TRUE));
?>
```

The example profiles the PHP code within the 'declare' block, recording the time at which every second low-level statement in the block was executed. This information can then be used to find the slow areas within particular segments of code. This process can be performed using other methods: using ticks is more convenient and easier to implement.

Ticks are well suited for debugging, implementing simple multitasking, backgrounded I/O and many other tasks.

See also **register_tick_function()** and **unregister_tick_function()**.

return

If called from within a function, the **return()** statement immediately ends execution of the current function, and returns its argument as the value of the function call. **return()** will also end the execution of an **eval()** statement or script file.

If called from the global scope, then execution of the current script file is ended. If the current script file was **include()**ed or **require()**ed, then control is passed back to the calling file. Furthermore, if the current script file was **include()**ed, then the value given to **return()** will be returned as the value of the **include()** call. If **return()** is called from within the main script file, then script execution ends. If the current script file was named by the auto_prepend_file or auto_append_file configura-tion options in php.ini, then that script file's execution is ended.

Note: Note that since **return()** is a language construct and not a function, the parentheses surrounding its argu-ments are *not* required–in fact, it is more common to leave them out than to use them, although it doesn't matter one way or the other.

require()

The **require()** statement includes and evaluates the specific file.

require() includes and evaluates a specific file. Detailed information on how this inclusion works is described in the docu-mentation for **include()**.

require() and **include()** are identical in every way except how they handle failure. **include()** produces a Warning while re-quire() results in a Fatal Error. In other words, don't hesitate to use require() if you want a missing file to halt processing of the page. **include()** does not behave this way, the script will continue regardless. Be sure to have an appropriate in-clude_path setting as well.

Example 12.2. Basic require() examples

```
<?php
require 'prepend.php';
require $somefile;
require ('somefile.txt');
?>
```

See the **include()** documentation for more examples.

Note: Prior to PHP 4.0.2, the following applies: **require()** will always attempt to read the target file, even if the line it's on never executes. The conditional statement won't affect **require()**. However, if the line on which the **re-quire()** occurs is not executed, neither will any of the code in the target file be executed. Similarly, looping struc-tures do not affect the behaviour of **require()**. Although the code contained in the target file is still subject to the loop, the **require()** itself happens only once.

Note: Because this is a language construct and not a function, it cannot be called using variable functions

Warning

Windows versions of PHP prior to PHP 4.3.0 do not support accessing remote files via this function, even if al-low_url_fopen is enabled.

See also **include()**, **require_once()**, **include_once()**, **eval()**, **file()**, **readfile()**, **virtual()** and include_path.

include()

The **include()** statement includes and evaluates the specified file.

The documentation below also applies to **require()**. The two constructs are identical in every way except how they handle failure. **include()** produces a Warning while **require()** results in a Fatal Error. In other words, use **require()** if you want a missing file to halt processing of the page. **include()** does not behave this way, the script will continue regardless. Be sure to have an appropriate include_path setting as well.

When a file is included, the code it contains inherits the variable scope of the line on which the include occurs. Any vari-

---

126

ables available at that line in the calling file will be available within the called file, from that point forward.

Example 12.3. Basic include() example

```
vars.php
<?php

$color = 'green';
$fruit = 'apple';

?>

test.php
<?php

echo "A $color $fruit"; // A

include 'vars.php';

echo "A $color $fruit"; // A green apple

?>
```

If the include occurs inside a function within the calling file, then all of the code contained in the called file will behave as though it had been defined inside that function. So, it will follow the variable scope of that function.

Example 12.4. Including within functions

```
<?php
function foo()
{
global $color;

    include 'vars.php';

    echo "A $color $fruit";
}

 /* vars.php is in the scope of foo() so        *
  * $fruit is NOT available outside of this      *
  * scope.  $color is because we declared it     *
  * as global.                                   */
foo();                          // A green apple
echo "A $color $fruit";         // A green

?>
```

When a file is included, parsing drops out of PHP mode and into HTML mode at the beginning of the target file, and re-sumes again at the end. For this reason, any code inside the target file which should be executed as PHP code must be en-closed within valid PHP start and end tags.

If "URL fopen wrappers" are enabled in PHP (which they are in the default configuration), you can specify the file to be in-cluded using an URL (via HTTP or other supported wrapper - see Appendix I, *List of Supported Protocols/Wrappers* for a list of protocols) instead of a local pathname. If the target server interprets the target file as PHP code, variables may be passed to the included file using an URL request string as used with HTTP GET. This is not strictly speaking the same thing as including the file and having it inherit the parent file's variable scope; the script is actually being run on the remote server and the result is then being included into the local script.

## 127

Warning

Windows versions of PHP prior to PHP 4.3.0 do not support accessing remote files via this function, even if al-low_url_fopen is enabled.

Example 12.5. include() through HTTP

```php
<?php

    /* This example assumes that www.example.com is configured to parse .php * * files
                    and not .txt files. Also, 'Works' here means that the variables *
   * $foo and $bar are available within the included file.                         */

   • Won't work; file.txt wasn't handled by www.example.com as PHP include
'http://www.example.com/file.txt?foo=1&bar=2';

   • Won't work; looks for a file named 'file.php?foo=1&bar=2' on the
   • local filesystem.
include 'file.php?foo=1&bar=2';

// Works.
include 'http://www.example.com/file.php?foo=1&bar=2';

$foo = 1;
$bar = 2;
include 'file.txt';        // Works.
include 'file.php';        // Works.

?>
```

See also Remote files, **fopen()** and **file()** for related information.

Because **include()** and **require()** are special language constructs, you must enclose them within a statement block if it's in-side a conditional block.

Example 12.6. include() and conditional blocks

```php
<?php

   • This is WRONG and will not work as desired. if
($condition)
      include $file;
else
     include $other;

   • This is CORRECT.
if ($condition) {
     include $file;
} else {
     include $other;
}

?>
```

Handling Returns: It is possible to execute a **return()** statement inside an included file in order to terminate processing in that file and return to the script which called it. Also, it's possible to return values from included files. You can take the value of the include call as you would a normal function.

Note: In PHP 3, the return may not appear inside a block unless it's a function block, in which case the **return()**

applies to that function and not the whole file.

Example 12.7. Include() and the return() statement

```
return.php
<?php

$var = 'PHP';

return $var;

?>
noreturn.php
<?php

$var = 'PHP';

?>
testreturns.php
<?php

$foo = include 'return.php';

echo $foo; // prints 'PHP'

$bar = include 'noreturn.php';

echo $bar; // prints 1

?>
```

$bar is the value 1 because the include was successful. Notice the difference between the above examples. The first uses **return()** within the included file while the other does not. A few other ways to "include" files into variables are with **fopen()**, **file()** or by using **include()** along with Output Control Functions.

Note: Because this is a language construct and not a function, it cannot be called using variable functions

See also **require()**, **require_once()**, **include_once()**, **readfile()**, **virtual()**, and include_path.

require_once()

The **require_once()** statement includes and evaluates the specified file during the execution of the script. This is a behavior similar to the **require()** statement, with the only difference being that if the code from a file has already been included, it will not be included again. See the documentation for **require()** for more information on how this statement works.

require_once() should be used in cases where the same file might be included and evaluated more than once during a par-ticular execution of a script, and you want to be sure that it is included exactly once to avoid problems with function re-definitions, variable value reassignments, etc.

For examples on using **require_once()** and **include_once()**, look at the PEAR [http:/ / pear.php.net/] code included in the latest PHP source code distributions.

Note: require_once() was added in PHP 4.0.1pl2

Note: Be aware, that the behaviour of **require_once()** and **include_once()** may not be what you expect on a non case sensitive operating system (such as Windows).

## 129

Example 12.8. require_once() is case sensitive

```
require_once("a.php"); // this will include a.php
require_once("A.php"); // this will include a.php again on Windows!
```

Warning

Windows versions of PHP prior to PHP 4.3.0 do not support accessing remote files via this function, even if al-low_url_fopen is enabled.

See also: **require()**, **include()**, **include_once()**, **get_required_files()**, **get_included_files()**, **readfile()**, and **virtual()**.

include_once()

The **include_once()** statement includes and evaluates the specified file during the execution of the script. This is a behavior similar to the **include()** statement, with the only difference being that if the code from a file has already been included, it will not be included again. As the name suggests, it will be included just once.

include_once() should be used in cases where the same file might be included and evaluated more than once during a par-ticular execution of a script, and you want to be sure that it is included exactly once to avoid problems with function re-definitions, variable value reassignments, etc.

For more examples on using **require_once()** and **include_once()**, look at the PEAR [http://pear.php.net/] code included in the latest PHP source code distributions.

Note: **include_once()** was added in PHP 4.0.1pl2

Note: Be aware, that the behaviour of **include_once()** and **require_once()** may not be what you expect on a non case sensitive operating system (such as Windows).

Example 12.9. include_once() is case sensitive

```
include_once("a.php"); // this will include a.php
include_once("A.php"); // this will include a.php again on Windows!
```

Warning

Windows versions of PHP prior to PHP 4.3.0 do not support accessing remote files via this function, even if al-low_url_fopen is enabled.

See also **include()**, **require()**, **require_once()**, **get_required_files()**, **get_included_files()**, **readfile()**, and **virtual()**.

130

Chapter 13. Functions

Table of Contents

User-defined functions

A function may be defined using syntax such as the following:

Example 13.1. Psuedo code to demonstrate function uses

```php
<?php
function foo ($arg_1, $arg_2, ..., $arg_n)
{
    echo "Example function.\n";
    return $retval;
}
?>
```

Any valid PHP code may appear inside a function, even other functions and class definitions.

In PHP 3, functions must be defined before they are referenced. No such requirement exists in PHP 4. *Except* when a func-tion is conditionally defined such as shown in the two examples below.

When a function is defined in a conditional manner such as the two examples shown. Its definition must be processed *prior* to being called.

Example 13.2. Conditional functions

```php
<?php

$makefoo = true;

/* We can't call foo() from here
    since it doesn't exist yet,
    but we can call bar() */

bar();

if ($makefoo) {
    function foo ()
    {
        echo "I don't exist until program execution reaches me.\n";
    }
}

/* Now we can safely call foo()
```

131

```
   since $makefoo evaluated to true */

if ($makefoo) foo();

function bar()
{
   echo "I exist immediately upon program start.\n";
}
?>
```

Example 13.3. Functions within functions

```
<?php
function foo()
{
   function bar()
   {
      echo "I don't exist until foo() is called.\n";
   }
}

/* We can't call bar() yet
   since it doesn't exist. */

foo();

/* Now we can call bar(),
   foo()'s processesing has
   made it accessable. */

bar();

?>
```

PHP does not support function overloading, nor is it possible to undefine or redefine previously-declared functions.

> **Note:** Function names are case-insensitive, though it is usually good form to call functions as they appear in their declaration.

PHP 3 does not support variable numbers of arguments to functions, although default arguments are supported (see Default argument values for more information). PHP 4 supports both: see Variable-length argument lists and the function references for **func_num_args()**, **func_get_arg()**, and **func_get_args()** for more information.

Function arguments

Information may be passed to functions via the argument list, which is a comma-delimited list of variables and/or constants.

PHP supports passing arguments by value (the default), passing by reference, and default argument values. Variable-length argument lists are supported only in PHP 4 and later; see Variable-length argument lists and the function references for **func_num_args()**, **func_get_arg()**, and **func_get_args()** for more information. A similar effect can be achieved in PHP 3 by passing an array of arguments to a function:

Example 13.4. Passing arrays to functions

```
function takes_array($input)
```

```
{
    echo "$input[0] + $input[1] = ", $input[0]+$input[1];
```

```
}
```

Making arguments be passed by reference

By default, function arguments are passed by value (so that if you change the value of the argument within the function, it does not get changed outside of the function). If you wish to allow a function to modify its arguments, you must pass them by reference.

If you want an argument to a function to always be passed by reference, you can prepend an ampersand (&) to the argument name in the function definition:

Example 13.5. Passing function parameters by reference

```php
<?php
function add_some_extra(&$string)
{
    $string .= 'and something extra.';
}
$str = 'This is a string, ';
add_some_extra($str);
echo $str; // outputs 'This is a string, and something extra.' ?>
```

Default argument values

A function may define C++-style default values for scalar arguments as follows:

Example 13.6. Use of default parameters in functions

```php
<?php
function makecoffee ($type = "cappuccino")
{
    return "Making a cup of $type.\n";
}
echo makecoffee ();
echo makecoffee ("espresso");
?>
```

The output from the above snippet is:

```
Making a cup of cappuccino.
Making a cup of espresso.
```

The default value must be a constant expression, not (for example) a variable or class member.

Note that when using default arguments, any defaults should be on the right side of any non-default arguments; otherwise, things will not work as expected. Consider the following code snippet:

Example 13.7. Incorrect usage of default function arguments

133

```
<?php
function makeyogurt ($type = "acidophilus", $flavour)
{
    return "Making a bowl of $type $flavour.\n";
}

echo makeyogurt ("raspberry"); // won't work as expected ?>
```

The output of the above example is:

Warning: Missing argument 2 in call to makeyogurt() in
/usr/local/etc/httpd/htdocs/php3test/functest.html on line 41 Making
a bowl of raspberry .

Now, compare the above with this:

Example 13.8. Correct usage of default function arguments

```
<?php
function makeyogurt ($flavour, $type = "acidophilus")
{
    return "Making a bowl of $type $flavour.\n";
}

echo makeyogurt ("raspberry"); // works as expected ?>
```

The output of this example is:

Making a bowl of acidophilus raspberry.

Variable-length argument lists

PHP 4 has support for variable-length argument lists in user-defined functions. This is really quite easy, using the **func_num_args()**, **func_get_arg()**, and **func_get_args()** functions.

No special syntax is required, and argument lists may still be explicitly provided with function definitions and will behave as normal.

Returning values

Values are returned by using the optional return statement. Any type may be returned, including lists and objects. This causes the function to end its execution immediately and pass control back to the line from which it was called. See **return()** for more information.

Example 13.9. Use of return()

```
<?php
function square ($num)
{
    return $num * $num;
```

134

```
}
echo square (4);        // outputs '16'.
?>
```

You can't return multiple values from a function, but similar results can be obtained by returning a list.

Example 13.10. Returning an array to get multiple values

```
<?php
function small_numbers()
{
    return array (0, 1, 2);
}
list ($zero, $one, $two) = small_numbers();
?>
```

To return a reference from a function, you have to use the reference operator & in both the function declaration and when assigning the returned value to a variable:

Example 13.11. Returning a reference from a function

```
<?php
function &returns_reference()
{
    return $someref;
}

$newref =& returns_reference();
?>
```

For more information on references, please check out References Explained.

Variable functions

PHP supports the concept of variable functions. This means that if a variable name has parentheses appended to it, PHP will look for a function with the same name as whatever the variable evaluates to, and will attempt to execute it. Among other things, this can be used to implement callbacks, function tables, and so forth.

Variable functions won't work with language constructs such as **echo()**, **print()**, **unset()**, **isset()**, **empty()**, **include()**, **re-quire()** and the like. You need to use your own wrapper function to utilize any of these constructs as variable functions.

Example 13.12. Variable function example

```
<?php
function foo()
{
    echo "In foo()<br>\n";
}

function bar($arg = '')
{
    echo "In bar(); argument was '$arg'.<br>\n";
}
```

```
•   This is a wrapper function around echo
function echoit($string)
{
    echo $string;
}

$func = 'foo';
$func();                // This calls foo()

$func = 'bar';
$func('test');          // This calls bar()

$func = 'echoit';
$func('test');          // This calls echoit()
?>
```

You can also call an object's method by using the variable functions feature.

Example 13.13. Variable method example

```
<?php
class Foo
{
    function Var()
    {
        $name = 'Bar';
        $this->$name(); // This calls the Bar() method
    }

    function Bar()
    {
        echo "This is Bar";
    }
}
$foo = new Foo();
$funcname = "Var";
$foo->$funcname();      // This calls $foo->Var()

?>
```

See also **call_user_func()**, variable variables and **function_exists()**.

Internal (built-in) functions

PHP comes standard with many functions and constructs. There are also functions that require specific PHP extensions compiled in otherwise you'll get fatal "undefined function" errors. For example, to use image functions such as **imagecreat-etruecolor()**, you'll need your PHP compiled with GD support. Or, to use **mysql_connect()** you'll need your PHP compiled in with MySQL support. There are many core functions that are included in every version of PHP like the string and vari-able functions. A call to **phpinfo()** or **get_loaded_extensions()** will show you which extensions are loaded into your PHP. Also note that many extensions are enabled by default and that the PHP manual is split up by extension. See the configura-tion, installation, and individual extension chapters, for information on how to setup your PHP.

Reading and understanding a function's prototype is explained within the manual section titled how to read a function defin-ition. It's important to realize what a function returns or if a function works directly on a passed in value. For example, **str_replace()** will return the modified string while **usort()** works on the actual passed in variable itself. Each manual page also has specific information on each function like information on function parameters, behavior changes, return values for both success and failure, and availability information. Knowing these important (yet often subtle) differences is crucial for writing correct PHP code.

## 136

See also **function_exists()**, the function reference, **get_extension_funcs()**, and **dl()**.

Chapter 14. Classes and Objects

Table of Contents

class

A class is a collection of variables and functions working with these variables. A class is defined using the following syntax:

```php
<?php
class Cart
{
    var $items;     // Items in our shopping cart

    // Add $num articles of $artnr to the cart

    function add_item ($artnr, $num)
    {
        $this->items[$artnr] += $num;
    }

    // Take $num articles of $artnr out of the cart

    function remove_item ($artnr, $num)
    {
        if ($this->items[$artnr] > $num) {
            $this->items[$artnr] -= $num;
            return true;
        } else {
            return false;
        }
    }
}
?>
```

This defines a class named Cart that consists of an associative array of articles in the cart and two functions to add and re-move items from this cart.

Caution

The following cautionary notes are valid for PHP 4.

The name stdClass is used interally by Zend and is reserved. You cannot have a class named stdClass in PHP.

The function names __sleep and __wakeup are magical in PHP classes. You cannot have functions with these names in any of your classes unless you want the magic functionality associated with them. See below for more in-

---

138

formation.

PHP reserves all function names starting with __ as magical. It is recommended that you do not use function names with __ in PHP unless you want some documented magic functionality.

Note: In PHP 4, only constant initializers for var variables are allowed. To initialize variables with non-constant values, you need an initialization function which is called automatically when an object is being constructed from the class. Such a function is called a constructor (see below).

```php
<?php
/* None of these will work in PHP 4. */
class Cart
{
    var $todays_date = date("Y-m-d");
    var $name = $firstname;
    var $owner = 'Fred ' . 'Jones';
    var $items = array("VCR", "TV");
}

/* This is how it should be done. */
class Cart
{
    var $todays_date;
    var $name;
    var $owner;
    var $items;

    function Cart()
    {
        $this->todays_date = date("Y-m-d");
        $this->name = $GLOBALS['firstname'];
        /* etc... */
    }
}
?>
```

Classes are types, that is, they are blueprints for actual variables. You have to create a variable of the desired type with the new operator.

```php
<?php
$cart = new Cart;
$cart->add_item("10", 1);

$another_cart = new Cart;
$another_cart->add_item("0815", 3);
```

This creates the objects $cart and $another_cart, both of the class Cart. The function add_item() of the $cart object is being called to add 1 item of article number 10 to the $cart. 3 items of article number 0815 are being added to $another_cart.

Both, $cart and $another_cart, have functions add_item(), remove_item() and a variable items. These are distinct functions and variables. You can think of the objects as something similar to directories in a filesystem. In a filesystem you can have two different files README.TXT, as long as they are in different directories. Just like with directories where you'll have to type the full pathname in order to reach each file from the toplevel directory, you have to specify the complete name of the function you want to call: In PHP terms, the toplevel directory would be the global namespace, and the pathname separator would be ->. Thus, the names $cart->items and $another_cart->items name two different variables. Note that the variable is named $cart->items, not $cart->$items, that is, a variable name in PHP has only a single dollar sign.

```php
// correct, single $
$cart->items = array("10" => 1);

• invalid, because $cart->$items becomes $cart->"" $cart-
>$items = array("10" => 1);
```

- correct, but may or may not be what was intended:
- $cart->$myvar becomes $cart->items
$myvar = 'items';

139

```
$cart->$myvar = array("10" => 1);
```

Within a class definition, you do not know under which name the object will be accessible in your program: at the time the Cart class was written, it was unknown that the object will be named $cart or $another_cart later. Thus, you cannot write $cart->items within the Cart class itself. Instead, in order to be able to access it's own functions and variables from within a class, one can use the pseudo-variable $this which can be read as 'my own' or 'current object'. Thus, '$this->items[$artnr] += $num' can be read as 'add $num to the $artnr counter of my own items array' or 'add $num to the $artnr counter of the items array within the current object'.

> **Note:** There are some nice functions to handle classes and objects. You might want to take a look at the Class/Ob-ject Functions

extends

Often you need classes with similar variables and functions to another existing class. In fact, it is good practice to define a generic class which can be used in all your projects and adapt this class for the needs of each of your specific projects. To facilitate this, classes can be extensions of other classes. The extended or derived class has all variables and functions of the base class (this is called 'inheritance' despite the fact that nobody died) and what you add in the extended definition. It is not possible to substract from a class, that is, to undefine any existing functions or variables. An extended class is always de-pendent on a single base class, that is, multiple inheritance is not supported. Classes are extended using the keyword 'ex-tends'.

```
class Named_Cart extends Cart
{
    var $owner;

    function set_owner ($name)
    {
        $this->owner = $name;
    }
}
```

This defines a class Named_Cart that has all variables and functions of Cart plus an additional variable $owner and an addi-tional function set_owner(). You create a named cart the usual way and can now set and get the carts owner. You can still use normal cart functions on named carts:

```
$ncart = new Named_Cart;          // Create a named cart
$ncart->set_owner("kris");        // Name that cart
print $ncart->owner;              // print the cart owners name
$ncart->add_item("10", 1);        // (inherited functionality from cart)
```

This is also called a "parent-child" relationship. You create a class, parent, and use extends to create a new class *based* on the parent class: the child class. You can even use this new child class and create another class based on this child class.

> **Note:** Classes must be defined before they are used! If you want the class Named_Cart to extend the class Cart, you will have to define the class Cart first. If you want to create another class called Yellow_named_cart based on the class Named_Cart you have to define Named_Cart first. To make it short: the order in which the classes are defined is important.

Constructors

Caution

In PHP 3 and PHP 4 constructors behave differently. The PHP 4 semantics are strongly preferred.

Constructors are functions in a class that are automatically called when you create a new instance of a class with new. In PHP 3, a function becomes a constructor when it has the same name as the class. In PHP 4, a function becomes a constructor, when it has the same name as the class it is defined in - the difference is subtle, but crucial (see below).

- Works in PHP 3 and PHP 4.

```
class Auto_Cart extends Cart
{
    function Auto_Cart()
    {
        $this->add_item ("10", 1);
    }
}
```

This defines a class Auto_Cart that is a Cart plus a constructor which initializes the cart with one item of article number "10" each time a new Auto_Cart is being made with "new". Constructors can take arguments and these arguments can be optional, which makes them much more useful. To be able to still use the class without parameters, all parameters to con-structors should be made optional by providing default values.

```
// Works in PHP 3 and PHP 4.
class Constructor_Cart extends Cart
{
    function Constructor_Cart($item = "10", $num = 1)
    {
        $this->add_item ($item, $num);
    }
}

// Shop the same old boring stuff.

$default_cart = new Constructor_Cart;

// Shop for real...

$different_cart = new Constructor_Cart("20", 17);
```

You also can use the @ operator to *mute* errors occuring in the constructor, e.g. @new.

Caution

In PHP 3, derived classes and constructors have a number of limitations. The following examples should be read carefully to understand these limitations.

```
class A
{
    function A()
    {
        echo "I am the constructor of A.<br>\n";
    }
}
class B extends A
{
    function C()
    {
        echo "I am a regular function.<br>\n";
    }
}
```

- no constructor is being called in PHP 3. $b =

new B;

In PHP 3, no constructor is being called in the above example. The rule in PHP 3 is: 'A constructor is a function of the same name as the class.'. The name of the class is B, and there is no function called B() in class B. Nothing happens.

This is fixed in PHP 4 by introducing another rule: If a class has no constructor, the constructor of the base class is being called, if it exists. The above example would have printed 'I am the constructor of A.
' in PHP 4.

141

```
class A
{
    function A()
    {
        echo "I am the constructor of A.<br>\n";
    }

    function B()
    {
        echo "I am a regular function named B in class A.<br>\n"; echo "I
        am not a constructor in A.<br>\n";
    }
}
class B extends A
{
    function C()
    {
        echo "I am a regular function.<br>\n";
    }
}
```

- This will call B() as a constructor. $b = new
B;

In PHP 3, the function B() in class A will suddenly become a constructor in class B, although it was never intended to be. The rule in PHP 3 is: 'A constructor is a function of the same name as the class.'. PHP 3 does not care if the function is being defined in class B, or if it has been inherited.

This is fixed in PHP 4 by modifying the rule to: 'A constructor is a function of the same name as the class it is being defined in.'. Thus in PHP 4, the class B would have no constructor function of its own and the constructor of the base class would have been called, printing 'I am the constructor of A.
'.

Caution

Neither PHP 3 nor PHP 4 call constructors of the base class automatically from a constructor of a derived class. It is your responsibility to propagate the call to constructors upstream where appropriate.

Note: There are no destructors in PHP 3 or PHP 4. You may use **register_shutdown_function()** instead to simu-late most effects of destructors.

Destructors are functions that are called automatically when an object is destroyed, either with **unset()** or by simply going out of scope. There are no destructors in PHP.

::

Caution

The following is valid for PHP 4 only.

Sometimes it is useful to refer to functions and variables in base classes or to refer to functions in classes that have not yet any instances. The :: operator is being used for this.

```
class A
{
    function example()
    {
        echo "I am the original function A::example().<br>\n";
    }
}
class B extends A
```

```
{
    function example()
    {
        echo "I am the redefined function B::example().<br>\n";
        A::example();
    }
}
```

- there is no object of class A.
- this will print
- I am the original function A::example().
A::example();

- create an object of class B.
$b = new B;

- this will print
- I am the redefined function B::example().
- I am the original function A::example().
 $b->example();

The above example calls the function example() in class A, but there is no object of class A, so that we cannot write $a->example() or similar. Instead we call example() as a 'class function', that is, as a function of the class itself, not any ob-ject of that class.

There are class functions, but there are no class variables. In fact, there is no object at all at the time of the call. Thus, a class function may not use any object variables (but it can use local and global variables), and it may no use $this at all.

In the above example, class B redefines the function example(). The original definition in class A is shadowed and no longer available, unless you are refering specifically to the implementation of example() in class A using the ::-operator. Write A::example() to do this (in fact, you should be writing parent::example(), as shown in the next section).

In this context, there is a current object and it may have object variables. Thus, when used from WITHIN an object function, you may use $this and object variables.

parent

You may find yourself writing code that refers to variables and functions in base classes. This is particularly true if your de-rived class is a refinement or specialisation of code in your base class.

Instead of using the literal name of the base class in your code, you should be using the special name parent, which refers to the name of your base class as given in the extends declaration of your class. By doing this, you avoid using the name of your base class in more than one place. Should your inheritance tree change during implementation, the change is easily made by simply changing the extends declaration of your class.

```
class A
{
    function example()
    {
        echo "I am A::example() and provide basic functionality.<br>\n";
    }
}

class B extends A
{
    function example()
    {
        echo "I am B::example() and provide additional functionality.<br>\n";
        parent::example();
    }
}
```

```
$b = new B;
```

## 143

- This will call B::example(), which will in turn call A::example(). $b->example();

Serializing objects - objects in sessions

Note: In PHP 3, objects will lose their class association throughout the process of serialization and unserialization. The resulting variable is of type object, but has no class and no methods, thus it is pretty useless (it has become just like an array with a funny syntax).

Caution

The following information is valid for PHP 4 only.

serialize() returns a string containing a byte-stream representation of any value that can be stored in PHP. **unserialize()** can use this string to recreate the original variable values. Using serialize to save an object will save all variables in an object. The functions in an object will not be saved, only the name of the class.

In order to be able to **unserialize()** an object, the class of that object needs to be defined. That is, if you have an object $a of class A on page1.php and serialize this, you'll get a string that refers to class A and contains all values of variabled con-tained in $a. If you want to be able to unserialize this on page2.php, recreating $a of class A, the definition of class A must be present in page2.php. This can be done for example by storing the class defintion of class A in an include file and includ-ing this file in both page1.php and page2.php.

```
classa.inc:
 class A
 {
     var $one = 1;

     function show_one()
     {
         echo $this->one;
     }
 }
page1.php:
 include("classa.inc");

 $a = new A;
 $s = serialize($a);
 • store $s somewhere where page2.php can find it. $fp =
 fopen("store", "w");
 fputs($fp, $s);
 fclose($fp);

page2.php:
 • this is needed for the unserialize to work properly.
 include("classa.inc");

 $s = implode("", @file("store"));
 $a = unserialize($s);

 • now use the function show_one() of the $a object. $a-
 >show_one();
```

If you are using sessions and use **session_register()** to register objects, these objects are serialized automatically at the end of each PHP page, and are unserialized automatically on each of the following pages. This basically means that these ob-jects can show up on any of your pages once they become part of your session.

It is strongly recommended that you include the class definitions of all such registered objects on all of your pages, even if you do not actually use these classes on all of your pages. If you don't and an object is being unserialized without its class definition being present, it will lose its class association and become an object of class stdClass without any functions available at all, that is, it will become quite useless.

## 144

So if in the example above $a became part of a session by running session_register("a"), you should include the file classa.inc on all of your pages, not only page1.php and page2.php.

The magic functions __sleep and __wakeup

serialize() checks if your class has a function with the magic name __sleep. If so, that function is being run prior to any serialization. It can clean up the object and is supposed to return an array with the names of all variables of that object that should be serialized.

The intended use of __sleep is to close any database connections that object may have, committing pending data or per-form similar cleanup tasks. Also, the function is useful if you have very large objects which need not be saved completely.

Conversely, unserialize() checks for the presence of a function with the magic name __wakeup. If present, this function can reconstruct any resources that object may have.

The intended use of __wakeup is to reestablish any database connections that may have been lost during serialization and perform other reinitialization tasks.

References inside the constructor

Creating references within the constructor can lead to confusing results. This tutorial-like section helps you to avoid prob-lems.

```
class Foo
{
    function Foo($name)
    {
        •   create a reference inside the global array $globalref global
        $globalref;
        $globalref[] = &$this;
        •   set name to passed value
        $this->setName($name);
        •   and put it out
        $this->echoName();
    }

    function echoName()
    {
        echo "<br>",$this->name;
    }

    function setName($name)
    {
        $this->name = $name;
    }
}
```

Let us check out if there is a difference between $bar1 which has been created using the copy = operator and $bar2 which has been created using the reference =& operator...

```
$bar1 = new Foo('set in constructor');
$bar1->echoName();
$globalref[0]->echoName();

/* output:
set in constructor
set in constructor
set in constructor */

$bar2 =& new Foo('set in constructor');
$bar2->echoName();
$globalref[1]->echoName();
```

```
/* output:
set in constructor
set in constructor
set in constructor */
```

Apparently there is no difference, but in fact there is a very significant one: $bar1 and $globalref[0] are _NOT_ refer-enced, they are NOT the same variable. This is because "new" does not return a reference by default, instead it returns a copy.

> **Note:** There is no performance loss (since PHP 4 and up use reference counting) returning copies instead of refer-ences. On the contrary it is most often better to simply work with copies instead of references, because creating ref-erences takes some time where creating copies virtually takes no time (unless none of them is a large array or ob-ject and one of them gets changed and the other(s) one(s) subsequently, then it would be wise to use references to change them all concurrently).

To prove what is written above let us watch the code below.

```
•   now we will change the name. what do you expect?
•   you could expect that both $bar1 and $globalref[0] change their names...
$bar1->setName('set from outside');

•   as mentioned before this is not the case.
$bar1->echoName();
$globalref[0]->echoName();

/* output:
set from outside
set in constructor */

•   let us see what is different with $bar2 and $globalref[1] $bar2-
>setName('set from outside');

•   luckily they are not only equal, they are the same variable
•   thus $bar2->name and $globalref[1]->name are the same too
$bar2->echoName();
$globalref[1]->echoName();

/* output:
set from outside
set from outside */
```

Another final example, try to understand it.

```
class A
{
    function A($i)
    {
        $this->value = $i;
        •   try to figure out why we do not need a reference here $this->b =
        new B($this);
    }

    function createRef()
    {
        $this->c = new B($this);
    }

    function echoValue()
    {
        echo "<br>","class ",get_class($this),': ',$this->value;
    }
}
```

```
class B
```

```
    function B(&$a)
    {
        $this->a = &$a;
    }

    function echoValue()
    {
        echo "<br>","class ",get_class($this),': ',$this->a->value;
    }
}
```

- try to undestand why using a simple copy here would yield
- in an undesired result in the *-marked line

```
$a =& new A(10);
$a->createRef();

$a->echoValue();
$a->b->echoValue();
$a->c->echoValue();

$a->value = 11;

$a->echoValue();
$a->b->echoValue(); // *
$a->c->echoValue();

/*
output:
class A: 10
class B: 10
class B: 10
class A: 11
class B: 11
class B: 11
*/
```

Comparing objects in PHP 4

In PHP 4, objects are compared in a very simple manner, namely: Two object instances are equal if they have the same at-tributes and values, and are instances of the same class. Similar rules are applied when comparing two objects using the identity operator (===).

If we were to execute the code in the example below:

Example 14.1. Example of object comparison in PHP 4

```
    function bool2str($bool) {
        if ($bool === false) {
            return 'FALSE';
        } else {
            return 'TRUE';
        }
}
function compareObjects(&$o1, &$o2) {
    echo 'o1 == o2 : '.bool2str($o1 == $o2)."\n";
    echo 'o1 != o2 : '.bool2str($o1 != $o2)."\n";
    echo 'o1 === o2 : '.bool2str($o1 === $o2)."\n";
    echo 'o1 !== o2 : '.bool2str($o1 !== $o2)."\n";
}

class Flag {
    var $flag;

    function Flag($flag=true) {
```

```
$this->flag = $flag;
```

147

```
    }
}
class SwitchableFlag extends Flag {

    function turnOn() {
        $this->flag = true;
    }

    function turnOff() {
        $this->flag = false;
    }
}

$o = new Flag();
$p = new Flag(false);
$q = new Flag();

$r = new SwitchableFlag();

echo "Compare instances created with the same parameters\n";
compareObjects($o, $q);

echo "\nCompare instances created with different parameters\n";
compareObjects($o, $p);

echo "\nCompare an instance of a parent class with one from a subclass\n";
compareObjects($o, $r);
```

We will see:

```
Compare instances created with the same parameters
o1 == o2 : TRUE
o1 != o2 : FALSE
o1 === o2 : TRUE
o1 !== o2 : FALSE

Compare instances created with different parameters
o1 == o2 : FALSE
o1 != o2 : TRUE
o1 === o2 : FALSE
o1 !== o2 : TRUE

Compare an instance of a parent class with one from a subclass
o1 == o2 : FALSE
o1 != o2 : TRUE
o1 === o2 : FALSE
o1 !== o2 : TRUE
```

Which is the output we will expect to obtain given the comparison rules above. Only instances with the same values for their attributes and from the same class are considered equal and identical.

Even in the cases where we have object composition, the same comparison rules apply. In the example below we create a container class that stores an associative array of Flag objects.

Example 14.2. Compound object comparisons in PHP 4

```
class FlagSet {
    var $set;

    function FlagSet($flagArr = array()) {
        $this->set = $flagArr;
    }

    function addFlag($name, $flag) {
        $this->set[$name] = $flag;
```

```
    function removeFlag($name) {
        if (array_key_exists($name, $this->set)) {
            unset($this->set[$name]);
        }
    }
}

$u = new FlagSet();
$u->addFlag('flag1', $o);
$u->addFlag('flag2', $p);
$v = new FlagSet(array('flag1'=>$q, 'flag2'=>$p)); $w = new
FlagSet(array('flag1'=>$q));

echo "\nComposite objects u(o,p) and v(q,p)\n";
compareObjects($u, $v);

echo "\nu(o,p) and w(q)\n";
compareObjects($u, $w);
```

Which gives the expected output:

```
Composite objects u(o,p) and v(q,p)
o1 == o2 : TRUE
o1 != o2 : FALSE
o1 === o2 : TRUE
o1 !== o2 : FALSE

u(o,p) and w(q)
o1 == o2 : FALSE
o1 != o2 : TRUE
o1 === o2 : FALSE
o1 !== o2 : TRUE
```

Comparing objects in PHP 5

Warning

This extension is *EXPERIMENTAL*. The behaviour of this extension – including the names of its functions and anything else documented about this extension – may change without notice in a future release of PHP. Use this extension at your own risk.

In PHP 5, object comparison is a more complicated than in PHP 4 and more in accordance to what one will expect from an Object Oriented Language (not that PHP 5 is such a language).

When using the comparison operator (==), object variables are compared in a simple manner, namely: Two object instances are equal if they have the same attributes and values, and are instances of the same class, defined in the same namespace.

On the other hand, when using the identity operator (===), object variables are identical if and only if they refer to the same instance of the same class (in a particular namespace).

An example will clarify these rules.

Example 14.3. Example of object comparison in PHP 5

```
    function bool2str($bool) {
        if ($bool === false) {
            return 'FALSE';
    } else {
            return 'TRUE';
    }
}
```

```
function   compareObjects(&$o1, &$o2) {
    echo 'o1 == o2      : '.bool2str($o1 == $o2)."\n";
    echo 'o1 != o2      : '.bool2str($o1 != $o2)."\n";
    echo 'o1 === o2   : '.bool2str($o1      === $o2)."\n";
    echo 'o1 !== o2   : '.bool2str($o1      !== $o2)."\n";
}

class Flag {
    var $flag;

    function Flag($flag=true) {
            $this->flag = $flag;
    }
}

namespace Other {

    class Flag {
        var $flag;

        function Flag($flag=true) {
                $this->flag = $flag;
        }
    }

}

$o = new Flag();
$p = new Flag();
$q = $o;
$r = new Other::Flag();

echo "Two instances of the same class\n";
compareObjects($o, $p);

echo "\nTwo references to the same instance\n";
compareObjects($o, $q);

echo "\nInstances of similarly named classes in different namespaces\n";
compareObjects($o, $r);
```

This example will output:

```
Two instances of the same class
o1 == o2 : TRUE
o1 != o2 : FALSE
o1 === o2 : FALSE
o1 !== o2 : TRUE

Two references to the same instance
o1 == o2 : TRUE
o1 != o2 : FALSE
o1 === o2 : TRUE
o1 !== o2 : FALSE

Instances of similarly named classes in different namespaces
o1 == o2 : FALSE
o1 != o2 : TRUE
o1 === o2 : FALSE
o1 !== o2 : TRUE
```

Chapter 15. References Explained

Table of Contents

What References Are

References in PHP are a means to access the same variable content by different names. They are not like C pointers, they are symbol table aliases. Note that in PHP, variable name and variable content are different, so the same content can have different names. The most close analogy is with Unix filenames and files - variable names are directory entries, while vari-able contents is the file itself. References can be thought of as hardlinking in Unix filesystem.

What References Do

PHP references allow you to make two variables to refer to the same content. Meaning, when you do:

```
$a =& $b
```

it means that $a and $b point to the same variable.

> **Note:** $a and $b are completely equal here, that's not $a is pointing to $b or vice versa, that's $a and $b pointing to the same place.

The same syntax can be used with functions, that return references, and with new operator (in PHP 4.0.4 and later):

```
$bar =& new fooclass();
$foo =& find_var ($bar);
```

> **Note:** Not using the & operator causes a copy of the object to be made. If you use $this in the class it will operate on the current instance of the class. The assignment without & will copy the instance (i.e. the object) and $this will operate on the copy, which is not always what is desired. Usually you want to have a single instance to work with, due to performance and memory consumption issues.
>
> While you can use the @ operator to *mute* any errors in the constructor when using it as @new, this does not work when using the &new statement. This is a limitation of the Zend Engine and will therefore result in a parser error.

The second thing references do is to pass variables by-reference. This is done by making a local variable in a function and a variable in the calling scope reference to the same content. Example:

```
function foo (&$var)
{
    $var++;
}

$a=5;
foo ($a);
```

151

will make $a to be 6. This happens because in the function foo the variable $var refers to the same content as $a. See also more detailed explanations about passing by reference.

The third thing reference can do is return by reference.

What References Are Not

As said before, references aren't pointers. That means, the following construct won't do what you expect:

```
function foo (&$var)
{
    $var =& $GLOBALS["baz"];
}
foo($bar);
```

What happens is that $var in foo will be bound with $bar in caller, but then it will be re-bound with $GLOBALS["baz"]. There's no way to bind $bar in the calling scope to something else using the reference mechanism, since $bar is not avail-able in the function foo (it is represented by $var, but $var has only variable contents and not name-to-value binding in the calling symbol table).

Passing by Reference

You can pass variable to function by reference, so that function could modify its arguments. The syntax is as follows:

```
function foo (&$var)
{
    $var++;
}

$a=5;
foo ($a);
// $a is 6 here
```

Note that there's no reference sign on function call - only on function definition. Function definition alone is enough to cor-rectly pass the argument by reference.

Following things can be passed by reference:

- Variable, i.e. foo($a)

- New statement, i.e. foo(new foobar())

- Reference, returned from a function, i.e.:

    ```
    function &bar()
    {
        $a = 5;
        return $a;
    }
    foo(bar());
    ```

    See also explanations about returning by reference.

Any other expression should not be passed by reference, as the result is undefined. For example, the following examples of passing by reference are invalid:

```
function bar() // Note the missing &
{
    $a = 5;
    return $a;
```

```
}
foo(bar());

foo($a = 5) // Expression, not variable
foo(5) // Constant, not variable
```

These requirements are for PHP 4.0.4 and later.

Returning References

Returning by-reference is useful when you want to use a function to find which variable a reference should be bound to.
When returning references, use this syntax:

```
function &find_var ($param)
{
    ...code...
    return $found_var;
}

$foo =& find_var ($bar);
$foo->x = 2;
```

In this example, the property of the object returned by the find_var function would be set, not the copy, as it would be without using reference syntax.

> **Note:** Unlike parameter passing, here you have to use & in both places - to indicate that you return by-reference, not a copy as usual, and to indicate that reference binding, rather than usual assignment, should be done for $foo.

Unsetting References

When you unset the reference, you just break the binding between variable name and variable content. This does not mean that variable content will be destroyed. For example:

```
$a = 1;
$b =& $a;
unset ($a);
```

won't unset $b, just $a.

Again, it might be useful to think about this as analogous to Unix **unlink** call.

Spotting References

Many syntax constructs in PHP are implemented via referencing mechanisms, so everything told above about reference binding also apply to these constructs. Some constructs, like passing and returning by-reference, are mentioned above. Other constructs that use references are:

global References

When you declare variable as **global $var** you are in fact creating reference to a global variable. That means, this is the same as:

```
$var =& $GLOBALS["var"];
```

That means, for example, that unsetting $var won't unset global variable.

$this

153

In an object method, $this is always reference to the caller object.

Part III. Features

Table of Contents

Chapter 16. HTTP authentication with PHP

The HTTP Authentication hooks in PHP are only available when it is running as an Apache module and is hence not avail-able in the CGI version. In an Apache module PHP script, it is possible to use the **header()** function to send an "Authentica-tion Required" message to the client browser causing it to pop up a Username/Password input window. Once the user has filled in a username and a password, the URL containing the PHP script will be called again with the predefined variables PHP_AUTH_USER, PHP_AUTH_PW, and AUTH_TYPE set to the user name, password and authentication type respectively. These predefined variables are found in the $_SERVER and $HTTP_SERVER_VARS arrays. Only "Basic" authentication is supported. See the **header()** function for more information.

> **PHP Version Note:** Autoglobals, such as $_SERVER, became available in PHP version 4.1.0 [http://www.php.net/release_4_1_0.php]. $HTTP_SERVER_VARS has been available since PHP 3.

An example script fragment which would force client authentication on a page is as follows:

Example 16.1. HTTP Authentication example

```php
<?php
  if (!isset($_SERVER['PHP_AUTH_USER'])) { header('WWW-
    Authenticate: Basic realm="My Realm"'); header('HTTP/1.0
    401 Unauthorized');
    echo 'Text to send if user hits Cancel button'; exit;
  } else {
    echo "<p>Hello {$_SERVER['PHP_AUTH_USER']}.</p>";
    echo "<p>You entered {$_SERVER['PHP_AUTH_PW']} as your password.</p>";
  }
?>
```

> **Compatibility Note:** Please be careful when coding the HTTP header lines. In order to guarantee maximum com-patibility with all clients, the keyword "Basic" should be written with an uppercase "B", the realm string must be enclosed in double (not single) quotes, and exactly one space should precede the 401 code in the HTTP/1.0 401 header line.

Instead of simply printing out PHP_AUTH_USER and PHP_AUTH_PW, as done in the above example, you may want to check the username and password for validity. Perhaps by sending a query to a database, or by looking up the user in a dbm file.

Watch out for buggy Internet Explorer browsers out there. They seem very picky about the order of the headers. Sending the WWW-Authenticate header before the HTTP/1.0 401 header seems to do the trick for now.

As of PHP 4.3.0, in order to prevent someone from writing a script which reveals the password for a page that was authen-ticated through a traditional external mechanism, the PHP_AUTH variables will not be set if external authentication is en-abled for that particular page and safe mode is enabled. Regardless, REMOTE_USER can be used to identify the externally-authenticated user. So, you can use $_SERVER['REMOTE_USER'].

> **Configuration Note:** PHP uses the presence of an AuthType directive to determine whether external authentica-tion is in effect.

Note, however, that the above does not prevent someone who controls a non-authenticated URL from stealing passwords from authenticated URLs on the same server.

Both Netscape Navigator and Internet Explorer will clear the local browser window's authentication cache for the realm upon receiving a server response of 401. This can effectively "log out" a user, forcing them to re-enter their username and

---

156

password. Some people use this to "time out" logins, or provide a "log-out" button.

Example 16.2. HTTP Authentication example forcing a new name/password

```php
<?php
  function authenticate() {
    header('WWW-Authenticate: Basic realm="Test Authentication System"');
    header('HTTP/1.0 401 Unauthorized');
    echo "You must enter a valid login ID and password to access this resource\n"; exit;
  }

  if (!isset($_SERVER['PHP_AUTH_USER']) ||
      ($_POST['SeenBefore'] == 1 && $_POST['OldAuth'] == $_SERVER['PHP_AUTH_USER'])) {
    authenticate();
  }
  else {
    echo "<p>Welcome: {$_SERVER['PHP_AUTH_USER']}<br>";
    echo "Old: {$_REQUEST['OldAuth']}";
    echo "<form action='{$_SERVER['PHP_SELF']}' METHOD='POST'>\n"; echo
    "<input type='hidden' name='SeenBefore' value='1'>\n";
    echo "<input type='hidden' name='OldAuth' value='{$_SERVER['PHP_AUTH_USER']}'>\n"; echo
    "<input type='submit' value='Re Authenticate'>\n"; echo "</form></p>\n";
  }
?>
```

This behavior is not required by the HTTP Basic authentication standard, so you should never depend on this. Testing with Lynx has shown that Lynx does not clear the authentication credentials with a 401 server response, so pressing back and then forward again will open the resource as long as the credential requirements haven't changed. The user can press the '_' key to clear their authentication information, however.

Also note that this does not work using Microsoft's IIS server and the CGI version of PHP due to a limitation of IIS. If you're using the IIS module (ISAPI), you may use the HTTP_AUTHORIZATION variable for example: list($user, $pw)

= explode(':', base64_decode(substr($_SERVER['HTTP_AUTHORIZATION'], 6)));

> **Note:** If safe mode is enabled, the uid of the script is added to the realm part of the WWW-Authenticate header.

## 157

Chapter 17. Cookies

PHP transparently supports HTTP cookies. Cookies are a mechanism for storing data in the remote browser and thus track-ing or identifying return users. You can set cookies using the **setcookie()** function. Cookies are part of the HTTP header, so **setcookie()** must be called before any output is sent to the browser. This is the same limitation that **header()** has. You can use the output buffering functions to delay the script output until you have decided whether or not to set any cookies or send any headers.

Any cookies sent to you from the client will automatically be turned into a PHP variable just like GET and POST method data, depending on the register_globals and variables_order configuration variables. If you wish to assign mul-tiple values to a single cookie, just add [] to the cookie name.

In PHP 4.1.0 and later, the $_COOKIE auto-global array will always be set with any cookies sent from the client.
$HTTP_COOKIE_VARS is also set in earlier versions of PHP when the track_vars configuration variable is set.

For more details, including notes on browser bugs, see the **setcookie()** function.

158

Chapter 18. Handling file uploads

Table of Contents

POST method uploads

PHP is capable of receiving file uploads from any RFC-1867 compliant browser (which includes Netscape Navigator 3 or later, Microsoft Internet Explorer 3 with a patch from Microsoft, or later without a patch). This feature lets people upload both text and binary files. With PHP's authentication and file manipulation functions, you have full control over who is al-lowed to upload and what is to be done with the file once it has been uploaded.

> **Related Configurations Note:** See also the file_uploads, upload_max_filesize, upload_tmp_dir, and post_max_size directives in php.ini

Note that PHP also supports PUT-method file uploads as used by Netscape Composer and W3C's Amaya clients. See the PUT Method Support for more details.

A file upload screen can be built by creating a special form which looks something like this:

Example 18.1. File Upload Form

```
<form enctype="multipart/form-data" action="_URL_" method="post">
<input type="hidden" name="MAX_FILE_SIZE" value="30000">
Send this file: <input name="userfile" type="file"> <input
type="submit" value="Send File"> </form>
```

The _URL_ should point to a PHP file. The MAX_FILE_SIZE hidden field must precede the file input field and its value is the maximum filesize accepted. The value is in bytes.

> **Warning**
>
> The MAX_FILE_SIZE is advisory to the browser. It is easy to circumvent this maximum. So don't count on it that the browser obeys your wish! The PHP-settings for maximum-size, however, cannot be fooled. But you should add MAX_FILE_SIZE anyway as it saves users the trouble to wait for a big file being transfered only to find out that it was too big afterwards.

The Variables defined for uploaded files differs depending on the PHP version and configuration. The autoglobal $_FILES exists as of PHP 4.1.0 The $HTTP_POST_FILES array has existed since PHP 4.0.0. These arrays will contain all your up-loaded file information. Using $_FILES is preferred. If the PHP directive register_globals is *on*, related variable names will also exist. register_globals defaults to *off* as of PHP 4.2.0 [http://www.php.net/release_4_2_0.php].

The contents of $_FILES from our example script is as follows. Note that this assumes the use of the file upload name *user-file*, as used in the example script above.

159

$_FILES['userfile']['name']
    The original name of the file on the client machine.

$_FILES['userfile']['type']
    The mime type of the file, if the browser provided this information. An example would be "image/gif".

$_FILES['userfile']['size']
    The size, in bytes, of the uploaded file.

$_FILES['userfile']['tmp_name']
    The temporary filename of the file in which the uploaded file was stored on the server.

$_FILES['userfile']['error']
    The error code associated with this file upload. ['error'] was added in PHP 4.2.0

Note: In PHP versions prior 4.1.0 this was named $HTTP_POST_FILES and it's not an autoglobal variable like $_FILES is. PHP 3 does not support $HTTP_POST_FILES.

When register_globals is turned *on* in php.ini, additional variables are available. For example, $userfile_name will equal $_FILES['userfile']['name'], $userfile_type will equal $_FILES['userfile']['type'], etc. Keep in mind that as of PHP 4.2.0, register_globals defaults to off. It's preferred to not rely on this directive.

Files will by default be stored in the server's default temporary directory, unless another location has been given with the upload_tmp_dir directive in php.ini. The server's default directory can be changed by setting the environment variable TMPDIR in the environment in which PHP runs. Setting it using **putenv()** from within a PHP script will not work. This en-vironment variable can also be used to make sure that other operations are working on uploaded files, as well.

Example 18.2. Validating file uploads

See also the function entries for **is_uploaded_file()** and **move_uploaded_file()** for further information. The following ex-ample will process the file upload that came from a form.

```
<?php
•  In PHP earlier then 4.1.0, $HTTP_POST_FILES should be used instead of $_FILES.
•  In PHP earlier then 4.0.3, use copy() and is_uploaded_file() instead of move_uploaded_file

$uploaddir = '/var/www/uploads/';

print "<pre>";
if (move_uploaded_file($_FILES['userfile']['tmp_name'], $uploaddir . $_FILES['userfile']['name'])) { print "File is valid, and
    was successfully uploaded. Here's some more debugging info:\n"; print_r($_FILES);
} else {
    print "Possible file upload attack! Here's some debugging info:\n";
    print_r($_FILES);
}
?>
```

The PHP script which receives the uploaded file should implement whatever logic is necessary for determining what should be done with the uploaded file. You can for example use the $_FILES['userfile']['size'] variable to throw away any files that are either too small or too big. You could use the $_FILES['userfile']['type'] variable to throw away any files that didn't match a certain type criteria. As of PHP 4.2.0, you could use $_FILES['userfile']['error'] and plan your logic according to the error codes. Whatever the logic, you should either delete the file from the temporary direct-ory or move it elsewhere.

The file will be deleted from the temporary directory at the end of the request if it has not been moved away or renamed.

## 160

Error Messages Explained

Since PHP 4.2.0, PHP returns an appropriate error code along with the file array. The error code can be found in the *['error']* segment of the file array that is created during the file upload by PHP. In otherwords, the error might be found in $_FILES['userfile']['error'].

UPLOAD_ERR_OK
   Value: 0; There is no error, the file uploaded with success.

UPLOAD_ERR_INI_SIZE
   Value: 1; The uploaded file exceeds the upload_max_filesize directive in php.ini.

UPLOAD_ERR_FORM_SIZE
   Value: 2; The uploaded file exceeds the *MAX_FILE_SIZE* directive that was specified in the html form.

UPLOAD_ERR_PARTIAL
   Value: 3; The uploaded file was only partially uploaded.

UPLOAD_ERR_NO_FILE
   Value: 4; No file was uploaded.

   Note: These became PHP constants in PHP 4.3.0

Common Pitfalls

The MAX_FILE_SIZE item cannot specify a file size greater than the file size that has been set in the upload_max_filesize ini-setting. The default is 2 Megabytes.

If memory limit is enabled, larger memory_limit may be needed. Make sure to set memory_limit large enough.

If max_execution_time is set too small, script execution may be exceeded the value. Make sure to set max_execution_time large enough.

   Note: max_execution_time **only** affects the execution time of the script itself. Any time spent on activity that hap-pens outside the execution of the script such as system calls using **system()**, the **sleep()** function, database queries, time taken by the file upload process, etc. is not included when determining the maximum time that the script has been running.

If post_max_size set too small, large files cannot be uploaded. Make sure to set post_max_size large enough.

Not validating which file you operate on may mean that users can access sensitive information in other directories.

Please note that the CERN httpd seems to strip off everything starting at the first whitespace in the content-type mime head-er it gets from the client. As long as this is the case, CERN httpd will not support the file upload feature.

Due to the large amount of directory listing styles we cannot guarantee that files with exotic names (like containing spaces) are handled properly.

Uploading multiple files

Multiple files can be uploaded using different name for input.

It is also possible to upload multiple files simultaneously and have the information organized automatically in arrays for you. To do so, you need to use the same array submission syntax in the HTML form as you do with multiple selects and

---

161

checkboxes:

> **Note:** Support for multiple file uploads was added in version 3.0.10.

Example 18.3. Uploading multiple files

```
<form action="file-upload.php" method="post" enctype="multipart/form-data"> Send
  these files:<br>
  <input name="userfile[]" type="file"><br>
  <input name="userfile[]" type="file"><br>
  <input type="submit" value="Send files">
</form>
```

When the above form is submitted, the arrays $_FILES['userfile'], $_FILES['userfile']['name'], and $_FILES['userfile']['size'] will be initialized (as well as in $HTTP_POST_FILES for PHP version prior 4.1.0). When register_globals is on, globals for uploaded files are also initialized. Each of these will be a numerically indexed array of the appropriate values for the submitted files.

For instance, assume that the filenames /home/test/review.html and /home/test/xwp.out are submitted. In this case, $_FILES['userfile']['name'][0]   would   contain   the   value   review.html,   and $_FILES['userfile']['name'][1] would contain the value xwp.out. Similarly, $_FILES['userfile']['size'][0] would contain review.html's filesize, and so forth.

$_FILES['userfile']['name'][0], $_FILES['userfile']['tmp_name'][0], $_FILES['userfile']['size'][0],   and $_FILES['userfile']['type'][0] are also set.

PUT method support

PUT method support has changed between PHP 3 and PHP 4. In PHP 4, one should use the standard input stream to read the contents of an HTTP PUT.

Example 18.4. Saving HTTP PUT files with PHP 4

```php
<?php
/* PUT data comes in on the stdin stream */
$putdata = fopen("php://stdin","r");

/* Open a file for writting */
$fp = fopen("myputfile.ext","w");

  /* Read the data 1kb at a time
     and write to the file */
while ($data = fread($putdata,1024))
  fwrite($fp,$data);

/* Close the streams */
fclose($fp);
fclose($putdata);
?>
```

> **Note:** All documentation below applies to PHP 3 only.

PHP provides support for the HTTP PUT method used by clients such as Netscape Composer and W3C Amaya. PUT re-quests are much simpler than a file upload and they look something like this:

PUT /path/filename.html HTTP/1.1

## 162

This would normally mean that the remote client would like to save the content that follows as: /path/filename.html in your web tree. It is obviously not a good idea for Apache or PHP to automatically let everybody overwrite any files in your web tree. So, to handle such a request you have to first tell your web server that you want a certain PHP script to handle the re-quest. In Apache you do this with the *Script* directive. It can be placed almost anywhere in your Apache configuration file. A common place is inside a <Directory> block or perhaps inside a <Virtualhost> block. A line like this would do the trick:

Script PUT /put.php

This tells Apache to send all PUT requests for URIs that match the context in which you put this line to the put.php script.
This assumes, of course, that you have PHP enabled for the .php extension and PHP is active.

Inside your put.php file you would then do something like this:

<?php copy($PHP_UPLOADED_FILE_NAME,$DOCUMENT_ROOT.$REQUEST_URI); ?>

This would copy the file to the location requested by the remote client. You would probably want to perform some checks and/or authenticate the user before performing this file copy. The only trick here is that when PHP sees a PUT-method re-quest it stores the uploaded file in a temporary file just like those handled but the POST-method. When the request ends, this temporary file is deleted. So, your PUT handling PHP script has to copy that file somewhere. The filename of this tem-porary file is in the $PHP_PUT_FILENAME variable, and you can see the suggested destination filename in the $REQUEST_URI (may vary on non-Apache web servers). This destination filename is the one that the remote client spe-cified. You do not have to listen to this client. You could, for example, copy all uploaded files to a special uploads directory.

## 163

Chapter 19. Using remote files

As long as *allow_url_fopen* is enabled in php.ini, you can use HTTP and FTP URLs with most of the functions that take a filename as a parameter. In addition, URLs can be used with the **include()**, **include_once()**, **require()** and **require_once()** statements. See Appendix I, *List of Supported Protocols/Wrappers* for more information about the protocols supported by PHP.

> **Note:** In PHP 4.0.3 and older, in order to use URL wrappers, you were required to configure PHP using the config-ure option –enable-url-fopen-wrapper.

> **Note:** The Windows versions of PHP earlier than PHP 4.3 did not support remote file accessing for the following functions: **include()**, **include_once()**, **require()**, **require_once()**, and the imagecreatefromXXX functions in the Image extension.

For example, you can use this to open a file on a remote web server, parse the output for the data you want, and then use that data in a database query, or simply to output it in a style matching the rest of your website.

Example 19.1. Getting the title of a remote page

```php
<?php
$file = fopen ("http://www.example.com/", "r"); if
(!$file) {
    echo "<p>Unable to open remote file.\n";
    exit;
}
while (!feof ($file)) {
    $line = fgets ($file, 1024);
    /* This only works if the title and its tags are on one line */ if (eregi
("<title>(.*)</title>", $line, $out)) {
        $title = $out[1];
        break;
    }
}
fclose($file);
?>
```

You can also write to files on an FTP server (provided that you have connected as a user with the correct access rights). You can only create new files using this method; if you try to overwrite a file that already exists, the **fopen()** call will fail.

To connect as a user other than 'anonymous', you need to specify the username (and possibly password) within the URL, such as 'ftp://user:password@ftp.example.com/path/to/file'. (You can use the same sort of syntax to access files via HTTP when they require Basic authentication.)

Example 19.2. Storing data on a remote server

```php
<?php
$file = fopen ("ftp://ftp.example.com/incoming/outputfile", "w"); if (!$file) {
    echo "<p>Unable to open remote file for writing.\n"; exit;
}
/* Write the data here. */
fputs ($file, $_SERVER['HTTP_USER_AGENT'] . "\n");
fclose ($file);
?>
```

164

Note: You might get the idea from the example above that you can use this technique to write to a remote log file. Unfortunately that would not work because the **fopen()** call will fail if the remote file already exists. To do distrib-uted logging like that, you should take a look at **syslog()**.

Chapter 20. Connection handling

Note: The following applies to 3.0.7 and later.

Internally in PHP a connection status is maintained. There are 3 possible states:

- 0 - NORMAL

- 1 - ABORTED

- 2 - TIMEOUT

When a PHP script is running normally the NORMAL state, is active. If the remote client disconnects the ABORTED state flag is turned on. A remote client disconnect is usually caused by the user hitting his STOP button. If the PHP-imposed time limit (see **set_time_limit()**) is hit, the TIMEOUT state flag is turned on.

You can decide whether or not you want a client disconnect to cause your script to be aborted. Sometimes it is handy to al-ways have your scripts run to completion even if there is no remote browser receiving the output. The default behaviour is however for your script to be aborted when the remote client disconnects. This behaviour can be set via the ig-nore_user_abort php.ini directive as well as through the corresponding "php_value ignore_user_abort" Apache .conf dir-ective or with the **ignore_user_abort()** function. If you do not tell PHP to ignore a user abort and the user aborts, your script will terminate. The one exception is if you have registered a shutdown function using **register_shutdown_function()**. With a shutdown function, when the remote user hits his STOP button, the next time your script tries to output something PHP will detect that the connection has been aborted and the shutdown function is called. This shutdown function will also get called at the end of your script terminating normally, so to do something different in case of a client disconnect you can use the **connection_aborted()** function. This function will return TRUE if the connection was aborted.

Your script can also be terminated by the built-in script timer. The default timeout is 30 seconds. It can be changed using the max_execution_time php.ini directive or the corresponding "php_value max_execution_time" Apache .conf directive as well as with the **set_time_limit() function. When the timer expires the script will be aborted and as with the above client disconnect case, if a shutdown function has been registered it will be called. Within this shutdown function you can check to see if a timeout caused the shutdown function to be called by calling the connection_timeout() function. This function will return TRUE if a timeout caused the shutdown function to be called.**

One thing to note is that both the ABORTED and the TIMEOUT states can be active at the same time. This is possible if you tell PHP to ignore user aborts. PHP will still note the fact that a user may have broken the connection, but the script will keep running. If it then hits the time limit it will be aborted and your shutdown function, if any, will be called. At this point you will find that **connection_timeout()** and **connection_aborted()** return TRUE. You can also check both states in a single call by using the **connection_status()**. This function returns a bitfield of the active states. So, if both states are active it would return 3, for example.

166

Chapter 21. Persistent Database Connections

Persistent connections are SQL links that do not close when the execution of your script ends. When a persistent connection is requested, PHP checks if there's already an identical persistent connection (that remained open from earlier) - and if it ex-ists, it uses it. If it does not exist, it creates the link. An 'identical' connection is a connection that was opened to the same host, with the same username and the same password (where applicable).

Note: There are other extensions that provide persistent connections, such as the IMAP extension.

People who aren't thoroughly familiar with the way web servers work and distribute the load may mistake persistent con-nects for what they're not. In particular, they do *not* give you an ability to open 'user sessions' on the same SQL link, they do *not* give you an ability to build up a transaction efficiently, and they don't do a whole lot of other things. In fact, to be ex-tremely clear about the subject, persistent connections don't give you *any* functionality that wasn't possible with their non-persistent brothers.

Why?

This has to do with the way web servers work. There are three ways in which your web server can utilize PHP to generate web pages.

The first method is to use PHP as a CGI "wrapper". When run this way, an instance of the PHP interpreter is created and destroyed for every page request (for a PHP page) to your web server. Because it is destroyed after every request, any re-sources that it acquires (such as a link to an SQL database server) are closed when it is destroyed. In this case, you do not gain anything from trying to use persistent connections – they simply don't persist.

The second, and most popular, method is to run PHP as a module in a multiprocess web server, which currently only in-cludes Apache. A multiprocess server typically has one process (the parent) which coordinates a set of processes (its chil-dren) who actually do the work of serving up web pages. When each request comes in from a client, it is handed off to one of the children that is not already serving another client. This means that when the same client makes a second request to the server, it may be serviced by a different child process than the first time. What a persistent connection does for you in this case it make it so each child process only needs to connect to your SQL server the first time that it serves a page that makes use of such a connection. When another page then requires a connection to the SQL server, it can reuse the connection that child established earlier.

The last method is to use PHP as a plug-in for a multithreaded web server. Currently PHP 4 has support for ISAPI, WSAPI, and NSAPI (on Windows), which all allow PHP to be used as a plug-in on multithreaded servers like Netscape FastTrack (iPlanet), Microsoft's Internet Information Server (IIS), and O'Reilly's WebSite Pro. The behavior is essentially the same as for the multiprocess model described before. Note that SAPI support is not available in PHP 3.

If persistent connections don't have any added functionality, what are they good for?

The answer here is extremely simple – efficiency. Persistent connections are good if the overhead to create a link to your SQL server is high. Whether or not this overhead is really high depends on many factors. Like, what kind of database it is, whether or not it sits on the same computer on which your web server sits, how loaded the machine the SQL server sits on is and so forth. The bottom line is that if that connection overhead is high, persistent connections help you considerably. They cause the child process to simply connect only once for its entire lifespan, instead of every time it processes a page that re-quires connecting to the SQL server. This means that for every child that opened a persistent connection will have its own open persistent connection to the server. For example, if you had 20 different child processes that ran a script that made a persistent connection to your SQL server, you'd have 20 different connections to the SQL server, one from each child.

Note, however, that this can have some drawbacks if you are using a database with connection limits that are exceeded by persistent child connections. If your database has a limit of 16 simultaneous connections, and in the course of a busy server session, 17 child threads attempt to connect, one will not be able to. If there are bugs in your scripts which do not allow the connections to shut down (such as infinite loops), the database with only 16 connections may be rapidly swamped. Check

your database documentation for information on handling abandoned or idle connections.

Warning

There are a couple of additional caveats to keep in mind when using persistent connections. One is that when using table locking on a persistent connection, if the script for whatever reason cannot release the lock, then subsequent scripts using the same connection will block indefinitely and may require that you either restart the httpd server or the database server. Another is that when using transactions, a transaction block will also carry over to the next script which uses that connection if script execution ends before the transaction block does. In either case, you can use **register_shutdown_function()** to register a simple cleanup function to unlock your tables or roll back your transactions. Better yet, avoid the problem entirely by not using persistent connections in scripts which use table locks or transactions (you can still use them elsewhere).

An important summary. Persistent connections were designed to have one-to-one mapping to regular connections. That means that you should *always* be able to replace persistent connections with non-persistent connections, and it won't change the way your script behaves. It *may* (and probably will) change the efficiency of the script, but not its behavior!

See also **fbsql_pconnect()**, **ibase_pconnect()**, **ifx_pconnect()**, **imap_popen()**, **ingres_pconnect()**, **msql_pconnect()**, **mssql_pconnect()**, **mysql_pconnect()**, **ociplogon()**, **odbc_pconnect()**, **ora_plogon()**, **pfsockopen()**, **pg_pconnect()**, and **sybase_pconnect()**.

Chapter 22. Safe Mode

Table of Contents

The PHP safe mode is an attempt to solve the shared-server security problem. It is architecturally incorrect to try to solve this problem at the PHP level, but since the alternatives at the web server and OS levels aren't very realistic, many people, especially ISP's, use safe mode for now.

Security and Safe Mode

Table 22.1. Security and Safe Mode Configuration Directives

Name	Default	Changeable
safe_mode	"0"	PHP_INI_SYSTEM
safe_mode_gid	"0"	PHP_INI_SYSTEM
safe_mode_include_dir	NULL	PHP_INI_SYSTEM
safe_mode_exec_dir	""	PHP_INI_SYSTEM
safe_mode_allowed_env_vars	PHP_	PHP_INI_SYSTEM
safe_mode_protected_env_vars	LD_LIBRARY_PATH	PHP_INI_SYSTEM
open_basedir	NULL	PHP_INI_SYSTEM
disable_functions	""	PHP_INI_SYSTEM
disable_classes	""	PHP_INI_SYSTEM

For further details and definition of the PHP_INI_* constants see **ini_set()**.

Here's a short explanation of the configuration directives.

safe_mode boolean
  Whether to enable PHP's safe mode. Read the Security and chapter for more information.

safe_mode_gid boolean
  By default, Safe Mode does a UID compare check when opening files. If you want to relax this to a GID compare, then turn on safe_mode_gid. Whether to use UID (FALSE) or GID (TRUE) checking upon file access.

safe_mode_include_dir string
  UID/GID checks are bypassed when including files from this directory and its subdirectories (directory must also be in include_path or full path must including).

  As of PHP 4.2.0, this directive can take a semi-colon separated path in a similar fashion to the include_path directive, rather than just a single directory.

The restriction specified is actually a prefix, not a directory name. This means that "safe_mode_include_dir = /dir/incl" also allows access to "/dir/include" and "/dir/incls" if they exist. When you want to restrict access to only the specified

---

169

directory, end with a slash. For example: "safe_mode_include_dir = /dir/incl/"

safe_mode_exec_dir string
> If PHP is used in safe mode, **system()** and the other functions executing system programs refuse to start programs that are not in this directory.

safe_mode_allowed_env_vars string
> Setting certain environment variables may be a potential security breach. This directive contains a comma-delimited list of prefixes. In Safe Mode, the user may only alter environment variables whose names begin with the prefixes supplied here. By default, users will only be able to set environment variables that begin with PHP_ (e.g. PHP_FOO=BAR).
>
> **Note:** If this directive is empty, PHP will let the user modify ANY environment variable!

safe_mode_protected_env_vars string
> This directive contains a comma-delimited list of environment variables that the end user won't be able to change using **putenv()**. These variables will be protected even if safe_mode_allowed_env_vars is set to allow to change them.

open_basedir string
> Limit the files that can be opened by PHP to the specified directory-tree, including the file itself. This directive is *NOT* affected by whether Safe Mode is turned On or Off.
>
> When a script tries to open a file with, for example, fopen or gzopen, the location of the file is checked. When the file is outside the specified directory-tree, PHP will refuse to open it. All symbolic links are resolved, so it's not possible to avoid this restriction with a symlink.
>
> The special value . indicates that the directory in which the script is stored will be used as base-directory.
>
> Under Windows, separate the directories with a semicolon. On all other systems, separate the directories with a colon.
> As an Apache module, open_basedir paths from parent directories are now automatically inherited.
>
> The restriction specified with open_basedir is actually a prefix, not a directory name. This means that "open_basedir = / dir/incl" also allows access to "/dir/include" and "/dir/incls" if they exist. When you want to restrict access to only the specified directory, end with a slash. For example: "open_basedir = /dir/incl/"
>
> **Note:** Support for multiple directories was added in 3.0.7.
>
> The default is to allow all files to be opened.

disable_functions string
> This directive allows you to disable certain functions for security reasons. It takes on a comma-dilimited list of function names. disable_functions is not affected by Safe Mode.
>
> This directive must be set in php.ini For example, you cannot set this in httpd.conf.

disable_classes string
> This directive allows you to disable certain classes for security reasons. It takes on a comma-dilimited list of class names. disable_classes is not affected by Safe Mode.
>
> This directive must be set in php.ini For example, you cannot set this in httpd.conf.
>
> **Availability note:** This directive became available in PHP 4.3.2

See also: register_globals, display_errors, and log_errors

When safe_mode is on, PHP checks to see if the owner of the current script matches the owner of the file to be operated on by a file function. For example:

```
-rw-rw-r   1 rasmus    rasmus       33 Jul  1 19:20 script.php
```

```
-rw-r--r--   1 root      root         1116 May 26 18:01 /etc/passwd
```

170

Running this script.php

```
<?php
 readfile('/etc/passwd');
?>
```

results in this error when safe mode is enabled:

Warning: SAFE MODE Restriction in effect. The script whose uid is 500 is not allowed to access /etc/passwd owned by uid 0 in /docroot/script.php on line 2

However, there may be environments where a strict UID check is not appropriate and a relaxed GID check is sufficient. This is supported by means of the safe_mode_gid switch. Setting it to On performs the relaxed GID checking, setting it to Off (the default) performs UID checking.

If instead of safe_mode, you set an open_basedir directory then all file operations will be limited to files under the specified directory For example (Apache httpd.conf example):

```
<Directory /docroot>
  php_admin_value open_basedir /docroot
</Directory>
```

If you run the same script.php with this open_basedir setting then this is the result:

Warning: open_basedir restriction in effect. File is in wrong directory in /docroot/script.php on line 2

You can also disable individual functions. Note that the disable_functions directive can not be used outside of the php.ini file which means that you cannot disable functions on a per-virtualhost or per-directory basis in your httpd.conf file. If we add this to our php.ini file:

disable_functions readfile,system

Then we get this output:

Warning: readfile() has been disabled for security reasons in /docroot/script.php on line 2

Functions restricted/disabled by safe mode

This is a still probably incomplete and possibly incorrect listing of the functions limited by safe mode.

Table 22.2. Safe mode limited functions

Function	Limitations
dbmopen()	Checks whether the files or directories you are about to oper- ate on have the same UID (owner) as the script that is being executed.
dbase_open()	Checks whether the files or directories you are about to oper- ate on have the same UID (owner) as the script that is being executed.
filepro()	Checks whether the files or directories you are about to oper- ate on have the same UID (owner) as the script that is being

	executed.
filepro_rowcount()	Checks whether the files or directories you are about to oper- ate on have the same UID (owner) as the script that is being executed.
filepro_retrieve()	Checks whether the files or directories you are about to oper-

171

Function	Limitations
	ate on have the same UID (owner) as the script that is being executed.
ifx_*()	sql_safe_mode restrictions, (!= safe mode)
ingres_*()	sql_safe_mode restrictions, (!= safe mode)
mysql_*()	sql_safe_mode restrictions, (!= safe mode)
pg_loimport()	Checks whether the files or directories you are about to oper- ate on have the same UID (owner) as the script that is being executed.
posix_mkfifo()	Checks whether the directory in which you are about to op- erate has the same UID (owner) as the script that is being ex- ecute d.
putenv()	Obeys the safe_mode_protected_env_var s and safe_mode_allowed_env_vars ini-directives. See also the documentation on **putenv()**
move_uploaded_file()	Checks whether the files or directories you are about to oper- ate on have the same UID (owner) as the script that is being executed.
chdir()	Checks whether the directory in which you are about to op- erate has the same UID (owner) as the script that is being ex- ecute d.
dl()	This function is disabled in safe mode.
backtick operator	This function is disabled in safe mode.
shell_exec() (functional equivalent of backticks)	This function is disabled in safe mode.
exec()	You ca n only execute s executable within the safe_mode_exec_dir. For practical reasons it's currently not allowed to have .. components in the path to the

	executable.
system()	ca executable You n only execute s within the safe_mode_exec_dir. For practical reasons it's currently not allowed to have .. components in the path to the executable.
passthru()	ca executable You n only execute s within the safe_mode_exec_dir. For practical reasons it's currently not allowed to have .. components in the path to the executable.
popen()	ca executable You n only execute s within the safe_mode_exec_dir. For practical reasons it's currently not allowed to have .. components in the path to the executable.
mkdir()	Checks whether the directory in which you are about to op- erate has the same UID (owner) as the script that is being ex- ecute d.
rmdir()	Checks whether the files or directories you are about to oper- ate on have the same UID (owner) as the script that is being executed.
rename()	Checks whether the files or directories you are about to oper- ate on have the same UID (owner) as the script that is being executed. Checks whether the directory in which you are about to operate has the same UID (owner) as the script that is being executed.
unlink()	Checks whether the files or directories you are about to oper- ate on have the same UID (owner) as the script that is being executed. Checks whether the directory in which you are about to operate has the same UID (owner) as the script that

Function	Limitations
	is being executed.
copy()	Checks whether the files or directories you are about to oper-ate on have the same UID (owner) as the script that is being executed. Checks whether the directory in which you are about to operate has the same UID (owner) as the script that is being executed. (on *source* and *target*)
chgrp()	Checks whether the files or directories you are about to oper-ate on have the same UID (owner) as the script that is being executed .
chown()	Checks whether the files or directories you are about to oper-ate on have the same UID (owner) as the script that is being executed .
chmod()	Checks whether the files or directories you are about to oper-ate on have the same UID (owner) as the script that is being executed. In addition, you cannot set the SUID, SGID and sticky bits
touch()	Checks whether the files or directories you are about to oper-ate on have the same UID (owner) as the script that is being executed. Checks whether the directory in which you are about to operate has the same UID (owner) as the script that is being executed.
symlink()	Checks whether the files or directories you are about to oper-ate on have the same UID (owner) as the script that is being executed. Checks whether the directory in which you are about to operate has the same UID (owner) as the script that is being executed. (note: only the target is checked)
link()	Checks whether the files or directories you are about to oper-

	ate on have the same UID (owner) as the script that is being executed. Checks whether the directory in which you are about to operate has the same UID (owner) as the script that is being executed. (note: only the target is checked)
getallheaders()	In safe mode, headers beginning with 'authorization' (case-insensitive) will not be returned. Warning: this is broken with the aol-server implementation of **getallheaders()**!
header()	In safe mode, the uid of the script is added to the realm part of the WWW-Authenticate header if you set this header (used for HTTP Authentication).
PHP_AUTH variables	In safe mode, the variables PHP_AUTH_USER, PHP_AUTH_PW, and AUTH_TYPE are not available in $_SERVER. Regardless, you can still use REMOTE_USER for the USER. (note: only affected since PHP 4.3.0)
highlight_file(), show_source()	Checks whether the files or directories you are about to oper- ate on have the same UID (owner) as the script that is being executed. Checks whether the directory in which you are about to operate has the same UID (owner) as the script that is being executed. (note: only affected since PHP 4.2.1)
parse_ini_file()	Checks whether the files or directories you are about to oper- ate on have the same UID (owner) as the script that is being executed. Checks whether the directory in which you are about to operate has the same UID (owner) as the script that is being executed. (note: only affected since PHP 4.2.1)

173

Function	Limitations
set_time_limit()	Has no affect when PHP is running in safe mode.
max_execution_time	Has no affect when PHP is running in safe mode.
Any function that uses php4/main/fopen_wrappers.c	??

Chapter 23.

As of version 4.3.0, PHP supports a new SAPI type (Server Application Programming Interface) named CLI which means *Command Line Interface*. As the name implies, this SAPI type main focus is on developing shell (or desktop as well) applic-ations with PHP. There are quite a few differences between the CLI SAPI and other SAPIs which are explained in this chapter. It's worth mentioning that CLI and CGI are different SAPI's although they do share many of the same behaviors.

The CLI SAPI was released for the first time with PHP 4.2.0, but was still experimental and had to be explicitly enabled with –enable-cli when running ./configure. Since PHP 4.3.0 the CLI SAPI is no longer experimental and the op-tion –enable-cli is on by default. You may use –disable-cli to disable it.

As of PHP 4.3.0, the name, location and existence of the CLI/CGI binaries will differ depending on how PHP is installed on your system. By default when executing make, both the CGI and CLI are built and placed as sapi/cgi/php and sapi/ cli/php respectively, in your php source directory. You will note that both are named php. What happens during make install depends on your configure line. If a module SAPI is chosen during configure, such as apxs, or the - -disable-cgi option is used, the CLI is copied to {PREFIX}/bin/php during make install otherwise the CGI is placed there. So, for example, if –with-apxs is in your configure line then the CLI is copied to {PREFIX}/bin/php during make install. If you want to override the installation of the CGI binary, use make install-cli after make install. Alternatively you can specify –disable-cgi in your configure line.

> **Note:** Because both –enable-cli and –enable-cgi are enabled by default, simply having –enable-cli in your configure line does not necessarily mean the CLI will be copied as {PREFIX}/bin/php during make in-stall.

The windows packages between PHP 4.2.0 and PHP 4.2.3 distributed the CLI as php-cli.exe,living in the same folder as the CGI php.exe. Starting with PHP 4.3.0 the windows package distributes the CLI as php.exe in a separate folder named cli, so cli/php.exe.

> **What SAPI do I have?:** From a shell, typing php -v will tell you whether php is CGI or CLI. See also the func-tion **php_sapi_name()** and the constant PHP_SAPI.

> **Note:** A unix manual page was added in PHP 4.3.2. You may view this by typing man php in your shell environ-ment.

Remarkable differences of the CLI SAPI compared to other SAPIs:

- Unlike the CGI SAPI, no headers are written to the output.

   Though the CGI SAPI provides a way to suppress HTTP headers, there's no equivalent switch to enable them in the CLI SAPI.

   CLI is started up in quiet mode by default, though the -q switch is kept for compatibility so that you can use older CGI scripts.

   It does not change the working directory to that of the script. (-C switch kept for

   compatibility) Plain text error messages (no HTML formatting).

- There are certain php.ini directives which are overriden by the CLI SAPI because they do not make sense in shell en-vironments:

Table 23.1. Overriden php.ini directives

175

Directive	CLI SAPI default value	Comment
html_errors	FALSE	It can be quite hard to read the error message in your shell when it's cluttered with all those meaningless HTML tags, therefore this directive defaults to FALSE.
implicit_flush	TRUE	It is desired that any output coming from **print()**, **echo()** and friends is immediately written to the output and not cached in any buffer. You still can use output buffering if you want to defer or manipulate standard output.
max_execution_time	0 (unlimited)	Due to endless possibilities of using PHP in shell environments, the max-imum execution time has been set to unlimited. Whereas applications written for the web are often ex-ecuted very quickly, shell applica-tion tend to have a much longer exe-cution time.
register_argc_argv	TRUE	Because this setting is TRUE you will always have access to *argc* (number of arguments passed to the application) and *argv* (array of the actual arguments) in the CLI SAPI. As of PHP 4.3.0, the PHP variables $argc and $argv are registered and filled in with the appropriate values when using the CLI SAPI. Prior to this version, the creation of these

		variables behaved as they do in CGI and MODULE versions which requires the PHP directive register_globals to be *on*. Regardless of version or re-gister_globals setting, you can al-ways go through either $_SERVER or $HTTP_SERVER_VARS. Example: $_SERVER['argv']

Note: These directives cannot be initialized with another value from the configuration file php.ini or a custom one (if specified). This is a limitation because those default values are applied after all configuration files have been parsed. However, their value can be changed during runtime (which does not make sense for all of those dir-ectives, e.g. register_argc_argv).

- To ease working in the shell environment, the following constants are defined:

Table 23.2. CLI specific Constants

Constant	Description
STDIN	An already opened stream to stdin. This saves opening it with

176

Constant	Description
	$stdin = fopen('php://stdin', 'r');
STDOUT	An already opened stream to stdout. This saves open- ing it with $stdout = fopen('php://stdout', 'w');
STDERR	An already opened stream to stderr. This saves open- ing it with $stderr = fopen('php://stderr', 'w');

Given the above, you don't need to open e.g. a stream for stderr yourself but simply use the constant instead of the stream resource:

```
php -r 'fwrite(STDERR, "stderr\n");'
```

You do not need to explicitly close these streams, as they are closed automatically by PHP when your script ends.

- The CLI SAPI does *not* change the current directory to the directory of the

executed script! Example showing the difference to the CGI SAPI:

```
<?php
    /* Our simple test application named test.php*/ echo
    getcwd(), "\n";
?>
```

When using the CGI version, the output is:

```
$
pwd
/tmp
```

```
$ php -q another_directory/test.php
/tmp/another_directory
```

This clearly shows that PHP changes its current directory to the one of the

executed script. Using the CLI SAPI yields:

```
$
pwd
/tmp
```

```
$ php -f another_directory/test.php /tmp
```

349

This allows greater flexibility when writing shell tools in PHP.

> **Note:** The CGI SAPI supports the CLI SAPI behaviour by means of the -C switch when run from the command line.

The list of command line options provided by the PHP binary can be queried anytime by running PHP with the -h switch:

```
Usage: php [options] [-f] <file> [args...]
       php [options] -r <code> [args...]
       php [options] [- args...]
  -s               Display   colour syntax highlighted source.
  -w               Display   source with stripped comments and whitespace.
```

-f <file>	Parse <file>.
-v	Version number
-c <path>|<file>	Look for php.ini file in this directory
-a	Run interactively
-d foo[=bar]	Define INI entry foo with value 'bar'
-e	Generate extended information for debugger/profiler
-z <file>	Load Zend extension <file>.
-l	Syntax check only (lint)
-m	Show compiled in modules
-i	PHP information
-r <code>	Run PHP <code> without using script tags <?..?>
-h	This help
args...	Arguments passed to script. Use -- args when first argument starts with - or script is read from stdin

The CLI SAPI has three different ways of getting the PHP code you want to execute:

- Telling PHP to execute a certain file.

  php my_script.php php -

  f my_script.php

  Both ways (whether using the -f switch or not) execute the file my_script.php. You can choose any file to execute - your PHP scripts do not have to end with the .php extension but can have any name or extension you wish.

- Pass the PHP code to execute directly on the command line.

  php -r 'print_r(get_defined_constants());'

  Special care has to be taken in regards of shell variable substitution and quoting usage.

  Note: Read the example carefully, there are no beginning or ending tags! The -r switch simply does not need them. Using them will lead to a parser error.

- Provide the PHP code to execute via standard input (stdin).

  This gives the powerful ability to dynamically create PHP code and feed it to the binary, as shown in this (fictional) ex-ample:

  $ some_application | some_filter | php | sort -u >final_output.txt

You cannot combine any of the three ways to execute code.

Like every shell application, the PHP binary accepts a number of arguments but your PHP script can also receive arguments. The number of arguments which can be passed to your script is not limited by PHP (the shell has a certain size limit in the number of characters which can be passed; usually you won't hit this limit). The arguments passed to your script are avail-able in the global array $argv. The zero index always contains the script name (which is - in case the PHP code is coming from either standard input or from the command line switch -r). The second registered global variable is $argc which con-tains the number of elements in the $argv array (not the number of arguments passed to the script).

As long as the arguments you want to pass to your script do not start with the - character, there's nothing special to watch out for. Passing an argument to your script which starts with a - will cause trouble because PHP itself thinks it has to handle it. To prevent this, use the argument list separator -. After this separator has been parsed by PHP, every argument follow-ing it is passed untouched to your script.

• This will not execute the given code but will show the PHP usage $ php -r 'var_dump($argv);' -h

```
Usage: php [options] [-f] <file> [args...]
[...]
```

• This will pass the '-h' argument to your script and prevent PHP from showing it's usage $ php -r
'var_dump($argv);' – -h
```
array(2) { [0]=>
  string(1) "-"
  [1]=> string(2) "-
  h"

}
```

However, there's another way of using PHP for shell scripting. You can write a script where the first line starts
with #!/usr/bin/php. Following this you can place normal PHP code included within the PHP starting and end
tags. Once you have set the execution attributes of the file appropriately (e.g. chmod +x test) your script can be
executed like a normal shell or perl script:

```
#!/usr/bin/php
<?php
    var_dump($argv);
?>
```

Assuming this file is named test in the current directory, we can now do the following:

```
$ chmod 755 test
$ ./test -h      – foo
array(4) {
  [0]=>
  string(6)    "./test"
  [1]=>
  string(2)    "-h"
  [2]=>
  string(2)    "–"
  [3]=>
  string(3)    "foo"
}
```

As you see, in this case no care needs to be taken when passing parameters which start with - to your script.

Table 23.3. Command line options

Option	Description
-s	Display colour syntax highlighted source. This option uses the internal mechanism to parse the file and produces a HTML highlighted version of it and writes it to standard output. Note that all it does it to generate a block of <code> [...] </code> HTML tags, no HTML headers. **Note:** This option does not work together with the - r option.
-w	Display source with stripped comments and whitespace. **Note:** This option does not work together with the - r option.

| -f | Parses and executed the given filename to the -f option.
This switch is optional and can be left out. Only providing
the filename to execute is sufficient. |

The PHP executable can be used to run PHP scripts absolutely independent from the web server. If you are on a Unix sys-tem, you should add a special first line to your PHP script, and make it executable, so the system will know, what program should run the script. On a Windows platform you can associate php.exe with the double click option of the .php files, or you can make a batch file to run the script through PHP. The first line added to the script to work on Unix won't hurt on Windows, so you can write cross platform programs this way. A simple example of writing a command line PHP program can be found below.

Example 23.1. Script intended to be run from command line (script.php)

```
#!/usr/bin/php
<?php

if ($argc != 2 || in_array($argv[1], array('--help', '-help', '-h', '-?'))) { ?>

This is a command line PHP script with one option.

  Usage:
  <?php echo $argv[0]; ?> <option>

  <option> can be some word you would like
  to print out. With the --help, -help, -h,
  or -? options, you can get this help.

<?php
} else {
    echo $argv[1];
}
?>
```

In the script above, we used the special first line to indicate that this file should be run by PHP. We work with a CLI version here, so there will be no HTTP header printouts. There are two variables you can use while writing command line applica-tions with PHP: $argc and $argv. The first is the number of arguments plus one (the name of the script running). The second is an array containing the arguments, starting with the script name as number zero ($argv[0]).

In the program above we checked if there are less or more than one arguments. Also if the argument was --help, -help, - h or -?, we printed out the help message, printing the script name dynamically. If we received some other argument we echoed that out.

182

If you would like to run the above script on Unix, you need to make it executable, and simply call it as script.php echothis or script.php -h. On Windows, you can make a batch file for this task:

Example 23.2. Batch file to run a command line PHP script (script.bat)

```
@c:\php\cli\php.exe script.php %1 %2 %3 %4
```

Assuming you named the above program script.php, and you have your CLI php.exe in c:\php\cli\php.exe this batch file will run it for you with your added options: script.bat echothis or script.bat -h.

See also the Readline extension documentation for more functions you can use to enhance your command line applications in PHP.

Chapter 1 Introduction to the MySQL PHP API

PHP is a server-side, HTML-embedded scripting language that may be used to create dynamic Web pages. It is available for most operating systems and Web servers, and can access most common databases, including MySQL. PHP may be run as a separate program or compiled as a module for use with a Web server.

PHP provides four different MySQL API extensions:

• Chapter 3, *MySQL Improved Extension*: Stands for "MySQL, Improved"; this extension is available as of PHP 5.0.0. It is intended for use with MySQL 4.1.1 and later. This extension fully supports the authentication protocol used in MySQL 5.0, as well as the Prepared Statements and Multiple Statements APIs. In addition, this extension provides an advanced, object-oriented programming interface.

• Chapter 4, *MySQL Functions (PDO_MYSQL)*: Not its own API, but instead it's a MySQL driver for the PHP database abstraction layer PDO (PHP Data Objects). The PDO MySQL driver sits in the layer below PDO itself, and provides MySQL-specific functionality. This extension is available as of PHP 5.1.0.

• Chapter 5, *Mysql_xdevapi*: This extension uses MySQL's X DevAPI and is available as a PECL extension named mysql_xdevapi. For general concepts and X DevAPI usage details, see X DevAPI User Guide.

• Chapter 6, *Original MySQL API*: Available for PHP versions 4 and 5, this extension is intended for use with MySQL versions prior to MySQL 4.1. This extension does not support the improved authentication protocol used in MySQL 4.1, nor does it support prepared statements or multiple statements. To use this extension with MySQL 4.1, you will likely configure the MySQL server to set the old_passwords system variable to 1 (see Client does not support authentication protocol).

Warning

This extension was removed from PHP 5.5.0. All users must migrate to either mysqli, PDO_MySQL, or mysql_xdevapi. For further information, see Section 2.3, "Choosing an API".

Note

This documentation, and other publications, sometimes uses the term Connector/ PHP. This term refers to the full set of MySQL related functionality in PHP, which includes the three APIs that are described in the preceding discussion, along with the mysqlnd core library and all of its plugins.

1

Table of Contents

2.1 Introduction

Depending on the version of PHP, there are either two or three PHP APIs for accessing the MySQL database. PHP 5 users can choose between the deprecated mysql extension, mysqli, or PDO_MySQL. PHP 7 removes the mysql extension, leaving only the latter two options.

This guide explains the terminology used to describe each API, information about choosing which API to use, and also information to help choose which MySQL library to use with the API.

2.2 Terminology overview

This section provides an introduction to the options available to you when developing a PHP application that needs to interact with a MySQL database.

What is an API?

An Application Programming Interface, or API, defines the classes, methods, functions and variables that your application will need to call in order to carry out its desired task. In the case of PHP applications that need to communicate with databases the necessary APIs are usually exposed via PHP extensions.

APIs can be procedural or object-oriented. With a procedural API you call functions to carry out tasks, with the object-oriented API you instantiate classes and then call methods on the resulting objects. Of the two the latter is usually the preferred interface, as it is more modern and leads to better organized code.

When writing PHP applications that need to connect to the MySQL server there are several API options available. This document discusses what is available and how to select the best solution for your application.

What is a Connector?

In the MySQL documentation, the term *connector* refers to a piece of software that allows your application to connect to the MySQL database server. MySQL provides connectors for a variety of languages, including PHP.

If your PHP application needs to communicate with a database server you will need to write PHP code to perform such activities as connecting to the database server, querying the database and other database-related functions. Software is required to provide the API that your PHP application will use, and also handle the communication between your application and the database server, possibly using other

intermediate libraries where necessary. This software is known generically as a connector, as it allows your application to *connect* to a database server.

What is a Driver?

A driver is a piece of software designed to communicate with a specific type of database server. The driver may also call a library, such as the MySQL Client Library or the MySQL Native Driver. These libraries implement the low-level protocol used to communicate with the MySQL database server.

By way of an example, the PHP Data Objects (PDO) database abstraction layer may use one of several database-specific drivers. One of the drivers it has available is the PDO MYSQL driver, which allows it to interface with the MySQL server.

Sometimes people use the terms connector and driver interchangeably, this can be confusing. In the MySQL-related documentation the term "driver"is reserved for software that provides the database-specific part of a connector package.

What is an Extension?

In the PHP documentation you will come across another term - *extension*. The PHP code consists of a core, with optional extensions to the core functionality. PHP's MySQL-related extensions, such as the mysqli extension, and the mysql extension, are implemented using the PHP extension framework.

An extension typically exposes an API to the PHP programmer, to allow its facilities to be used programmatically. However, some extensions which use the PHP extension framework do not expose an API to the PHP programmer.

The PDO MySQL driver extension, for example, does not expose an API to the PHP programmer, but provides an interface to the PDO layer above it.

The terms API and extension should not be taken to mean the same thing, as an extension may not necessarily expose an API to the programmer.

2.3 Choosing an API

PHP offers three different APIs to connect to MySQL. Below we show the APIs provided by the mysql, mysqli, and PDO extensions. Each code snippet creates a connection to a MySQL server running on "example.com" using the username "user" and the password "password". And a query is run to greet the user.

Example 2.1 Comparing the three MySQL APIs

```php
<?php
// mysqli
$mysqli = new mysqli("example.com", "user", "password", "database");
$result = $mysqli->query("SELECT 'Hello, dear MySQL user!' AS _message FROM DUAL");
$row = $result->fetch_assoc();
echo htmlentities($row['_message']);

// PDO
$pdo = new PDO('mysql:host=example.com;dbname=database', 'user', 'password');
$statement = $pdo->query("SELECT 'Hello, dear MySQL user!' AS _message FROM
DUAL"); $row = $statement->fetch(PDO::FETCH_ASSOC); echo
htmlentities($row['_message']);

// mysql
```

```
$c = mysql_connect("example.com", "user", "password");
```

4 _____

```
mysql_select_db("database");
$result = mysql_query("SELECT 'Hello, dear MySQL user!' AS _message FROM DUAL");
$row = mysql_fetch_assoc($result);
echo htmlentities($row['_message']);
?>
```

Recommended API

It is recommended to use either the mysqli or PDO_MySQL extensions. It is not recommended to use the old mysql extension for new development, as it was deprecated in PHP 5.5.0 and was removed in PHP 7. A detailed feature comparison matrix is provided below. The overall performance of all three extensions is considered to be about the same. Although the performance of the extension contributes only a fraction of the total run time of a PHP web request. Often, the impact is as low as 0.1%.

Feature comparison

	ext/mysqli	PDO_MySQL	ext/mysql
PHP version introduced	5.0	5.1	2.0
Included with PHP 5.x	Yes	Yes	Yes
Included with PHP 7.x	Yes	Yes	No
Development status	Active	Active	Maintenance only in 5.x; removed in 7.x
Lifecycle	Active	Active	Deprecated in 5.x; removed in 7.x
Recommended for new projects	Yes	Yes	No
OOP Interface	Yes	Yes	No
Procedural Interface	Yes	No	Yes
API supports non-blocking, asynchronous queries with mysqlnd	Yes	No	No
Persistent Connections	Yes	Yes	Yes
API supports Charsets	Yes	Yes	Yes
API supports server-side Prepared Statements	Yes	Yes	No
API supports client-side Prepared Statements	No	Yes	No
API supports Stored Procedures	Yes	Yes	No
API supports Multiple	Yes	Most	No

Statements			
API supports Transactions	Yes	Yes	No
Transactions can be controlled with SQL	Yes	Yes	Yes
Supports all MySQL 5.1+ functionality	Yes	Most	No

5

2.4 Choosing a library

The mysqli, PDO_MySQL and mysql PHP extensions are lightweight wrappers on top of a C client library. The extensions can either use the mysqlnd library or the libmysqlclient library. Choosing a library is a compile time decision.

The mysqlnd library is part of the PHP distribution since 5.3.0. It offers features like lazy connections and query caching, features that are not available with libmysqlclient, so using the built-in mysqlnd library is highly recommended. See the mysqlnd documentation for additional details, and a listing of features and functionality that it offers.

Example 2.2 Configure commands for using mysqlnd or libmysqlclient

```
// Recommended, compiles with mysqlnd
$ ./configure –with-mysqli=mysqlnd –with-pdo-mysql=mysqlnd –with-mysql=mysqlnd
```

- Alternatively recommended, compiles with mysqlnd as of PHP 5.4

```
$ ./configure –with-mysqli –with-pdo-mysql –with-mysql
```

- Not recommended, compiles with libmysqlclient

```
$ ./configure –with-mysqli=/path/to/mysql_config –with-pdo-mysql=/path/to/mysql_config –with-mysql=/path/to
```

Library feature comparison

It is recommended to use the mysqlnd library instead of the MySQL Client Server library (libmysqlclient). Both libraries are supported and constantly being improved.

	MySQL native driver (mysqlnd)	MySQL client server library (libmysqlclient)
Part of the PHP distribution	Yes	No
PHP version introduced	5.3.0	N/A
License	PHP License 3.01	Dual-License
Development status	Active	Active
Lifecycle	No end announced	No end announced
PHP 5.4 and above; compile default (for all MySQL extensions)	Yes	No
PHP 5.3; compile default (for all MySQL extensions)	No	Yes
Compression protocol support	Yes (5.3.1+)	Yes
SSL support	Yes (5.3.3+)	Yes
Named pipe support	Yes (5.3.4+)	Yes
Non-blocking, asynchronous	Yes	No

queries		
Performance statistics	Yes	No
LOAD LOCAL INFILE respects the open_basedir directive	Yes	No

6

	MySQL native driver (mysqlnd)	MySQL client server library (libmysqlclient)
Uses PHP's native memory management system (e.g., follows PHP memory limits)	Yes	No
Return numeric column as double (COM_QUERY)	Yes	No
Return numeric column as string (COM_QUERY)	Yes	Yes
Plugin API	Yes	Limited
Read/Write splitting for MySQL Replication	Yes, with plugin	No
Load Balancing	Yes, with plugin	No
Fail over	Yes, with plugin	No
Lazy connections	Yes, with plugin	No
Query caching	Yes, with plugin	No
Transparent query manipulations (E.g., auto-EXPLAIN or monitoring)	Yes, with plugin	No
Automatic reconnect	No	Optional

2.5 Concepts

These concepts are specific to the MySQL drivers for PHP.

2.5.1 Buffered and Unbuffered queries

Queries are using the buffered mode by default. This means that query results are immediately transferred from the MySQL Server to PHP and then are kept in the memory of the PHP process. This allows additional operations like counting the number of rows, and moving (seeking) the current result pointer. It also allows issuing further queries on the same connection while working on the result set. The downside of the buffered mode is that larger result sets might require quite a lot memory. The memory will be
kept occupied till all references to the result set are unset or the result set was explicitly freed, which will automatically happen during request end the latest. The terminology "store result" is also used for buffered mode, as the whole result set is stored at once.

Note

When using libmysqlclient as library PHP's memory limit won't count the memory used for result sets unless the data is fetched into PHP variables. With mysqlnd the memory accounted for will include the full result set.

Unbuffered MySQL queries execute the query and then return a resource while the data is still waiting on the MySQL server for being fetched. This uses less memory on the PHP-side, but can increase the load on the server. Unless the full result set was fetched from the server no further queries can be sent over the same connection. Unbuffered queries can also be referred to as "use result".

7

Following these characteristics buffered queries should be used in cases where you expect only a limited result set or need to know the amount of returned rows before reading all rows. Unbuffered mode should be used when you expect larger results.

Because buffered queries are the default, the examples below will demonstrate how to execute unbuffered queries with each API.

Example 2.3 Unbuffered query example: mysqli

```php
<?php
$mysqli = new mysqli("localhost", "my_user", "my_password", "world");
$uresult = $mysqli->query("SELECT   Name   FROM   City",
MYSQLI_USE_RESULT);

if ($uresult) {
    while ($row = $uresult->fetch_assoc()) {
        echo $row['Name'] . PHP_EOL;
    }
}
$uresult->close();
?>
```

Example 2.4 Unbuffered query example: pdo_mysql

```php
<?php
$pdo = new PDO("mysql:host=localhost;dbname=world", 'my_user',
'my_pass'); $pdo->setAttribute(PDO::MYSQL_ATTR_USE_BUFFERED_QUERY,
false);

$uresult = $pdo->query("SELECT Name FROM City");
if ($uresult) {
    while ($row = $uresult->fetch(PDO::FETCH_ASSOC)) {
        echo $row['Name'] . PHP_EOL;
    }
}
?>
```

Example 2.5 Unbuffered query example: mysql

```php
<?php
$conn = mysql_connect("localhost", "my_user", "my_pass");
$db = mysql_select_db("world");

$uresult = mysql_unbuffered_query("SELECT Name FROM
City"); if ($uresult) {
    while ($row = mysql_fetch_assoc($uresult)) {
        echo $row['Name'] . PHP_EOL;
    }
}
?>
```

2.5.2 Character sets

8

Ideally a proper character set will be set at the server level, and doing this is described within the Character Set Configuration section of the MySQL Server manual. Alternatively, each MySQL API offers a method to set the character set at runtime.

The character set and character escaping

The character set should be understood and defined, as it has an affect on every action, and includes security implications. For example, the escaping mechanism (e.g., mysqli_real_escape_string for mysqli, mysql_real_escape_string for mysql, and PDO::quote for PDO_MySQL) will adhere to this setting. It is important to realize that these functions will not use the character set that is defined with a query, so for example the following will not have an effect on them:

Example 2.6 Problems with setting the character set with SQL

```
<?php

$mysqli = new mysqli("localhost", "my_user", "my_password", "world");

•       Will NOT affect $mysqli->real_escape_string();
$mysqli->query("SET NAMES utf8");

•       Will NOT affect $mysqli->real_escape_string();
$mysqli->query("SET CHARACTER SET utf8");

•       But, this will affect $mysqli->real_escape_string();
$mysqli->set_charset('utf8');

•       But, this will NOT affect it (utf-8 vs utf8) – don't use dashes here $mysqli->set_charset('utf-8');

?>
```

Below are examples that demonstrate how to properly alter the character set at runtime using each API.

Possible UTF-8 confusion

Because character set names in MySQL do not contain dashes, the string "utf8" is valid in MySQL to set the character set to UTF-8. The string "utf-8" is not valid, as using "utf-8" will fail to change the character set.

Example 2.7 Setting the character set example: mysqli

```
<?php
$mysqli = new mysqli("localhost", "my_user", "my_password", "world");

printf("Initial character set: %s\n", $mysqli->character_set_name());

if (!$mysqli->set_charset('utf8')) {
    printf("Error loading character set utf8: %s\n", $mysqli->error); exit;
}

echo "New character set information:\n";
print_r( $mysqli->get_charset() );
```

Example 2.8 Setting the character set example: pdo_mysql

Note: This only works as of PHP 5.3.6.

```php
<?php
$pdo = new PDO("mysql:host=localhost;dbname=world;charset=utf8", 'my_user', 'my_pass');
?>
```

Example 2.9 Setting the character set example: mysql

```php
<?php
$conn = mysql_connect("localhost", "my_user", "my_pass");
$db = mysql_select_db("world");

echo 'Initial character set: ' .          mysql_client_encoding($conn) . "\n";

if (!mysql_set_charset('utf8', $conn)) {
    echo "Error: Unable to set the character set.\n";
    exit;
}

echo 'Your current character set is: ' . mysql_client_encoding($conn); ?>
```

Table of Contents

1
1

12

1
3

The mysqli extension allows you to access the functionality provided by MySQL 4.1 and above. More information about the MySQL Database server can be found at http://www.mysql.com/

An overview of software available for using MySQL from PHP can be found at Section 3.1, "Overview"

Documentation for MySQL can be found at http://dev.mysql.com/doc/.

Parts of this documentation included from MySQL manual with permissions of Oracle Corporation.

Examples use either the world or sakila database, which are freely available.

3.1 Overview

This section provides an introduction to the options available to you when developing a PHP application that needs to interact with a MySQL database.

What is an API?

An Application Programming Interface, or API, defines the classes, methods, functions and variables that your application will need to call in order to carry out its desired task. In the case of PHP applications that need to communicate with databases the necessary APIs are usually exposed via PHP extensions.

APIs can be procedural or object-oriented. With a procedural API you call functions to carry out tasks, with the object-oriented API you instantiate classes and then call methods on the resulting objects. Of the two the latter is usually the preferred interface, as it is more modern and leads to better organized code.

When writing PHP applications that need to connect to the MySQL server there are several API options available. This document discusses what is available and how to select the best solution for your application.

What is a Connector?

In the MySQL documentation, the term *connector* refers to a piece of software that allows your application to connect to the MySQL database server. MySQL provides connectors for a variety of languages, including PHP.

If your PHP application needs to communicate with a database server you will need to write PHP code to perform such activities as connecting to the database server, querying the database and other database-related functions. Software is required to provide the API that your PHP application will use, and also handle the communication between your application and the database server, possibly using other

14 _____

intermediate libraries where necessary. This software is known generically as a connector, as it allows your application to *connect* to a database server.

What is a Driver?

A driver is a piece of software designed to communicate with a specific type of database server. The driver may also call a library, such as the MySQL Client Library or the MySQL Native Driver. These libraries implement the low-level protocol used to communicate with the MySQL database server.

By way of an example, the PHP Data Objects (PDO) database abstraction layer may use one of several database-specific drivers. One of the drivers it has available is the PDO MYSQL driver, which allows it to interface with the MySQL server.

Sometimes people use the terms connector and driver interchangeably, this can be confusing. In the MySQL-related documentation the term "driver"is reserved for software that provides the database-specific part of a connector package.

What is an Extension?

In the PHP documentation you will come across another term - *extension*. The PHP code consists of a core, with optional extensions to the core functionality. PHP's MySQL-related extensions, such as the mysqli extension, and the mysql extension, are implemented using the PHP extension framework.

An extension typically exposes an API to the PHP programmer, to allow its facilities to be used programmatically. However, some extensions which use the PHP extension framework do not expose an API to the PHP programmer.

The PDO MySQL driver extension, for example, does not expose an API to the PHP programmer, but provides an interface to the PDO layer above it.

The terms API and extension should not be taken to mean the same thing, as an extension may not necessarily expose an API to the programmer.

What are the main PHP API offerings for using MySQL?

There are three main API options when considering connecting to a MySQL database server:

- PHP's MySQL Extension

- PHP's mysqli Extension

- PHP Data Objects (PDO)

Each has its own advantages and disadvantages. The following discussion aims to give a brief introduction to the key aspects of each API.

What is PHP's MySQL Extension?

This is the original extension designed to allow you to develop PHP applications that interact with a MySQL database. The mysql extension provides a procedural interface and is intended for use only with MySQL versions older than 4.1.3. This extension can be used with versions of MySQL 4.1.3 or newer, but not all of the latest MySQL server features will be available.

> **Note**
>
> If you are using MySQL versions 4.1.3 or later it is *strongly* recommended that you use the mysqli extension instead.

The mysql extension source code is located in the PHP extension directory ext/mysql.

For further information on the mysql extension, see Chapter 6, Original MySQL API.

What is PHP's mysqli Extension?

The mysqli extension, or as it is sometimes known, the MySQL *improved* extension, was developed to take advantage of new features found in MySQL systems versions 4.1.3 and newer. The mysqli extension is included with PHP versions 5 and later.

The mysqli extension has a number of benefits, the key enhancements over the mysql extension being:

- Object-oriented interface

- Support for Prepared Statements

- Support for Multiple Statements

- Support for Transactions

- Enhanced debugging capabilities

- Embedded server support

> **Note**
>
> If you are using MySQL versions 4.1.3 or later it is *strongly* recommended that you use this extension.

As well as the object-oriented interface the extension also provides a procedural interface.

The mysqli extension is built using the PHP extension framework, its source code is located in the directory ext/mysqli.

For further information on the mysqli extension, see Chapter 3, MySQL Improved Extension.

What is PDO?

PHP Data Objects, or PDO, is a database abstraction layer specifically for PHP applications. PDO provides a consistent API for your PHP application regardless of the type of database server your application will connect to. In theory, if you are using the PDO API, you could switch the database server you used, from say Firebird to MySQL, and only need to make minor changes to your PHP code.

Other examples of database abstraction layers include JDBC for Java applications and DBI for Perl.

While PDO has its advantages, such as a clean, simple, portable API, its main disadvantage is that it doesn't allow you to use all of the advanced features that are available in the latest versions of MySQL server. For example, PDO does not allow you to use MySQL's support for Multiple Statements.

PDO is implemented using the PHP extension framework, its source code is located in the directory ext/pdo.

For further information on PDO, see the http://www.php.net/book.pdo.

What is the PDO MYSQL driver?

The PDO MYSQL driver is not an API as such, at least from the PHP programmer's perspective. In fact the PDO MYSQL driver sits in the layer below PDO itself and provides MySQL-specific functionality. The

16

programmer still calls the PDO API, but PDO uses the PDO MYSQL driver to carry out communication with the MySQL server.

The PDO MYSQL driver is one of several available PDO drivers. Other PDO drivers available include those for the Firebird and PostgreSQL database servers.

The PDO MYSQL driver is implemented using the PHP extension framework. Its source code is located in the directory ext/pdo_mysql. It does not expose an API to the PHP programmer.

For further information on the PDO MYSQL driver, see Chapter 4, MySQL Functions (PDO_MYSQL).

What is PHP's MySQL Native Driver?

In order to communicate with the MySQL database server the mysql extension, mysqli and the PDO MYSQL driver each use a low-level library that implements the required protocol. In the past, the only available library was the MySQL Client Library, otherwise known as libmysqlclient.

However, the interface presented by libmysqlclient was not optimized for communication with PHP applications, as libmysqlclient was originally designed with C applications in mind. For this reason the MySQL Native Driver, mysqlnd, was developed as an alternative to libmysqlclient for PHP applications.

The mysql extension, the mysqli extension and the PDO MySQL driver can each be individually configured to use either libmysqlclient or mysqlnd. As mysqlnd is designed specifically to be utilised in the PHP system it has numerous memory and speed enhancements over libmysqlclient. You are strongly encouraged to take advantage of these improvements.

> **Note**
>
> The MySQL Native Driver can only be used with MySQL server versions 4.1.3 and later.

The MySQL Native Driver is implemented using the PHP extension framework. The source code is located in ext/mysqlnd. It does not expose an API to the PHP programmer.

Comparison of Features

The following table compares the functionality of the three main methods of connecting to MySQL from PHP:

Table 3.1 Comparison of MySQL API options for PHP

	PHP's mysqli Extension	PDO (Using PDO MySQL Driver and MySQL Native Driver)	PHP's MySQL Extension
PHP version introduced	5.0	5.0	Prior to 3.0
Included with PHP 5.x	yes	yes	Yes
MySQL development status	Active development	Active development as of PHP 5.3	Maintenance only
Recommended by MySQL for new projects	Yes - preferred option	Yes	No
API supports Charsets	Yes	Yes	No
API supports server-side Prepared Statements	Yes	Yes	No

	PHP's mysqli ExtensionPDO (Using PDO MySQL Driver and MySQL Native Driver)		PHP's MySQL Extension
API supports client-side Prepared Statements	No	Yes	No
API supports Stored Procedures	Yes	Yes	No
API supports Multiple Statements	Yes	Most	No
Supports all MySQL 4.1+ functionality	Yes	Most	No

3.2 Quick start guide

This quick start guide will help with choosing and gaining familiarity with the PHP MySQL API.

This quick start gives an overview on the mysqli extension. Code examples are provided for all major aspects of the API. Database concepts are explained to the degree needed for presenting concepts specific to MySQL.

Required: A familiarity with the PHP programming language, the SQL language, and basic knowledge of the MySQL server.

3.2.1 Dual procedural and object-oriented interface

The mysqli extension features a dual interface. It supports the procedural and object-oriented programming paradigm.

Users migrating from the old mysql extension may prefer the procedural interface. The procedural interface is similar to that of the old mysql extension. In many cases, the function names differ only by prefix. Some mysqli functions take a connection handle as their first argument, whereas matching functions in the old mysql interface take it as an optional last argument.

Example 3.1 Easy migration from the old mysql extension

```php
<?php
$mysqli = mysqli_connect("example.com", "user", "password", "database");
$res = mysqli_query($mysqli, "SELECT 'Please, do not use ' AS _msg FROM DUAL");
$row = mysqli_fetch_assoc($res);
echo $row['_msg'];

$mysql = mysql_connect("example.com", "user", "password");
mysql_select_db("test");
$res = mysql_query("SELECT 'the mysql extension for new developments.' AS _msg FROM DUAL", $mysql);
$row = mysql_fetch_assoc($res);
echo $row['_msg'];
?>
```

The above example will output:

_____

Please, do not use the mysql extension for new developments.

The object-oriented interface

In addition to the classical procedural interface, users can choose to use the object-oriented interface. The documentation is organized using the object-oriented interface. The object-oriented interface shows functions grouped by their purpose, making it easier to get started. The reference section gives examples for both syntax variants.

There are no significant performance differences between the two interfaces. Users can base their choice on personal preference.

Example 3.2 Object-oriented and procedural interface

```php
<?php
$mysqli = mysqli_connect("example.com", "user", "password", "database");
if (mysqli_connect_errno($mysqli)) {
    echo "Failed to connect to MySQL: " . mysqli_connect_error();
}

$res = mysqli_query($mysqli, "SELECT 'A world full of ' AS _msg FROM DUAL");
$row = mysqli_fetch_assoc($res);
echo $row['_msg'];

$mysqli = new mysqli("example.com", "user", "password", "database");
if ($mysqli->connect_errno) {
    echo "Failed to connect to MySQL: " . $mysqli->connect_error;
}

$res = $mysqli->query("SELECT 'choices to please everybody.' AS _msg FROM DUAL");
$row = $res->fetch_assoc();
echo $row['_msg'];
?>
```

The above example will output:

A world full of choices to please everybody.

The object oriented interface is used for the quickstart because the reference section is organized that way.

Mixing styles

It is possible to switch between styles at any time. Mixing both styles is not recommended for code clarity and coding style reasons.

Example 3.3 Bad coding style

```php
<?php
$mysqli = new mysqli("example.com", "user", "password", "database");
if ($mysqli->connect_errno) {
    echo "Failed to connect to MySQL: " . $mysqli->connect_error;
}

$res = mysqli_query($mysqli, "SELECT 'Possible but bad style.' AS _msg FROM DUAL"); if
(!$res) {
    echo "Failed to run query: (" . $mysqli->errno . ") " . $mysqli->error;
}

if ($row = $res->fetch_assoc()) {
    echo $row['_msg'];
}
?>
```

The above example will output:

Possible but bad style.

See also

mysqli::__construct
mysqli::query
mysqli_result::fetch_assoc
$mysqli::connect_errno
$mysqli::connect_error
$mysqli::errno
$mysqli::error
The MySQLi Extension Function Summary

3.2.2 Connections

The MySQL server supports the use of different transport layers for connections. Connections use TCP/IP, Unix domain sockets or Windows named pipes.

The hostname localhost has a special meaning. It is bound to the use of Unix domain sockets. It is not possible to open a TCP/IP connection using the hostname localhost you must use 127.0.0.1 instead.

Example 3.4 Special meaning of localhost

```php
<?php
$mysqli = new mysqli("localhost", "user", "password", "database"); if
($mysqli->connect_errno) {
    echo "Failed to connect to MySQL: (" . $mysqli->connect_errno . ") " . $mysqli->connect_error;
}
echo $mysqli->host_info . "\n";

$mysqli = new mysqli("127.0.0.1", "user", "password", "database", 3306); if
($mysqli->connect_errno) {
```

```
        echo "Failed to connect to MySQL: (" . $mysqli->connect_errno . ") " . $mysqli->connect_error;
    }
```

20

———————

```
echo $mysqli->host_info . "\n";
?>
```

The above example will output:

```
Localhost via UNIX socket
127.0.0.1 via TCP/IP
```

Connection parameter defaults

Depending on the connection function used, assorted parameters can be omitted. If a parameter is not provided, then the extension attempts to use the default values that are set in the PHP configuration file.

Example 3.5 Setting defaults

```
mysqli.default_host=192.168.2.27
mysqli.default_user=root
mysqli.default_pw=""
mysqli.default_port=3306
mysqli.default_socket=/tmp/mysql.sock
```

The resulting parameter values are then passed to the client library that is used by the extension. If the client library detects empty or unset parameters, then it may default to the library built-in values.

Built-in connection library defaults

If the host value is unset or empty, then the client library will default to a Unix socket connection on localhost. If socket is unset or empty, and a Unix socket connection is requested, then a connection to the default socket on /tmp/mysql.sock is attempted.

On Windows systems, the host name . is interpreted by the client library as an attempt to open a Windows named pipe based connection. In this case the socket parameter is interpreted as the pipe name. If not given or empty, then the socket (pipe name) defaults to \\.\pipe\MySQL.

If neither a Unix domain socket based not a Windows named pipe based connection is to be established and the port parameter value is unset, the library will default to port 3306.

The mysqlnd library and the MySQL Client Library (libmysqlclient) implement the same logic for determining defaults.

Connection options

Connection options are available to, for example, set init commands which are executed upon connect, or for requesting use of a certain charset. Connection options must be set before a network connection is established.

For setting a connection option, the connect operation has to be performed in three steps: creating a connection handle with mysqli_init, setting the requested options using mysqli_options, and establishing the network connection with mysqli_real_connect.

Connection pooling

The mysqli extension supports persistent database connections, which are a special kind of pooled connections. By default, every database connection opened by a script is either explicitly closed by the user during runtime or released automatically at the end of the script. A persistent connection is not. Instead it is put into a pool for later reuse, if a connection to the same server using the same username, password, socket, port and default database is opened. Reuse saves connection overhead.

Every PHP process is using its own mysqli connection pool. Depending on the web server deployment model, a PHP process may serve one or multiple requests. Therefore, a pooled connection may be used by one or more scripts subsequently.

Persistent connection

If a unused persistent connection for a given combination of host, username, password, socket, port and default database can not be found in the connection pool, then mysqli opens a new connection. The use of persistent connections can be enabled and disabled using the PHP directive mysqli.allow_persistent. The total number of connections opened by a script can be limited with mysqli.max_links. The maximum number of persistent connections per PHP process can be restricted with mysqli.max_persistent. Please note, that the web server may spawn many PHP processes.

A common complain about persistent connections is that their state is not reset before reuse. For example, open and unfinished transactions are not automatically rolled back. But also, authorization changes which happened in the time between putting the connection into the pool and reusing it are not reflected. This may be seen as an unwanted side-effect. On the contrary, the name persistent may be understood as a promise that the state is persisted.

The mysqli extension supports both interpretations of a persistent connection: state persisted, and state reset before reuse. The default is reset. Before a persistent connection is reused, the mysqli extension implicitly calls mysqli_change_user to reset the state. The persistent connection appears to the user as if it was just opened. No artifacts from previous usages are visible.

The mysqli_change_user function is an expensive operation. For best performance, users may want to recompile the extension with the compile flag MYSQLI_NO_CHANGE_USER_ON_PCONNECT being set.

It is left to the user to choose between safe behavior and best performance. Both are valid optimization goals. For ease of use, the safe behavior has been made the default at the expense of maximum performance.

See also

mysqli::__construct
mysqli::init
mysqli::options
mysqli::real_connect
mysqli::change_user
$mysqli::host_info
MySQLi Configuration Options
Persistent Database Connections

3.2.3 Executing statements

Statements can be executed with the mysqli_query, mysqli_real_query and mysqli_multi_query functions. The mysqli_query function is the most common, and combines the

22

executing statement with a buffered fetch of its result set, if any, in one call. Calling mysqli_query is identical to calling mysqli_real_query followed by mysqli_store_result.

Example 3.6 Connecting to MySQL

```php
<?php
$mysqli = new mysqli("example.com", "user", "password", "database");
if ($mysqli->connect_errno) {
    echo "Failed to connect to MySQL: (" . $mysqli->connect_errno . ") " . $mysqli->connect_error;
}

if (!$mysqli->query("DROP TABLE IF EXISTS test") ||
    !$mysqli->query("CREATE TABLE test(id INT)") ||
    !$mysqli->query("INSERT INTO test(id) VALUES (1)")) {
    echo "Table creation failed: (" . $mysqli->errno . ") " . $mysqli->error;
}
?>
```

Buffered result sets

After statement execution results can be retrieved at once to be buffered by the client or by read row by row. Client-side result set buffering allows the server to free resources associated with the statement results as early as possible. Generally speaking, clients are slow consuming result sets. Therefore, it is recommended to use buffered result sets. mysqli_query combines statement execution and result set buffering.

PHP applications can navigate freely through buffered results. Navigation is fast because the result sets are held in client memory. Please, keep in mind that it is often easier to scale by client than it is to scale the server.

Example 3.7 Navigation through buffered results

```php
<?php
$mysqli = new mysqli("example.com", "user", "password", "database");
if ($mysqli->connect_errno) {
    echo "Failed to connect to MySQL: (" . $mysqli->connect_errno . ") " . $mysqli->connect_error;
}

if (!$mysqli->query("DROP TABLE IF EXISTS test") ||
    !$mysqli->query("CREATE TABLE test(id INT)") ||
    !$mysqli->query("INSERT INTO test(id) VALUES (1), (2), (3)")) {
    echo "Table creation failed: (" . $mysqli->errno . ") " . $mysqli->error;
}

$res = $mysqli->query("SELECT id FROM test ORDER BY id ASC");

echo "Reverse order...\n";
for ($row_no = $res->num_rows - 1; $row_no >= 0; $row_no--) {
    $res->data_seek($row_no);
    $row = $res->fetch_assoc();
    echo " id = " . $row['id'] . "\n";
}

echo "Result set order...\n";
```

```
$res->data_seek(0);
while ($row = $res->fetch_assoc()) {
    echo " id = " . $row['id'] . "\n";
}
```

2
3

```
?>
```

The above example will output:

```
Reverse order...
 id = 3
 id = 2
 id = 1
Result set order...
 id = 1
 id = 2
 id = 3
```

Unbuffered result sets

If client memory is a short resource and freeing server resources as early as possible to keep server load low is not needed, unbuffered results can be used. Scrolling through unbuffered results is not possible before all rows have been read.

Example 3.8 Navigation through unbuffered results

```php
<?php
$mysqli->real_query("SELECT id FROM test ORDER BY id
ASC"); $res = $mysqli->use_result();

echo "Result set order...\n";
while ($row = $res->fetch_assoc()) {
    echo " id = " . $row['id'] . "\n";
}
?>
```

Result set values data types

The mysqli_query, mysqli_real_query and mysqli_multi_query functions are used to execute non-prepared statements. At the level of the MySQL Client Server Protocol, the command COM_QUERY and the text protocol are used for statement execution. With the text protocol, the MySQL server converts all data of a result sets into strings before sending. This conversion is done regardless of the SQL result set column data type. The mysql client libraries receive all column values as strings. No further client-side casting is done to convert columns back to their native types. Instead, all values are provided as PHP strings.

Example 3.9 Text protocol returns strings by default

```php
<?php
$mysqli = new mysqli("example.com", "user", "password", "database");
if ($mysqli->connect_errno) {
    echo "Failed to connect to MySQL: (" . $mysqli->connect_errno . ") " . $mysqli->connect_error;
}

if (!$mysqli->query("DROP TABLE IF EXISTS test") ||
    !$mysqli->query("CREATE TABLE test(id INT, label CHAR(1))") ||
    !$mysqli->query("INSERT INTO test(id, label) VALUES (1, 'a')")) {
```

24

```
    echo "Table creation failed: (" . $mysqli->errno . ") " . $mysqli->error;
}

$res = $mysqli->query("SELECT id, label FROM test WHERE id = 1");
$row = $res->fetch_assoc();

printf("id = %s (%s)\n", $row['id'], gettype($row['id'])); printf("label = %s
(%s)\n", $row['label'], gettype($row['label'])); ?>
```

The above example will output:

```
id = 1 (string)
label = a (string)
```

It is possible to convert integer and float columns back to PHP numbers by setting the
MYSQLI_OPT_INT_AND_FLOAT_NATIVE connection option, if using the mysqlnd library. If set, the
mysqlnd library will check the result set meta data column types and convert numeric SQL columns to
PHP numbers, if the PHP data type value range allows for it. This way, for example, SQL INT columns are
returned as integers.

Example 3.10 Native data types with mysqlnd and connection option

```
<?php
$mysqli = mysqli_init();
$mysqli->options(MYSQLI_OPT_INT_AND_FLOAT_NATIVE, 1);
$mysqli->real_connect("example.com", "user", "password", "database");

if ($mysqli->connect_errno) {
    echo "Failed to connect to MySQL: (" . $mysqli->connect_errno . ") " . $mysqli->connect_error;
}

if (!$mysqli->query("DROP TABLE IF EXISTS test") ||
    !$mysqli->query("CREATE TABLE test(id INT, label CHAR(1))") ||
    !$mysqli->query("INSERT INTO test(id, label) VALUES (1, 'a')")) {
    echo "Table creation failed: (" . $mysqli->errno . ") " . $mysqli->error;
}

$res = $mysqli->query("SELECT id, label FROM test WHERE id = 1");
$row = $res->fetch_assoc();

printf("id = %s (%s)\n", $row['id'], gettype($row['id'])); printf("label = %s
(%s)\n", $row['label'], gettype($row['label'])); ?>
```

The above example will output:

```
id = 1 (integer)
label = a (string)
```

See also

3.2.4 Prepared Statements

The MySQL database supports prepared statements. A prepared statement or a parameterized statement is used to execute the same statement repeatedly with high efficiency.

Basic workflow

The prepared statement execution consists of two stages: prepare and execute. At the prepare stage a statement template is sent to the database server. The server performs a syntax check and initializes server internal resources for later use.

The MySQL server supports using anonymous, positional placeholder with ?.

Example 3.11 First stage: prepare

```php
<?php
$mysqli = new mysqli("example.com", "user", "password", "database");
if ($mysqli->connect_errno) {
    echo "Failed to connect to MySQL: (" . $mysqli->connect_errno . ") " . $mysqli->connect_error;
}

/* Non-prepared statement */
if (!$mysqli->query("DROP TABLE IF EXISTS test") || !$mysqli->query("CREATE TABLE test(id INT)")) { echo
    "Table creation failed: (" . $mysqli->errno . ") " . $mysqli->error;
}

/* Prepared statement, stage 1: prepare */
if (!($stmt = $mysqli->prepare("INSERT INTO test(id) VALUES (?)"))) { echo
    "Prepare failed: (" . $mysqli->errno . ") " . $mysqli->error;
}
?>
```

Prepare is followed by execute. During execute the client binds parameter values and sends them to the server. The server creates a statement from the statement template and the bound values to execute it using the previously created internal resources.

Example 3.12 Second stage: bind and execute

```php
<?php
```

```
/* Prepared statement, stage 2: bind and execute */
$id = 1;
if (!$stmt->bind_param("i", $id)) {
```

```
        echo "Binding parameters failed: (" . $stmt->errno . ") " . $stmt->error;
}

if (!$stmt->execute()) {
    echo "Execute failed: (" . $stmt->errno . ") " . $stmt->error;
}
?>
```

Repeated execution

A prepared statement can be executed repeatedly. Upon every execution the current value of the bound variable is evaluated and sent to the server. The statement is not parsed again. The statement template is not transferred to the server again.

Example 3.13 INSERT prepared once, executed multiple times

```
<?php
$mysqli = new mysqli("example.com", "user", "password", "database");
if ($mysqli->connect_errno) {
    echo "Failed to connect to MySQL: (" . $mysqli->connect_errno . ") " . $mysqli->connect_error;
}

/* Non-prepared statement */
if (!$mysqli->query("DROP TABLE IF EXISTS test") || !$mysqli->query("CREATE TABLE test(id INT)")) { echo
    "Table creation failed: (" . $mysqli->errno . ") " . $mysqli->error;
}

/* Prepared statement, stage 1: prepare */
if (!($stmt = $mysqli->prepare("INSERT INTO test(id) VALUES (?)"))) { echo
    "Prepare failed: (" . $mysqli->errno . ") " . $mysqli->error;
}

/* Prepared statement, stage 2: bind and execute */
$id = 1;
if (!$stmt->bind_param("i", $id)) {
    echo "Binding parameters failed: (" . $stmt->errno . ") " . $stmt->error;
}

if (!$stmt->execute()) {
    echo "Execute failed: (" . $stmt->errno . ") " . $stmt->error;
}

/* Prepared statement: repeated execution, only data transferred from client to server */ for
($id = 2; $id < 5; $id++) {
    if (!$stmt->execute()) {
        echo "Execute failed: (" . $stmt->errno . ") " . $stmt->error;
    }
}

/* explicit close recommended */
$stmt->close();

/* Non-prepared statement */
```

```
$res = $mysqli->query("SELECT id FROM test");
var_dump($res->fetch_all());
?>
```

The above example will output:

```
array(4) {
  [0]=>
  array(1) {
    [0]=>
    string(1) "1"
  }
  [1]=>
  array(1) {
    [0]=>
    string(1) "2"
  }
  [2]=>
  array(1) {
    [0]=>
    string(1) "3"
  }
  [3]=>
  array(1) {
    [0]=>
    string(1) "4"
  }
}
```

Every prepared statement occupies server resources. Statements should be closed explicitly immediately after use. If not done explicitly, the statement will be closed when the statement handle is freed by PHP.

Using a prepared statement is not always the most efficient way of executing a statement. A prepared statement executed only once causes more client-server round-trips than a non-prepared statement. This is why the SELECT is not run as a prepared statement above.

Also, consider the use of the MySQL multi-INSERT SQL syntax for INSERTs. For the example, multi-INSERT requires less round-trips between the server and client than the prepared statement shown above.

Example 3.14 Less round trips using multi-INSERT SQL

```php
<?php
if (!$mysqli->query("INSERT INTO test(id) VALUES (1), (2), (3), (4)")) { echo "Multi-
    INSERT failed: (" . $mysqli->errno . ") " . $mysqli->error;
}
?>
```

Result set values data types

The MySQL Client Server Protocol defines a different data transfer protocol for prepared statements and non-prepared statements. Prepared statements are using the so called binary protocol. The MySQL server sends result set data "as is" in binary format. Results are not serialized into strings before sending. The client libraries do not receive strings only. Instead, they will receive binary data and try to convert the values into appropriate PHP data types. For example, results from an SQL INT column will be provided as PHP integer variables.

Example 3.15 Native datatypes

```php
<?php
$mysqli = new mysqli("example.com", "user", "password", "database");
```

```
if ($mysqli->connect_errno) {
    echo "Failed to connect to MySQL: (" . $mysqli->connect_errno . ") " . $mysqli->connect_error;
}

if (!$mysqli->query("DROP TABLE IF EXISTS test") ||
    !$mysqli->query("CREATE TABLE test(id INT, label CHAR(1))") ||
    !$mysqli->query("INSERT INTO test(id, label) VALUES (1, 'a')")) {
    echo "Table creation failed: (" . $mysqli->errno . ") " . $mysqli->error;
}

$stmt = $mysqli->prepare("SELECT id, label FROM test WHERE id = 1");
$stmt->execute();
$res = $stmt->get_result();
$row = $res->fetch_assoc();

printf("id = %s (%s)\n", $row['id'], gettype($row['id'])); printf("label = %s
(%s)\n", $row['label'], gettype($row['label'])); ?>
```

The above example will output:

```
id = 1 (integer)
label = a (string)
```

This behavior differs from non-prepared statements. By default, non-prepared statements return all results as strings. This default can be changed using a connection option. If the connection option is used, there are no differences.

Fetching results using bound variables

Results from prepared statements can either be retrieved by binding output variables, or by requesting a mysqli_result object.

Output variables must be bound after statement execution. One variable must be bound for every column of the statements result set.

Example 3.16 Output variable binding

```
<?php
$mysqli = new mysqli("example.com", "user", "password", "database");
if ($mysqli->connect_errno) {
    echo "Failed to connect to MySQL: (" . $mysqli->connect_errno . ") " . $mysqli->connect_error;
}

if (!$mysqli->query("DROP TABLE IF EXISTS test") ||
    !$mysqli->query("CREATE TABLE test(id INT, label CHAR(1))") ||
    !$mysqli->query("INSERT INTO test(id, label) VALUES (1, 'a')")) {
    echo "Table creation failed: (" . $mysqli->errno . ") " . $mysqli->error;
}

if (!($stmt = $mysqli->prepare("SELECT id, label FROM test"))) {
    echo "Prepare failed: (" . $mysqli->errno . ") " . $mysqli->error;
}
```

```
if (!$stmt->execute()) {
    echo "Execute failed: (" . $mysqli->errno . ") " . $mysqli->error;
}
```

```
$out_id    = NULL;
$out_label = NULL;
if (!$stmt->bind_result($out_id, $out_label)) {
    echo "Binding output parameters failed: (" . $stmt->errno . ") " . $stmt->error;
}

while ($stmt->fetch()) {
    printf("id = %s (%s), label = %s (%s)\n", $out_id, gettype($out_id), $out_label, gettype($out_label));
}
?>
```

The above example will output:

```
id = 1 (integer), label = a (string)
```

Prepared statements return unbuffered result sets by default. The results of the statement are not implicitly fetched and transferred from the server to the client for client-side buffering. The result set takes server resources until all results have been fetched by the client. Thus it is recommended to consume results timely. If a client fails to fetch all results or the client closes the statement before having fetched all data, the data has to be fetched implicitly by mysqli.

It is also possible to buffer the results of a prepared statement using mysqli_stmt_store_result.

Fetching results using mysqli_result interface

Instead of using bound results, results can also be retrieved through the mysqli_result interface. mysqli_stmt_get_result returns a buffered result set.

Example 3.17 Using mysqli_result to fetch results

```
<?php
$mysqli = new mysqli("example.com", "user", "password", "database");
if ($mysqli->connect_errno) {
    echo "Failed to connect to MySQL: (" . $mysqli->connect_errno . ") " . $mysqli->connect_error;
}

if (!$mysqli->query("DROP TABLE IF EXISTS test") ||
    !$mysqli->query("CREATE TABLE test(id INT, label CHAR(1))") ||
    !$mysqli->query("INSERT INTO test(id, label) VALUES (1, 'a')")) {
    echo "Table creation failed: (" . $mysqli->errno . ") " . $mysqli->error;
}

if (!($stmt = $mysqli->prepare("SELECT id, label FROM test ORDER BY id ASC"))) {
    echo "Prepare failed: (" . $mysqli->errno . ") " . $mysqli->error;
}

if (!$stmt->execute()) {
    echo "Execute failed: (" . $stmt->errno . ") " . $stmt->error;
}

if (!($res = $stmt->get_result())) {
```

```
        echo "Getting result set failed: (" . $stmt->errno . ") " . $stmt->error;
}

var_dump($res->fetch_all());
```

30

```
?>
```

The above example will output:

```
array(1) {
  [0]=>
  array(2) {
    [0]=>
    int(1)
    [1]=>
    string(1) "a"
  }
}
```

Using the mysqli_result interface offers the additional benefit of flexible client-side result set navigation.

Example 3.18 Buffered result set for flexible read out

```php
<?php
$mysqli = new mysqli("example.com", "user", "password", "database");
if ($mysqli->connect_errno) {
    echo "Failed to connect to MySQL: (" . $mysqli->connect_errno . ") " . $mysqli->connect_error;
}

if (!$mysqli->query("DROP TABLE IF EXISTS test") ||
    !$mysqli->query("CREATE TABLE test(id INT, label CHAR(1))") ||
    !$mysqli->query("INSERT INTO test(id, label) VALUES (1, 'a'), (2, 'b'), (3, 'c')")) { echo "Table
    creation failed: (" . $mysqli->errno . ") " . $mysqli->error;
}

if (!($stmt = $mysqli->prepare("SELECT id, label FROM test"))) {
    echo "Prepare failed: (" . $mysqli->errno . ") " . $mysqli->error;
}

if (!$stmt->execute()) {
    echo "Execute failed: (" . $stmt->errno . ") " . $stmt->error;
}

if (!($res = $stmt->get_result())) {
    echo "Getting result set failed: (" . $stmt->errno . ") " . $stmt->error;
}

for ($row_no = ($res->num_rows - 1); $row_no >= 0; $row_no--) {
    $res->data_seek($row_no);
    var_dump($res->fetch_assoc());
}
$res->close();
?>
```

The above example will output:

```
array(2) {
  ["Id"]=>
```

```
   int(3)
   ["label"]=>
   string(1) "c"
}
array(2) {
   ["id"]=>
   int(2)
   ["label"]=>
   string(1) "b"
}
array(2) {
   ["id"]=>
   int(1)
   ["label"]=>
   string(1) "a"
}
```

Escaping and SQL injection

Bound variables are sent to the server separately from the query and thus cannot interfere with it. The server uses these values directly at the point of execution, after the statement template is parsed. Bound parameters do not need to be escaped as they are never substituted into the query string directly. A hint must be provided to the server for the type of bound variable, to create an appropriate conversion. See the mysqli_stmt_bind_param function for more information.

Such a separation sometimes considered as the only security feature to prevent SQL injection, but the same degree of security can be achieved with non-prepared statements, if all the values are formatted correctly. It should be noted that correct formatting is not the same as escaping and involves more logic than simple escaping. Thus, prepared statements are simply a more convenient and less error-prone approach to this element of database security.

Client-side prepared statement emulation

The API does not include emulation for client-side prepared statement emulation.

Quick prepared - non-prepared statement comparison

The table below compares server-side prepared and non-prepared statements.

Table 3.2 Comparison of prepared and non-prepared statements

	Prepared Statement	Non-prepared statement
Client-server round trips, SELECT, single execution	2	1
Statement string transferred from client to server	1	1
Client-server round trips, SELECT, repeated (n) execution	1 + n	n
Statement string transferred from client to server	1 template, n times bound parameter, if any	n times together with parameter, if any
Input parameter binding API	Yes, automatic input escaping	No, manual input escaping
Output variable binding API	Yes	No
Supports use of mysqli_result API	Yes, use mysqli_stmt_get_result	Yes

32

	Prepared Statement	Non-prepared statement
Buffered result sets	Yes, use mysqli_stmt_get_result or binding with mysqli_stmt_store_result	Yes, default of mysqli_query
Unbuffered result sets	Yes, use output binding API	Yes, use mysqli_real_query with mysqli_use_result
MySQL Client Server protocol data transfer flavor	Binary protocol	Text protocol
Result set values SQL data types	Preserved when fetching	Converted to string or preserved when fetching
Supports all SQL statements	Recent MySQL versions support most but not all	Yes

See also

mysqli::__construct
mysqli::query
mysqli::prepare
mysqli_stmt::prepare
mysqli_stmt::execute
mysqli_stmt::bind_param
mysqli_stmt::bind_result

3.2.5 Stored Procedures

The MySQL database supports stored procedures. A stored procedure is a subroutine stored in the database catalog. Applications can call and execute the stored procedure. The CALL SQL statement is used to execute a stored procedure.

Parameter

Stored procedures can have IN, INOUT and OUT parameters, depending on the MySQL version. The mysqli interface has no special notion for the different kinds of parameters.

IN parameter

Input parameters are provided with the CALL statement. Please, make sure values are escaped correctly.

Example 3.19 Calling a stored procedure

```php
<?php
$mysqli = new mysqli("example.com", "user", "password", "database");
if ($mysqli->connect_errno) {
    echo "Failed to connect to MySQL: (" . $mysqli->connect_errno . ") " . $mysqli->connect_error;
}

if (!$mysqli->query("DROP TABLE IF EXISTS test") || !$mysqli->query("CREATE TABLE test(id INT)")) { echo
    "Table creation failed: (" . $mysqli->errno . ") " . $mysqli->error;
}
```

3
3

```php
if (!$mysqli->query("DROP PROCEDURE IF EXISTS p") ||
    !$mysqli->query("CREATE PROCEDURE p(IN id_val INT) BEGIN INSERT INTO test(id) VALUES(id_val); END;")) {
    echo "Stored procedure creation failed: (" . $mysqli->errno . ") " . $mysqli->error;
}

if (!$mysqli->query("CALL p(1)")) {
    echo "CALL failed: (" . $mysqli->errno . ") " . $mysqli->error;
}

if (!($res = $mysqli->query("SELECT id FROM test"))) {
    echo "SELECT failed: (" . $mysqli->errno . ") " . $mysqli->error;
}

var_dump($res->fetch_assoc());
?>
```

The above example will output:

```
array(1) {
  ["id"]=>
  string(1) "1"
}
```

INOUT/OUT parameter

The values of INOUT/OUT parameters are accessed using session variables.

Example 3.20 Using session variables

```php
<?php
$mysqli = new mysqli("example.com", "user", "password", "database");
if ($mysqli->connect_errno) {
    echo "Failed to connect to MySQL: (" . $mysqli->connect_errno . ") " . $mysqli->connect_error;
}

if (!$mysqli->query("DROP PROCEDURE IF EXISTS p") ||
    !$mysqli->query('CREATE PROCEDURE p(OUT msg VARCHAR(50)) BEGIN SELECT "Hi!" INTO msg;
    END;')) { echo "Stored procedure creation failed: (" . $mysqli->errno . ") " . $mysqli->error;
}

if (!$mysqli->query("SET @msg = ''") || !$mysqli->query("CALL p(@msg)")) {
    echo "CALL failed: (" . $mysqli->errno . ") " . $mysqli->error;
}

if (!($res = $mysqli->query("SELECT @msg as _p_out"))) {
    echo "Fetch failed: (" . $mysqli->errno . ") " . $mysqli->error;
}

$row = $res->fetch_assoc();
echo $row['_p_out'];
?>
```

The above example will output:

Hi!

Application and framework developers may be able to provide a more convenient API using a mix of session variables and databased catalog inspection. However, please note the possible performance impact of a custom solution based on catalog inspection.

Handling result sets

Stored procedures can return result sets. Result sets returned from a stored procedure cannot be fetched correctly using mysqli_query. The mysqli_query function combines statement execution and fetching the first result set into a buffered result set, if any. However, there are additional stored procedure result sets hidden from the user which cause mysqli_query to fail returning the user expected result sets.

Result sets returned from a stored procedure are fetched using mysqli_real_query or mysqli_multi_query. Both functions allow fetching any number of result sets returned by a statement, such as CALL. Failing to fetch all result sets returned by a stored procedure causes an error.

Example 3.21 Fetching results from stored procedures

```php
<?php
$mysqli = new mysqli("example.com", "user", "password", "database");
if ($mysqli->connect_errno) {
    echo "Failed to connect to MySQL: (" . $mysqli->connect_errno . ") " . $mysqli->connect_error;
}

if (!$mysqli->query("DROP TABLE IF EXISTS test") ||
    !$mysqli->query("CREATE TABLE test(id INT)") ||
    !$mysqli->query("INSERT INTO test(id) VALUES (1), (2), (3)")) {
    echo "Table creation failed: (" . $mysqli->errno . ") " . $mysqli->error;
}

if (!$mysqli->query("DROP PROCEDURE IF EXISTS p") ||
    !$mysqli->query('CREATE PROCEDURE p() READS SQL DATA BEGIN SELECT id FROM test; SELECT id + 1
    FROM tes echo "Stored procedure creation failed: (" . $mysqli->errno . ") " . $mysqli->error;
}

if (!$mysqli->multi_query("CALL p()")) {
    echo "CALL failed: (" . $mysqli->errno . ") " . $mysqli->error;
}

do {
    if ($res = $mysqli->store_result()) {
        printf("—\n");
        var_dump($res->fetch_all());
        $res->free();
    } else {
        if ($mysqli->errno) {
            echo "Store failed: (" . $mysqli->errno . ") " . $mysqli->error;
        }
    }
} while ($mysqli->more_results() && $mysqli->next_result()); ?>
```

The above example will output:

```
—
array(3) {
  [0]=>
  array(1) {
    [0]=>
    string(1) "1"
  }
  [1]=>
  array(1) {
    [0]=>
    string(1) "2"
  }
  [2]=>
  array(1) {
    [0]=>
    string(1) "3"
  }
}
—
array(3) {
  [0]=>
  array(1) {
    [0]=>
    string(1) "2"
  }
  [1]=>
  array(1) {
    [0]=>
    string(1) "3"
  }
  [2]=>
  array(1) {
    [0]=>
    string(1) "4"
  }
}
```

Use of prepared statements

No special handling is required when using the prepared statement interface for fetching results from the same stored procedure as above. The prepared statement and non-prepared statement interfaces are similar. Please note, that not every MYSQL server version may support preparing the CALL SQL statement.

Example 3.22 Stored Procedures and Prepared Statements

```php
<?php
$mysqli = new mysqli("example.com", "user", "password", "database");
if ($mysqli->connect_errno) {
    echo "Failed to connect to MySQL: (" . $mysqli->connect_errno . ") " . $mysqli->connect_error;
}

if (!$mysqli->query("DROP TABLE IF EXISTS test") ||
    !$mysqli->query("CREATE TABLE test(id INT)") ||
    !$mysqli->query("INSERT INTO test(id) VALUES (1), (2), (3)")) {
    echo "Table creation failed: (" . $mysqli->errno . ") " . $mysqli->error;
}

if (!$mysqli->query("DROP PROCEDURE IF EXISTS p") ||
    !$mysqli->query('CREATE PROCEDURE p() READS SQL DATA BEGIN SELECT id FROM test; SELECT id + 1 FROM
test; E echo "Stored procedure creation failed: (" . $mysqli->errno . ") " . $mysqli->error;
}
```

36

Multiple Statements

```php
if (!($stmt = $mysqli->prepare("CALL p()"))) {
    echo "Prepare failed: (" . $mysqli->errno . ") " . $mysqli->error;
}

if (!$stmt->execute()) {
    echo "Execute failed: (" . $stmt->errno . ") " . $stmt->error;
}

do {
    if ($res = $stmt->get_result()) {
        printf("—\n");
        var_dump(mysqli_fetch_all($res));
        mysqli_free_result($res);
    } else {
        if ($stmt->errno) {
            echo "Store failed: (" . $stmt->errno . ") " . $stmt->error;
        }
    }
} while ($stmt->more_results() && $stmt->next_result()); ?>
```

Of course, use of the bind API for fetching is supported as well.

Example 3.23 Stored Procedures and Prepared Statements using bind API

```php
<?php
if (!($stmt = $mysqli->prepare("CALL p()"))) {
    echo "Prepare failed: (" . $mysqli->errno . ") " . $mysqli->error;
}

if (!$stmt->execute()) {
    echo "Execute failed: (" . $stmt->errno . ") " . $stmt->error;
}

do {

    $id_out = NULL;
    if (!$stmt->bind_result($id_out)) {
        echo "Bind failed: (" . $stmt->errno . ") " . $stmt->error;
    }

    while ($stmt->fetch()) {
        echo "id = $id_out\n";
    }
} while ($stmt->more_results() && $stmt->next_result()); ?>
```

See also

mysqli::query
mysqli::multi_query
mysqli_result::next-result
mysqli_result::more-results

3.2.6 Multiple Statements

MySQL optionally allows having multiple statements in one statement string. Sending multiple statements at once reduces client-server round trips but requires special handling.

Multiple statements or multi queries must be executed with mysqli_multi_query. The individual statements of the statement string are separated by semicolon. Then, all result sets returned by the executed statements must be fetched.

The MySQL server allows having statements that do return result sets and statements that do not return result sets in one multiple statement.

Example 3.24 Multiple Statements

```php
<?php
$mysqli = new mysqli("example.com", "user", "password", "database");
if ($mysqli->connect_errno) {
    echo "Failed to connect to MySQL: (" . $mysqli->connect_errno . ") " . $mysqli->connect_error;
}

if (!$mysqli->query("DROP TABLE IF EXISTS test") || !$mysqli->query("CREATE TABLE test(id INT)")) { echo
    "Table creation failed: (" . $mysqli->errno . ") " . $mysqli->error;
}

$sql = "SELECT COUNT(*) AS _num FROM test; ";
$sql.= "INSERT INTO test(id) VALUES (1); ";
$sql.= "SELECT COUNT(*) AS _num FROM test; ";

if (!$mysqli->multi_query($sql)) {
    echo "Multi query failed: (" . $mysqli->errno . ") " . $mysqli->error;
}

do {
    if ($res = $mysqli->store_result()) {
        var_dump($res->fetch_all(MYSQLI_ASSOC));
        $res->free();
    }
} while ($mysqli->more_results() && $mysqli->next_result()); ?>
```

The above example will output:

```
array(1) {
  [0]=>
  array(1) {
    ["_num"]=>
    string(1) "0"
  }
}
array(1) {
  [0]=>
  array(1) {
    ["_num"]=>
    string(1) "1"
  }
}
```

8

The API functions mysqli_query and mysqli_real_query do not set a connection flag necessary for activating multi queries in the server. An extra API call is used for multiple statements to reduce the likeliness of accidental SQL injection attacks. An attacker may try to add statements such as ; DROP DATABASE mysql or ; SELECT SLEEP(999). If the attacker succeeds in adding SQL to the statement string but mysqli_multi_query is not used, the server will not execute the second, injected and malicious SQL statement.

Example 3.25 SQL Injection

```
<?php
$mysqli = new mysqli("example.com", "user", "password", "database");
$res = $mysqli->query("SELECT 1; DROP TABLE mysql.user"); if
(!$res) {
    echo "Error executing query: (" . $mysqli->errno . ") " . $mysqli->error;
}
?>
```

The above example will output:

```
Error executing query: (1064) You have an error in your SQL syntax;
check the manual that corresponds to your MySQL server version for the right syntax to
use near 'DROP TABLE mysql.user' at line 1
```

Prepared statements

Use of the multiple statement with prepared statements is not supported.

See also

mysqli::query
mysqli::multi_query
mysqli_result::next-result
mysqli_result::more-results

3.2.7 API support for transactions

The MySQL server supports transactions depending on the storage engine used. Since MySQL 5.5, the default storage engine is InnoDB. InnoDB has full ACID transaction support.

Transactions can either be controlled using SQL or API calls. It is recommended to use API calls for enabling and disabling the auto commit mode and for committing and rolling back transactions.

Example 3.26 Setting auto commit mode with SQL and through the API

```
<?php
$mysqli = new mysqli("example.com", "user", "password", "database");
if ($mysqli->connect_errno) {
        echo "Failed to connect to MySQL: (" . $mysqli->connect_errno . ") " . $mysqli->connect_error;
```

```
/* Recommended: using API to control transactional settings */
$mysqli->autocommit(false);

/* Won't be monitored and recognized by the replication and the load balancing plugin */ if
(!$mysqli->query('SET AUTOCOMMIT = 0')) {
    echo "Query failed: (" . $mysqli->errno . ") " . $mysqli->error;
}
?>
```

Optional feature packages, such as the replication and load balancing plugin, can easily monitor API calls. The replication plugin offers transaction aware load balancing, if transactions are controlled with API calls. Transaction aware load balancing is not available if SQL statements are used for setting auto commit mode, committing or rolling back a transaction.

Example 3.27 Commit and rollback

```
<?php
$mysqli = new mysqli("example.com", "user", "password", "database");
$mysqli->autocommit(false);

$mysqli->query("INSERT INTO test(id) VALUES (1)");
$mysqli->rollback();

$mysqli->query("INSERT INTO test(id) VALUES (2)");
$mysqli->commit();
?>
```

Please note, that the MySQL server cannot roll back all statements. Some statements cause an implicit commit.

See also

mysqli::autocommit
mysqli_result::commit
mysqli_result::rollback

3.2.8 Metadata

A MySQL result set contains metadata. The metadata describes the columns found in the result set. All metadata sent by MySQL is accessible through the mysqli interface. The extension performs no or negligible changes to the information it receives. Differences between MySQL server versions are not aligned.

Meta data is access through the mysqli_result interface.

Example 3.28 Accessing result set meta data

```
<?php
```

```php
$mysqli = new mysqli("example.com", "user", "password", "database");
if ($mysqli->connect_errno) {
```

```php
    echo "Failed to connect to MySQL: (" . $mysqli->connect_errno . ") " . $mysqli->connect_error;
}

$res = $mysqli->query("SELECT 1 AS _one, 'Hello' AS _two FROM DUAL");
var_dump($res->fetch_fields());
?>
```

The above example will output:

```
array(2) {
  [0]=>
  object(stdClass)#3 (13) {
    ["name"]=>
    string(4) "_one"
    ["orgname"]=>
    string(0) ""
    ["table"]=>
    string(0) ""
    ["orgtable"]=>
    string(0) ""
    ["def"]=>
    string(0) ""
    ["db"]=>
    string(0) ""
    ["catalog"]=>
    string(3) "def"
    ["max_length"]=>
    int(1)
    ["length"]=>
    int(1)
    ["charsetnr"]=>
    int(63)
    ["flags"]=>
    int(32897)
    ["type"]=>
    int(8)
    ["decimals"]=>
    int(0)
  }
  [1]=>
  object(stdClass)#4 (13) {
    ["name"]=>
    string(4) "_two"
    ["orgname"]=>
    string(0) ""
    ["table"]=>
    string(0) ""
    ["orgtable"]=>
    string(0) ""
    ["def"]=>
    string(0) ""
```

```
["db"]=>
string(0) ""
["catalog"]=>
string(3) "def"
["max_length"]=>
int(5)
["length"]=>
int(5)
["charsetnr"]=>
int(8)
["flags"]=>
int(1)
```

_____
4
1

```
      ["type"]=>
      int(253)
      ["decimals"]=>
      int(31)
   }
}
```

Prepared statements

Meta data of result sets created using prepared statements are accessed the same way. A suitable mysqli_result handle is returned by mysqli_stmt_result_metadata.

Example 3.29 Prepared statements metadata

```php
<?php
$stmt = $mysqli->prepare("SELECT 1 AS _one, 'Hello' AS _two FROM DUAL");
$stmt->execute();
$res = $stmt->result_metadata();
var_dump($res->fetch_fields());
?>
```

See also

mysqli::query
mysqli_result::fetch_fields

3.3 Installing/Configuring

3.3.1 Requirements

In order to have these functions available, you must compile PHP with support for the mysqli extension.

MySQL 8

When running a PHP version before 7.1.16, or PHP 7.2 before 7.2.4, set MySQL 8 Server's default password plugin to *mysql_native_password* or else you will see errors similar to *The server requested authentication method unknown to the client [caching_sha2_password]* even when *caching_sha2_password* is not used.

This is because MySQL 8 defaults to caching_sha2_password, a plugin that is not recognized by the older PHP (mysqlnd) releases. Instead, change it by setting default_authentication_plugin=mysql_native_password in my.cnf. The *caching_sha2_password* plugin will be supported in a future PHP release. In the meantime, the mysql_xdevapi extension does support it.

3.3.2 Installation

The mysqli extension was introduced with PHP version 5.0.0. The MySQL Native Driver was included in PHP version 5.3.0.

3.3.2.1 Installation on Linux

The common Unix distributions include binary versions of PHP that can be installed. Although these binary versions are typically built with support for the MySQL extensions, the extension libraries themselves may need to be installed using an additional package. Check the package manager that comes with your chosen distribution for availability.

For example, on Ubuntu the php5-mysql package installs the ext/mysql, ext/mysqli, and pdo_mysql PHP extensions. On CentOS, the php-mysql package also installs these three PHP extensions.

Alternatively, you can compile this extension yourself. Building PHP from source allows you to specify the MySQL extensions you want to use, as well as your choice of client library for each extension.

The MySQL Native Driver is the recommended client library option, as it results in improved performance and gives access to features not available when using the MySQL Client Library. Refer to What is PHP's MySQL Native Driver? for a brief overview of the advantages of MySQL Native Driver.

The /path/to/mysql_config represents the location of the mysql_config program that comes with MySQL Server.

Table 3.3 mysqli compile time support matrix

PHP Version	Default	Configure Options: mysqlnd	Configure Options: libmysqlclient	Changelog
5.4.x and above	mysqlnd	–with-mysqli	–with-mysqli=/path/to/mysql_config	mysqlnd is the default
5.3.x	libmysqlclient	–with-mysqli=mysqlnd	–with-mysqli=/path/to/mysql_config	mysqlnd is supported
5.0.x, 5.1.x, 5.2.x	libmysqlclient	Not Available	–with-mysqli=/path/to/mysql_config	mysqlnd is not supported

Note that it is possible to freely mix MySQL extensions and client libraries. For example, it is possible to enable the MySQL extension to use the MySQL Client Library (libmysqlclient), while configuring the mysqli extension to use the MySQL Native Driver. However, all permutations of extension and client library are possible.

3.3.2.2 Installation on Windows Systems

On Windows, PHP is most commonly installed using the binary installer.

PHP 5.3.0 and newer

On Windows, for PHP versions 5.3 and newer, the mysqli extension is enabled and uses the MySQL Native Driver by default. This means you don't need to worry about configuring access to libmysql.dll.

PHP 5.0, 5.1, 5.2

On these old unsupported PHP versions (PHP 5.2 reached EOL on '6 Jan 2011'), additional configuration procedures are required to enable mysqli and specify the client library you want it to use.

The mysqli extension is not enabled by default, so the php_mysqli.dll DLL must be enabled inside of php.ini. In order to do this you need to find the php.ini file (typically located in c:\php), and make sure you remove the comment (semi-colon) from the start of the line extension=php_mysqli.dll, in the section marked [PHP_MYSQLI].

Also, if you want to use the MySQL Client Library with mysqli, you need to make sure PHP can access the client library file. The MySQL Client Library is included as a file named libmysql.dll in the Windows PHP distribution. This file needs to be available in the Windows system's PATH environment variable, so that it can be successfully loaded. See the FAQ titled "How do I add my PHP directory to the PATH on Windows" for information on how to do this. Copying libmysql.dll to the Windows system directory (typically c:\Windows\system) also works, as the system directory is by default in the system's PATH. However, this practice is strongly discouraged.

As with enabling any PHP extension (such as php_mysqli.dll), the PHP directive extension_dir should be set to the directory where the PHP extensions are located. See also the Manual Windows Installation Instructions. An example extension_dir value for PHP 5 is c:\php\ext.

Note

If when starting the web server an error similar to the following occurs: "Unable to load dynamic library './php_mysqli.dll'", this is because php_mysqli.dll and/or libmysql.dll cannot be found by the system.

3.3.3 Runtime Configuration

The behaviour of these functions is affected by settings in php.ini.

Table 3.4 MySQLi Configuration Options

Name	Default	Changeable	Changelog
mysqli.allow_local_infile	"0"	PHP_INI_SYSTEM	Available as of PHP 5.2.4. Before PHP 7.2.16 and 7.3.3 the default was "1".
mysqli.allow_persistent	"1"	PHP_INI_SYSTEM	Available as of PHP 5.3.0.
mysqli.max_persistent	"-1"	PHP_INI_SYSTEM	Available as of PHP 5.3.0.
mysqli.max_links	"-1"	PHP_INI_SYSTEM	
mysqli.default_port	"3306"	PHP_INI_ALL	

Name	Default	Changeable	Changelog
mysqli.default_socket	NULL	PHP_INI_ALL	
mysqli.default_host	NULL	PHP_INI_ALL	
mysqli.default_user	NULL	PHP_INI_ALL	
mysqli.default_pw	NULL	PHP_INI_ALL	
mysqli.reconnect	"0"	PHP_INI_SYSTEM	
mysqli.rollback_on_cached	TRUEplink —	PHP_INI_SYSTEM	Available as of PHP 5.6.0.

For further details and definitions of the preceding PHP_INI_* constants, see the chapter on configuration changes.

Here's a short explanation of the configuration directives.

mysqli.allow_local_infile integer — Allow accessing, from PHP's perspective, local files with LOAD DATA statements

mysqli.allow_persistent integer — Enable the ability to create persistent connections using mysqli_connect.

mysqli.max_persistent integer — Maximum of persistent connections that can be made. Set to 0 for unlimited.

mysqli.max_links integer — The maximum number of MySQL connections per process.

mysqli.default_port integer — The default TCP port number to use when connecting to the database server if no other port is specified. If no default is specified, the port will be obtained from the MYSQL_TCP_PORT environment variable, the mysql-tcp entry in /etc/services or the compile-time MYSQL_PORT constant, in that order. Win32 will only use the MYSQL_PORT constant.

mysqli.default_socket string — The default socket name to use when connecting to a local database server if no other socket name is specified.

mysqli.default_host string — The default server host to use when connecting to the database server if no other host is specified. Doesn't apply insafe mode.

mysqli.default_user string — The default user name to use when connecting to the database server if no other name is specified. Doesn't apply insafe mode.

mysqli.default_pw string — The default password to use when connecting to the database server if no other password is specified. Doesn't apply insafe mode.

mysqli.reconnect integer — Automatically reconnect if the connection was lost.

> **Note**
>
> This php.ini setting is ignored by the mysqlnd driver.

mysqli.rollback_on_cached_link bool *If* *plink* this option is enabled, closing a persistent connection will rollback any pending transactions of this connection before it is put back into the persistent connection pool. Otherwise, pending transactions will be

4
5

rolled back only when the connection is reused, or when it is actually closed.

Users cannot set MYSQL_OPT_READ_TIMEOUT through an API call or runtime configuration setting. Note that if it were possible there would be differences between how libmysqlclient and streams would interpret the value of MYSQL_OPT_READ_TIMEOUT.

3.3.4 Resource Types

This extension has no resource types defined.

3.4 The mysqli Extension and Persistent Connections

Persistent connection support was introduced in PHP 5.3 for the mysqli extension. Support was already present in PDO MYSQL and ext/mysql. The idea behind persistent connections is that a connection between a client process and a database can be reused by a client process, rather than being created and destroyed multiple times. This reduces the overhead of creating fresh connections every time one is required, as unused connections are cached and ready to be reused.

Unlike the mysql extension, mysqli does not provide a separate function for opening persistent connections. To open a persistent connection you must prepend p: to the hostname when connecting.

The problem with persistent connections is that they can be left in unpredictable states by clients. For example, a table lock might be activated before a client terminates unexpectedly. A new client process reusing this persistent connection will get the connection "as is".Any cleanup would need to be done by the new client process before it could make good use of the persistent connection, increasing the burden on the programmer.

The persistent connection of the mysqli extension however provides built-in cleanup handling code. The cleanup carried out by mysqli includes:

- Rollback active transactions

- Close and drop temporary tables

- Unlock tables

- Reset session variables

- Close prepared statements (always happens with PHP)

- Close handler

- Release locks acquired with GET_LOCK

This ensures that persistent connections are in a clean state on return from the connection pool, before the client process uses them.

The mysqli extension does this cleanup by automatically calling the C-API function mysql_change_user().

The automatic cleanup feature has advantages and disadvantages though. The advantage is that the programmer no longer needs to worry about adding cleanup code, as it is called automatically. However,

the disadvantage is that the code could *potentially* be a little slower, as the code to perform the cleanup needs to run each time a connection is returned from the connection pool.

It is possible to switch off the automatic cleanup code, by compiling PHP with MYSQLI_NO_CHANGE_USER_ON_PCONNECT defined.

> **Note**
>
> The mysqli extension supports persistent connections when using either MySQL Native Driver or MySQL Client Library.

3.5 Predefined Constants

The constants below are defined by this extension, and will only be available when the extension has either been compiled into PHP or dynamically loaded at runtime.

MYSQLI_READ_DEFAULT_GROUP	Read options from the named group from my.cnf or the file specified with MYSQLI_READ_DEFAULT_FILE
MYSQLI_READ_DEFAULT_FILE	Read options from the named option file instead of from my.cnf
MYSQLI_OPT_CONNECT_TIMEOUT	Connect timeout in seconds
MYSQLI_OPT_LOCAL_INFILE	Enables command LOAD LOCAL INFILE
MYSQLI_INIT_COMMAND	Command to execute when connecting to MySQL server. Will automatically be re-executed when reconnecting.
MYSQLI_CLIENT_SSL	Use SSL (encrypted protocol). This option should not be set by application programs; it is set internally in the MySQL client library
MYSQLI_CLIENT_COMPRESS	Use compression protocol
MYSQLI_CLIENT_INTERACTIVE	Allow interactive_timeout seconds (instead of wait_timeout seconds) of inactivity before closing the connection. The client's session wait_timeout variable will be set to the value of the session interactive_timeout variable.
MYSQLI_CLIENT_IGNORE_SPACE	Allow spaces after function names. Makes all functions names reserved words.
MYSQLI_CLIENT_NO_SCHEMA	Don't allow the db_name.tbl_name.col_name syntax.
MYSQLI_CLIENT_MULTI_QUERIES	Allows multiple semicolon-delimited queries in a single mysqli_query call.
MYSQLI_STORE_RESULT	For using buffered resultsets
MYSQLI_USE_RESULT	For using unbuffered resultsets
MYSQLI_ASSOC	Columns are returned into the array having the fieldname as the array index.
MYSQLI_NUM	Columns are returned into the array having an enumerated index.
MYSQLI_BOTH	Columns are returned into the array having both a numerical index and the fieldname as the associative index.

4
7

MYSQLI_NOT_NULL_FLAG	Indicates that a field is defined as NOT NULL
MYSQLI_PRI_KEY_FLAG	Field is part of a primary index
MYSQLI_UNIQUE_KEY_FLAG	Field is part of a unique index.
MYSQLI_MULTIPLE_KEY_FLAG	Field is part of an index.
MYSQLI_BLOB_FLAG	Field is defined as BLOB
MYSQLI_UNSIGNED_FLAG	Field is defined as UNSIGNED
MYSQLI_ZEROFILL_FLAG	Field is defined as ZEROFILL
MYSQLI_AUTO_INCREMENT_FLAG	Field is defined as AUTO_INCREMENT
MYSQLI_TIMESTAMP_FLAG	Field is defined as TIMESTAMP
MYSQLI_SET_FLAG	Field is defined as SET
MYSQLI_NUM_FLAG	Field is defined as NUMERIC
MYSQLI_PART_KEY_FLAG	Field is part of an multi-index
MYSQLI_GROUP_FLAG	Field is part of GROUP BY
MYSQLI_TYPE_DECIMAL	Field is defined as DECIMAL
MYSQLI_TYPE_NEWDECIMAL	Precision math DECIMAL or NUMERIC field (MySQL 5.0.3 and up)
MYSQLI_TYPE_BIT	Field is defined as BIT (MySQL 5.0.3 and up)
MYSQLI_TYPE_TINY	Field is defined as TINYINT
MYSQLI_TYPE_SHORT	Field is defined as SMALLINT
MYSQLI_TYPE_LONG	Field is defined as INT
MYSQLI_TYPE_FLOAT	Field is defined as FLOAT
MYSQLI_TYPE_DOUBLE	Field is defined as DOUBLE
MYSQLI_TYPE_NULL	Field is defined as DEFAULT NULL
MYSQLI_TYPE_TIMESTAMP	Field is defined as TIMESTAMP
MYSQLI_TYPE_LONGLONG	Field is defined as BIGINT
MYSQLI_TYPE_INT24	Field is defined as MEDIUMINT
MYSQLI_TYPE_DATE	Field is defined as DATE
MYSQLI_TYPE_TIME	Field is defined as TIME
MYSQLI_TYPE_DATETIME	Field is defined as DATETIME
MYSQLI_TYPE_YEAR	Field is defined as YEAR
MYSQLI_TYPE_NEWDATE	Field is defined as DATE

48

MYSQLI_TYPE_INTERVAL	Field is defined as INTERVAL
MYSQLI_TYPE_ENUM	Field is defined as ENUM
MYSQLI_TYPE_SET	Field is defined as SET
MYSQLI_TYPE_TINY_BLOB	Field is defined as TINYBLOB
MYSQLI_TYPE_MEDIUM_BLOB	Field is defined as MEDIUMBLOB
MYSQLI_TYPE_LONG_BLOB	Field is defined as LONGBLOB
MYSQLI_TYPE_BLOB	Field is defined as BLOB
MYSQLI_TYPE_VAR_STRING	Field is defined as VARCHAR
MYSQLI_TYPE_STRING	Field is defined as CHAR or BINARY
MYSQLI_TYPE_CHAR	Field is defined as TINYINT. For CHAR, see MYSQLI_TYPE_STRING
MYSQLI_TYPE_GEOMETRY	Field is defined as GEOMETRY
MYSQLI_NEED_DATA	More data available for bind variable
MYSQLI_NO_DATA	No more data available for bind variable
MYSQLI_DATA_TRUNCATED	Data truncation occurred. Available since PHP 5.1.0 and MySQL 5.0.5.
MYSQLI_ENUM_FLAG	Field is defined as ENUM. Available since PHP 5.3.0.
MYSQLI_BINARY_FLAG	Field is defined as BINARY. Available since PHP 5.3.0.
MYSQLI_CURSOR_TYPE_FOR_UPDATE	
MYSQLI_CURSOR_TYPE_NO_CURSOR	
MYSQLI_CURSOR_TYPE_READ_ONLY	
MYSQLI_CURSOR_TYPE_SCROLLABLE	
MYSQLI_STMT_ATTR_CURSOR_TYPE	
MYSQLI_STMT_ATTR_PREFETCH_ROWS	
MYSQLI_STMT_ATTR_UPDATE_MAX_LENGTH	
MYSQLI_SET_CHARSET_NAME	
MYSQLI_REPORT_INDEX	Report if no index or bad index was used in a query.
MYSQLI_REPORT_ERROR	Report errors from mysqli function calls.
MYSQLI_REPORT_STRICT	Throw a mysqli_sql_exception for errors instead of warnings.
MYSQLI_REPORT_ALL	Set all options on (report all).
MYSQLI_REPORT_OFF	Turns reporting off.
MYSQLI_DEBUG_TRACE_ENABLED	Is set to 1 if mysqli_debug functionality is enabled.

MYSQLI_SERVER_QUERY_NO_GOOD_INDEX_USED

MYSQLI_SERVER_QUERY_NO_INDEX_USED

MYSQLI_REFRESH_GRANT	Refreshes the grant tables.
MYSQLI_REFRESH_LOG	Flushes the logs, like executing the FLUSH LOGS SQL statement.
MYSQLI_REFRESH_TABLES	Flushes the table cache, like executing the FLUSH TABLES SQL statement.
MYSQLI_REFRESH_HOSTS	Flushes the host cache, like executing the FLUSH HOSTS SQL statement.
MYSQLI_REFRESH_STATUS	Reset the status variables, like executing the FLUSH STATUS SQL statement.
MYSQLI_REFRESH_THREADS	Flushes the thread cache.
MYSQLI_REFRESH_SLAVE and	On a slave replication server: resets the master server information, restarts the slave. Like executing the RESET SLAVE SQL statement.
MYSQLI_REFRESH_MASTER the	On a master replication server: removes the binary log files listed in binary log index, and truncates the index file. Like executing the RESET MASTER SQL statement.

MYSQLI_TRANS_COR_AND_CHAIN Appends "AND CHAIN" to mysqli_commit or mysqli_rollback.

MYSQLI_TRANS_COR_AND_NO_CH Appends IN "AND NO CHAIN" to mysqli_commit or mysqli_rollback.

MYSQLI_TRANS_COR_RELEASE   Appends "RELEASE" to mysqli_commit or mysqli_rollback.

MYSQLI_TRANS_COR_NO_RELEASE Appends "NO RELEASE" to mysqli_commit or mysqli_rollback.

MYSQLI_TRANS_START_READ_ONLY Start the transaction as "START TRANSACTION READ ONLY" with mysqli_begin_transaction.

MYSQLI_TRANS_START_READ_WRITE Start the transaction as "START TRANSACTION READ WRITE" with mysqli_begin_transaction.

MYSQLI_TRANS_START_CONSISTENT Start_the SNAPSHOT transaction as "START TRANSACTION WITH CONSISTENT
SNAPSHOT" with mysqli_begin_transaction.

3.6 Notes

Some implementation notes:

- Support was added for MYSQL_TYPE_GEOMETRY to the MySQLi extension in PHP 5.3.

- Note there are different internal implementations within libmysqlclient and mysqlnd for handling columns of type MYSQL_TYPE_GEOMETRY. Generally speaking, mysqlnd will allocate significantly less memory. For example, if there is a POINT column in a result set, libmysqlclient may pre-allocate up to 4GB of RAM although less than 50 bytes are needed for holding a POINT column in memory. Memory allocation is much lower, less than 50 bytes, if using mysqlnd.

3.7 The MySQLi Extension Function Summary

Table 3.5 Summary of mysqli methods

mysqli Class			
OOP Interface	**Procedural Interface** **Alias (Do not use)**		**Description**
Properties			
$mysqli::affected_rows	mysqli_affected_rows N/A		Gets the number of affected rows in a previous MySQL operation
$mysqli::client_info	mysqli_get_client_infoN/A		Returns the MySQL client version as a string
$mysqli::client_version	mysqli_get_client_versionN/A		Returns MySQL client version info as an integer
$mysqli::connect_errno	mysqli_connect_errnoN/A		Returns the error code from last connect call
$mysqli::connect_error	mysqli_connect_errorN/A		Returns a string description of the last connect error
$mysqli::errno	mysqli_errno N/A		Returns the error code for the most recent function call
$mysqli::error	mysqli_error N/A		Returns a string description of the last error
$mysqli::field_count	mysqli_field_count N/A		Returns the number of columns for the most recent query
$mysqli::host_info	mysqli_get_host_infoN/A		Returns a string representing the type of connection used
$mysqli::protocol_version	mysqli_get_proto_infoN/A		Returns the version of the MySQL protocol used
$mysqli::server_info	mysqli_get_server_infoN/A		Returns the version of the MySQL server
$mysqli::server_version	mysqli_get_server_versionN/A		Returns the version of the MySQL server as an integer

$mysqli::info	mysqli_info	N/A	Retrieves information about the most recently executed query
$mysqli::insert_id	mysqli_insert_id	N/A	Returns the auto generated id used in the last query

5
1

mysqli Class			
OOP Interface	**Procedural Interface**	**Alias (Do not use)**	**Description**
$mysqli::sqlstate	mysqli_sqlstate	N/A	Returns the SQLSTATE error from previous MySQL operation
$mysqli::warning_count	mysqli_warning_count	N/A	Returns the number of warnings from the last query for the given link
Methods			
mysqli::autocommit	mysqli_autocommit	N/A	Turns on or off auto-committing database modifications
mysqli::change_user	mysqli_change_user	N/A	Changes the user of the specified database connection
mysqli::character_setmysqliname, mysqli::client_encoding	character_setmysqliname_client_encoding		Returns the default character set for the database connection
mysqli::close	mysqli_close	N/A	Closes a previously opened database connection
mysqli::commit	mysqli_commit	N/A	Commits the current transaction
mysqli::__construct	mysqli_connect	N/A	Open a new connection to the MySQL server [Note: static (i.e. class) method]
mysqli::debug	mysqli_debug	N/A	Performs debugging operations
mysqli::dump_debug_infomysqli_dump_debug_info		N/A	Dump debugging information into the log
mysqli::get_charset	mysqli_get_charset	N/A	Returns a character set object
mysqli::get_connectionmysqlistatsget_connectionstats		N/A	Returns client connection statistics. Available only with mysqlnd.
mysqli::get_client_infomysqli_get_client_info		N/A	Returns the MySQL client version as a string
mysqli::get_client_statsmysqli_get_client_stats		N/A	Returns client per-process statistics.

			Available only with mysqlnd.
mysqli::get_cache_statsmysqli_get_cache_stats**N/A**			**Returns client Zval cache statistics. Available only with mysqlnd.**
mysqli::get_server_infomysqli_get_server_info**N/A**			**Returns a string representing the version**

52

mysqli Class			
OOP Interface	**Procedural Interface**	**Alias (Do not use)**	**Description**
			of the MySQL server that the MySQLi extension is connected to
mysqli::get_warningsmysqli_get_warnings		N/A	**NOT DOCUMENTED**
mysqli::init	mysqli_init	N/A	Initializes MySQLi and returns a resource for use with mysqli_real_connect. [Not called on an object, as it returns a $mysqli object.]
mysqli::kill	mysqli_kill	N/A	Asks the server to kill a MySQL thread
mysqli::more_resultsmysqli_more_results		N/A	Check if there are any more query results from a multi query
mysqli::multi_query mysqli_multi_query		N/A	Performs a query on the database
mysqli::next_result mysqli_next_result		N/A	Prepare next result from multi_query
mysqli::options	mysqli_options	mysqli_set_opt	Set options
mysqli::ping	mysqli_ping	N/A	Pings a server connection, or tries to reconnect if the connection has gone down
mysqli::prepare	mysqli_prepare	N/A	Prepare an SQL statement for execution
mysqli::query	mysqli_query	N/A	Performs a query on the database
mysqli::real_connectmysqli_real_connect		N/A	Opens a connection to a mysql server
mysqli::real_escape_mysqlistring, real_escape_ mysqli::escape_string		stringmysqli_escape_string	Escapes special characters in a string for use in an SQL statement, taking into account the current charset of the connection
mysqli::real_query	mysqli_real_query	N/A	Execute an SQL query

mysqli::refresh	mysqli_refresh	N/A	Flushes tables or caches, or resets the replication server information
mysqli::rollback	mysqli_rollback	N/A	Rolls back current transaction

5
3

mysqli Class			
OOP Interface	Procedural Interface	Alias (Do not use)	Description
mysqli::select_db	mysqli_select_db	N/A	Selects the default database for database queries
mysqli::set_charset	mysqli_set_charset	N/A	Sets the default client character set
mysqli::set_local_	infilemysqlidefaultsetlocal_infileN/A_default		Unsets user defined handler for load local infile command
mysqli::set_local_	infilemysqlihandlersetlocal_infileN/A_handler		Set callback function for LOAD DATA LOCAL INFILE command
mysqli::ssl_set	mysqli_ssl_set	N/A	Used for establishing secure connections using SSL
mysqli::stat	mysqli_stat	N/A	Gets the current system status
mysqli::stmt_init	mysqli_stmt_init	N/A	Initializes a statement and returns an object for use with mysqli_stmt_prepare
mysqli::store_resultmysqli_store_result N/A			Transfers a result set from the last query
mysqli::thread_id	mysqli_thread_id	N/A	Returns the thread ID for the current connection
mysqli::thread_safe mysqli_thread_safe		N/A	Returns whether thread safety is given or not
mysqli::use_result	mysqli_use_result	N/A	Initiate a result set retrieval

Table 3.6 Summary of mysqli_stmt methods

MySQL_STMT			
OOP Interface	Procedural Interface	Alias (Do not use)	Description
Properties			
$mysqli_stmt::affected_rowsmysqli_stmt_affected		N/Arows	Returns the total number of rows changed, deleted, or inserted by the last executed

			statement
$mysqli_stmt::errno	mysqli_stmt_errno	N/A	Returns the error code for the most recent statement call
$mysqli_stmt::error	mysqli_stmt_error	N/A	Returns a string description for last statement error

54

MySQL_STMT			
OOP Interface	**Procedural Interface**	**Alias (Do not use)**	**Description**
$mysqli_stmt::field_count	mysqli_stmt_field_count	N/A	Returns the number of field in the given statement - not documented
$mysqli_stmt::insert_id	mysqli_stmt_insert_id	N/A	Get the ID generated from the previous INSERT operation
$mysqli_stmt::num_rows	mysqli_stmt_num_rows	N/A	Return the number of rows in statements result set
$mysqli_stmt::param_count	mysqli_stmt_param_count	mysqli_param_count	Returns the number of parameter for the given statement
$mysqli_stmt::sqlstate	mysqli_stmt_sqlstate	N/A	Returns SQLSTATE error from previous statement operation
Methods			
mysqli_stmt::attr_	getmysqli_stmt_attr_get	N/A	Used to get the current value of a statement attribute
mysqli_stmt::attr_	setmysqli_stmt_attr_set	N/A	Used to modify the behavior of a prepared statement
mysqli_stmt::bind_	parammysqli_stmt_bind_param	mysqli_bind_param	Binds variables to a prepared statement as parameters
mysqli_stmt::bind_	resultmysqli_stmt_bind_result	mysqli_bind_result	Binds variables to a prepared statement for result storage
mysqli_stmt::close	mysqli_stmt_close	N/A	Closes a prepared statement
mysqli_stmt::data_	seekmysqli_stmt_data_seek	N/A	Seeks to an arbitrary row in statement result set
mysqli_stmt::executemysqli_stmt_execute	mysqli_execute		Executes a prepared Query
mysqli_stmt::fetch	mysqli_stmt_fetch	mysqli_fetch	Fetch results from a prepared statement into

			the bound variables
mysqli_stmt::free_resultmysqli_stmt_free_resultN/A			Frees stored result memory for the given statement handle
mysqli_stmt::get_resultmysqli_stmt_get_resultN/A			Gets a result set from a prepared statement. Available only with mysqlnd.

5
5

MySQL_STMT			
OOP Interface	Procedural Interface	Alias (Do not use)	Description
mysqli_stmt::get_warningsmysqli_stmt_get_warningsN/A			NOT DOCUMENTED
mysqli_stmt::more_resultsmysqli_stmt_more_resultsN/A			Checks if there are more query results from a multiple query
mysqli_stmt::next_resultmysqli_stmt_next_resultN/A			Reads the next result from a multiple query
mysqli_stmt::num_rowsmysqli_stmt_num_rowsN/A			See also property $mysqli_stmt::num_rows
mysqli_stmt::preparemysqli_stmt_prepare N/A			Prepare an SQL statement for execution
mysqli_stmt::reset	mysqli_stmt_reset	N/A	Resets a prepared statement
mysqli_stmt::result_mysqlietadatastmt_result_metadatamysqli_get_metadata			Returns result set metadata from a prepared statement
mysqli_stmt::send_longmysqlidatastmt_send_longmysqlidata_send_long_dataSend data in blocks			
mysqli_stmt::store_resultmysqli_stmt_store_resultN/A			Transfers a result set from a prepared statement

Table 3.7 Summary of mysqli_result methods

mysqli_result			
OOP Interface	Procedural Interface	Alias (Do not use)	Description
Properties			
$mysqli_result::current_fieldmysqli_field_tell		N/A	Get current field offset of a result pointer
$mysqli_result::field_countmysqli_num_fields		N/A	Get the number of fields in a result
$mysqli_result::lengths	mysqli_fetch_lengths	N/A	Returns the lengths of the columns of the current row in the result set
$mysqli_result::num_rows mysqli_num_rows		N/A	Gets the number of rows in a result
Methods			

461

mysqli_result::data_mysqliseek_data_seek	N/A	Adjusts the result pointer to an arbitrary row in the result
mysqli_result::fetchmysqliall_fetch_all	N/A	Fetches all result rows and returns the result set as an associative array, a numeric array, or both. Available only with mysqlnd.

mysqli_result			
OOP Interface	**Procedural Interface**	**Alias (Do not use)**	**Description**
mysqli_result::fetchmysqliarray_fetch_array		N/A	Fetch a result row as an associative, a numeric array, or both
mysqli_result::fetchmysqliasoc_fetch_assoc		N/A	Fetch a result row as an associative array
mysqli_result::fetchmysqlified_fetchdirectfield_		directN/A	Fetch meta-data for a single field
mysqli_result::fetchmysqlified_fetch_field		N/A	Returns the next field in the result set
mysqli_result::fetchmysqlifiedsfetch_fields		N/A	Returns an array of objects representing the fields in a result set
mysqli_result::fetchmysqliobjectfetch_object		N/A	Returns the current row of a result set as an object
mysqli_result::fetchmysqlirow_fetch_row		N/A	Get a result row as an enumerated array
mysqli_result::fieldmysqliseek_field_seek		N/A	Set result pointer to a specified field offset
mysqli_result::free, mysqli_free_result mysqli_result::close, mysqli_result::free_result		N/A	Frees the memory associated with a result

Table 3.8 Summary of mysqli_driver methods

MySQL_Driver			
OOP Interface	**Procedural Interface**	**Alias (Do not use)**	**Description**
Properties			
N/A			
Methods			
mysqli_driver::embeddedmysqliserverembeddedend_serverN/A_end			NOT DOCUMENTED
mysqli_driver::embeddedmysqliserverembeddedstartserverN/A_start			NOT DOCUMENTED

Note

463

Alias functions are provided for backward compatibility purposes only. Do not use them in new projects.

3.8 Examples

3.8.1 MySQLi extension basic examples

5
7

This example shows how to connect, execute a query, use basic error handling, print resulting rows, and disconnect from a MySQL database.

This example uses the freely available Sakila database that can be downloaded from dev.mysql.com, as described here. To get this example to work, (a) install sakila and (b) modify the connection variables (host, your_user, your_pass).

Example 3.30 MySQLi extension overview example

```php
<?php
    Let's pass in a $_GET variable to our example, in this case
    it's aid for actor_id in our Sakila database. Let's make it
    default to 1, and cast it to an integer as to avoid SQL injection
    and/or related security problems. Handling all of this goes beyond
    the scope of this simple example. Example:
        http://example.org/script.php?aid=42
if (isset($_GET['aid']) && is_numeric($_GET['aid'])) {
    $aid = (int) $_GET['aid'];
} else {
    $aid = 1;
}


    Connecting to and selecting a MySQL database named sakila
    Hostname: 127.0.0.1, username: your_user, password: your_pass, db: sakila
$mysqli = new mysqli('127.0.0.1', 'your_user', 'your_pass', 'sakila');

    Oh no! A connect_errno exists so the connection attempt failed!
if ($mysqli->connect_errno) {
        The connection failed. What do you want to do?
        You could contact yourself (email?), log the error, show a nice page, etc.
        You do not want to reveal sensitive information

        Let's try this:
    echo "Sorry, this website is experiencing problems.";

        Something you should not do on a public site, but this example will show you
        anyways, is print out MySQL error related information – you might log this echo
"Error: Failed to make a MySQL connection, here is why: \n";
    echo "Errno: " . $mysqli->connect_errno . "\n";
    echo "Error: " . $mysqli->connect_error . "\n";

        You might want to show them something nice, but we will simply exit
    exit;
}

// Perform an SQL query
$sql = "SELECT actor_id, first_name, last_name FROM actor WHERE actor_id = $aid";
if (!$result = $mysqli->query($sql)) {
    // Oh no! The query failed.
    echo "Sorry, the website is experiencing problems.";

        Again, do not do this on a public site, but we'll show you how
        to get the error information
    echo "Error: Our query failed to execute and here is why: \n";
    echo "Query: " . $sql . "\n";
    echo "Errno: " . $mysqli->errno . "\n";
    echo "Error: " . $mysqli->error . "\n";
```

```
        exit;
}
```

>>>   Phew, we made it. We know our MySQL connection and query
>>>   succeeded, but do we have a result?

```
if ($result->num_rows === 0) {
    // Oh, no rows! Sometimes that's expected and okay, sometimes
```

58   _____

- it is not. You decide. In this case, maybe actor_id was too
- large?

```
    echo "We could not find a match for ID $aid, sorry about that. Please try again."; exit;
}
```

- Now, we know only one result will exist in this example so let's
- fetch it into an associated array where the array's keys are the
- table's column names

```
$actor = $result->fetch_assoc();
echo "Sometimes I see " . $actor['first_name'] . " " . $actor['last_name'] . " on TV.";
```

- Now, let's fetch five random actors and output their names to a list.
- We'll add less error handling here as you can do that on your own now

```
$sql = "SELECT actor_id, first_name, last_name FROM actor ORDER BY rand() LIMIT 5";
if (!$result = $mysqli->query($sql)) {
    echo "Sorry, the website is experiencing problems.";
    exit;
}
```

- Print our 5 random actors in a list, and link to each actor echo

```
"<ul>\n";
while ($actor = $result->fetch_assoc()) {
    echo "<li><a href='" . $_SERVER['SCRIPT_FILENAME'] . "?aid=" . $actor['actor_id'] . "'>\n"; echo
        $actor['first_name'] . ' ' . $actor['last_name'];
    echo "</a></li>\n";
}
echo "</ul>\n";
```

- The script will automatically free the result and close the MySQL
- connection when it exits, but let's just do it anyways

```
$result->free();
$mysqli->close();
?>
```

3.9 The mysqli class

Represents a connection between PHP and a MySQL database.

```
mysqli {
mysqli

    Properties

int
   mysqli->affected_rows ;

int
   mysqli->connect_errno ;

string
   mysqli->connect_error ;

int
   mysqli->errno ;
```

array
  mysqli->error_list ;

string

```
  mysqli->error ;

int
  mysqli->field_count ;

string
  mysqli->client_info ;

int
  mysqli->client_version ;

string
  mysqli->host_info ;

string
  mysqli->protocol_version ;

string
  mysqli->server_info ;

int
  mysqli->server_version ;

string
  mysqli->info ;

mixed
  mysqli->insert_id ;

string
  mysqli->sqlstate ;

int
  mysqli->thread_id ;

int
  mysqli->warning_count ;

Methods

mysqli::__construct(
  string host
                =ini_get("mysqli.default_host"),
string username
                =ini_get("mysqli.default_user"),
string passwd
                =ini_get("mysqli.default_pw"),
string dbname
                ="",
  int port
                =ini_get("mysqli.default_port"),
string socket
                =ini_get("mysqli.default_socket"));

bool mysqli::autocommit(
  bool mode);

bool mysqli::change_user(
  string user,
```

```
    string password,
    string database);

string mysqli::character_set_name();

bool mysqli::close();

bool mysqli::commit(
    int flags
```

60

-              =0,
  string name);

  void mysqli::connect(
    string host
-             =ini_get("mysqli.default_host"),
  string username
-             =ini_get("mysqli.default_user"),
  string passwd
-             =ini_get("mysqli.default_pw"),
  string dbname
-             ="",
  int port
-             =ini_get("mysqli.default_port"),
  string socket
-             =ini_get("mysqli.default_socket"));

  bool mysqli::debug(
    string message);

  bool mysqli::dump_debug_info();

  object mysqli::get_charset();

  string mysqli::get_client_info();

  bool mysqli::get_connection_stats();

  string mysqli_stmt::get_server_info();

  mysqli_warning mysqli::get_warnings();

  mysqli mysqli::init();

  bool mysqli::kill(
    int processid);

  bool mysqli::more_results();

  bool mysqli::multi_query(
    string query);

  bool mysqli::next_result();

  bool mysqli::options(
    int option,
    mixed value);

  bool mysqli::ping();

  public static int mysqli::poll(
    array read,
    array error,
    array reject,
    int sec,
    int usec
-             =0);

  mysqli_stmt mysqli::prepare(

471

```
        string query);

    mixed mysqli::query(
        string query,
        int resultmode
                =MYSQLI_STORE_RES

ULT); bool mysqli::real_connect(
```

6
1

```
    string host,
    string username,
    string passwd,
    string dbname,
    int port,
    string socket,
    int flags);

string mysqli::escape_string(
    string escapestr);

string mysqli::real_escape_string(
    string escapestr);

bool mysqli::real_query(
    string query);

public mysqli_result mysqli::reap_async_query();

public bool mysqli::refresh(
    int options);

bool mysqli::rollback(
    int flags
            =0,
    string name);

int mysqli::rpl_query_type(
    string query);

bool mysqli::select_db(
    string dbname);

bool mysqli::send_query(
    string query);

bool mysqli::set_charset(
    string charset);

bool mysqli::set_local_infile_handler(
    mysqli link,
    callable read_func);

bool mysqli::ssl_set(
    string key,
    string cert,
    string ca,
    string capath,
    string cipher);

string mysqli::stat();

mysqli_stmt mysqli::stmt_init();

mysqli_result mysqli::store_result(
    int option);

mysqli_result mysqli::use_result();
}
```

3.9.1 mysqli::$affected_rows, mysqli_affected_rows

-     mysqli::$affected_rows

62

mysqli_affected_rows

Gets the number of affected rows in a previous MySQL operation

Description

Object oriented style

```
int
    mysqli->affected_rows ;
```

Procedural style

```
int mysqli_affected_rows(
    mysqli link);
```

Returns the number of rows affected by the last INSERT, UPDATE, REPLACE or DELETE query.

For SELECT statements mysqli_affected_rows works like mysqli_num_rows.

Parameters

link	Procedural style only: A link identifier returned by mysqli_connect or mysqli_init

Return Values

An integer greater than zero indicates the number of rows affected or retrieved. Zero indicates that no records were updated for an UPDATE statement, no rows matched the WHERE clause in the query or that no query has yet been executed. -1 indicates that the query returned an error.

> **Note**
>
> If the number of affected rows is greater than the maximum integer value(PHP_INT_MAX), the number of affected rows will be returned as a string.

Examples

Example 3.31 $mysqli->affected_rows **example**

Object oriented style

```php
<?php
$mysqli = new mysqli("localhost", "my_user", "my_password", "world");

/* check connection */
if (mysqli_connect_errno()) {
    printf("Connect failed: %s\n", mysqli_connect_error());
    exit();
}

/* Insert rows */
$mysqli->query("CREATE TABLE Language SELECT * from
CountryLanguage"); printf("Affected rows (INSERT): %d\n", $mysqli-
>affected_rows);

$mysqli->query("ALTER TABLE Language ADD Status int default 0");

/* update rows */
```

```
$mysqli->query("UPDATE Language SET Status=1 WHERE Percentage >
50"); printf("Affected rows (UPDATE): %d\n", $mysqli->affected_rows);
```

6
3

```php
/* delete rows */
$mysqli->query("DELETE FROM Language WHERE Percentage <
50"); printf("Affected rows (DELETE): %d\n", $mysqli-
>affected_rows);

/* select all rows */
$result = $mysqli->query("SELECT CountryCode FROM Language");
printf("Affected rows (SELECT): %d\n", $mysqli->affected_rows);

$result->close();

/* Delete table Language */
$mysqli->query("DROP TABLE Language");

/* close connection */
$mysqli->close();
?>
```

Procedural style

```php
<?php
$link = mysqli_connect("localhost", "my_user", "my_password", "world");

if (!$link) {
    printf("Can't connect to localhost. Error: %s\n", mysqli_connect_error()); exit();
}

/* Insert rows */
mysqli_query($link, "CREATE TABLE Language SELECT * from
CountryLanguage"); printf("Affected rows (INSERT): %d\n",
mysqli_affected_rows($link));

mysqli_query($link, "ALTER TABLE Language ADD Status int default 0");

/* update rows */
mysqli_query($link, "UPDATE Language SET Status=1 WHERE Percentage >
50"); printf("Affected rows (UPDATE): %d\n", mysqli_affected_rows($link));

/* delete rows */
mysqli_query($link, "DELETE FROM Language WHERE Percentage <
50"); printf("Affected rows (DELETE): %d\n",
mysqli_affected_rows($link));

/* select all rows */
$result = mysqli_query($link, "SELECT CountryCode FROM Language");
printf("Affected rows (SELECT): %d\n", mysqli_affected_rows($link));

mysqli_free_result($result);

/* Delete table Language */
mysqli_query($link, "DROP TABLE Language");

/* close connection */
mysqli_close($link);
```

```
?>
```

The above examples will output:

```
Affected rows (INSERT): 984
Affected rows (UPDATE): 168
```

64

Affected rows (DELETE): 815
Affected rows (SELECT): 169

See Also

mysqli_num_rows
mysqli_info

3.9.2 mysqli::autocommit, mysqli_autocommit

•   mysqli::autocommit

mysqli_autocommit

Turns on or off auto-committing database modifications

Description

Object oriented style

```
bool mysqli::autocommit(
    bool mode);
```

Procedural style

```
bool mysqli_autocommit(
    mysqli link,
    bool mode);
```

Turns on or off auto-commit mode on queries for the database connection.

To determine the current state of autocommit use the SQL command SELECT @@autocommit.

Parameters

link	Procedural style only: A link identifier returned by mysqli_connect or mysqli_init
mode	Whether to turn on auto-commit or not.

Return Values

Returns TRUE on success or FALSE on failure.

Notes

> **Note**
>
> This function doesn't work with non transactional table types (like MyISAM or ISAM).

Examples

Example 3.32 mysqli::autocommit example

Object oriented style

```php
<?php
$mysqli = new mysqli("localhost", "my_user", "my_password", "world");

if (mysqli_connect_errno()) {
    printf("Connect failed: %s\n", mysqli_connect_error());
    exit();
}

/* turn autocommit on */
$mysqli->autocommit(TRUE);

if ($result = $mysqli->query("SELECT @@autocommit")) {
    $row = $result->fetch_row(); printf("Autocommit is
%s\n", $row[0]); $result->free();

}

/* close connection */
$mysqli->close();
?>
```

Procedural style

```php
<?php
$link = mysqli_connect("localhost", "my_user", "my_password", "world");

if (!$link) {
    printf("Can't connect to localhost. Error: %s\n", mysqli_connect_error()); exit();
}

/* turn autocommit on */
mysqli_autocommit($link, TRUE);

if ($result = mysqli_query($link, "SELECT @@autocommit")) {
    $row = mysqli_fetch_row($result); printf("Autocommit is
%s\n", $row[0]); mysqli_free_result($result);

}

/* close connection */
mysqli_close($link);
?>
```

The above examples will output:

Autocommit is 1

See Also

mysqli_begin_transaction
mysqli_commit
mysqli_rollback

66

_____

3.9.3 mysqli::begin_transaction, mysqli_begin_transaction

- mysqli::begin_transaction

mysqli_begin_transaction

Starts a transaction

Description

Object oriented style (method):

```
public bool mysqli::begin_transaction(
    int flags
        =0,
    string name);
```

Procedural style:

```
bool mysqli_begin_transaction(
    mysqli link,
    int flags
        =0,
    string name);
```

Begins a transaction. Requires the InnoDB engine (it is enabled by default). For additional details about how MySQL transactions work, see http://dev.mysql.com/doc/mysql/en/commit.html.

Parameters

link	Procedural style only: A link identifier returned by mysqli_connect or mysqli_init
flags	Valid flags are:

- MYSQLI_TRANS_START_READ_ONLY: Start the transaction as "START TRANSACTION READ ONLY". Requires MySQL 5.6 and above.

- MYSQLI_TRANS_START_READ_WRITE: Start the transaction as "START TRANSACTION READ WRITE". Requires MySQL 5.6 and above.

- MYSQLI_TRANS_START_WITH_CONSISTENT_SNAPSHOT: Start the transaction as "START TRANSACTION WITH CONSISTENT SNAPSHOT".

name	Savepoint name for the transaction.

Return Values

Returns TRUE on success or FALSE on failure.

Examples

Example 3.33 $mysqli->begin_transaction example

Object oriented style

```php
<?php
$mysqli = new mysqli("127.0.0.1", "my_user", "my_password", "sakila");

if ($mysqli->connect_errno) {
    printf("Connect failed: %s\n", $mysqli->connect_error);
    exit();
}

$mysqli->begin_transaction(MYSQLI_TRANS_START_READ_ONLY);

$mysqli->query("SELECT first_name, last_name FROM
actor"); $mysqli->commit();

$mysqli->close();
?>
```

Procedural style

```php
<?php
$link = mysqli_connect("127.0.0.1", "my_user", "my_password", "sakila");

if (mysqli_connect_errno()) {
    printf("Connect failed: %s\n", mysqli_connect_error());
    exit();
}

mysqli_begin_transaction($link, MYSQLI_TRANS_START_READ_ONLY);

mysqli_query($link, "SELECT first_name, last_name FROM actor LIMIT 1");
mysqli_commit($link);

mysqli_close($link);
?>
```

See Also

mysqli_autocommit
mysqli_commit
mysqli_rollback

3.9.4 mysqli::change_user, mysqli_change_user

>>>   mysqli::change_user

mysqli_change_user

Changes the user of the specified database connection

Description

Object oriented style

```
bool mysqli::change_user(
    string user,
```

```
    string password,
    string database);
```

Procedural style

```
bool mysqli_change_user(
    mysqli link,
    string user,
    string password,
    string database);
```

Changes the user of the specified database connection and sets the current database.

In order to successfully change users a valid *username* and *password* parameters must be provided and that user must have sufficient permissions to access the desired database. If for any reason authorization fails, the current user authentication will remain.

Parameters

link	Procedural style only: A link identifier returned by mysqli_connect or mysqli_init
user	The MySQL user name.
password	The MySQL password.
database	The database to change to.
	If desired, the NULL value may be passed resulting in only changing the user and not selecting a database. To select a database in this case use the mysqli_select_db function.

Return Values

Returns TRUE on success or FALSE on failure.

Notes

> **Note**
>
> Using this command will always cause the current database connection to behave as if was a completely new database connection, regardless of if the operation was completed successfully. This reset includes performing a rollback on any active transactions, closing all temporary tables, and unlocking all locked tables.

Examples

Example 3.34 mysqli::change_user example

Object oriented style

```php
<?php

/* connect database test */
$mysqli = new mysqli("localhost", "my_user", "my_password", "test");

/* check connection */
if (mysqli_connect_errno()) {
```

```
printf("Connect failed: %s\n", mysqli_connect_error());
exit();
```

6
9

```
}
/* Set Variable a */
$mysqli->query("SET @a:=1");

/* reset all and select a new database */
$mysqli->change_user("my_user", "my_password", "world");

if ($result = $mysqli->query("SELECT DATABASE()")) {
    $row = $result->fetch_row();
    printf("Default database: %s\n", $row[0]);
    $result->close();
}

if ($result = $mysqli->query("SELECT @a")) {
    $row = $result->fetch_row();
    if ($row[0] === NULL) {
        printf("Value of variable a is NULL\n");
    }
    $result->close();
}
```
```
/* close connection */
$mysqli->close();
?>
```

Procedural style

```
<?php
/* connect database test */
$link = mysqli_connect("localhost", "my_user", "my_password", "test");

/* check connection */
if (!$link) {
    printf("Connect failed: %s\n", mysqli_connect_error());
    exit();
}

/* Set Variable a */
mysqli_query($link, "SET @a:=1");

/* reset all and select a new database */
mysqli_change_user($link, "my_user", "my_password", "world");

if ($result = mysqli_query($link, "SELECT DATABASE()")) {
    $row = mysqli_fetch_row($result); printf("Default
    database: %s\n", $row[0]); mysqli_free_result($result);
}

if ($result = mysqli_query($link, "SELECT @a")) {
    $row = mysqli_fetch_row($result);
    if ($row[0] === NULL) {
        printf("Value of variable a is NULL\n");
    }
    mysqli_free_result($result);
```

```
}

/* close connection */
mysqli_close($link);
?>
```

70

The above examples will output:

Default database: world
Value of variable a is NULL

See Also

mysqli_connect
mysqli_select_db

3.9.5 mysqli::character_set_name, mysqli_character_set_name

- mysqli::character_set_name

mysqli_character_set_name

Returns the default character set for the database connection

Description

Object oriented style

```
string mysqli::character_set_name();
```

Procedural style

```
string mysqli_character_set_name(
    mysqli link);
```

Returns the current character set for the database connection.

Parameters

link   Procedural style only: A link identifier returned by mysqli_connect or
                              mysqli_init

Return Values

The default character set for the current connection

Examples

Example 3.35 mysqli::character_set_name example

Object oriented style

```
<?php
/* Open a connection */
$mysqli = new mysqli("localhost", "my_user", "my_password", "world");

/* check connection */
if (mysqli_connect_errno()) {
    printf("Connect failed: %s\n", mysqli_connect_error());
    exit();
```

```
}
/* Print current character set */
$charset = $mysqli->character_set_name();
printf ("Current character set is %s\n", $charset);

$mysqli->close();
?>
```

Procedural style

```
<?php
/* Open a connection */
$link = mysqli_connect("localhost", "my_user", "my_password", "world");

/* check connection */
if (!$link) {
    printf("Connect failed: %s\n", mysqli_connect_error());
    exit();
}

/* Print current character set */
$charset = mysqli_character_set_name($link);
printf ("Current character set is %s\n",$charset);

/* close connection */
mysqli_close($link);
?>
```

The above examples will output:

```
Current character set is latin1_swedish_ci
```

See Also

mysqli_set_charset
mysqli_client_encoding
mysqli_real_escape_string

3.9.6 mysqli::close, mysqli_close

>>>   mysqli::close

mysqli_close

Closes a previously opened database connection

Description

Object oriented style

```
bool mysqli::close();
```

72

494

Procedural style

```
bool mysqli_close(
    mysqli link);
```

Closes a previously opened database connection.

Open non-persistent MySQL connections and result sets are automatically destroyed when a PHP script finishes its execution. So, while explicitly closing open connections and freeing result sets is optional, doing so is recommended. This will immediately return resources to PHP and MySQL, which can improve performance. For related information, see freeing resources

Parameters

link   Procedural style only: A link identifier returned by mysqli_connect or
                                    mysqli_init

Return Values

Returns TRUE on success or FALSE on failure.

Examples

See mysqli_connect.

Notes

> **Note**
>
> mysqli_close will not close persistent connections. For additional details, see the
> manual page on persistent connections.

See Also

mysqli::__construct
mysqli_init
mysqli_real_connect
mysqli_free_result

3.9.7 mysqli::commit, mysqli_commit

>>>   mysqli::commit

mysqli_commit

Commits the current transaction

Description

Object oriented style

```
bool mysqli::commit(
    int flags
        =0,
    string name);
```

Procedural style

```
bool mysqli_commit(
    mysqli link,
    int flags
            =0,
    string name);
```

Commits the current transaction for the database connection.

Parameters

link	Procedural style only: A link identifier returned by mysqli_connect or mysqli_init
flags	A bitmask of MYSQLI_TRANS_COR_* constants.
name	If provided then COMMIT/*name*/ is executed.

Return Values

Returns TRUE on success or FALSE on failure.

Changelog

Version	Description
5.5.0	Added *flags* and *name* parameters.

Examples

Example 3.36 mysqli::commit example

Object oriented style

```php
<?php
$mysqli = new mysqli("localhost", "my_user", "my_password", "world");

/* check connection */
if (mysqli_connect_errno()) {
    printf("Connect failed: %s\n", mysqli_connect_error());
    exit();
}

$mysqli->query("CREATE TABLE Language LIKE CountryLanguage");

/* set autocommit to off */
$mysqli->autocommit(FALSE);

/* Insert some values */
$mysqli->query("INSERT INTO Language VALUES ('DEU', 'Bavarian', 'F', 11.2)");
$mysqli->query("INSERT INTO Language VALUES ('DEU', 'Swabian', 'F', 9.4)");

/* commit transaction */
if (!$mysqli->commit()) {
    print("Transaction commit failed\n");
    exit();
}

/* drop table */
```

```
$mysqli->query("DROP TABLE Language");

/* close connection */
$mysqli->close();
```

74

```
?>
```

Procedural style

```php
<?php
$link = mysqli_connect("localhost", "my_user", "my_password", "test");

/* check connection */
if (!$link) {
    printf("Connect failed: %s\n", mysqli_connect_error());
    exit();
}

/* set autocommit to off */
mysqli_autocommit($link, FALSE);

mysqli_query($link, "CREATE TABLE Language LIKE CountryLanguage");

/* Insert some values */
mysqli_query($link, "INSERT INTO Language VALUES ('DEU', 'Bavarian', 'F', 11.2)");
mysqli_query($link, "INSERT INTO Language VALUES ('DEU', 'Swabian', 'F', 9.4)");

/* commit transaction */
if (!mysqli_commit($link)) {
    print("Transaction commit failed\n");
    exit();
}
```

```php
/* close connection */
mysqli_close($link);
?>
```

See Also

mysqli_autocommit
mysqli_begin_transaction
mysqli_rollback
mysqli_savepoint

3.9.8 mysqli::$connect_errno, mysqli_connect_errno

- mysqli::$connect_errno

  mysqli_connect_errno

  Returns the error code from last connect call

Description

Object oriented style

```
int
    mysqli->connect_errno ;
```

Procedural style

$$\frac{\quad\quad\quad}{\begin{array}{r} 7 \\ 5 \end{array}}$$

```
int mysqli_connect_errno();
```

Returns the last error code number from the last call to mysqli_connect.

> **Note**
>
> Client error message numbers are listed in the MySQL errmsg.h header file,
> server error message numbers are listed in mysqld_error.h. In the MySQL
> source distribution you can find a complete list of error messages and error
> numbers in the file Docs/mysqld_error.txt.

Return Values

An error code value for the last call to mysqli_connect, if it failed. zero means no error occurred.

Examples

Example 3.37 $mysqli->connect_errno **example**

Object oriented style

```php
<?php
$mysqli = @new mysqli('localhost', 'fake_user', 'my_password', 'my_db');

if ($mysqli->connect_errno) {
    die('Connect Error: ' . $mysqli->connect_errno);
}
?>
```

Procedural style

```php
<?php
$link = @mysqli_connect('localhost', 'fake_user', 'my_password', 'my_db');

if (!$link) {
    die('Connect Error: ' . mysqli_connect_errno());
}
?>
```

The above examples will output:

```
Connect Error: 1045
```

See Also

mysqli_connect
mysqli_connect_error
mysqli_errno
mysqli_error
mysqli_sqlstate

3.9.9 mysqli::$connect_error, mysqli_connect_error

>>> mysqli::$connect_error

mysqli_connect_error

Returns a string description of the last connect error

Description

Object oriented style

```
string
    mysqli->connect_error ;
```

Procedural style

```
string mysqli_connect_error();
```

Returns the last error message string from the last call to mysqli_connect.

Return Values

A string that describes the error. NULL is returned if no error occurred.

Examples

Example 3.38 $mysqli->connect_error **example**

Object oriented style

```php
<?php
$mysqli = @new mysqli('localhost', 'fake_user', 'my_password', 'my_db');
```
>>> Works as of PHP 5.2.9 and 5.3.0.
```php
if ($mysqli->connect_error) {
    die('Connect Error: ' . $mysqli->connect_error);
}
?>
```

Procedural style

```php
<?php
$link = @mysqli_connect('localhost', 'fake_user', 'my_password', 'my_db');

if (!$link) {
    die('Connect Error: ' . mysqli_connect_error());
}
?>
```

The above examples will output:

Connect Error: Access denied for user 'fake_user'@'localhost' (using password: YES)

Notes

Warning

The mysqli->connect_error property only works properly as of PHP versions 5.2.9 and 5.3.0. Use the mysqli_connect_error function if compatibility with earlier PHP versions is required.

See Also

mysqli_connect
mysqli_connect_errno
mysqli_errno
mysqli_error
mysqli_sqlstate

3.9.10 mysqli::__construct, mysqli::connect, mysqli_connect

\#   mysqli::__construct

mysqli::connect

mysqli_connect

Open a new connection to the MySQL server

Description

Object oriented style

```
            mysqli::__construct(
               string host
•                     =ini_get("mysqli.default_host"),
string username
•                     =ini_get("mysqli.default_user"),
string passwd
•                     =ini_get("mysqli.default_pw"),
string dbname
•                     ="",
               int port
•                     =ini_get("mysqli.default_port"),
string socket
•                     =ini_get("mysqli.default_socket"));

            void mysqli::connect(
               string host
•                     =ini_get("mysqli.default_host"),
string username
•                     =ini_get("mysqli.default_user"),
string passwd
•                     =ini_get("mysqli.default_pw"),
string dbname
•                     ="",
```

```
            int port
>>>                  =ini_get("mysqli.default_port"),
string socket
```

78

_____

5.   =ini_get("mysqli.default_socket"));

Procedural style

```
mysqli mysqli_connect(
    string host
```
5.   =ini_get("mysqli.default_host"),
string username
6.   =ini_get("mysqli.default_user"),
string passwd
7.   =ini_get("mysqli.default_pw"),
string dbname
8.   ="",
    int port
3.   =ini_get("mysqli.default_port"),
string socket
4.   =ini_get("mysqli.default_socket"));

Opens a connection to the MySQL Server.

Parameters

host	Can be either a host name or an IP address. Passing the NULL value or the string "localhost" to this parameter, the local host is assumed. When possible, pipes will be used instead of the TCP/IP protocol.
	Prepending host by p: opens a persistent connection. mysqli_change_user is automatically called on connections opened from the connection pool.
username	The MySQL user name.
passwd	If not provided or NULL, the MySQL server will attempt to authenticate the user against those user records which have no password only. This allows one username to be used with different permissions (depending on if a password is provided or not).
dbname	If provided will specify the default database to be used when performing queries.
port	Specifies the port number to attempt to connect to the MySQL server.
socket	Specifies the socket or named pipe that should be used.

> **Note**
>
> Specifying the *socket* parameter will not explicitly determine the type of connection to be used when connecting to the MySQL server. How the connection is made to the MySQL database is determined by the *host* parameter.

Return Values

Returns an object which represents the connection to a MySQL Server.

Changelog

Version	Description
5.3.0	Added the ability of persistent connections.

7
9

Examples

Example 3.39 mysqli::__construct example

Object oriented style

```php
<?php
$mysqli = new mysqli('localhost', 'my_user', 'my_password', 'my_db');

/*
    This is the "official" OO way to do it,
    BUT $connect_error was broken until PHP 5.2.9 and 5.3.0.
 */
if ($mysqli->connect_error) {
    die('Connect Error (' . $mysqli->connect_errno . ') '
            . $mysqli->connect_error);
}

/*
    Use this instead of $connect_error if you need to ensure
    compatibility with PHP versions prior to 5.2.9 and 5.3.0.
 */
if (mysqli_connect_error()) {
    die('Connect Error (' . mysqli_connect_errno() . ') '
            . mysqli_connect_error());
}

echo 'Success... ' . $mysqli->host_info . "\n";

$mysqli->close();
?>
```

Object oriented style when extending mysqli class

```php
<?php

class foo_mysqli extends mysqli {
    public function __construct($host, $user, $pass, $db) {
        parent::__construct($host, $user, $pass, $db);

        if (mysqli_connect_error()) {
            die('Connect Error (' . mysqli_connect_errno() . ') '
                    . mysqli_connect_error());
        }
    }
}

$db = new foo_mysqli('localhost', 'my_user', 'my_password', 'my_db');

echo 'Success... ' . $db->host_info . "\n";

$db->close();
?>
```

Procedural style

80

```
<?php
$link = mysqli_connect('localhost', 'my_user', 'my_password', 'my_db');

if (!$link) {
    die('Connect Error (' . mysqli_connect_errno() . ') '
            . mysqli_connect_error());
}

echo 'Success... ' . mysqli_get_host_info($link) . "\n";

mysqli_close($link);
?>
```

The above examples will output:

Success... MySQL host info: localhost via TCP/IP

Notes

> **Note**
>
> MySQLnd always assumes the server default charset. This charset is sent during connection hand-shake/authentication, which mysqlnd will use.
>
> Libmysqlclient uses the default charset set in the my.cnf or by an explicit call to mysqli_options prior to calling mysqli_real_connect, but after mysqli_init.

> **Note**

•   syntax only: If a connection fails an object is still returned. To check if the connection failed then use either the mysqli_connect_error function or the mysqli->connect_error property as in the preceding examples.

> **Note**
>
> If it is necessary to set options, such as the connection timeout, mysqli_real_connect must be used instead.

> **Note**
>
> Calling the constructor with no parameters is the same as calling mysqli_init.

> **Note**
>
> Error "Can't create TCP/IP socket (10106)" usually means that the variables_order configure directive doesn't contain characterE. On Windows, if the environment is not copied the SYSTEMROOT environment variable won't be available and PHP will have problems loading Winsock.

See Also

mysqli_real_connect
mysqli_options
mysqli_connect_errno

mysqli_connect_error
mysqli_close

3.9.11 mysqli::debug, mysqli_debug

>>>   mysqli::debug

mysqli_debug

Performs debugging operations

Description

Object oriented style

```
bool mysqli::debug(
    string message);
```

Procedural style

```
bool mysqli_debug(
    string message);
```

Performs debugging operations using the Fred Fish debugging library.

Parameters

message   A string representing the debugging operation to perform

Return Values

Returns TRUE.

Notes

> **Note**
>
> To use the mysqli_debug function you must compile the MySQL client library to support debugging.

Examples

Example 3.40 Generating a Trace File

```php
<?php

/* Create a trace file in '/tmp/client.trace' on the local (client) machine: */
mysqli_debug("d:t:o,/tmp/client.trace");

?>
```

See Also

mysqli_dump_debug_info
mysqli_report

513

3.9.12 mysqli::dump_debug_info, mysqli_dump_debug_info

- mysqli::dump_debug_info

mysqli_dump_debug_info

Dump debugging information into the log

Description

Object oriented style

```
bool mysqli::dump_debug_info();
```

Procedural style

```
bool mysqli_dump_debug_info(
    mysqli link);
```

This function is designed to be executed by an user with the SUPER privilege and is used to dump debugging information into the log for the MySQL Server relating to the connection.

Parameters

link   Procedural style only: A link identifier returned by mysqli_connect or
                              mysqli_init

Return Values

Returns TRUE on success or FALSE on failure.

See Also

mysqli_debug

3.9.13 mysqli::$errno, mysqli_errno

>>>   mysqli::$errno

mysqli_errno

Returns the error code for the most recent function call

Description

Object oriented style

```
int
    mysqli->errno ;
```

Procedural style

```
int mysqli_errno(
    mysqli link);
```

Returns the last error code for the most recent MySQLi function call that can succeed or fail.

Client error message numbers are listed in the MySQL errmsg.h header file, server error message numbers are listed in mysqld_error.h. In the MySQL source distribution you can find a complete list of error messages and error numbers in the file Docs/mysqld_error.txt.

Parameters

link   Procedural style only: A link identifier returned by mysqli_connect or mysqli_init

Return Values

An error code value for the last call, if it failed. zero means no error occurred.

Examples

Example 3.41 $mysqli->errno **example**

Object oriented style

```php
<?php
$mysqli = new mysqli("localhost", "my_user", "my_password", "world");

/* check connection */
if ($mysqli->connect_errno) {
    printf("Connect failed: %s\n", $mysqli->connect_error);
    exit();
}

if (!$mysqli->query("SET a=1")) {
    printf("Errorcode: %d\n", $mysqli->errno);
}

/* close connection */
$mysqli->close();
?>
```

Procedural style

```php
<?php
$link = mysqli_connect("localhost", "my_user", "my_password", "world");

/* check connection */
if (mysqli_connect_errno()) {
    printf("Connect failed: %s\n", mysqli_connect_error());
    exit();
}

if (!mysqli_query($link, "SET a=1")) {
    printf("Errorcode: %d\n", mysqli_errno($link));
}

/* close connection */
mysqli_close($link);
?>
```

The above examples will output:

_____

Errorcode: 1193

See Also

mysqli_connect_errno
mysqli_connect_error
mysqli_error
mysqli_sqlstate

3.9.14 mysqli::$error_list, mysqli_error_list

•   mysqli::$error_list

mysqli_error_list

Returns a list of errors from the last command executed

Description

Object oriented style

```
array
    mysqli->error_list ;
```

Procedural style

```
array mysqli_error_list(
    mysqli link);
```

Returns a array of errors for the most recent MySQLi function call that can succeed or fail.

Parameters

link   Procedural style only: A link identifier returned by mysqli_connect or mysqli_init

Return Values

A list of errors, each as an associative array containing the errno, error, and sqlstate.

Examples

Example 3.42 $mysqli->error_list **example**

Object oriented style

```php
<?php
$mysqli = new mysqli("localhost", "nobody", "");

/* check connection */
if (mysqli_connect_errno()) {
    printf("Connect failed: %s\n", mysqli_connect_error());
    exit();
```

```
}
    if (!$mysqli->query("SET a=1")) {
        print_r($mysqli->error_list);
}

/* close connection */
$mysqli->close();
?>
```

Procedural style

```php
<?php
$link = mysqli_connect("localhost", "my_user", "my_password", "world");

/* check connection */
if (mysqli_connect_errno()) {
    printf("Connect failed: %s\n", mysqli_connect_error());
    exit();
}

    if (!mysqli_query($link, "SET a=1")) {
        print_r(mysqli_error_list($link));
}

/* close connection */
mysqli_close($link);
?>
```

The above examples will output:

```
Array
(
    => Array
        (
            [errno] => 1193
            [sqlstate] => HY000
            [error] => Unknown system variable 'a'
        )

)
```

>>>

See Also

mysqli_connect_errno
mysqli_connect_error
mysqli_error
mysqli_sqlstate

3.9.15 mysqli::$error, mysqli_error

- mysqli::$error

86

mysqli_error

Returns a string description of the last error

Description

Object oriented style

```
string
   mysqli->error ;
```

Procedural style

```
string mysqli_error(
   mysqli link);
```

Returns the last error message for the most recent MySQLi function call that can succeed or fail.

Parameters

link Procedural style only: A link identifier returned by mysqli_connect or mysqli_init

Return Values

A string that describes the error. An empty string if no error occurred.

Examples

Example 3.43 $mysqli->error **example**

Object oriented style

```php
<?php
$mysqli = new mysqli("localhost", "my_user", "my_password", "world");

/* check connection */
if ($mysqli->connect_errno) {
    printf("Connect failed: %s\n", $mysqli->connect_error);
    exit();
}

if (!$mysqli->query("SET a=1")) {
    printf("Error message: %s\n", $mysqli->error);
}

/* close connection */
$mysqli->close();
?>
```

Procedural style

```php
<?php
$link = mysqli_connect("localhost", "my_user", "my_password", "world");

/* check connection */
if (mysqli_connect_errno()) {
```

```
printf("Connect failed: %s\n", mysqli_connect_error());
```

8
7

```
    exit();
}

if (!mysqli_query($link, "SET a=1")) {
    printf("Error message: %s\n", mysqli_error($link));
}

/* close connection */
mysqli_close($link);
?>
```

The above examples will output:

Error message: Unknown system variable 'a'

See Also

mysqli_connect_errno
mysqli_connect_error
mysqli_errno
mysqli_sqlstate

3.9.16 mysqli::$field_count, mysqli_field_count

>>>   mysqli::$field_count

           mysqli_field_count

           Returns the number of columns for the most recent query

Description

Object oriented style

```
int
    mysqli->field_count ;
```

Procedural style

```
int mysqli_field_count(
    mysqli link);
```

Returns the number of columns for the most recent query on the connection represented by the *link* parameter. This function can be useful when using the mysqli_store_result function to determine if the query should have produced a non-empty result set or not without knowing the nature of the query.

Parameters

link   Procedural style only: A link identifier returned by mysqli_connect or
                                mysqli_init

Return Values

An integer representing the number of fields in a result set.

525

Examples

Example 3.44 $mysqli->field_count **example**

Object oriented style

```php
<?php
$mysqli = new mysqli("localhost", "my_user", "my_password", "test");

$mysqli->query( "DROP TABLE IF EXISTS friends");
$mysqli->query( "CREATE TABLE friends (id int, name varchar(20))");

$mysqli->query( "INSERT INTO friends VALUES (1,'Hartmut'), (2, 'Ulf')");


$mysqli->real_query("SELECT * FROM friends");

if ($mysqli->field_count) {
    /* this was a select/show or describe query */
    $result = $mysqli->store_result();

    /* process resultset */
    $row = $result->fetch_row();

    /* free resultset */
    $result->close();
}
/* close connection */
$mysqli->close();
?>
```

Procedural style

```php
<?php
$link = mysqli_connect("localhost", "my_user", "my_password", "test");

mysqli_query($link, "DROP TABLE IF EXISTS friends");
mysqli_query($link, "CREATE TABLE friends (id int, name varchar(20))");

mysqli_query($link, "INSERT INTO friends VALUES (1,'Hartmut'), (2, 'Ulf')");

mysqli_real_query($link, "SELECT * FROM friends");

if (mysqli_field_count($link)) {
    /* this was a select/show or describe query */
    $result = mysqli_store_result($link);

    /* process resultset */
    $row = mysqli_fetch_row($result);

    /* free resultset */
    mysqli_free_result($result);
}
```

```
/* close connection */
mysqli_close($link);
?>
```

8
9

3.9.17 mysqli::get_charset, mysqli_get_charset

- mysqli::get_charset

mysqli_get_charset

Returns a character set object

Description

Object oriented style

```
object mysqli::get_charset();
```

Procedural style

```
object mysqli_get_charset(
    mysqli link);
```

Returns a character set object providing several properties of the current active character set.

Parameters

link	Procedural style only: A link identifier returned by mysqli_connect or mysqli_init

Return Values

The function returns a character set object with the following properties:

charset	Character set name
collation dir	Collation name
	Directory the charset description was fetched from (?) or "" for built-in character sets
min_length	Minimum character length in bytes
max_length	Maximum character length in bytes
number state	Internal character set number
	Character set status (?)

Examples

Example 3.45 mysqli::get_charset **example** Object oriented style

```
<?ph
p $db = mysqli_init();
  $db->real_connect("localhost","root","","test");
  var_dump($db->get_charset());

?>
```

Procedural style

```
<?php
  $db = mysqli_init();
  mysqli_real_connect($db, "localhost","root","","test");
  var_dump(mysqli_get_charset($db));
?>
```

The above examples will output:

```
object(stdClass)#2 (7) {
  ["charset"]=>
  string(6) "latin1"
  ["collation"]=>
  string(17) "latin1_swedish_ci"
  ["dir"]=>
  string(0) ""
  ["min_length"]=>
  int(1)
  ["max_length"]=>
  int(1)
  ["number"]=>
  int(8)
  ["state"]=>
  int(801)
}
```

See Also

mysqli_character_set_name
mysqli_set_charset

3.9.18 mysqli::$client_info, mysqli::get_client_info, mysqli_get_client_info

>>>   mysqli::$client_info

mysqli::get_client_info

mysqli_get_client_info

Get MySQL client info

Description

Object oriented style

```
string
  mysqli->client_info ;
```

```
string mysqli::get_client_info();
```

Procedural style

```
string mysqli_get_client_info(
    mysqli link);
```

Returns a string that represents the MySQL client library version.

Return Values

A string that represents the MySQL client library version

Examples

Example 3.46 mysqli_get_client_info

```
<?php

/* We don't need a connection to determine
    the version of mysql client library */

printf("Client library version: %s\n", mysqli_get_client_info()); ?>
```

See Also

mysqli_get_client_version
mysqli_get_server_info
mysqli_get_server_version

3.9.19 mysqli::$client_version, mysqli_get_client_version

• 　　　　　mysqli::$client_version

mysqli_get_client_version

Returns the MySQL client version as an integer

Description

Object oriented style

```
int
    mysqli->client_version ;
```

Procedural style

```
int mysqli_get_client_version(
    mysqli link);
```

Returns client version number as an integer.

Return Values

A number that represents the MySQL client library version in format: main_version*10000 + minor_version *100 + sub_version. For example, 4.1.0 is returned as 40100.

This is useful to quickly determine the version of the client library to know if some capability exists.

Examples

Example 3.47 mysqli_get_client_version

```php
<?php

/* We don't need a connection to determine
   the version of mysql client library */

printf("Client library version: %d\n", mysqli_get_client_version()); ?>
```

See Also

mysqli_get_client_info
mysqli_get_server_info
mysqli_get_server_version

3.9.20 mysqli::get_connection_stats, mysqli_get_connection_stats

- mysqli::get_connection_stats

mysqli_get_connection_stats

Returns statistics about the client connection

Description

Object oriented style

```
bool mysqli::get_connection_stats();
```

Procedural style

```
array mysqli_get_connection_stats(
    mysqli link);
```

Returns statistics about the client connection. Available only with mysqlnd.

Parameters

link   Procedural style only: A link identifier returned by mysqli_connect or
mysqli_init

Return Values

Returns an array with connection stats if success, FALSE otherwise.

Examples

Example 3.48 A mysqli_get_connection_stats example

```php
<?php
$link = mysqli_connect();
print_r(mysqli_get_connection_stats($link));
```

```
?>
```

The above example will output something similar to:

```
Array
(
    [bytes_sent] => 43
    [bytes_received] => 80
    [packets_sent] => 1
    [packets_received] => 2
    [protocol_overhead_in] => 8
    [protocol_overhead_out] => 4
    [bytes_received_ok_packet] => 11
    [bytes_received_eof_packet] => 0
    [bytes_received_rset_header_packet] => 0
    [bytes_received_rset_field_meta_packet] => 0
    [bytes_received_rset_row_packet] => 0
    [bytes_received_prepare_response_packet] => 0
    [bytes_received_change_user_packet] => 0
    [packets_sent_command] => 0
    [packets_received_ok] => 1
    [packets_received_eof] => 0
    [packets_received_rset_header] => 0
    [packets_received_rset_field_meta] => 0
    [packets_received_rset_row] => 0
    [packets_received_prepare_response] => 0
    [packets_received_change_user] => 0
    [result_set_queries] => 0
    [non_result_set_queries] => 0
    [no_index_used] => 0
    [bad_index_used] => 0
    [slow_queries] => 0
    [buffered_sets] => 0
    [unbuffered_sets] => 0
    [ps_buffered_sets] => 0
    [ps_unbuffered_sets] => 0
    [flushed_normal_sets] => 0
    [flushed_ps_sets] => 0
    [ps_prepared_never_executed] => 0
    [ps_prepared_once_executed] => 0
    [rows_fetched_from_server_normal] => 0
    [rows_fetched_from_server_ps] => 0
    [rows_buffered_from_client_normal] => 0
    [rows_buffered_from_client_ps] => 0
    [rows_fetched_from_client_normal_buffered] => 0
    [rows_fetched_from_client_normal_unbuffered] => 0
    [rows_fetched_from_client_ps_buffered] => 0
    [rows_fetched_from_client_ps_unbuffered] => 0
    [rows_fetched_from_client_ps_cursor] => 0
    [rows_skipped_normal] => 0
    [rows_skipped_ps] => 0
    [copy_on_write_saved] => 0
    [copy_on_write_performed] => 0
```

```
[command_buffer_too_small] => 0
[connect_success] => 1
[connect_failure] => 0
[connection_reused] => 0
[reconnect] => 0
[pconnect_success] => 0
[active_connections] => 1
[active_persistent_connections] => 0
[explicit_close] => 0
[implicit_close] => 0
```

94

```
[disconnect_close] => 0
[in_middle_of_command_close] => 0
[explicit_free_result] => 0
[implicit_free_result] => 0
[explicit_stmt_close] => 0
[implicit_stmt_close] => 0
[mem_emalloc_count] => 0
[mem_emalloc_ammount] => 0
[mem_ecalloc_count] => 0
[mem_ecalloc_ammount] => 0
[mem_erealloc_count] => 0
[mem_erealloc_ammount] => 0
[mem_efree_count] => 0
[mem_malloc_count] => 0
[mem_malloc_ammount] => 0
[mem_calloc_count] => 0
[mem_calloc_ammount] => 0
[mem_realloc_count] => 0
[mem_realloc_ammount] => 0
[mem_free_count] => 0
[proto_text_fetched_null] => 0
[proto_text_fetched_bit] => 0
[proto_text_fetched_tinyint] => 0
[proto_text_fetched_short] => 0
[proto_text_fetched_int24] => 0
[proto_text_fetched_int] => 0
[proto_text_fetched_bigint] => 0
[proto_text_fetched_decimal] => 0
[proto_text_fetched_float] => 0
[proto_text_fetched_double] => 0
[proto_text_fetched_date] => 0
[proto_text_fetched_year] => 0
[proto_text_fetched_time] => 0
[proto_text_fetched_datetime] => 0
[proto_text_fetched_timestamp] => 0
[proto_text_fetched_string] => 0
[proto_text_fetched_blob] => 0
[proto_text_fetched_enum] => 0
[proto_text_fetched_set] => 0
[proto_text_fetched_geometry] => 0
[proto_text_fetched_other] => 0
[proto_binary_fetched_null] => 0
[proto_binary_fetched_bit] => 0
[proto_binary_fetched_tinyint] => 0
[proto_binary_fetched_short] => 0
[proto_binary_fetched_int24] => 0
[proto_binary_fetched_int] => 0
[proto_binary_fetched_bigint] => 0
[proto_binary_fetched_decimal] => 0
[proto_binary_fetched_float] => 0
[proto_binary_fetched_double] => 0
[proto_binary_fetched_date] => 0
[proto_binary_fetched_year] => 0
[proto_binary_fetched_time] => 0
[proto_binary_fetched_datetime] => 0
[proto_binary_fetched_timestamp] => 0
```

```
    [proto_binary_fetched_string] => 0
    [proto_binary_fetched_blob] => 0
    [proto_binary_fetched_enum] => 0
    [proto_binary_fetched_set] => 0
    [proto_binary_fetched_geometry] => 0
    [proto_binary_fetched_other] => 0
)
```

See Also

9
5

3.9.21 mysqli::$host_info, mysqli_get_host_info

>>>   mysqli::$host_info

mysqli_get_host_info

Returns a string representing the type of connection used

Description

Object oriented style

```
string
    mysqli->host_info ;
```

Procedural style

```
string mysqli_get_host_info(
    mysqli link);
```

Returns a string describing the connection represented by the *link* parameter (including the server host name).

Parameters

link   Procedural style only: A link identifier returned by mysqli_connect or mysqli_init

Return Values

A character string representing the server hostname and the connection type.

Examples

Example 3.49 $mysqli->host_info **example**

Object oriented style

```php
<?php
$mysqli = new mysqli("localhost", "my_user", "my_password", "world");

/* check connection */
if (mysqli_connect_errno()) {
    printf("Connect failed: %s\n", mysqli_connect_error());
    exit();
}

/* print host information */
printf("Host info: %s\n", $mysqli->host_info);

/* close connection */
$mysqli->close();
?>
```

Procedural style

```php
<?php
$link = mysqli_connect("localhost", "my_user", "my_password", "world");

/* check connection */
if (mysqli_connect_errno()) {
    printf("Connect failed: %s\n", mysqli_connect_error());
    exit();
}

/* print host information */
printf("Host info: %s\n", mysqli_get_host_info($link));

/* close connection */
mysqli_close($link);
?>
```

The above examples will output:

Host info: Localhost via UNIX socket

See Also

mysqli_get_proto_info

3.9.22 mysqli::$protocol_version, mysqli_get_proto_info

>>>   mysqli::$protocol_version

mysqli_get_proto_info

Returns the version of the MySQL protocol used

Description

Object oriented style

```
string
    mysqli->protocol_version ;
```

Procedural style

```
int mysqli_get_proto_info(
    mysqli link);
```

Returns an integer representing the MySQL protocol version used by the connection represented by the *link* parameter.

Parameters

link	**Procedural style only: A link identifier returned by** mysqli_connect **or** mysqli_init

Return Values

Returns an integer representing the protocol version.

Examples

Example 3.50 $mysqli->protocol_version **example**

Object oriented style

```php
<?php
$mysqli = new mysqli("localhost", "my_user", "my_password");

/* check connection */
if (mysqli_connect_errno()) {
    printf("Connect failed: %s\n", mysqli_connect_error());
    exit();
}

/* print protocol version */
printf("Protocol version: %d\n", $mysqli->protocol_version);

/* close connection */
$mysqli->close();
?>
```

Procedural style

```php
<?php
$link = mysqli_connect("localhost", "my_user", "my_password");

/* check connection */
if (mysqli_connect_errno()) {
    printf("Connect failed: %s\n", mysqli_connect_error());
    exit();
}

/* print protocol version */
printf("Protocol version: %d\n", mysqli_get_proto_info($link));

/* close connection */
mysqli_close($link);
?>
```

The above examples will output:

```
Protocol version: 10
```

See Also

---

mysqli_get_host_info

3.9.23 mysqli::$server_info, mysqli::get_server_info, mysqli_get_server_info

\#   mysqli::$server_info

            mysqli::get_server_info

            mysqli_get_server_info

            Returns the version of the MySQL server

Description

Object oriented style

```
string
    mysqli->server_info ;
```

```
string mysqli_stmt::get_server_info();
```

Procedural style

```
string mysqli_get_server_info(
    mysqli link);
```

Returns a string representing the version of the MySQL server that the MySQLi extension is connected to.

Parameters

link   Procedural style only: A link identifier returned by mysqli_connect or
                                mysqli_init

Return Values

A character string representing the server version.

Examples

Example 3.51 $mysqli->server_info **example**

Object oriented style

```
<?php
$mysqli = new mysqli("localhost", "my_user", "my_password");

/* check connection */
if (mysqli_connect_errno()) {
    printf("Connect failed: %s\n", mysqli_connect_error());
    exit();
}

/* print server version */
printf("Server version: %s\n", $mysqli->server_info);
```

```
/* close connection */
$mysqli->close();
?>
```

Procedural style

```php
<?php
$link = mysqli_connect("localhost", "my_user", "my_password");

/* check connection */
if (mysqli_connect_errno()) {
    printf("Connect failed: %s\n", mysqli_connect_error());
    exit();
}

/* print server version */
printf("Server version: %s\n", mysqli_get_server_info($link));

/* close connection */
mysqli_close($link);
?>
```

The above examples will output:

Server version: 4.1.2-alpha-debug

See Also

mysqli_get_client_info
mysqli_get_client_version
mysqli_get_server_version

3.9.24 mysqli::$server_version, mysqli_get_server_version

• mysqli::$server_version

mysqli_get_server_version

Returns the version of the MySQL server as an integer

Description

Object oriented style

```
int
    mysqli->server_version ;
```

Procedural style

int mysqli_get_server_version(

100

```
    mysqli link);
```

The mysqli_get_server_version function returns the version of the server connected to (represented by
the *link* parameter) as an integer.

Parameters

link   Procedural style only: A link identifier returned by mysqli_connect or
                                        mysqli_init

Return Values

An integer representing the server version.

The form of this version number is main_version * 10000 + minor_version * 100 +
sub_version (i.e. version 4.1.0 is 40100).

Examples

Example 3.52 $mysqli->server_version **example**

Object oriented style

```php
<?php
$mysqli = new mysqli("localhost", "my_user", "my_password");

/* check connection */
if (mysqli_connect_errno()) {
    printf("Connect failed: %s\n", mysqli_connect_error());
    exit();
}

/* print server version */
printf("Server version: %d\n", $mysqli->server_version);

/* close connection */
$mysqli->close();
?>
```

Procedural style

```php
<?php
$link = mysqli_connect("localhost", "my_user", "my_password");

/* check connection */
if (mysqli_connect_errno()) {
    printf("Connect failed: %s\n", mysqli_connect_error());
    exit();
}

/* print server version */
printf("Server version: %d\n", mysqli_get_server_version($link));

/* close connection */
mysqli_close($link);
?>
```

The above examples will output:

Server version: 40102

See Also

mysqli_get_client_info
mysqli_get_client_version
mysqli_get_server_info

3.9.25 mysqli::get_warnings, mysqli_get_warnings

- mysqli::get_warnings

  mysqli_get_warnings

  Get result of SHOW WARNINGS

  Description

  Object oriented style

  mysqli_warning mysqli::get_warnings();

  Procedural style

  mysqli_warning mysqli_get_warnings(
      mysqli link);

  Warning

  This function is currently not documented; only its argument list is available.

3.9.26 mysqli::$info, mysqli_info

- mysqli::$info

  mysqli_info

  Retrieves information about the most recently executed query

  Description

  Object oriented style

  string
      mysqli->info ;

  Procedural style

  string mysqli_info(
      mysqli link);

The mysqli_info function returns a string providing information about the last query executed. The nature of this string is provided below:

Table 3.9 Possible mysqli_info return values

Query type	Example result string
INSERT INTO...SELECT...	Records: 100 Duplicates: 0 Warnings: 0
INSERT INTO...VALUES (...),(...),(...)	Records: 3 Duplicates: 0 Warnings: 0
LOAD DATA INFILE ...	Records: 1 Deleted: 0 Skipped: 0 Warnings: 0
ALTER TABLE ...	Records: 3 Duplicates: 0 Warnings: 0
UPDATE ...	Rows matched: 40 Changed: 40 Warnings: 0

> **Note**
>
> Queries which do not fall into one of the preceding formats are not supported. In these situations, mysqli_info will return an empty string.

Parameters

link   Procedural style only: A link identifier returned by mysqli_connect or
                                         mysqli_init

Return Values

A character string representing additional information about the most recently executed query.

Examples

Example 3.53 $mysqli->info **example**

Object oriented style

```php
<?php
$mysqli = new mysqli("localhost", "my_user", "my_password", "world");

/* check connection */
if (mysqli_connect_errno()) {
    printf("Connect failed: %s\n", mysqli_connect_error());
    exit();
}

$mysqli->query("CREATE TEMPORARY TABLE t1 LIKE City");

/* INSERT INTO .. SELECT */
$mysqli->query("INSERT INTO t1 SELECT * FROM City ORDER BY ID LIMIT
150"); printf("%s\n", $mysqli->info);

/* close connection */
$mysqli->close();
?>
```

Procedural style

```php
<?php
```

10
3

```
$link = mysqli_connect("localhost", "my_user", "my_password", "world");

/* check connection */
if (mysqli_connect_errno()) {
    printf("Connect failed: %s\n", mysqli_connect_error());
    exit();
}

mysqli_query($link, "CREATE TEMPORARY TABLE t1 LIKE City");

/* INSERT INTO .. SELECT */
mysqli_query($link, "INSERT INTO t1 SELECT * FROM City ORDER BY ID LIMIT 150");
printf("%s\n", mysqli_info($link));

/* close connection */
mysqli_close($link);
?>
```

The above examples will output:

Records: 150 Duplicates: 0   Warnings: 0

See Also

mysqli_affected_rows
mysqli_warning_count
mysqli_num_rows

3.9.27 mysqli::init, mysqli_init

- mysqli::init

  mysqli_init

  Initializes MySQLi and returns a resource for use with mysqli_real_connect()

  Description

  Object oriented style

    mysqli mysqli::init();

  Procedural style

    mysqli mysqli_init();

  Allocates or initializes a MYSQL object suitable for mysqli_options and mysqli_real_connect.

  > **Note**
  >
  > Any subsequent calls to any mysqli function (except mysqli_options) will fail
  > until mysqli_real_connect was called.

  Return Values

Returns an object.

Examples

See mysqli_real_connect.

See Also

mysqli_options
mysqli_close
mysqli_real_connect
mysqli_connect

3.9.28 mysqli::$insert_id, mysqli_insert_id

* mysqli::$insert_id

   mysqli_insert_id

   Returns the auto generated id used in the latest query

Description

Object oriented style

```
mixed
   mysqli->insert_id ;
```

Procedural style

```
mixed mysqli_insert_id(
   mysqli link);
```

The mysqli_insert_id function returns the ID generated by a query (usually INSERT) on a table with a column having the AUTO_INCREMENT attribute. If no INSERT or UPDATE statements were sent via this connection, or if the modified table does not have a column with the AUTO_INCREMENT attribute, this function will return zero.

> **Note**
>
> Performing an INSERT or UPDATE statement using the LAST_INSERT_ID() function will also modify the value returned by the mysqli_insert_id function.

Parameters

link   Procedural style only: A link identifier returned by mysqli_connect or
                                mysqli_init

Return Values

The value of the AUTO_INCREMENT field that was updated by the previous query. Returns zero if there was no previous query on the connection or if the query did not update an AUTO_INCREMENT value.

> **Note**
>
> If the number is greater than maximal int value, mysqli_insert_id will return a string.

Examples

Example 3.54 $mysqli->insert_id **example**

Object oriented style

```php
<?php
$mysqli = new mysqli("localhost", "my_user", "my_password", "world");

/* check connection */
if (mysqli_connect_errno()) {
    printf("Connect failed: %s\n", mysqli_connect_error());
    exit();
}

$mysqli->query("CREATE TABLE myCity LIKE City");

$query = "INSERT INTO myCity VALUES (NULL, 'Stuttgart', 'DEU', 'Stuttgart', 617000)";
$mysqli->query($query);

printf ("New Record has id %d.\n", $mysqli->insert_id);

/* drop table */
$mysqli->query("DROP TABLE myCity");

/* close connection */
$mysqli->close();
?>
```

Procedural style

```php
<?php
$link = mysqli_connect("localhost", "my_user", "my_password", "world");

/* check connection */
if (mysqli_connect_errno()) {
    printf("Connect failed: %s\n", mysqli_connect_error());
    exit();
}

mysqli_query($link, "CREATE TABLE myCity LIKE City");

$query = "INSERT INTO myCity VALUES (NULL, 'Stuttgart', 'DEU', 'Stuttgart', 617000)";
mysqli_query($link, $query);

printf ("New Record has id %d.\n", mysqli_insert_id($link));

/* drop table */
mysqli_query($link, "DROP TABLE myCity");

/* close connection */
mysqli_close($link);
?>
```

The above examples will output:

106

New Record has id 1.

3.9.29 mysqli::kill, mysqli_kill

- mysqli::kill mysqli_kill

    Asks the server to kill a MySQL thread

    Description

    Object oriented style

    ```
    bool mysqli::kill(
        int processid);
    ```

    Procedural style

    ```
    bool mysqli_kill(
        mysqli link,
        int processid);
    ```

    This function is used to ask the server to kill a MySQL thread specified by the *processid* parameter. This value must be retrieved by calling the mysqli_thread_id function.

    To stop a running query you should use the SQL command KILL QUERY processid.

    Parameters

link	Procedural style only: A link identifier returned by mysqli_connect or mysqli_init

    Return Values

    Returns TRUE on success or FALSE on failure.

    Examples

    Example 3.55 mysqli::kill example

    Object oriented style

    ```php
    <?php
    $mysqli = new mysqli("localhost", "my_user", "my_password", "world");

    /* check connection */
    if (mysqli_connect_errno()) {
        printf("Connect failed: %s\n", mysqli_connect_error());
        exit();
    }

    /* determine our thread id */
    $thread_id = $mysqli->thread_id;
    ```

```php
/* Kill connection */
$mysqli->kill($thread_id);

/* This should produce an error */
if (!$mysqli->query("CREATE TABLE myCity LIKE City")) {
    printf("Error: %s\n", $mysqli->error);
    exit;
}

/* close connection */
$mysqli->close();
?>
```

Procedural style

```php
<?php
$link = mysqli_connect("localhost", "my_user", "my_password", "world");

/* check connection */
if (mysqli_connect_errno()) {
    printf("Connect failed: %s\n", mysqli_connect_error());
    exit();
}

/* determine our thread id */
$thread_id = mysqli_thread_id($link);

/* Kill connection */
mysqli_kill($link, $thread_id);

/* This should produce an error */
if (!mysqli_query($link, "CREATE TABLE myCity LIKE City")) {
    printf("Error: %s\n", mysqli_error($link));
    exit;
}

/* close connection */
mysqli_close($link);
?>
```

The above examples will output:

```
Error: MySQL server has gone away
```

See Also

mysqli_thread_id

3.9.30 mysqli::more_results, mysqli_more_results

- mysqli::more_results

mysqli_more_results

108

Check if there are any more query results from a multi query

Description

Object oriented style

```
bool mysqli::more_results();
```

Procedural style

```
bool mysqli_more_results(
    mysqli link);
```

Indicates if one or more result sets are available from a previous call to mysqli_multi_query.

Parameters

link   Procedural style only: A link identifier returned by mysqli_connect or
                                  mysqli_init

Return Values

Returns TRUE if one or more result sets are available from a previous call to mysqli_multi_query, otherwise FALSE.

Examples

See mysqli_multi_query.

See Also

mysqli_multi_query
mysqli_next_result
mysqli_store_result
mysqli_use_result

3.9.31 mysqli::multi_query, mysqli_multi_query

• mysqli::multi_query

mysqli_multi_query

Performs a query on the database

Description

Object oriented style

```
bool mysqli::multi_query(
    string query);
```

Procedural style

```
bool mysqli_multi_query(
    mysqli link,
    string query);
```

Executes one or multiple queries which are concatenated by a semicolon.

To retrieve the resultset from the first query you can use mysqli_use_result or mysqli_store_result. All subsequent query results can be processed using mysqli_more_results and mysqli_next_result.

Parameters

link	Procedural style only: A link identifier returned by mysqli_connect or mysqli_init
query	The query, as a string.
	Data inside the query should be properly escaped.

Return Values

Returns FALSE if the first statement failed. To retrieve subsequent errors from other statements you have to call mysqli_next_result first.

Examples

Example 3.56 mysqli::multi_query example

Object oriented style

```php
<?php
$mysqli = new mysqli("localhost", "my_user", "my_password", "world");

/* check connection */
if (mysqli_connect_errno()) {
    printf("Connect failed: %s\n", mysqli_connect_error());
    exit();
}

$query  = "SELECT CURRENT_USER();";
$query .= "SELECT Name FROM City ORDER BY ID LIMIT 20, 5";

/* execute multi query */
if ($mysqli->multi_query($query)) {
    do {
        /* store first result set */
        if ($result = $mysqli->store_result()) {
            while ($row = $result->fetch_row()) {
                printf("%s\n", $row[0]);
            }
            $result->free();
        }
        /* print divider */
        if ($mysqli->more_results()) {
            printf("-----------\n");
        }
    } while ($mysqli->next_result());
}

/* close connection */
$mysqli->close();
?>
```

Procedural style

```php
<?php
$link = mysqli_connect("localhost", "my_user", "my_password", "world");

/* check connection */
if (mysqli_connect_errno()) {
    printf("Connect failed: %s\n", mysqli_connect_error());
    exit();
}

$query  = "SELECT CURRENT_USER();";
$query .= "SELECT Name FROM City ORDER BY ID LIMIT 20, 5";

/* execute multi query */
if (mysqli_multi_query($link, $query)) {
    do {
        /* store first result set */
        if ($result = mysqli_store_result($link)) {
            while ($row = mysqli_fetch_row($result)) {
                printf("%s\n", $row[0]);
            }
            mysqli_free_result($result);
        }
        /* print divider */
        if (mysqli_more_results($link)) {
            printf("————\n");
        }
    } while (mysqli_next_result($link));
}

/* close connection */
mysqli_close($link);
?>
```

The above examples will output something similar to:

```
my_user@localhost
————
Amersfoort
Maastricht
Dordrecht
Leiden
Haarlemmermeer
```

See Also

mysqli_query
mysqli_use_result
mysqli_store_result
mysqli_next_result
mysqli_more_results

3.9.32 mysqli::next_result, mysqli_next_result

- mysqli::next_result

$$\frac{11}{1}$$

mysqli_next_result

Prepare next result from multi_query

Description

Object oriented style

```
bool mysqli::next_result();
```

Procedural style

```
bool mysqli_next_result(
    mysqli link);
```

Prepares next result set from a previous call to mysqli_multi_query which can be retrieved by mysqli_store_result or mysqli_use_result.

Parameters

link   Procedural style only: A link identifier returned by mysqli_connect or
                                        mysqli_init

Return Values

Returns TRUE on success or FALSE on failure.

Examples

See mysqli_multi_query.

See Also

mysqli_multi_query
mysqli_more_results
mysqli_store_result
mysqli_use_result

3.9.33 mysqli::options, mysqli_options

- mysqli::options

    mysqli_options

    Set options

    Description

    Object oriented style

    ```
    bool mysqli::options(
        int option,
        mixed value);
    ```

    Procedural style

```
bool mysqli_options(
    mysqli link,
    int option,
    mixed value);
```

Used to set extra connect options and affect behavior for a connection.

This function may be called multiple times to set several options.

mysqli_options should be called after mysqli_init and before mysqli_real_connect.

Parameters

link
: Procedural style only: A link identifier returned by mysqli_connect or mysqli_init

option
: The option that you want to set. It can be one of the following values:

Table 3.10 Valid options

Name	Description
MYSQLI_OPT_CONNECT_TIMEOUT	connection timeout in seconds (supported on Windows with TCP/IP since PHP 5.3.1)
MYSQLI_OPT_LOCAL_INFILE	enable/disable use of LOAD LOCAL INFILE
MYSQLI_INIT_COMMAND	command to execute after when connecting to MySQL server
MYSQLI_READ_DEFAULT_FILE	Read options from named option file instead of my.cnf
MYSQLI_READ_DEFAULT_GROUP	Read options from the named group from my.cnf or the file specified with MYSQL_READ_DEFAULT_FILE.
MYSQLI_SERVER_PUBLIC_KEY	RSA public key file used with the SHA-256 based authentication.
MYSQLI_OPT_NET_CMD_BUFFER_SIZE	The size of the internal command/network buffer. Only valid for mysqlnd.
MYSQLI_OPT_NET_READ_BUFFER_SIZE	Maximum read chunk size in bytes when reading the body of a MySQL command packet. Only valid for mysqlnd.
MYSQLI_OPT_INT_AND_FLOAT_NATIVE	Convert integer and float columns back to PHP numbers. Only valid for mysqlnd.
MYSQLI_OPT_SSL_VERIFY_SERVER_CERT	

value   The value for the option.

Return Values

Returns TRUE on success or FALSE on failure.

Changelog

Version	Description
5.5.0	The MYSQLI_SERVER_PUBLIC_KEY and MYSQLI_SERVER_PUBLIC_KEY options were added.
5.3.0	The MYSQLI_OPT_INT_AND_FLOAT_NATIVE, MYSQLI_OPT_NET_CMD_BUFFER_SIZE, MYSQLI_OPT_NET_READ_BUFFER_SIZE, and MYSQLI_OPT_SSL_VERIFY_SERVER_CERT options were added.

Examples

See mysqli_real_connect.

Notes

> **Note**
>
> MySQLnd always assumes the server default charset. This charset is sent during connection hand-shake/authentication, which mysqlnd will use.
>
> Libmysqlclient uses the default charset set in the my.cnf or by an explicit call to mysqli_options prior to calling mysqli_real_connect, but after mysqli_init.

See Also

mysqli_init
mysqli_real_connect

3.9.34 mysqli::ping, mysqli_ping

- mysqli::ping

  mysqli_ping

  Pings a server connection, or tries to reconnect if the connection has gone down

Description

Object oriented style

```
bool mysqli::ping();
```

Procedural style

```
bool mysqli_ping(
    mysqli link);
```

Checks whether the connection to the server is working. If it has gone down and global option mysqli.reconnect is enabled, an automatic reconnection is attempted.

Note

The php.ini setting mysqli.reconnect is ignored by the mysqlnd driver, so automatic reconnection is never attempted.

This function can be used by clients that remain idle for a long while, to check whether the server has closed the connection and reconnect if necessary.

Parameters

link   Procedural style only: A link identifier returned by mysqli_connect or mysqli_init

Return Values

Returns TRUE on success or FALSE on failure.

Examples

Example 3.57 mysqli::ping example

Object oriented style

```php
<?php
$mysqli = new mysqli("localhost", "my_user", "my_password", "world");

/* check connection */
if ($mysqli->connect_errno) {
    printf("Connect failed: %s\n", $mysqli->connect_error);
    exit();
}

/* check if server is alive */
if ($mysqli->ping()) {
    printf ("Our connection is ok!\n");
} else {
    printf ("Error: %s\n", $mysqli->error);
}

/* close connection */
$mysqli->close();
?>
```

Procedural style

```php
<?php
$link = mysqli_connect("localhost", "my_user", "my_password", "world");

/* check connection */
if (mysqli_connect_errno()) {
    printf("Connect failed: %s\n", mysqli_connect_error());
    exit();
}

/* check if server is alive */
```

```
if (mysqli_ping($link)) {
    printf ("Our connection is ok!\n");
} else {
```

11
5

```
      printf ("Error: %s\n", mysqli_error($link));
}

/* close connection */
mysqli_close($link);
?>
```

The above examples will output:

```
Our connection is ok!
```

3.9.35 mysqli::poll, mysqli_poll

* mysqli::poll mysqli_poll

    Poll connections

    Description

    Object oriented style

    ```
    public static int mysqli::poll(
        array read,
        array error,
        array reject,
        int sec,
        int usec
    ```
* =0);

    Procedural style

    ```
    int mysqli_poll(
        array read,
        array error,
        array reject,
        int sec,
        int usec
    ```
* =0);

    Poll connections. Available only with mysqlnd. The method can be used as static.

    Parameters

read	List of connections to check for outstanding results that can be read.
error failure	List of connections on which an error occured, for example, query or lost connection.
reject	List of connections rejected because no asynchronous query has been run on for which the function could poll results.
sec	Maximum number of seconds to wait, must be non-negative.

usec	Maximum number of microseconds to wait, must be non-negative.

Return Values

Returns number of ready connections upon success, FALSE otherwise.

Examples

Example 3.58 A mysqli_poll example

```php
<?php
$link1 = mysqli_connect();
$link1->query("SELECT 'test'", MYSQLI_ASYNC);
$all_links = array($link1);
$processed = 0;
do {
    $links = $errors = $reject = array();
    foreach ($all_links as $link) {
        $links[] = $errors[] = $reject[] = $link;
    }
    if (!mysqli_poll($links, $errors, $reject, 1)) {
        continue;
    }
    foreach ($links as $link) {
        if ($result = $link->reap_async_query()) {
            print_r($result->fetch_row());
            if (is_object($result))
                mysqli_free_result($result);
        } else die(sprintf("MySQLi Error: %s", mysqli_error($link)));
        $processed++;
    }
} while ($processed < count($all_links)); ?>
```

The above example will output:

```
Array
(
    [0] => test
)
```

See Also

mysqli_query
mysqli_reap_async_query

3.9.36 mysqli::prepare, mysqli_prepare

- mysqli::prepare

mysqli_prepare

Prepare an SQL statement for execution

Description

Object oriented style

```
mysqli_stmt mysqli::prepare(
    string query);
```

Procedural style

```
mysqli_stmt mysqli_prepare(
    mysqli link,
    string query);
```

Prepares the SQL query, and returns a statement handle to be used for further operations on the statement. The query must consist of a single SQL statement.

The parameter markers must be bound to application variables using mysqli_stmt_bind_param and/or mysqli_stmt_bind_result before executing the statement or fetching rows.

Parameters

link   Procedural style only: A link identifier returned by mysqli_connect or mysqli_init

query   The query, as a string.

> **Note**
>
> You should not add a terminating semicolon or \g to the statement.

This parameter can include one or more parameter markers in the SQL statement by embedding question mark (?) characters at the appropriate positions.

> **Note**
>
> The markers are legal only in certain places in SQL statements. For example, they are allowed in the VALUES() list of an INSERT statement (to specify column values for a row), or in a comparison with a column in a WHERE clause to specify a comparison value.
>
> However, they are not allowed for identifiers (such as table or column names), in the select list that names the columns to be returned by a SELECT statement, or to specify both operands of a binary operator such as the = equal sign. The latter restriction is necessary because it would be impossible to determine the parameter type. It's not allowed to compare marker with NULL by ? IS NULL too. In general, parameters are legal only in Data Manipulation Language (DML) statements, and not in Data Definition Language (DDL) statements.

Return Values

mysqli_prepare returns a statement object or FALSE if an error occurred.

Examples

Example 3.59 mysqli::prepare **example**

Object oriented style

```php
<?php
$mysqli = new mysqli("localhost", "my_user", "my_password", "world");

/* check connection */
if (mysqli_connect_errno()) {
    printf("Connect failed: %s\n", mysqli_connect_error());
    exit();
}

$city = "Amersfoort";

/* create a prepared statement */
if ($stmt = $mysqli->prepare("SELECT District FROM City WHERE Name=?")) {

    /* bind parameters for markers */
    $stmt->bind_param("s", $city);

    /* execute query */
    $stmt->execute();

    /* bind result variables */
    $stmt->bind_result($district);

    /* fetch value */
    $stmt->fetch();

    printf("%s is in district %s\n", $city, $district);

    /* close statement */
    $stmt->close();
}

/* close connection */
$mysqli->close();
?>
```

Procedural style

```php
<?php
$link = mysqli_connect("localhost", "my_user", "my_password", "world");

/* check connection */
if (mysqli_connect_errno()) {
    printf("Connect failed: %s\n", mysqli_connect_error());
    exit();
}
```

```
$city = "Amersfoort";

/* create a prepared statement */
if ($stmt = mysqli_prepare($link, "SELECT District FROM City WHERE Name=?")) {
```

11
9

```
        /* bind parameters for markers */
        mysqli_stmt_bind_param($stmt, "s", $city);

        /* execute query */
        mysqli_stmt_execute($stmt);

        /* bind result variables */
        mysqli_stmt_bind_result($stmt, $district);

        /* fetch value */
        mysqli_stmt_fetch($stmt);

        printf("%s is in district %s\n", $city, $district);

        /* close statement */
        mysqli_stmt_close($stmt);
}

/* close connection */
mysqli_close($link);
?>
```

The above examples will output:

Amersfoort is in district Utrecht

See Also

mysqli_stmt_execute
mysqli_stmt_fetch
mysqli_stmt_bind_param
mysqli_stmt_bind_result
mysqli_stmt_close

3.9.37 mysqli::query, mysqli_query

- mysqli::query

mysqli_query

Performs a query on the database

Description

Object oriented style

```
mixed mysqli::query(
    string query,
    int resultmode
```
- =MYSQLI_STORE_RESULT);

Procedural style

```
mixed mysqli_query(
```

mysqli link,

```
    string query,
    int resultmode
•  =MYSQLI_STORE_RESULT);
```

Performs a *query* against the database.

For non-DML queries (not INSERT, UPDATE or DELETE), this function is similar to calling mysqli_real_query followed by either mysqli_use_result or mysqli_store_result.

Note

In the case where you pass a statement to mysqli_query that is longer than max_allowed_packet of the server, the returned error codes are different depending on whether you are using MySQL Native Driver (mysqlnd) or MySQL Client Library (libmysqlclient). The behavior is as follows:

• mysqlnd on Linux returns an error code of 1153. The error message means "got a packet bigger than max_allowed_packet bytes".

• mysqlnd on Windows returns an error code 2006. This error message means "server has gone away".

• libmysqlclient on all platforms returns an error code 2006. This error message means "server has gone away".

Parameters

link	Procedural style only: A link identifier returned by mysqli_connect or mysqli_init
query	The query string.
	Data inside the query should be properly escaped.
resultmode	Either the constant MYSQLI_USE_RESULT or MYSQLI_STORE_RESULT depending on the desired behavior. By default, MYSQLI_STORE_RESULT is used.
	If you use MYSQLI_USE_RESULT all subsequent calls will return error Commands out of sync unless you call mysqli_free_result
	With MYSQLI_ASYNC (available with mysqlnd), it is possible to perform query asynchronously. mysqli_poll is then used to get results from such queries.

Return Values

Returns FALSE on failure. For successful SELECT, SHOW, DESCRIBE or EXPLAIN queries mysqli_query will return a mysqli_result object. For other successful queries mysqli_query will return TRUE.

Changelog

Version	Description
5.3.0	Added the ability of async queries.

Examples

Example 3.60 mysqli::query example

Object oriented style

```php
<?php
$mysqli = new mysqli("localhost", "my_user", "my_password", "world");

/* check connection */
if ($mysqli->connect_errno) {
    printf("Connect failed: %s\n", $mysqli->connect_error);
    exit();
}

/* Create table doesn't return a resultset */
if ($mysqli->query("CREATE TEMPORARY TABLE myCity LIKE City") === TRUE)
    { printf("Table myCity successfully created.\n");
}

/* Select queries return a resultset */
if ($result = $mysqli->query("SELECT Name FROM City LIMIT 10")) {
    printf("Select returned %d rows.\n", $result->num_rows);

    /* free result set */
    $result->close();
}

/* If we have to retrieve large amount of data we use MYSQLI_USE_RESULT */
if ($result = $mysqli->query("SELECT * FROM City", MYSQLI_USE_RESULT)) {

    /* Note, that we can't execute any functions which interact with the
       server until result set was closed. All calls will return an 'out of sync'
       error */
    if (!$mysqli->query("SET @a:='this will not work'")) {
        printf("Error: %s\n", $mysqli->error);
    }
    $result->close();
}

$mysqli->close();
?>
```

Procedural style

```php
<?php
$link = mysqli_connect("localhost", "my_user", "my_password", "world");

/* check connection */
if (mysqli_connect_errno()) {
    printf("Connect failed: %s\n", mysqli_connect_error());
    exit();
}

/* Create table doesn't return a resultset */
```

```php
if (mysqli_query($link, "CREATE TEMPORARY TABLE myCity LIKE City") === TRUE) {
    printf("Table myCity successfully created.\n");
}

/* Select queries return a resultset */
if ($result = mysqli_query($link, "SELECT Name FROM City LIMIT 10")) {
    printf("Select returned %d rows.\n", mysqli_num_rows($result));
```

122

```
    /* free result set */
    mysqli_free_result($result);
}

/* If we have to retrieve large amount of data we use MYSQLI_USE_RESULT */ if
($result = mysqli_query($link, "SELECT * FROM City", MYSQLI_USE_RESULT)) {

    /* Note, that we can't execute any functions which interact with the
       server until result set was closed. All calls will return an 'out of sync'
       error */
    if (!mysqli_query($link, "SET @a:='this will not work'")) {
        printf("Error: %s\n", mysqli_error($link));
    }
    mysqli_free_result($result);
}

mysqli_close($link);
?>
```

The above examples will output:

```
Table myCity successfully created.
Select returned 10 rows.
Error: Commands out of sync;   You can't run this command now
```

See Also

mysqli_real_query
mysqli_multi_query
mysqli_free_result

3.9.38 mysqli::real_connect, mysqli_real_connect

• mysqli::real_connect

        mysqli_real_connect

    Opens a connection to a mysql server

Description

Object oriented style

```
bool mysqli::real_connect(
    string host,
    string username,
    string passwd,
    string dbname,
    int port,
    string socket,
    int flags);
```

Procedural style

bool mysqli_real_connect(

$$\frac{}{\begin{array}{r}12\\3\end{array}}$$

```
mysqli link,
string host,
string username,
string passwd,
string dbname,
int port,
string socket,
int flags);
```

Establish a connection to a MySQL database engine.

This function differs from mysqli_connect:

- mysqli_real_connect needs a valid object which has to be created by function mysqli_init.

- With the mysqli_options function you can set various options for connection.

- There is a *flags* parameter.

Parameters

link
: Procedural style only: A link identifier returned by mysqli_connect or mysqli_init

host
: Can be either a host name or an IP address. Passing the NULL value or the string "localhost" to this parameter, the local host is assumed. When possible, pipes will be used instead of the TCP/IP protocol.

username
: The MySQL user name.

passwd
: If provided or NULL, the MySQL server will attempt to authenticate the user against those user records which have no password only. This allows one username to be used with different permissions (depending on if a password as provided or not).
: If provided will specify the default database to be used when

dbname
: performing queries.

port
: Specifies the port number to attempt to connect to the MySQL server.

socket
: Specifies the socket or named pipe that should be used.

> **Note**
>
> Specifying the *socket* parameter will not explicitly determine the type of connection to be used when connecting to the MySQL server. How the connection is made to the MySQL database is determined by the *host* parameter.

flags
: With the parameter *flags* you can set different connection options:

Table 3.11 Supported flags

Name	Description
MYSQLI_CLIENT_COMPRESS	Use compression protocol
MYSQLI_CLIENT_FOUND_ROWS	return number of matched rows,

		not the number of affected rows

124

Name	Description
MYSQLI_CLIENT_IGNORE_SPACE	Allow spaces after function names. Makes all function names reserved words.
MYSQLI_CLIENT_INTERACTIVE	Allow interactive_timeout seconds (instead of wait_timeout seconds) of inactivity before closing the connection
MYSQLI_CLIENT_SSL	Use SSL (encryption)
MYSQLI_CLIENT_SSL_DONT_VERIFY_SERVER	Like MYSQLI_CLIENT_SSL, but disables validation of the provided SSL certificate. This is only for installations using MySQL Native Driver and MySQL 5.6 or later.

Note

For security reasons the MULTI_STATEMENT flag is not supported in PHP. If you want to execute multiple queries use the mysqli_multi_query function.

Changelog

Version	Description
5.6.16	Added the MYSQLI_CLIENT_SSL_DONT_VERIFY_SERVER_CERT flag for MySQL Native Driver

Return Values

Returns TRUE on success or FALSE on failure.

Examples

Example 3.61 mysqli::real_connect example

Object oriented style

```php
<?php

$mysqli = mysqli_init();
if (!$mysqli) {
    die('mysqli_init failed');
}

if (!$mysqli->options(MYSQLI_INIT_COMMAND, 'SET AUTOCOMMIT =
    0')) { die('Setting MYSQLI_INIT_COMMAND failed');
}
```

```php
if (!$mysqli->options(MYSQLI_OPT_CONNECT_TIMEOUT,
    5)) { die('Setting MYSQLI_OPT_CONNECT_TIMEOUT
    failed');
}
```

125

```
if (!$mysqli->real_connect('localhost', 'my_user', 'my_password', 'my_db')) {
    die('Connect Error (' . mysqli_connect_errno() . ') '
            . mysqli_connect_error());
}

echo 'Success... ' . $mysqli->host_info . "\n";

$mysqli->close();
?>
```

Object oriented style when extending mysqli class

```
<?php

class foo_mysqli extends mysqli {
    public function __construct($host, $user, $pass, $db) {
        parent::init();

        if (!parent::options(MYSQLI_INIT_COMMAND, 'SET AUTOCOMMIT = 0'))
            { die('Setting MYSQLI_INIT_COMMAND failed');
        }

        if (!parent::options(MYSQLI_OPT_CONNECT_TIMEOUT, 5))
            { die('Setting MYSQLI_OPT_CONNECT_TIMEOUT
            failed');
        }

        if (!parent::real_connect($host, $user, $pass, $db)) {
            die('Connect Error (' . mysqli_connect_errno() . ') '
                    . mysqli_connect_error());
        }
    }
}

$db = new foo_mysqli('localhost', 'my_user', 'my_password', 'my_db');

echo 'Success... ' . $db->host_info . "\n";

$db->close();
?>
```

Procedural style

```
<?php

$link = mysqli_init();
if (!$link) {
    die('mysqli_init failed');
}

if (!mysqli_options($link, MYSQLI_INIT_COMMAND, 'SET AUTOCOMMIT = 0')) {
    die('Setting MYSQLI_INIT_COMMAND failed');
}
```

```php
if (!mysqli_options($link, MYSQLI_OPT_CONNECT_TIMEOUT, 5))
    { die('Setting MYSQLI_OPT_CONNECT_TIMEOUT failed');
}

if (!mysqli_real_connect($link, 'localhost', 'my_user', 'my_password', 'my_db')) {
    die('Connect Error (' . mysqli_connect_errno() . ') '
```

126

```
                    . mysqli_connect_error());
}

echo 'Success...' . mysqli_get_host_info($link) . "\n";

mysqli_close($link);
?>
```

The above examples will output:

```
Success... MySQL host info: localhost via TCP/IP
```

Notes

> **Note**
>
> MySQLnd always assumes the server default charset. This charset is sent during connection hand-shake/authentication, which mysqlnd will use.
>
> Libmysqlclient uses the default charset set in the my.cnf or by an explicit call to mysqli_options prior to calling mysqli_real_connect, but after mysqli_init.

See Also

mysqli_connect
mysqli_init
mysqli_options
mysqli_ssl_set
mysqli_close

3.9.39 mysqli::real_escape_string, mysqli::escape_string, mysqli_real_escape_string

• mysqli::real_escape_string

mysqli::escape_string

mysqli_real_escape_string

Escapes special characters in a string for use in an SQL statement, taking into account the current charset of the connection

Description

Object oriented style

```
string mysqli::escape_string(
    string escapestr);
```

```
string mysqli::real_escape_string(
    string escapestr);
```

Procedural style

```
string mysqli_real_escape_string(
    mysqli link,
    string escapestr);
```

This function is used to create a legal SQL string that you can use in an SQL statement. The given string is encoded to an escaped SQL string, taking into account the current character set of the connection.

> **Security: the default character set**
>
> The character set must be set either at the server level, or with the API function mysqli_set_charset for it to affect mysqli_real_escape_string. See the concepts section on character sets for more information.

Parameters

link   Procedural style only: A link identifier returned by mysqli_connect or mysqli_init

escapestr   The string to be escaped.

                                          Characters encoded are NUL (ASCII 0), \n, \r, \, ', ", and Control-Z.

Return Values

Returns an escaped string.

Errors/Exceptions

Executing this function without a valid MySQLi connection passed in will return NULL and emit E_WARNING level errors.

Examples

Example 3.62 mysqli::real_escape_string example

Object oriented style

```php
<?php
$mysqli = new mysqli("localhost", "my_user", "my_password", "world");

/* check connection */
if (mysqli_connect_errno()) {
    printf("Connect failed: %s\n", mysqli_connect_error());
    exit();
}

$mysqli->query("CREATE TEMPORARY TABLE myCity LIKE City");

$city = "'s Hertogenbosch";

/* this query will fail, cause we didn't escape $city */
if (!$mysqli->query("INSERT into myCity (Name) VALUES ('$city')")) {
    printf("Error: %s\n", $mysqli->sqlstate);
}

$city = $mysqli->real_escape_string($city);
```

```
/* this query with escaped $city will work */
if ($mysqli->query("INSERT into myCity (Name) VALUES ('$city')")) {
    printf("%d Row inserted.\n", $mysqli->affected_rows);
}

$mysqli->close();
?>
```

Procedural style

```
<?php
$link = mysqli_connect("localhost", "my_user", "my_password", "world");

/* check connection */
if (mysqli_connect_errno()) {
    printf("Connect failed: %s\n", mysqli_connect_error());
    exit();
}

mysqli_query($link, "CREATE TEMPORARY TABLE myCity LIKE City");

$city = "'s Hertogenbosch";

/* this query will fail, cause we didn't escape $city */
if (!mysqli_query($link, "INSERT into myCity (Name) VALUES ('$city')")) {
    printf("Error: %s\n", mysqli_sqlstate($link));
}

$city = mysqli_real_escape_string($link, $city);

/* this query with escaped $city will work */
if (mysqli_query($link, "INSERT into myCity (Name) VALUES ('$city')")) {
    printf("%d Row inserted.\n", mysqli_affected_rows($link));
}

mysqli_close($link);
?>
```

The above examples will output:

```
Error: 42000
1 Row inserted.
```

Notes

> **Note**
>
> For those accustomed to using mysql_real_escape_string, note that the
> arguments of mysqli_real_escape_string differ from what
> mysql_real_escape_string expects. The *link* identifier comes first in

mysqli_real_escape_string, whereas the string to be escaped comes first in mysql_real_escape_string.

See Also

_____

12
9

mysqli_set_charset
mysqli_character_set_name

3.9.40 mysqli::real_query, mysqli_real_query

- mysqli::real_query

  mysqli_real_query

  Execute an SQL query

  Description

  Object oriented style

  ```
  bool mysqli::real_query(
      string query);
  ```

  Procedural style

  ```
  bool mysqli_real_query(
      mysqli link,
      string query);
  ```

  Executes a single query against the database whose result can then be retrieved or stored using the mysqli_store_result or mysqli_use_result functions.

  In order to determine if a given query should return a result set or not, see mysqli_field_count.

  Parameters

link	Procedural style only: A link identifier returned by mysqli_connect or mysqli_init
query	The query, as a string.
	Data inside the query should be properly escaped.

  Return Values

  Returns TRUE on success or FALSE on failure.

  See Also

  mysqli_query
  mysqli_store_result
  mysqli_use_result

3.9.41 mysqli::reap_async_query, mysqli_reap_async_query

- mysqli::reap_async_query

mysqli_reap_async_query

  Get result from async query

130

Description

Object oriented style

```
public mysqli_result mysqli::reap_async_query();
```

Procedural style

```
mysqli_result mysqli_reap_async_query(
    mysqli link);
```

Get result from async query. Available only with mysqlnd.

Parameters

link   Procedural style only: A link identifier returned by mysqli_connect or
                                      mysqli_init

Return Values

Returns mysqli_result in success, FALSE otherwise.

See Also

mysqli_poll

3.9.42 mysqli::refresh, mysqli_refresh

• mysqli::refresh

mysqli_refresh

Refreshes

Description

Object oriented style

```
public bool mysqli::refresh(
    int options);
```

Procedural style

```
bool mysqli_refresh(
    resource link,
    int options);
```

Flushes tables or caches, or resets the replication server information.

Parameters

link   Procedural style only: A link identifier returned by mysqli_connect or
                                      mysqli_init

options   The options to refresh, using the MYSQLI_REFRESH_* constants as
                                      documented within the MySQLi constants documentation.

                                      See also the official MySQL Refresh documentation.

Return Values

TRUE if the refresh was a success, otherwise FALSE

See Also

mysqli_poll

3.9.43 mysqli::release_savepoint, mysqli_release_savepoint

• mysqli::release_savepoint

mysqli_release_savepoint

Removes the named savepoint from the set of savepoints of the current transaction

Description

Object oriented style (method):

```
public bool mysqli::release_savepoint(
    string name);
```

Procedural style:

```
bool mysqli_release_savepoint(
    mysqli link,
    string name);
```

> **Warning**
>
> This function is currently not documented; only its argument list is available.

Parameters

link	Procedural style only: A link identifier returned by mysqli_connect or mysqli_init
name	

Return Values

Returns TRUE on success or FALSE on failure.

See Also

mysqli_rollback

3.9.44 mysqli::rollback, mysqli_rollback

• mysqli::rollback

mysqli_rollback

Rolls back current transaction

132

Description

Object oriented style

```
bool mysqli::rollback(
    int flags
=0,
    string name);
```

Procedural style

```
bool mysqli_rollback(
    mysqli link,
    int flags
=0,
    string name);
```

Rollbacks the current transaction for the database.

Parameters

link	Procedural style only: A link identifier returned by mysqli_connect or mysqli_init
flags	A bitmask of MYSQLI_TRANS_COR_* constants.
name	If provided then ROLLBACK/*name*/ is executed.

Return Values

Returns TRUE on success or FALSE on failure.

Changelog

Version	Description
5.5.0	Added *flags* and *name* parameters.

Examples

Example 3.63 mysqli::rollback **example**

Object oriented style

```
<?php
$mysqli = new mysqli("localhost", "my_user", "my_password", "world");

/* check connection */
if (mysqli_connect_errno()) {
    printf("Connect failed: %s\n", mysqli_connect_error());
    exit();
}

/* disable autocommit */
$mysqli->autocommit(FALSE);

$mysqli->query("CREATE TABLE myCity LIKE City");
```

```
$mysqli->query("ALTER TABLE myCity Type=InnoDB");
$mysqli->query("INSERT INTO myCity SELECT * FROM City LIMIT 50");
```

13
3

```php
/* commit insert */
$mysqli->commit();

/* delete all rows */
$mysqli->query("DELETE FROM myCity");

if ($result = $mysqli->query("SELECT COUNT(*) FROM myCity")) {
    $row = $result->fetch_row();
    printf("%d rows in table myCity.\n", $row[0]);
    /* Free result */
    $result->close();
}

/* Rollback */
$mysqli->rollback();

if ($result = $mysqli->query("SELECT COUNT(*) FROM myCity")) {
    $row = $result->fetch_row();
    printf("%d rows in table myCity (after rollback).\n", $row[0]);
    /* Free result */
    $result->close();
}

/* Drop table myCity */
$mysqli->query("DROP TABLE myCity");

$mysqli->close();
?>
```

Procedural style

```php
<?php
$link = mysqli_connect("localhost", "my_user", "my_password", "world");

/* check connection */
if (mysqli_connect_errno()) {
    printf("Connect failed: %s\n", mysqli_connect_error());
    exit();
}

/* disable autocommit */
mysqli_autocommit($link, FALSE);

mysqli_query($link, "CREATE TABLE myCity LIKE City");
mysqli_query($link, "ALTER TABLE myCity Type=InnoDB");
mysqli_query($link, "INSERT INTO myCity SELECT * FROM City LIMIT 50");

/* commit insert */
mysqli_commit($link);

/* delete all rows */
mysqli_query($link, "DELETE FROM myCity");

if ($result = mysqli_query($link, "SELECT COUNT(*) FROM myCity")) {
    $row = mysqli_fetch_row($result);
    printf("%d rows in table myCity.\n", $row[0]);
```

```
        /* Free result */
        mysqli_free_result($result);
}

/* Rollback */
mysqli_rollback($link);
```

134

```
if ($result = mysqli_query($link, "SELECT COUNT(*) FROM myCity")) {
    $row = mysqli_fetch_row($result);
    printf("%d rows in table myCity (after rollback).\n", $row[0]); /*
    Free result */
    mysqli_free_result($result);
}

/* Drop table myCity */
mysqli_query($link, "DROP TABLE myCity");

mysqli_close($link);
?>
```

The above examples will output:

```
0 rows in table myCity.
50 rows in table myCity (after rollback).
```

See Also

mysqli_begin_transaction
mysqli_commit
mysqli_autocommit
mysqli_release_savepoint

3.9.45 mysqli::rpl_query_type, mysqli_rpl_query_type

- mysqli::rpl_query_type

    mysqli_rpl_query_type

    Returns RPL query type

Description

Object oriented style

```
int mysqli::rpl_query_type(
    string query);
```

Procedural style

```
int mysqli_rpl_query_type(
    mysqli link,
    string query);
```

Returns MYSQLI_RPL_MASTER, MYSQLI_RPL_SLAVE or MYSQLI_RPL_ADMIN depending on a query type. INSERT, UPDATE and similar are *master* queries, SELECT is *slave*, and FLUSH, REPAIR and similar are *admin*.

> **Warning**
>
> This function is currently not documented; only its argument list is available.

> **Warning**
>
> This function has been *DEPRECATED* and *REMOVED* as of PHP 5.3.0.

3.9.46 mysqli::savepoint, mysqli_savepoint

- mysqli::savepoint

  mysqli_savepoint

  Set a named transaction savepoint

  Description

  Object oriented style (method):

  ```
  public bool mysqli::savepoint(
      string name);
  ```

  Procedural style:

  ```
  bool mysqli_savepoint(
      mysqli link,
      string name);
  ```

> **Warning**
>
> This function is currently not documented; only its argument list is available.

  Parameters

  link   Procedural style only: A link identifier returned by mysqli_connect or
                    mysqli_init

  name

  Return Values

  Returns TRUE on success or FALSE on failure.

  See Also

  mysqli_commit

3.9.47 mysqli::select_db, mysqli_select_db

- mysqli::select_db

  mysqli_select_db

  Selects the default database for database queries

  Description

  Object oriented style

```
bool mysqli::select_db(
    string dbname);
```

Procedural style

```
bool mysqli_select_db(
    mysqli link,
    string dbname);
```

Selects the default database to be used when performing queries against the database connection.

Note

This function should only be used to change the default database for the connection. You can select the default database with 4th parameter in mysqli_connect.

Parameters

link   Procedural style only: A link identifier returned by mysqli_connect or mysqli_init

dbname   The database name.

Return Values

Returns TRUE on success or FALSE on failure.

Examples

Example 3.64 mysqli::select_db example

Object oriented style

```php
<?php
$mysqli = new mysqli("localhost", "my_user", "my_password", "test");

/* check connection */
if (mysqli_connect_errno()) {
    printf("Connect failed: %s\n", mysqli_connect_error());
    exit();
}

/* return name of current default database */
if ($result = $mysqli->query("SELECT DATABASE()")) {
    $row = $result->fetch_row();
    printf("Default database is %s.\n", $row[0]);
    $result->close();
}

/* change db to world db */
$mysqli->select_db("world");

/* return name of current default database */
if ($result = $mysqli->query("SELECT DATABASE()")) {
    $row = $result->fetch_row();
    printf("Default database is %s.\n", $row[0]);
    $result->close();
```

619

```
}
$mysqli->close();
```

13
7

```
?>
```

Procedural style

```php
<?php
$link = mysqli_connect("localhost", "my_user", "my_password", "test");

/* check connection */
if (mysqli_connect_errno()) {
    printf("Connect failed: %s\n", mysqli_connect_error());
    exit();
}

/* return name of current default database */
if ($result = mysqli_query($link, "SELECT DATABASE()")) {
    $row = mysqli_fetch_row($result); printf("Default
    database is %s.\n", $row[0]);
    mysqli_free_result($result);
}

/* change db to world db */
mysqli_select_db($link, "world");

/* return name of current default database */
if ($result = mysqli_query($link, "SELECT DATABASE()")) {
    $row = mysqli_fetch_row($result); printf("Default
    database is %s.\n", $row[0]);
    mysqli_free_result($result);
}

mysqli_close($link);
?>
```

The above examples will output:

```
Default database is test.
Default database is world.
```

See Also

mysqli_connect
mysqli_real_connect

3.9.48 mysqli::send_query, mysqli_send_query

- mysqli::send_query

mysqli_send_query

> Send the query and return

Description

138

_____

Object oriented style

```
bool mysqli::send_query(
    string query);
```

Procedural style

```
bool mysqli_send_query(
    mysqli link,
    string query);
```

Warning

This function is currently not documented; only its argument list is available.

Warning

This function has been *DEPRECATED* and *REMOVED* as of PHP 5.3.0.

3.9.49 mysqli::set_charset, mysqli_set_charset

• mysqli::set_charset

mysqli_set_charset

Sets the default client character set

Description

Object oriented style

```
bool mysqli::set_charset(
    string charset);
```

Procedural style

```
bool mysqli_set_charset(
    mysqli link,
    string charset);
```

Sets the default character set to be used when sending data from and to the database server.

Parameters

link   Procedural style only: A link identifier returned by mysqli_connect or
                                  mysqli_init

charset   The charset to be set as default.

Return Values

Returns TRUE on success or FALSE on failure.

Notes

Note

To use this function on a Windows platform you need MySQL client library
version 4.1.11 or above (for MySQL 5.0 you need 5.0.6 or above).

Note

> This is the preferred way to change the charset. Using mysqli_query to set it (such as SET NAMES utf8) is not recommended. See the MySQL character set concepts section for more information.

Examples

Example 3.65 mysqli::set_charset example

Object oriented style

```php
<?php
$mysqli = new mysqli("localhost", "my_user", "my_password", "test");

/* check connection */
if (mysqli_connect_errno()) {
    printf("Connect failed: %s\n", mysqli_connect_error());
    exit();
}

printf("Initial character set: %s\n", $mysqli->character_set_name());

/* change character set to utf8 */
if (!$mysqli->set_charset("utf8")) {
    printf("Error loading character set utf8: %s\n", $mysqli->error); exit();
} else {
    printf("Current character set: %s\n", $mysqli->character_set_name());
}

$mysqli->close();
?>
```

Procedural style

```php
<?php
$link = mysqli_connect('localhost', 'my_user', 'my_password', 'test');

/* check connection */
if (mysqli_connect_errno()) {
    printf("Connect failed: %s\n", mysqli_connect_error());
    exit();
}

printf("Initial character set: %s\n", mysqli_character_set_name($link));

/* change character set to utf8 */
if (!mysqli_set_charset($link, "utf8")) {
    printf("Error loading character set utf8: %s\n", mysqli_error($link)); exit();
} else {
    printf("Current character set: %s\n", mysqli_character_set_name($link));
}

mysqli_close($link);
```

?>

140

_____

The above examples will output something similar to:

```
Initial character set: latin1
Current character set: utf8
```

See Also

mysqli_character_set_name
mysqli_real_escape_string
MySQL character set concepts
List of character sets that MySQL supports

3.9.50 mysqli::set_local_infile_default, mysqli_set_local_infile_default

* mysqli::set_local_infile_default

mysqli_set_local_infile_default

Unsets user defined handler for load local infile command

Description

```
void mysqli_set_local_infile_default(
    mysqli link);
```

Deactivates a LOAD DATA INFILE LOCAL handler previously set with
mysqli_set_local_infile_handler.

Parameters

link   Procedural style only: A link identifier returned by mysqli_connect or
                          mysqli_init

Return Values

No value is returned.

Examples

See mysqli_set_local_infile_handler examples

See Also

mysqli_set_local_infile_handler

3.9.51 mysqli::set_local_infile_handler, mysqli_set_local_infile_handler

* mysqli::set_local_infile_handler

mysqli_set_local_infile_handler

Set callback function for LOAD DATA LOCAL INFILE command

Description

Object oriented style

```
bool mysqli::set_local_infile_handler(
    mysqli link,
    callable read_func);
```

Procedural style

```
bool mysqli_set_local_infile_handler(
    mysqli link,
    callable read_func);
```

Set callback function for **LOAD DATA LOCAL INFILE** command

The callbacks task is to read input from the file specified in the LOAD DATA LOCAL INFILE and to reformat it into the format understood by LOAD DATA INFILE.

The returned data needs to match the format specified in the LOAD DATA

Parameters

link	Procedural style only: A link identifier returned by mysqli_connect or mysqli_init
read_func	A callback function or object method taking the following parameters:

	stream	A PHP stream associated with the SQL commands INFILE
	&buffer	A string buffer to store the rewritten input into
	buflen	The maximum number of characters to be stored in the buffer
	&errormsg	If an error occurs you can store an error message in here

The callback function should return the number of characters stored in the *buffer* or a negative value if an error occurred.

Return Values

Returns TRUE on success or FALSE on failure.

Examples

Example 3.66 mysqli::set_local_infile_handler **example**

Object oriented style

```php
<?php
$db = mysqli_init();
$db->real_connect("localhost","root","","test");

function callme($stream, &$buffer, $buflen, &$errmsg)
{
   $buffer = fgets($stream);

   echo $buffer;
```

- convert to upper case and replace "," delimiter with [TAB] $buffer = strtoupper(str_replace(",", "\t", $buffer));

```php
   return strlen($buffer);
}

echo "Input:\n";

$db->set_local_infile_handler("callme");
$db->query("LOAD DATA LOCAL INFILE 'input.txt' INTO TABLE t1");
$db->set_local_infile_default();

$res = $db->query("SELECT * FROM t1");

echo "\nResult:\n";
while ($row = $res->fetch_assoc()) {
   echo join(",", $row)."\n";
}
?>
```

Procedural style

```php
<?php
$db = mysqli_init();
mysqli_real_connect($db, "localhost","root","","test");

function callme($stream, &$buffer, $buflen, &$errmsg)
{
   $buffer = fgets($stream);

   echo $buffer;
```

- convert to upper case and replace "," delimiter with [TAB] $buffer = strtoupper(str_replace(",", "\t", $buffer));

```php
   return strlen($buffer);
}

echo "Input:\n";

mysqli_set_local_infile_handler($db, "callme");
mysqli_query($db, "LOAD DATA LOCAL INFILE 'input.txt' INTO TABLE t1");
mysqli_set_local_infile_default($db);
```

```php
$res = mysqli_query($db, "SELECT * FROM t1");

echo "\nResult:\n";
while ($row = mysqli_fetch_assoc($res)) {
  echo join(",", $row)."\n";
```

14
3

```
    }
?>
```

The above examples will output:

```
Input:
23,foo
42,bar

Output:
23,FOO
42,BAR
```

See Also

mysqli_set_local_infile_default

3.9.52 mysqli::$sqlstate, mysqli_sqlstate

- mysqli::$sqlstate

mysqli_sqlstate

Returns the SQLSTATE error from previous MySQL operation

Description

Object oriented style

```
string
    mysqli->sqlstate ;
```

Procedural style

```
string mysqli_sqlstate(
    mysqli link);
```

Returns a string containing the SQLSTATE error code for the last error. The error code consists of five characters. '00000' means no error. The values are specified by ANSI SQL and ODBC. For a list of possible values, see http://dev.mysql.com/doc/mysql/en/error-handling.html.

> **Note**
>
> Note that not all MySQL errors are yet mapped to SQLSTATE's. The valueHY000 (general error) is used for unmapped errors.

Parameters

link   Procedural style only: A link identifier returned by mysqli_connect or
                                    mysqli_init

Return Values

Returns a string containing the SQLSTATE error code for the last error. The error code consists of five characters. '00000' means no error.

Examples

Example 3.67 $mysqli->sqlstate **example**

Object oriented style

```php
<?php
$mysqli = new mysqli("localhost", "my_user", "my_password", "world");

/* check connection */
if (mysqli_connect_errno()) {
    printf("Connect failed: %s\n", mysqli_connect_error());
    exit();
}

/* Table City already exists, so we should get an error */
if (!$mysqli->query("CREATE TABLE City (ID INT, Name VARCHAR(30))")) {
    printf("Error - SQLSTATE %s.\n", $mysqli->sqlstate);
}

$mysqli->close();
?>
```

Procedural style

```php
<?php
$link = mysqli_connect("localhost", "my_user", "my_password", "world");

/* check connection */
if (mysqli_connect_errno()) {
    printf("Connect failed: %s\n", mysqli_connect_error());
    exit();
}

/* Table City already exists, so we should get an error */
if (!mysqli_query($link, "CREATE TABLE City (ID INT, Name VARCHAR(30))")) {
    printf("Error - SQLSTATE %s.\n", mysqli_sqlstate($link));
}

mysqli_close($link);
?>
```

The above examples will output:

```
Error - SQLSTATE 42S01.
```

See Also

<u>mysqli_errno</u>
<u>mysqli_error</u>

3.9.53 mysqli::ssl_set, mysqli_ssl_set

- mysqli::ssl_set

mysqli_ssl_set

Used for establishing secure connections using SSL

Description

Object oriented style

```
bool mysqli::ssl_set(
    string key,
    string cert,
    string ca,
    string capath,
    string cipher);
```

Procedural style

```
bool mysqli_ssl_set(
    mysqli link,
    string key,
    string cert,
    string ca,
    string capath,
    string cipher);
```

Used for establishing secure connections using SSL. It must be called before mysqli_real_connect. This function does nothing unless OpenSSL support is enabled.

Note that MySQL Native Driver does not support SSL before PHP 5.3.3, so calling this function when using MySQL Native Driver will result in an error. MySQL Native Driver is enabled by default on Microsoft Windows from PHP version 5.3 onwards.

Parameters

link	Procedural style only: A link identifier returned by mysqli_connect or mysqli_init
key	The path name to the key file.
cert	The path name to the certificate file.
ca	The path name to the certificate authority file.
capath in	The pathname to a directory that contains trusted SSL CA certificates PEM format.
cipher	A list of allowable ciphers to use for SSL encryption.

Any unused SSL parameters may be given as NULL

Return Values

This function always returns TRUE value. If SSL setup is incorrect mysqli_real_connect will return an error when you attempt to connect.

See Also

mysqli_options
mysqli_real_connect

3.9.54 mysqli::stat, mysqli_stat

* mysqli::stat

    mysqli_stat

    Gets the current system status

    Description

    Object oriented style

    string mysqli::stat();

    Procedural style

    ```
    string mysqli_stat(
        mysqli link);
    ```

    mysqli_stat returns a string containing information similar to that provided by the 'mysqladmin status' command. This includes uptime in seconds and the number of running threads, questions, reloads, and open tables.

    Parameters

    link   Procedural style only: A link identifier returned by mysqli_connect or
                                          mysqli_init

    Return Values

    A string describing the server status. FALSE if an error occurred.

    Examples

    Example 3.68 mysqli::stat example

    Object oriented style

    ```php
    <?php
    $mysqli = new mysqli("localhost", "my_user", "my_password", "world");

    /* check connection */
    if (mysqli_connect_errno()) {
        printf("Connect failed: %s\n", mysqli_connect_error());
        exit();
    }

    printf ("System status: %s\n", $mysqli->stat());

    $mysqli->close();
    ?>
    ```

Procedural style

```php
<?php
$link = mysqli_connect("localhost", "my_user", "my_password", "world");

/* check connection */
if (mysqli_connect_errno()) {
    printf("Connect failed: %s\n", mysqli_connect_error());
    exit();
}

printf("System status: %s\n", mysqli_stat($link));

mysqli_close($link);
?>
```

The above examples will output:

```
System status: Uptime: 272  Threads: 1   Questions: 5340  Slow queries: 0
Opens: 13  Flush tables: 1    Open tables: 0   Queries per second avg: 19.632
Memory in use: 8496K Max memory used: 8560K
```

See Also

mysqli_get_server_info

3.9.55 mysqli::stmt_init, mysqli_stmt_init

* mysqli::stmt_init

mysqli_stmt_init

Initializes a statement and returns an object for use with mysqli_stmt_prepare

Description

Object oriented style

```
mysqli_stmt mysqli::stmt_init();
```

Procedural style

```
mysqli_stmt mysqli_stmt_init(
    mysqli link);
```

Allocates and initializes a statement object suitable for mysqli_stmt_prepare.

> **Note**
>
> Any subsequent calls to any mysqli_stmt function will fail
> until mysqli_stmt_prepare was called.

Parameters

link   Procedural style only: A link identifier returned by mysqli_connect or mysqli_init

Return Values

Returns an object.

See Also

mysqli_stmt_prepare

3.9.56 mysqli::store_result, mysqli_store_result

- mysqli::store_result

    mysqli_store_result

    Transfers a result set from the last query

Description

Object oriented style

```
mysqli_result mysqli::store_result(
    int option);
```

Procedural style

```
mysqli_result mysqli_store_result(
    mysqli link,
    int option);
```

Transfers the result set from the last query on the database connection represented by the *link* parameter to be used with the mysqli_data_seek function.

Parameters

link   Procedural style only: A link identifier returned by mysqli_connect or mysqli_init

option   The option that you want to set. It can be one of the following values:

Table 3.12 Valid options

Name	Description
MYSQLI_STORE_RESULT_COPY_DATA	Copy results from the internal mysqlnd buffer into the PHP variables fetched. By default, mysqlnd will use a reference logic to avoid copying and duplicating results held in memory. For certain result sets, for example, result sets with many small rows, the copy approach can reduce the

Name	Description
	overall memory usage because PHP variables holding results may be released earlier (available with mysqlnd only, since PHP 5.6.0)

Return Values

Returns a buffered result object or FALSE if an error occurred.

> **Note**
>
> mysqli_store_result returns FALSE in case the query didn't return a result set (if the query was, for example an INSERT statement). This function also returns FALSE if the reading of the result set failed. You can check if you have got an error by checking if mysqli_error doesn't return an empty string, if mysqli_errno returns a non zero value, or if mysqli_field_count returns a non zero value. Also possible reason for this function returning FALSE after successful call to mysqli_query can be too large result set (memory for it cannot be allocated).
> If mysqli_field_count returns a non-zero value, the statement should have produced a non-empty result set.

Notes

> **Note**
>
> Although it is always good practice to free the memory used by the result of a query using the mysqli_free_result function, when transferring large result sets using the mysqli_store_result this becomes particularly important.

Examples

See mysqli_multi_query.

See Also

mysqli_real_query
mysqli_use_result

3.9.57 mysqli::$thread_id, mysqli_thread_id

• mysqli::$thread_id

mysqli_thread_id

Returns the thread ID for the current connection

Description

Object oriented style

```
int
    mysqli->thread_id ;
```

Procedural style

```
int mysqli_thread_id(
    mysqli link);
```

The mysqli_thread_id function returns the thread ID for the current connection which can then be killed using the mysqli_kill function. If the connection is lost and you reconnect with mysqli_ping, the thread ID will be other. Therefore you should get the thread ID only when you need it.

Note

The thread ID is assigned on a connection-by-connection basis. Hence, if the connection is broken and then re-established a new thread ID will be assigned.

To kill a running query you can use the SQL command KILL QUERY processid.

Parameters

link   Procedural style only: A link identifier returned by mysqli_connect or mysqli_init

Return Values

Returns the Thread ID for the current connection.

Examples

Example 3.69 $mysqli->thread_id example

Object oriented style

```php
<?php
$mysqli = new mysqli("localhost", "my_user", "my_password", "world");

/* check connection */
if (mysqli_connect_errno()) {
    printf("Connect failed: %s\n", mysqli_connect_error());
    exit();
}

/* determine our thread id */
$thread_id = $mysqli->thread_id;

/* Kill connection */
$mysqli->kill($thread_id);

/* This should produce an error */
if (!$mysqli->query("CREATE TABLE myCity LIKE City")) {
    printf("Error: %s\n", $mysqli->error);
    exit;
}

/* close connection */
$mysqli->close();
?>
```

Procedural style

```php
<?php
```

```
    $link = mysqli_connect("localhost", "my_user", "my_password", "world");

/* check connection */
if (mysqli_connect_errno()) {
    printf("Connect failed: %s\n", mysqli_connect_error());
    exit();
}

/* determine our thread id */
$thread_id = mysqli_thread_id($link);

/* Kill connection */
mysqli_kill($link, $thread_id);

/* This should produce an error */
if (!mysqli_query($link, "CREATE TABLE myCity LIKE City")) {
    printf("Error: %s\n", mysqli_error($link));
    exit;
}

/* close connection */
mysqli_close($link);
?>
```

The above examples will output:

Error: MySQL server has gone away

See Also

mysqli_kill

3.9.58 mysqli::thread_safe, mysqli_thread_safe

- mysqli::thread_safe

mysqli_thread_safe

Returns whether thread safety is given or not

Description

Procedural style

```
bool mysqli_thread_safe();
```

Tells whether the client library is compiled as thread-safe.

Return Values

TRUE if the client library is thread-safe, otherwise FALSE.

3.9.59 mysqli::use_result, mysqli_use_result

- mysqli::use_result

mysqli_use_result

Initiate a result set retrieval

Description

Object oriented style

```
mysqli_result mysqli::use_result();
```

Procedural style

```
mysqli_result mysqli_use_result(
    mysqli link);
```

Used to initiate the retrieval of a result set from the last query executed using the mysqli_real_query function on the database connection.

Either this or the mysqli_store_result function must be called before the results of a query can be retrieved, and one or the other must be called to prevent the next query on that database connection from failing.

> **Note**
>
> The mysqli_use_result function does not transfer the entire result set from the database and hence cannot be used functions such as mysqli_data_seek to move to a particular row within the set. To use this functionality, the result set must be stored using mysqli_store_result. One should not use mysqli_use_result if a lot of processing on the client side is performed, since this will tie up the server and prevent other threads from updating any tables from which the data is being fetched.

Return Values

Returns an unbuffered result object or FALSE if an error occurred.

Examples

Example 3.70 mysqli::use_result example

Object oriented style

```php
<?php
$mysqli = new mysqli("localhost", "my_user", "my_password", "world");

/* check connection */
if (mysqli_connect_errno()) {
    printf("Connect failed: %s\n", mysqli_connect_error());
    exit();
}

$query  = "SELECT CURRENT_USER();";
$query .= "SELECT Name FROM City ORDER BY ID LIMIT 20, 5";

/* execute multi query */
if ($mysqli->multi_query($query)) {
    do {
```

```php
        /* store first result set */
        if ($result = $mysqli->use_result()) {
            while ($row = $result->fetch_row()) {
                printf("%s\n", $row[0]);
            }
            $result->close();
        }
        /* print divider */
        if ($mysqli->more_results()) {
            printf("—————\n");
        }
    } while ($mysqli->next_result());
}

/* close connection */
$mysqli->close();
?>
```

Procedural style

```php
<?php
$link = mysqli_connect("localhost", "my_user", "my_password", "world");

/* check connection */
if (mysqli_connect_errno()) {
    printf("Connect failed: %s\n", mysqli_connect_error());
    exit();
}

$query  = "SELECT CURRENT_USER();";
$query .= "SELECT Name FROM City ORDER BY ID LIMIT 20, 5";

/* execute multi query */
if (mysqli_multi_query($link, $query)) {
    do {
        /* store first result set */
        if ($result = mysqli_use_result($link)) {
            while ($row = mysqli_fetch_row($result)) {
                printf("%s\n", $row[0]);
            }
            mysqli_free_result($result);
        }
        /* print divider */
        if (mysqli_more_results($link)) {
            printf("—————\n");
        }
    } while (mysqli_next_result($link));
}

/* close connection */
mysqli_close($link);
?>
```

The above examples will output:

```
my_user@localhost
---------
Amersfoort
Maastricht
```

154

Dordrecht
Leiden
Haarlemmermeer

See Also

mysqli_real_query
mysqli_store_result

3.9.60 mysqli::$warning_count, mysqli_warning_count

- mysqli::$warning_count

    mysqli_warning_count

    Returns the number of warnings from the last query for the given link

Description

Object oriented style

```
int
    mysqli->warning_count ;
```

Procedural style

```
int mysqli_warning_count(
    mysqli link);
```

Returns the number of warnings from the last query in the connection.

> **Note**
>
> For retrieving warning messages you can use the SQL command SHOW
> WARNINGS [limit row_count].

Parameters

link   Procedural style only: A link identifier returned by mysqli_connect or
                              mysqli_init

Return Values

Number of warnings or zero if there are no warnings.

Examples

Example 3.71 $mysqli->warning_count **example**

Object oriented style

```php
<?php
$mysqli = new mysqli("localhost", "my_user", "my_password", "world");

/* check connection */
```

```php
if (mysqli_connect_errno()) {
    printf("Connect failed: %s\n", mysqli_connect_error());
    exit();
}

$mysqli->query("CREATE TABLE myCity LIKE City");

/* a remarkable city in Wales */
$query = "INSERT INTO myCity (CountryCode, Name) VALUES('GBR',
        'Llanfairpwllgwyngyllgogerychwyrndrobwllllantysiliogogogoch')";

$mysqli->query($query);

if ($mysqli->warning_count) {
    if ($result = $mysqli->query("SHOW WARNINGS")) {
        $row = $result->fetch_row();
        printf("%s (%d): %s\n", $row[0], $row[1], $row[2]);
        $result->close();
    }
}

/* close connection */
$mysqli->close();
?>
```

Procedural style

```php
<?php
$link = mysqli_connect("localhost", "my_user", "my_password", "world");

/* check connection */
if (mysqli_connect_errno()) {
    printf("Connect failed: %s\n", mysqli_connect_error());
    exit();
}

mysqli_query($link, "CREATE TABLE myCity LIKE City");

/* a remarkable long city name in Wales */
$query = "INSERT INTO myCity (CountryCode, Name) VALUES('GBR',
        'Llanfairpwllgwyngyllgogerychwyrndrobwllllantysiliogogogoch')";

mysqli_query($link, $query);

if (mysqli_warning_count($link)) {
    if ($result = mysqli_query($link, "SHOW WARNINGS")) {
        $row = mysqli_fetch_row($result);
        printf("%s (%d): %s\n", $row[0], $row[1], $row[2]);
        mysqli_free_result($result);
    }
}

/* close connection */
mysqli_close($link);
?>
```

The above examples will output:

Warning (1264): Data truncated for column 'Name' at row 1

See Also

mysqli_errno
mysqli_error
mysqli_sqlstate

3.10 The mysqli_stmt class

Represents a prepared statement.

```
mysqli_stmt {
mysqli_stmt

      Properties
  int
    mysqli_stmt->affected_rows ;

  int
    mysqli_stmt->errno ;

  array
    mysqli_stmt->error_list ;

  string
    mysqli_stmt->error ;

  int
    mysqli_stmt->field_count ;

  int
    mysqli_stmt->insert_id ;

  int
    mysqli_stmt->num_rows ;

  int
    mysqli_stmt->param_count ;

  string
    mysqli_stmt->sqlstate ;

Methods

  mysqli_stmt::__construct(
    mysqli link,
    string query);

  int mysqli_stmt::attr_get(
    int attr);

  bool mysqli_stmt::attr_set(
    int attr,
    int mode);
```

```
bool mysqli_stmt::bind_param(
    string types,
    mixed var1,
```

```
    mixed ...);

bool mysqli_stmt::bind_result(
    mixed var1,
    mixed ...);

bool mysqli_stmt::close();

void mysqli_stmt::data_seek(
    int offset);

bool mysqli_stmt::execute();

bool mysqli_stmt::fetch();

void mysqli_stmt::free_result();

mysqli_result mysqli_stmt::get_result();

object mysqli_stmt::get_warnings();

int mysqli_stmt::num_rows();

mixed mysqli_stmt::prepare(
    string query);

bool mysqli_stmt::reset();

mysqli_result mysqli_stmt::result_metadata();

bool mysqli_stmt::send_long_data(
    int param_nr,
    string data);

bool mysqli_stmt::store_result();

}
```

3.10.1 mysqli_stmt::$affected_rows, mysqli_stmt_affected_rows

- mysqli_stmt::$affected_rows

mysqli_stmt_affected_rows

Returns the total number of rows changed, deleted, or inserted by the last executed statement

Description

Object oriented style

```
int
    mysqli_stmt->affected_rows ;
```

Procedural style

```
int mysqli_stmt_affected_rows(
    mysqli_stmt stmt);
```

Returns the number of rows affected by INSERT, UPDATE, or DELETE query.

This function only works with queries which update a table. In order to get the number of rows from a SELECT query, use mysqli_stmt_num_rows instead.

158

Parameters

stmt   Procedural style only: A statement identifier returned by
                             mysqli_stmt_init.

Return Values

An integer greater than zero indicates the number of rows affected or retrieved. Zero indicates that no
records where updated for an UPDATE/DELETE statement, no rows matched the WHERE clause in the
query or that no query has yet been executed. -1 indicates that the query has returned an error. NULL
indicates an invalid argument was supplied to the function.

> **Note**
>
> If the number of affected rows is greater than maximal PHP int value, the number
> of affected rows will be returned as a string value.

Examples

Example 3.72 Object oriented style

```php
<?php
$mysqli = new mysqli("localhost", "my_user", "my_password", "world");

/* check connection */
if (mysqli_connect_errno()) {
    printf("Connect failed: %s\n", mysqli_connect_error());
    exit();
}

/* create temp table */
$mysqli->query("CREATE TEMPORARY TABLE myCountry LIKE Country");

$query = "INSERT INTO myCountry SELECT * FROM Country WHERE Code LIKE ?";

/* prepare statement */
if ($stmt = $mysqli->prepare($query)) {

    /* Bind variable for placeholder */
    $code = 'A%';
    $stmt->bind_param("s", $code);

    /* execute statement */
    $stmt->execute();

    printf("rows inserted: %d\n", $stmt->affected_rows);

    /* close statement */
    $stmt->close();
}

/* close connection */
$mysqli->close();
?>
```

Example 3.73 Procedural style

```php
<?php
```

```
$link = mysqli_connect("localhost", "my_user", "my_password", "world");

/* check connection */
if (mysqli_connect_errno()) {
    printf("Connect failed: %s\n", mysqli_connect_error());
    exit();
}

/* create temp table */
mysqli_query($link, "CREATE TEMPORARY TABLE myCountry LIKE Country");

$query = "INSERT INTO myCountry SELECT * FROM Country WHERE Code LIKE ?";

/* prepare statement */
if ($stmt = mysqli_prepare($link, $query)) {

    /* Bind variable for placeholder */
    $code = 'A%';
    mysqli_stmt_bind_param($stmt, "s", $code);

    /* execute statement */
    mysqli_stmt_execute($stmt);

    printf("rows inserted: %d\n", mysqli_stmt_affected_rows($stmt));

    /* close statement */
    mysqli_stmt_close($stmt);
}

/* close connection */
mysqli_close($link);
?>
```

The above examples will output:

```
rows inserted: 17
```

See Also

mysqli_stmt_num_rows
mysqli_prepare

3.10.2 mysqli_stmt::attr_get, mysqli_stmt_attr_get

- mysqli_stmt::attr_get

mysqli_stmt_attr_get

Used to get the current value of a statement attribute

Description

Object oriented style

```
int mysqli_stmt::attr_get(
    int attr);
```

160

Procedural style

```
int mysqli_stmt_attr_get(
    mysqli_stmt stmt,
    int attr);
```

Gets the current value of a statement attribute.

Parameters

stmt   Procedural style only: A statement identifier returned by
mysqli_stmt_init.

attr   The attribute that you want to get.

Return Values

Returns FALSE if the attribute is not found, otherwise returns the value of the attribute.

3.10.3 mysqli_stmt::attr_set, mysqli_stmt_attr_set

• mysqli_stmt::attr_set

mysqli_stmt_attr_set

Used to modify the behavior of a prepared statement

Description

Object oriented style

```
bool mysqli_stmt::attr_set(
    int attr,
    int mode);
```

Procedural style

```
bool mysqli_stmt_attr_set(
    mysqli_stmt stmt,
    int attr,
    int mode);
```

Used to modify the behavior of a prepared statement. This function may be called multiple times to set several attributes.

Parameters

stmt   Procedural style only: A statement identifier returned by
mysqli_stmt_init.

attr   The attribute that you want to set. It can have one of the following
values:

Table 3.13 Attribute values

Character	Description
MYSQLI_STMT_ATTR_UPDATE_	MAXSettingLENGTHtoTRUE causes mysqli_stmt_store_result

Character	Description
	to update the metadata MYSQL_FIELD->max_length value.
MYSQLI_STMT_ATTR_CURSOR_TYPE	Type of cursor to open for statement when mysqli_stmt_execute is invoked. *mode* can be MYSQLI_CURSOR_TYPE_NO_CURSOR (the default) or MYSQLI_CURSOR_TYPE_READ_ONLY.
MYSQLI_STMT_ATTR_PREFETCH_ROWS	Number of rows to fetch from server at a time when using a cursor. *mode* can be in the range from 1 to the maximum value of unsigned long. The default is 1.

If you use the MYSQLI_STMT_ATTR_CURSOR_TYPE option with MYSQLI_CURSOR_TYPE_READ_ONLY, a cursor is opened for the statement when you invoke mysqli_stmt_execute. If there is already an open cursor from a previous mysqli_stmt_execute call, it closes the cursor before opening a new one. mysqli_stmt_reset also closes any open cursor before preparing the statement for re-execution. mysqli_stmt_free_result closes any open cursor.

If you open a cursor for a prepared statement, mysqli_stmt_store_result is unnecessary.

| mode | The value to assign to the attribute. |

See Also

Connector/MySQL mysqli_stmt_attr_set()

3.10.4 mysqli_stmt::bind_param, mysqli_stmt_bind_param

• mysqli_stmt::bind_param

mysqli_stmt_bind_param

Binds variables to a prepared statement as parameters

Description

Object oriented style

```
bool mysqli_stmt::bind_param(
    string types,
    mixed var1,
    mixed ...);
```

Procedural style

```
bool mysqli_stmt_bind_param(
```

```
mysqli_stmt stmt,
string types,
mixed var1,
mixed ...);
```

Bind variables for the parameter markers in the SQL statement that was passed to mysqli_prepare.

> **Note**
>
> If data size of a variable exceeds max. allowed packet size (max_allowed_packet), you have to specify b in *types* and use mysqli_stmt_send_long_data to send the data in packets.

> **Note**
>
> Care must be taken when using mysqli_stmt_bind_param in conjunction with call_user_func_array. Note that mysqli_stmt_bind_param requires parameters to be passed by reference, whereas call_user_func_array can accept as a parameter a list of variables that can represent references or values.

Parameters

stmt

Procedural style only: A statement identifier returned by mysqli_stmt_init.

types

A string that contains one or more characters which specify the types for the corresponding bind variables:

Table 3.14 Type specification chars

Character	Description
i	corresponding variable has type integer
d	corresponding variable has type double
s	corresponding variable has type string
b	corresponding variable is a blob and will be sent in packets

var1

The number of variables and length of string *types* must match the parameters in the statement.

Return Values

Returns TRUE on success or FALSE on failure.

Examples

Example 3.74 Object oriented style

```php
<?php
$mysqli = new mysqli('localhost', 'my_user', 'my_password', 'world');
```

```
/* check connection */
if (mysqli_connect_errno()) {
```

```php
    printf("Connect failed: %s\n", mysqli_connect_error());
    exit();
}

$stmt = $mysqli->prepare("INSERT INTO CountryLanguage VALUES (?, ?, ?, ?)");
$stmt->bind_param('sssd', $code, $language, $official, $percent);

$code = 'DEU';
$language = 'Bavarian';
$official = "F";
$percent = 11.2;

/* execute prepared statement */
$stmt->execute();

printf("%d Row inserted.\n", $stmt->affected_rows);

/* close statement and connection */
$stmt->close();

/* Clean up table CountryLanguage */
$mysqli->query("DELETE FROM CountryLanguage WHERE
Language='Bavarian'"); printf("%d Row deleted.\n", $mysqli-
>affected_rows);

/* close connection */
$mysqli->close();
?>
```

Example 3.75 Procedural style

```php
<?php
$link = mysqli_connect('localhost', 'my_user', 'my_password', 'world');

/* check connection */
if (!$link) {
    printf("Connect failed: %s\n", mysqli_connect_error());
    exit();
}

$stmt = mysqli_prepare($link, "INSERT INTO CountryLanguage VALUES (?, ?, ?, ?)");
mysqli_stmt_bind_param($stmt, 'sssd', $code, $language, $official, $percent);

$code = 'DEU';
$language = 'Bavarian';
$official = "F";
$percent = 11.2;

/* execute prepared statement */
mysqli_stmt_execute($stmt);

printf("%d Row inserted.\n", mysqli_stmt_affected_rows($stmt));

/* close statement and connection */
mysqli_stmt_close($stmt);
```

```php
/* Clean up table CountryLanguage */
mysqli_query($link, "DELETE FROM CountryLanguage WHERE
Language='Bavarian'"); printf("%d Row deleted.\n", mysqli_affected_rows($link));

/* close connection */
mysqli_close($link);
?>
```

164

The above examples will output:

1 Row inserted.
1 Row deleted.

See Also

mysqli_stmt_bind_result
mysqli_stmt_execute
mysqli_stmt_fetch
mysqli_prepare
mysqli_stmt_send_long_data
mysqli_stmt_errno
mysqli_stmt_error

3.10.5 mysqli_stmt::bind_result, mysqli_stmt_bind_result

- mysqli_stmt::bind_result

mysqli_stmt_bind_result

Binds variables to a prepared statement for result storage

Description

Object oriented style

```
bool mysqli_stmt::bind_result(
    mixed var1,
    mixed ...);
```

Procedural style

```
bool mysqli_stmt_bind_result(
    mysqli_stmt stmt,
    mixed var1,
    mixed ...);
```

Binds columns in the result set to variables.

When mysqli_stmt_fetch is called to fetch data, the MySQL client/server protocol places the data for the bound columns into the specified variables *var1, ...*

> **Note**
>
> Note that all columns must be bound after mysqli_stmt_execute and prior to calling mysqli_stmt_fetch. Depending on column types bound variables can silently change to the corresponding PHP type.
>
> A column can be bound or rebound at any time, even after a result set has been partially retrieved. The new binding takes effect the next time mysqli_stmt_fetch is called.

Parameters

stmt	Procedural style only: A statement identifier returned by mysqli_stmt_init.
var1	The variable to be bound.

Return Values

Returns TRUE on success or FALSE on failure.

Examples

Example 3.76 Object oriented style

```php
<?php
$mysqli = new mysqli("localhost", "my_user", "my_password", "world");

if (mysqli_connect_errno()) {
    printf("Connect failed: %s\n", mysqli_connect_error());
    exit();
}

/* prepare statement */
if ($stmt = $mysqli->prepare("SELECT Code, Name FROM Country ORDER BY Name LIMIT
    5")) { $stmt->execute();

    /* bind variables to prepared statement */
    $stmt->bind_result($col1, $col2);

    /* fetch values */
    while ($stmt->fetch()) {
        printf("%s %s\n", $col1, $col2);
    }

    /* close statement */
    $stmt->close();
}
/* close connection */
$mysqli->close();

?>
```

Example 3.77 Procedural style

```php
<?php
$link = mysqli_connect("localhost", "my_user", "my_password", "world");

/* check connection */
if (!$link) {
    printf("Connect failed: %s\n", mysqli_connect_error());
    exit();
}

/* prepare statement */
```

```
if ($stmt = mysqli_prepare($link, "SELECT Code, Name FROM Country ORDER BY Name LIMIT 5"))
  { mysqli_stmt_execute($stmt);

  /* bind variables to prepared statement */
```

166

```
    mysqli_stmt_bind_result($stmt, $col1, $col2);

    /* fetch values */
    while (mysqli_stmt_fetch($stmt)) {
        printf("%s %s\n", $col1, $col2);
    }

    /* close statement */
    mysqli_stmt_close($stmt);
}

/* close connection */
mysqli_close($link);
?>
```

The above examples will output:

```
AFG Afghanistan
ALB Albania
DZA Algeria
ASM American Samoa
AND Andorra
```

See Also

mysqli_stmt_get_result
mysqli_stmt_bind_param
mysqli_stmt_execute
mysqli_stmt_fetch
mysqli_prepare
mysqli_stmt_prepare
mysqli_stmt_init
mysqli_stmt_errno
mysqli_stmt_error

3.10.6 mysqli_stmt::close, mysqli_stmt_close

- mysqli_stmt::close

mysqli_stmt_close

Closes a prepared statement

Description

Object oriented style

```
bool mysqli_stmt::close();
```

Procedural style

```
bool mysqli_stmt_close(
```

678

mysqli_stmt stmt);

Closes a prepared statement. mysqli_stmt_close also deallocates the statement handle. If the current statement has pending or unread results, this function cancels them so that the next query can be executed.

Parameters

stmt   Procedural style only: A statement identifier returned by
                                               mysqli_stmt_init.

Return Values

Returns TRUE on success or FALSE on failure.

See Also

mysqli_prepare

3.10.7 mysqli_stmt::__construct

- mysqli_stmt::__construct

    Constructs a new mysqli_stmt object

Description

```
mysqli_stmt::__construct(
    mysqli link,
    string query);
```

This method constructs a new mysqli_stmt object.

> **Note**
>
> In general, you should use either mysqli_prepare or mysqli_stmt_init to create a mysqli_stmt object, rather than directly instantiating the object with new mysqli_stmt. This method (and the ability to directly instantiate mysqli_stmt objects) may be deprecated and removed in the future.

Parameters

link   Procedural style only: A link identifier returned by mysqli_connect or
                                               mysqli_init

query   The query, as a string. If this parameter is omitted, then the constructor
                                               behaves identically to mysqli_stmt_init, if provided, then it behaves
                                               as per mysqli_prepare.

See Also

mysqli_prepare
mysqli_stmt_init

3.10.8 mysqli_stmt::data_seek, mysqli_stmt_data_seek

- mysqli_stmt::data_seek

mysqli_stmt_data_seek

Seeks to an arbitrary row in statement result set

Description

Object oriented style

```
void mysqli_stmt::data_seek(
    int offset);
```

Procedural style

```
void mysqli_stmt_data_seek(
    mysqli_stmt stmt,
    int offset);
```

Seeks to an arbitrary result pointer in the statement result set.

mysqli_stmt_store_result must be called prior to mysqli_stmt_data_seek.

Parameters

stmt	Procedural style only: A statement identifier returned by mysqli_stmt_init.
offset	Must be between zero and the total number of rows minus one (0.. mysqli_stmt_num_rows - 1).

Return Values

No value is returned.

Examples

Example 3.78 Object oriented style

```php
<?php
/* Open a connection */
$mysqli = new mysqli("localhost", "my_user", "my_password", "world");

/* check connection */
if (mysqli_connect_errno()) {
    printf("Connect failed: %s\n", mysqli_connect_error());
    exit();
}

$query = "SELECT Name, CountryCode FROM City ORDER BY
Name"; if ($stmt = $mysqli->prepare($query)) {

    /* execute query */
    $stmt->execute();

    /* bind result variables */
    $stmt->bind_result($name, $code);

    /* store result */
```

681

```
$stmt->store_result();
```

16
9

```
    /* seek to row no. 400 */
    $stmt->data_seek(399);

    /* fetch values */
    $stmt->fetch();

    printf ("City: %s        Countrycode: %s\n", $name, $code);

    /* close statement */
    $stmt->close();
}

/* close connection */
$mysqli->close();
?>
```

Example 3.79 Procedural style

```
<?php
/* Open a connection */
$link = mysqli_connect("localhost", "my_user", "my_password", "world");

/* check connection */
if (mysqli_connect_errno()) {
    printf("Connect failed: %s\n", mysqli_connect_error());
    exit();
}

$query = "SELECT Name, CountryCode FROM City ORDER BY
Name"; if ($stmt = mysqli_prepare($link, $query)) {

    /* execute query */
    mysqli_stmt_execute($stmt);

    /* bind result variables */
    mysqli_stmt_bind_result($stmt, $name, $code);

    /* store result */
    mysqli_stmt_store_result($stmt);

    /* seek to row no. 400 */
    mysqli_stmt_data_seek($stmt, 399);

    /* fetch values */
    mysqli_stmt_fetch($stmt);

    printf ("City: %s        Countrycode: %s\n", $name, $code);

    /* close statement */
    mysqli_stmt_close($stmt);
}

/* close connection */
mysqli_close($link);
?>
```

The above examples will output:

170

City: Benin City   Countrycode: NGA

See Also

mysqli_prepare

3.10.9 mysqli_stmt::$errno, mysqli_stmt_errno

- mysqli_stmt::$errno

mysqli_stmt_errno

> Returns the error code for the most recent statement call

Description

Object oriented style

```
int
    mysqli_stmt->errno ;
```

Procedural style

```
int mysqli_stmt_errno(
    mysqli_stmt stmt);
```

Returns the error code for the most recently invoked statement function that can succeed or fail.

Client error message numbers are listed in the MySQL errmsg.h header file, server error message numbers are listed in mysqld_error.h. In the MySQL source distribution you can find a complete list of error messages and error numbers in the file Docs/mysqld_error.txt.

Parameters

stmt   Procedural style only: A statement identifier returned by
                                  mysqli_stmt_init.

Return Values

An error code value. Zero means no error occurred.

Examples

Example 3.80 Object oriented style

```php
<?php
/* Open a connection */
$mysqli = new mysqli("localhost", "my_user", "my_password", "world");

/* check connection */
if (mysqli_connect_errno()) {
    printf("Connect failed: %s\n", mysqli_connect_error());
    exit();
}
```

```php
$mysqli->query("CREATE TABLE myCountry LIKE Country");
$mysqli->query("INSERT INTO myCountry SELECT * FROM Country");

$query = "SELECT Name, Code FROM myCountry ORDER BY
Name"; if ($stmt = $mysqli->prepare($query)) {

    /* drop table */
    $mysqli->query("DROP TABLE myCountry");

    /* execute query */
    $stmt->execute();

    printf("Error: %d.\n", $stmt->errno);

    /* close statement */
    $stmt->close();
}

/* close connection */
$mysqli->close();
?>
```

Example 3.81 Procedural style

```php
<?php
/* Open a connection */
$link = mysqli_connect("localhost", "my_user", "my_password", "world");

/* check connection */
if (mysqli_connect_errno()) {
    printf("Connect failed: %s\n", mysqli_connect_error());
    exit();
}

mysqli_query($link, "CREATE TABLE myCountry LIKE Country");
mysqli_query($link, "INSERT INTO myCountry SELECT * FROM Country");

$query = "SELECT Name, Code FROM myCountry ORDER BY
Name"; if ($stmt = mysqli_prepare($link, $query)) {

    /* drop table */
    mysqli_query($link, "DROP TABLE myCountry");

    /* execute query */
    mysqli_stmt_execute($stmt);

    printf("Error: %d.\n", mysqli_stmt_errno($stmt));

    /* close statement */
    mysqli_stmt_close($stmt);
}

/* close connection */
mysqli_close($link);
?>
```

The above examples will output:

172

Error: 1146.

See Also

mysqli_stmt_error
mysqli_stmt_sqlstate

3.10.10 mysqli_stmt::$error_list, mysqli_stmt_error_list

• mysqli_stmt::$error_list

mysqli_stmt_error_list

Returns a list of errors from the last statement executed

Description

Object oriented style

```
array
    mysqli_stmt->error_list ;
```

Procedural style

```
array mysqli_stmt_error_list(
    mysqli_stmt stmt);
```

Returns an array of errors for the most recently invoked statement function that can succeed or fail.

Parameters

stmt   Procedural style only: A statement identifier returned by
                              mysqli_stmt_init.

Return Values

A list of errors, each as an associative array containing the errno, error, and sqlstate.

Examples

Example 3.82 Object oriented style

```php
<?php
/* Open a connection */
$mysqli = new mysqli("localhost", "my_user", "my_password", "world");

/* check connection */
if (mysqli_connect_errno()) {
    printf("Connect failed: %s\n", mysqli_connect_error());
    exit();
}

$mysqli->query("CREATE TABLE myCountry LIKE Country");
$mysqli->query("INSERT INTO myCountry SELECT * FROM Country");
```

```
$query = "SELECT Name, Code FROM myCountry ORDER BY
Name"; if ($stmt = $mysqli->prepare($query)) {

    /* drop table */
    $mysqli->query("DROP TABLE myCountry");

    /* execute query */
    $stmt->execute();

    echo "Error:\n";
    print_r($stmt->error_list);

    /* close statement */
    $stmt->close();
}

/* close connection */
$mysqli->close();
?>
```

Example 3.83 Procedural style

```
<?php
/* Open a connection */
$link = mysqli_connect("localhost", "my_user", "my_password", "world");

/* check connection */
if (mysqli_connect_errno()) {
    printf("Connect failed: %s\n", mysqli_connect_error());
    exit();
}

mysqli_query($link, "CREATE TABLE myCountry LIKE Country");
mysqli_query($link, "INSERT INTO myCountry SELECT * FROM Country");

$query = "SELECT Name, Code FROM myCountry ORDER BY
Name"; if ($stmt = mysqli_prepare($link, $query)) {

    /* drop table */
    mysqli_query($link, "DROP TABLE myCountry");

    /* execute query */
    mysqli_stmt_execute($stmt);

    echo "Error:\n";
    print_r(mysql_stmt_error_list($stmt));

    /* close statement */
    mysqli_stmt_close($stmt);
}

/* close connection */
mysqli_close($link);
?>
```

The above examples will output:

174

```
Array
(
    => Array
        (
            [errno] => 1146
            [sqlstate] => 42S02
            [error] => Table 'world.myCountry' doesn't exist
        )

)
```

See Also

mysqli_stmt_error
mysqli_stmt_errno
mysqli_stmt_sqlstate

3.10.11 mysqli_stmt::$error, mysqli_stmt_error

• mysqli_stmt::$error

mysqli_stmt_error

Returns a string description for last statement error

Description

Object oriented style

```
string
    mysqli_stmt->error ;
```

Procedural style

```
string mysqli_stmt_error(
    mysqli_stmt stmt);
```

Returns a string containing the error message for the most recently invoked statement function that can succeed or fail.

Parameters

stmt   Procedural style only: A statement identifier returned by
                                mysqli_stmt_init.

Return Values

A string that describes the error. An empty string if no error occurred.

Examples

Example 3.84 Object oriented style

```php
<?php
/* Open a connection */
$mysqli = new mysqli("localhost", "my_user", "my_password", "world");

/* check connection */
if (mysqli_connect_errno()) {
    printf("Connect failed: %s\n", mysqli_connect_error());
    exit();
}

$mysqli->query("CREATE TABLE myCountry LIKE Country");
$mysqli->query("INSERT INTO myCountry SELECT * FROM Country");


$query = "SELECT Name, Code FROM myCountry ORDER BY
Name"; if ($stmt = $mysqli->prepare($query)) {

    /* drop table */
    $mysqli->query("DROP TABLE myCountry");

    /* execute query */
    $stmt->execute();

    printf("Error: %s.\n", $stmt->error);

    /* close statement */
    $stmt->close();
}

/* close connection */
$mysqli->close();
?>
```

Example 3.85 Procedural style

```php
<?php
/* Open a connection */
$link = mysqli_connect("localhost", "my_user", "my_password", "world");

/* check connection */
if (mysqli_connect_errno()) {
    printf("Connect failed: %s\n", mysqli_connect_error());
    exit();
}

mysqli_query($link, "CREATE TABLE myCountry LIKE Country");
mysqli_query($link, "INSERT INTO myCountry SELECT * FROM Country");


$query = "SELECT Name, Code FROM myCountry ORDER BY
Name"; if ($stmt = mysqli_prepare($link, $query)) {

    /* drop table */
    mysqli_query($link, "DROP TABLE myCountry");

    /* execute query */
```

```
    mysqli_stmt_execute($stmt);

    printf("Error: %s.\n", mysqli_stmt_error($stmt));

    /* close statement */
    mysqli_stmt_close($stmt);
}
```

176 _____

```
/* close connection */
mysqli_close($link);
?>
```

The above examples will output:

```
Error: Table 'world.myCountry' doesn't exist.
```

See Also

mysqli_stmt_errno
mysqli_stmt_sqlstate

3.10.12 mysqli_stmt::execute, mysqli_stmt_execute

* mysqli_stmt::execute

mysqli_stmt_execute

Executes a prepared Query

Description

Object oriented style

```
bool mysqli_stmt::execute();
```

Procedural style

```
bool mysqli_stmt_execute(
    mysqli_stmt stmt);
```

Executes a query that has been previously prepared using the mysqli_prepare function. When executed any parameter markers which exist will automatically be replaced with the appropriate data.

If the statement is UPDATE, DELETE, or INSERT, the total number of affected rows can be determined by using the mysqli_stmt_affected_rows function. Likewise, if the query yields a result set the mysqli_stmt_fetch function is used.

> **Note**
>
> When using mysqli_stmt_execute, the mysqli_stmt_fetch function must be used to fetch the data prior to performing any additional queries.

Parameters

stmt   Procedural style only: A statement identifier returned by
                                    mysqli_stmt_init.

Return Values

Returns TRUE on success or FALSE on failure.

Examples

Example 3.86 Object oriented style

```php
<?php
$mysqli = new mysqli("localhost", "my_user", "my_password", "world");

/* check connection */
if (mysqli_connect_errno()) {
    printf("Connect failed: %s\n", mysqli_connect_error());
    exit();
}

$mysqli->query("CREATE TABLE myCity LIKE City");

/* Prepare an insert statement */
$query = "INSERT INTO myCity (Name, CountryCode, District) VALUES (?,?,?)";
$stmt = $mysqli->prepare($query);

$stmt->bind_param("sss", $val1, $val2, $val3);

$val1 = 'Stuttgart';
$val2 = 'DEU';
$val3 = 'Baden-Wuerttemberg';

/* Execute the statement */
$stmt->execute();

$val1 = 'Bordeaux';
$val2 = 'FRA';
$val3 = 'Aquitaine';

/* Execute the statement */
$stmt->execute();

/* close statement */
$stmt->close();

/* retrieve all rows from myCity */
$query = "SELECT Name, CountryCode, District FROM
myCity"; if ($result = $mysqli->query($query)) {
    while ($row = $result->fetch_row()) {
        printf("%s (%s,%s)\n", $row[0], $row[1], $row[2]);
    }
    /* free result set */
    $result->close();
}

/* remove table */
$mysqli->query("DROP TABLE myCity");

/* close connection */
$mysqli->close();
?>
```

Example 3.87 Procedural style

```php
<?php
```

178

```php
$link = mysqli_connect("localhost", "my_user", "my_password", "world");

/* check connection */
if (mysqli_connect_errno()) {
    printf("Connect failed: %s\n", mysqli_connect_error());
    exit();
}

mysqli_query($link, "CREATE TABLE myCity LIKE City");

/* Prepare an insert statement */
$query = "INSERT INTO myCity (Name, CountryCode, District) VALUES (?,?,?)";
$stmt = mysqli_prepare($link, $query);

mysqli_stmt_bind_param($stmt, "sss", $val1, $val2, $val3);

$val1 = 'Stuttgart';
$val2 = 'DEU';
$val3 = 'Baden-Wuerttemberg';

/* Execute the statement */
mysqli_stmt_execute($stmt);

$val1 = 'Bordeaux';
$val2 = 'FRA';
$val3 = 'Aquitaine';

/* Execute the statement */
mysqli_stmt_execute($stmt);

/* close statement */
mysqli_stmt_close($stmt);

/* retrieve all rows from myCity */
$query = "SELECT Name, CountryCode, District FROM
myCity"; if ($result = mysqli_query($link, $query)) {
    while ($row = mysqli_fetch_row($result)) {
        printf("%s (%s,%s)\n", $row[0], $row[1], $row[2]);
    }
    /* free result set */
    mysqli_free_result($result);
}

/* remove table */
mysqli_query($link, "DROP TABLE myCity");

/* close connection */
mysqli_close($link);
?>
```

The above examples will output:

```
Stuttgart (DEU,Baden-Wuerttemberg)
Bordeaux (FRA,Aquitaine)
```

See Also

mysqli_prepare
mysqli_stmt_bind_param
mysqli_stmt_get_result

17
9

3.10.13 mysqli_stmt::fetch, mysqli_stmt_fetch

* mysqli_stmt::fetch

mysqli_stmt_fetch

Fetch results from a prepared statement into the bound variables

Description

Object oriented style

```
bool mysqli_stmt::fetch();
```

Procedural style

```
bool mysqli_stmt_fetch(
    mysqli_stmt stmt);
```

Fetch the result from a prepared statement into the variables bound by mysqli_stmt_bind_result.

> **Note**
>
> Note that all columns must be bound by the application before calling mysqli_stmt_fetch.

> **Note**
>
> Data are transferred unbuffered without calling mysqli_stmt_store_result which can decrease performance (but reduces memory cost).

Parameters

stmt Procedural style only: A statement identifier returned by mysqli_stmt_init.

Return Values

Table 3.15 Return Values

Value	Description
TRUE	Success. Data has been fetched
FALSE	Error occurred
NULL	No more rows/data exists or data truncation occurred

Examples

Example 3.88 Object oriented style

```php
<?php
$mysqli = new mysqli("localhost", "my_user", "my_password", "world");
```

703

```php
/* check connection */
if (mysqli_connect_errno()) {
    printf("Connect failed: %s\n", mysqli_connect_error());
    exit();
}

$query = "SELECT Name, CountryCode FROM City ORDER by ID DESC LIMIT 150,5";

if ($stmt = $mysqli->prepare($query)) {

    /* execute statement */
    $stmt->execute();

    /* bind result variables */
    $stmt->bind_result($name, $code);

    /* fetch values */
    while ($stmt->fetch()) {
        printf ("%s (%s)\n", $name, $code);
    }

    /* close statement */
    $stmt->close();
}

/* close connection */
$mysqli->close();
?>
```

Example 3.89 Procedural style

```php
<?php
$link = mysqli_connect("localhost", "my_user", "my_password", "world");

/* check connection */
if (mysqli_connect_errno()) {
    printf("Connect failed: %s\n", mysqli_connect_error());
    exit();
}

$query = "SELECT Name, CountryCode FROM City ORDER by ID DESC LIMIT 150,5";

if ($stmt = mysqli_prepare($link, $query)) {

    /* execute statement */
    mysqli_stmt_execute($stmt);

    /* bind result variables */
    mysqli_stmt_bind_result($stmt, $name, $code);

    /* fetch values */
    while (mysqli_stmt_fetch($stmt)) {
        printf ("%s (%s)\n", $name, $code);
    }

    /* close statement */
```

```
    mysqli_stmt_close($stmt);
}

/* close connection */
mysqli_close($link);
?>
```

18
1

The above examples will output:

```
Rockford (USA)
Tallahassee (USA)
Salinas (USA)
Santa Clarita (USA)
Springfield (USA)
```

See Also

mysqli_prepare
mysqli_stmt_errno
mysqli_stmt_error
mysqli_stmt_bind_result

3.10.14 mysqli_stmt::$field_count, mysqli_stmt_field_count

* mysqli_stmt::$field_count

mysqli_stmt_field_count

Returns the number of field in the given statement

Description

Object oriented style

```
int
    mysqli_stmt->field_count ;
```

Procedural style

```
int mysqli_stmt_field_count(
    mysqli_stmt stmt);
```

Warning

This function is currently not documented; only its argument list is available.

3.10.15 mysqli_stmt::free_result, mysqli_stmt_free_result

* mysqli_stmt::free_result

mysqli_stmt_free_result

Frees stored result memory for the given statement handle

Description

Object oriented style

```
void mysqli_stmt::free_result();
```

Procedural style

```
void mysqli_stmt_free_result(
    mysqli_stmt stmt);
```

Frees the result memory associated with the statement, which was allocated by mysqli_stmt_store_result.

Parameters

stmt   Procedural style only: A statement identifier returned by mysqli_stmt_init.

Return Values

No value is returned.

See Also

mysqli_stmt_store_result

3.10.16 mysqli_stmt::get_result, mysqli_stmt_get_result

- mysqli_stmt::get_result

mysqli_stmt_get_result

Gets a result set from a prepared statement

Description

Object oriented style

```
mysqli_result mysqli_stmt::get_result();
```

Procedural style

```
mysqli_result mysqli_stmt_get_result(
    mysqli_stmt stmt);
```

Call to return a result set from a prepared statement query.

Parameters

stmt   Procedural style only: A statement identifier returned by mysqli_stmt_init.

Return Values

Returns a resultset for successful SELECT queries, or FALSE for other DML queries or on failure. The mysqli_errno function can be used to distinguish between the two types of failure.

MySQL Native Driver Only

Available only with mysqlnd.

Examples

Example 3.90 Object oriented style

```php
<?php

$mysqli = new mysqli("127.0.0.1", "user", "password", "world");

if($mysqli->connect_error)
{
    die("$mysqli->connect_errno: $mysqli->connect_error");
}

$query = "SELECT Name, Population, Continent FROM Country WHERE Continent=? ORDER BY Name
LIMIT 1";

$stmt = $mysqli->stmt_init();
if(!$stmt->prepare($query))
{
    print "Failed to prepare statement\n";
}
else
{
    $stmt->bind_param("s", $continent);

    $continent_array = array('Europe','Africa','Asia','North America');

    foreach($continent_array as $continent)
    {
        $stmt->execute();
        $result = $stmt->get_result();
        while ($row = $result->fetch_array(MYSQLI_NUM))
        {
            foreach ($row as $r)
            {
                print "$r ";
            }
            print "\n";
        }
    }
}

$stmt->close();
$mysqli->close();
?>
```

Example 3.91 Procedural style

```php
<?php

$link = mysqli_connect("127.0.0.1", "user", "password", "world");

if (!$link)
```

```
{
    $error = mysqli_connect_error();
    $errno = mysqli_connect_errno();
    print "$errno: $error\n";
    exit();
}

$query = "SELECT Name, Population, Continent FROM Country WHERE Continent=? ORDER BY Name
LIMIT 1";
```

```
$stmt = mysqli_stmt_init($link);
if(!mysqli_stmt_prepare($stmt, $query))
{
    print "Failed to prepare statement\n";
}
else
{
    mysqli_stmt_bind_param($stmt, "s", $continent);

    $continent_array = array('Europe','Africa','Asia','North America');

    foreach($continent_array as $continent)
    {
        mysqli_stmt_execute($stmt);
        $result = mysqli_stmt_get_result($stmt);
        while ($row = mysqli_fetch_array($result, MYSQLI_NUM))
        {
            foreach ($row as $r)
            {
                print "$r ";
            }
            print "\n";
        }
    }
}
mysqli_stmt_close($stmt);
mysqli_close($link);
?>
```

The above examples will output:

```
Albania 3401200 Europe
Algeria 31471000 Africa
Afghanistan 22720000 Asia
Anguilla 8000 North America
```

See Also

mysqli_prepare
mysqli_stmt_result_metadata

3.10.17 mysqli_stmt::get_warnings, mysqli_stmt_get_warnings

- mysqli_stmt::get_warnings

mysqli_stmt_get_warnings

Object oriented style

```
object mysqli_stmt::get_warnings();
```

Procedural style

```
object mysqli_stmt_get_warnings(
    mysqli_stmt stmt);
```

Warning

This function is currently not documented; only its argument list is available.

3.10.18 mysqli_stmt::$insert_id, mysqli_stmt_insert_id

* mysqli_stmt::$insert_id

mysqli_stmt_insert_id

Get the ID generated from the previous INSERT operation

Description

Object oriented style

```
int
    mysqli_stmt->insert_id ;
```

Procedural style

```
mixed mysqli_stmt_insert_id(
    mysqli_stmt stmt);
```

Warning

This function is currently not documented; only its argument list is available.

3.10.19 mysqli_stmt::more_results, mysqli_stmt_more_results

* mysqli_stmt::more_results

mysqli_stmt_more_results

Check if there are more query results from a multiple query

Description

Object oriented style (method):

```
public bool mysqli_stmt::more_results();
```

Procedural style:

```
bool mysqli_stmt_more_results(
    mysql_stmt stmt);
```

Checks if there are more query results from a multiple query.

Parameters

stmt   Procedural style only: A statement identifier returned by
                                  mysqli_stmt_init.

Return Values

Returns TRUE if more results exist, otherwise FALSE.

MySQL Native Driver Only

Available only with mysqlnd.

See Also

mysqli_stmt::next_result
mysqli::multi_query

3.10.20 mysqli_stmt::next_result, mysqli_stmt_next_result

* mysqli_stmt::next_result

mysqli_stmt_next_result

Reads the next result from a multiple query

Description

Object oriented style (method):

```
public bool mysqli_stmt::next_result();
```

Procedural style:

```
bool mysqli_stmt_next_result(
    mysql_stmt stmt);
```

Reads the next result from a multiple query.

Parameters

stmt   Procedural style only: A statement identifier returned by
                                  mysqli_stmt_init.

Return Values

Returns TRUE on success or FALSE on failure.

Errors/Exceptions

Emits an E_STRICT level error if a result set does not exist, and suggests using
          mysqli_stmt::more_results in these cases, before calling mysqli_stmt::next_result.

MySQL Native Driver Only

Available only with mysqlnd.

See Also

mysqli_stmt::more_results
mysqli::multi_query

3.10.21 mysqli_stmt::$num_rows, mysqli_stmt::num_rows, mysqli_stmt_num_rows

• mysqli_stmt::$num_rows

mysqli_stmt::num_rows

mysqli_stmt_num_rows

Return the number of rows in statements result set

Description

Object oriented style

```
int
    mysqli_stmt->num_rows ;
```

```
int mysqli_stmt::num_rows();
```

Procedural style

```
int mysqli_stmt_num_rows(
    mysqli_stmt stmt);
```

Returns the number of rows in the result set. The use of mysqli_stmt_num_rows depends on whether or not you used mysqli_stmt_store_result to buffer the entire result set in the statement handle.

If you use mysqli_stmt_store_result, mysqli_stmt_num_rows may be called immediately.

Parameters

stmt   Procedural style only: A statement identifier returned by
                                        mysqli_stmt_init.

Return Values

An integer representing the number of rows in result set.

Examples

Example 3.92 Object oriented style

```php
<?php
/* Open a connection */
$mysqli = new mysqli("localhost", "my_user", "my_password", "world");

/* check connection */
```

188

```php
if (mysqli_connect_errno()) {
    printf("Connect failed: %s\n", mysqli_connect_error());
    exit();
}

$query = "SELECT Name, CountryCode FROM City ORDER BY Name LIMIT
20"; if ($stmt = $mysqli->prepare($query)) {

    /* execute query */
    $stmt->execute();

    /* store result */
    $stmt->store_result();

    printf("Number of rows: %d.\n", $stmt->num_rows);

    /* close statement */
    $stmt->close();
}
/* close connection */
$mysqli->close();
?>
```

Example 3.93 Procedural style

```php
<?php
/* Open a connection */
$link = mysqli_connect("localhost", "my_user", "my_password", "world");

/* check connection */
if (mysqli_connect_errno()) {
    printf("Connect failed: %s\n", mysqli_connect_error());
    exit();
}

$query = "SELECT Name, CountryCode FROM City ORDER BY Name LIMIT
20"; if ($stmt = mysqli_prepare($link, $query)) {

    /* execute query */
    mysqli_stmt_execute($stmt);

    /* store result */
    mysqli_stmt_store_result($stmt);

    printf("Number of rows: %d.\n", mysqli_stmt_num_rows($stmt));

    /* close statement */
    mysqli_stmt_close($stmt);
}
/* close connection */
mysqli_close($link);
?>
```

The above examples will output:

Number of rows: 20.

$$\begin{array}{r} \hline 18 \\ 9 \end{array}$$

See Also

mysqli_stmt_affected_rows
mysqli_prepare
mysqli_stmt_store_result

3.10.22 mysqli_stmt::$param_count, mysqli_stmt_param_count

• mysqli_stmt::$param_count

mysqli_stmt_param_count

Returns the number of parameter for the given statement

Description

Object oriented style

```
int
    mysqli_stmt->param_count ;
```

Procedural style

```
int mysqli_stmt_param_count(
    mysqli_stmt stmt);
```

Returns the number of parameter markers present in the prepared statement.

Parameters

stmt   Procedural style only: A statement identifier returned by
                                mysqli_stmt_init.

Return Values

Returns an integer representing the number of parameters.

Examples

Example 3.94 Object oriented style

```php
<?php
$mysqli = new mysqli("localhost", "my_user", "my_password", "world");

/* check connection */
if (mysqli_connect_errno()) {
    printf("Connect failed: %s\n", mysqli_connect_error());
    exit();
}

if ($stmt = $mysqli->prepare("SELECT Name FROM Country WHERE Name=? OR Code=?")) {

    $marker = $stmt->param_count;
    printf("Statement has %d markers.\n", $marker);

    /* close statement */
```

```
    $stmt->close();
}

/* close connection */
$mysqli->close();
?>
```

Example 3.95 Procedural style

```
<?php
$link = mysqli_connect("localhost", "my_user", "my_password", "world");

/* check connection */
if (mysqli_connect_errno()) {
    printf("Connect failed: %s\n", mysqli_connect_error());
    exit();
}

if ($stmt = mysqli_prepare($link, "SELECT Name FROM Country WHERE Name=? OR Code=?")) {

    $marker = mysqli_stmt_param_count($stmt);
    printf("Statement has %d markers.\n", $marker);

    /* close statement */
    mysqli_stmt_close($stmt);
}

/* close connection */
mysqli_close($link);
?>
```

The above examples will output:

```
Statement has 2 markers.
```

See Also

mysqli_prepare

3.10.23 mysqli_stmt::prepare, mysqli_stmt_prepare

• mysqli_stmt::prepare

mysqli_stmt_prepare

> Prepare an SQL statement for execution

Description

Object oriented style

mixed mysqli_stmt::prepare(

```
string query);
```

Procedural style

```
bool mysqli_stmt_prepare(
    mysqli_stmt stmt,
    string query);
```

Prepares the SQL query pointed to by the null-terminated string query.

The parameter markers must be bound to application variables using mysqli_stmt_bind_param and/or mysqli_stmt_bind_result before executing the statement or fetching rows.

> **Note**
>
> In the case where you pass a statement to mysqli_stmt_prepare that is longer than max_allowed_packet of the server, the returned error codes are different depending on whether you are using MySQL Native Driver (mysqlnd) or MySQL Client Library (libmysqlclient). The behavior is as follows:

• mysqlnd on Linux returns an error code of 1153. The error message means "got a packet bigger than max_allowed_packet bytes".

• mysqlnd on Windows returns an error code 2006. This error message means "server has gone away".

• libmysqlclient on all platforms returns an error code 2006. This error message means "server has gone away".

Parameters

stmt	Procedural style only: A statement identifier returned by mysqli_stmt_init.
query	The query, as a string. It must consist of a single SQL statement.
	You can include one or more parameter markers in the SQL statement by embedding question mark (?) characters at the appropriate positions.

> **Note**
>
> You should not add a terminating semicolon or \g to the statement.

> **Note**
>
> The markers are legal only in certain places in SQL statements. For example, they are allowed in the VALUES() list of an INSERT statement (to specify column values for a row), or in a comparison with a column in a WHERE clause to specify a comparison value.
>
> However, they are not allowed for identifiers (such as table or column names), in the select list that names the columns to be returned by a SELECT statement), or to specify both operands of a binary operator such as the = equal sign.

> The latter restriction is necessary because it would be impossible to determine the parameter type. In general, parameters are legal only in Data Manipulation Language (DML) statements, and not in Data Definition Language (DDL) statements.

Return Values

Returns TRUE on success or FALSE on failure.

Examples

Example 3.96 Object oriented style

```php
<?php
$mysqli = new mysqli("localhost", "my_user", "my_password", "world");

/* check connection */
if (mysqli_connect_errno()) {
    printf("Connect failed: %s\n", mysqli_connect_error());
    exit();
}

$city = "Amersfoort";

/* create a prepared statement */
$stmt =  $mysqli->stmt_init();
if ($stmt->prepare("SELECT District FROM City WHERE Name=?")) {

    /* bind parameters for markers */
    $stmt->bind_param("s", $city);

    /* execute query */
    $stmt->execute();

    /* bind result variables */
    $stmt->bind_result($district);

    /* fetch value */
    $stmt->fetch();

    printf("%s is in district %s\n", $city, $district);

    /* close statement */
    $stmt->close();
}

/* close connection */
$mysqli->close();
?>
```

Example 3.97 Procedural style

```php
<?php
$link = mysqli_connect("localhost", "my_user", "my_password", "world");

/* check connection */
if (mysqli_connect_errno()) {
```

```
    printf("Connect failed: %s\n", mysqli_connect_error());
    exit();
}

$city = "Amersfoort";

/* create a prepared statement */
$stmt = mysqli_stmt_init($link);
 if (mysqli_stmt_prepare($stmt, 'SELECT District FROM City WHERE Name=?')) {

    /* bind parameters for markers */
    mysqli_stmt_bind_param($stmt, "s", $city);

    /* execute query */
    mysqli_stmt_execute($stmt);

    /* bind result variables */
    mysqli_stmt_bind_result($stmt, $district);

    /* fetch value */
    mysqli_stmt_fetch($stmt);

    printf("%s is in district %s\n", $city, $district);

    /* close statement */
    mysqli_stmt_close($stmt);
}
/* close connection */
mysqli_close($link);
?>
```

The above examples will output:

Amersfoort is in district Utrecht

See Also

mysqli_stmt_init
mysqli_stmt_execute
mysqli_stmt_fetch
mysqli_stmt_bind_param
mysqli_stmt_bind_result
mysqli_stmt_get_result
mysqli_stmt_close

3.10.24 mysqli_stmt::reset, mysqli_stmt_reset

- mysqli_stmt::reset

mysqli_stmt_reset

Resets a prepared statement

Description

Object oriented style

```
bool mysqli_stmt::reset();
```

Procedural style

```
bool mysqli_stmt_reset(
    mysqli_stmt stmt);
```

Resets a prepared statement on client and server to state after prepare.

It resets the statement on the server, data sent using mysqli_stmt_send_long_data, unbuffered result sets and current errors. It does not clear bindings or stored result sets. Stored result sets will be cleared when executing the prepared statement (or closing it).

To prepare a statement with another query use function mysqli_stmt_prepare.

Parameters

stmt   Procedural style only: A statement identifier returned by
                                   mysqli_stmt_init.

Return Values

Returns TRUE on success or FALSE on failure.

See Also

mysqli_prepare

3.10.25 mysqli_stmt::result_metadata, mysqli_stmt_result_metadata

• mysqli_stmt::result_metadata

mysqli_stmt_result_metadata

Returns result set metadata from a prepared statement

Description

Object oriented style

```
mysqli_result mysqli_stmt::result_metadata();
```

Procedural style

```
mysqli_result mysqli_stmt_result_metadata(
    mysqli_stmt stmt);
```

If a statement passed to mysqli_prepare is one that produces a result set, mysqli_stmt_result_metadata returns the result object that can be used to process the meta information such as total number of fields and individual field information.

> **Note**
>
> This result set pointer can be passed as an argument to any of the field-based functions that process result set metadata, such as:

- mysqli_num_fields

- mysqli_fetch_field

- mysqli_fetch_field_direct

- mysqli_fetch_fields

- mysqli_field_count

- mysqli_field_seek

- mysqli_field_tell

- mysqli_free_result

The result set structure should be freed when you are done with it, which you can do by passing it to mysqli_free_result

Note

The result set returned by mysqli_stmt_result_metadata contains only metadata. It does not contain any row results. The rows are obtained by using the statement handle with mysqli_stmt_fetch.

Parameters

stmt   Procedural style only: A statement identifier returned by mysqli_stmt_init.

Return Values

Returns a result object or FALSE if an error occurred.

Examples

Example 3.98 Object oriented style

```php
<?php
$mysqli = new mysqli("localhost", "my_user", "my_password", "test");

$mysqli->query("DROP TABLE IF EXISTS friends");
$mysqli->query("CREATE TABLE friends (id int, name varchar(20))");

$mysqli->query("INSERT INTO friends VALUES (1,'Hartmut'), (2, 'Ulf')");

$stmt = $mysqli->prepare("SELECT id, name FROM friends");
$stmt->execute();

/* get resultset for metadata */
$result = $stmt->result_metadata();

/* retrieve field information from metadata result set */
$field = $result->fetch_field();

printf("Fieldname: %s\n", $field->name);

/* close resultset */
$result->close();
```

```
/* close connection */
$mysqli->close();
?>
```

Example 3.99 Procedural style

```php
<?php
$link = mysqli_connect("localhost", "my_user", "my_password", "test");

mysqli_query($link, "DROP TABLE IF EXISTS friends");
mysqli_query($link, "CREATE TABLE friends (id int, name varchar(20))");

mysqli_query($link, "INSERT INTO friends VALUES (1,'Hartmut'), (2, 'Ulf')");

$stmt = mysqli_prepare($link, "SELECT id, name FROM friends");
mysqli_stmt_execute($stmt);

/* get resultset for metadata */
$result = mysqli_stmt_result_metadata($stmt);

/* retrieve field information from metadata result set */
$field = mysqli_fetch_field($result);

printf("Fieldname: %s\n", $field->name);

/* close resultset */
mysqli_free_result($result);

/* close connection */
mysqli_close($link);
?>
```

See Also

mysqli_prepare
mysqli_free_result

3.10.26 mysqli_stmt::send_long_data, mysqli_stmt_send_long_data

- mysqli_stmt::send_long_data

mysqli_stmt_send_long_data

Send data in blocks

Description

Object oriented style

```
bool mysqli_stmt::send_long_data(
    int param_nr,
    string data);
```

Procedural style

```
bool mysqli_stmt_send_long_data(
   mysqli_stmt stmt,
   int param_nr,
   string data);
```

Allows to send parameter data to the server in pieces (or chunks), e.g. if the size of a blob exceeds the size of max_allowed_packet. This function can be called multiple times to send the parts of a character or binary data value for a column, which must be one of the TEXT or BLOB datatypes.

Parameters

stmt   Procedural style only: A statement identifier returned by
                             mysqli_stmt_init.

param_nr   Indicates which parameter to associate the data with. Parameters are
                             numbered beginning with 0.

data   A string containing data to be sent.

Return Values

Returns TRUE on success or FALSE on failure.

Examples

Example 3.100 Object oriented style

```php
<?php
$stmt = $mysqli->prepare("INSERT INTO messages (message) VALUES
(?)"); $null = NULL;
$stmt->bind_param("b", $null);
$fp = fopen("messages.txt", "r");
while (!feof($fp)) {
    $stmt->send_long_data(0, fread($fp, 8192));
}
fclose($fp);
$stmt->execute();
?>
```

See Also

mysqli_prepare
mysqli_stmt_bind_param

3.10.27 mysqli_stmt::$sqlstate, mysqli_stmt_sqlstate

• mysqli_stmt::$sqlstate

mysqli_stmt_sqlstate

Returns SQLSTATE error from previous statement operation

Description

Object oriented style

```
string
    mysqli_stmt->sqlstate ;
```

Procedural style

```
string mysqli_stmt_sqlstate(
    mysqli_stmt stmt);
```

Returns a string containing the SQLSTATE error code for the most recently invoked prepared statement function that can succeed or fail. The error code consists of five characters. '00000' means no error. The values are specified by ANSI SQL and ODBC. For a list of possible values, see http://dev.mysql.com/doc/mysql/en/error-handling.html.

Parameters

stmt   Procedural style only: A statement identifier returned by
                                  mysqli_stmt_init.

Return Values

Returns a string containing the SQLSTATE error code for the last error. The error code consists of five characters. '00000' means no error.

Notes

> **Note**
>
> Note that not all MySQL errors are yet mapped to SQLSTATE's. The valueHY000 (general error) is used for unmapped errors.

Examples

Example 3.101 Object oriented style

```php
<?php
/* Open a connection */
$mysqli = new mysqli("localhost", "my_user", "my_password", "world");

/* check connection */
if (mysqli_connect_errno()) {
    printf("Connect failed: %s\n", mysqli_connect_error());
    exit();
}

$mysqli->query("CREATE TABLE myCountry LIKE Country");
$mysqli->query("INSERT INTO myCountry SELECT * FROM Country");


$query = "SELECT Name, Code FROM myCountry ORDER BY
Name"; if ($stmt = $mysqli->prepare($query)) {

    /* drop table */
    $mysqli->query("DROP TABLE myCountry");

    /* execute query */
    $stmt->execute();

    printf("Error: %s.\n", $stmt->sqlstate);

    /* close statement */
```

```
    $stmt->close();
}

/* close connection */
$mysqli->close();
?>
```

Example 3.102 Procedural style

```
<?php
/* Open a connection */
$link = mysqli_connect("localhost", "my_user", "my_password", "world");

/* check connection */
if (mysqli_connect_errno()) {
    printf("Connect failed: %s\n", mysqli_connect_error());
    exit();
}

mysqli_query($link, "CREATE TABLE myCountry LIKE Country");
mysqli_query($link, "INSERT INTO myCountry SELECT * FROM Country");


$query = "SELECT Name, Code FROM myCountry ORDER BY
Name"; if ($stmt = mysqli_prepare($link, $query)) {

    /* drop table */
    mysqli_query($link, "DROP TABLE myCountry");

    /* execute query */
    mysqli_stmt_execute($stmt);

    printf("Error: %s.\n", mysqli_stmt_sqlstate($stmt));

    /* close statement */
    mysqli_stmt_close($stmt);
}
/* close connection */
mysqli_close($link);
?>
```

The above examples will output:

```
Error: 42S02.
```

See Also

mysqli_stmt_errno
mysqli_stmt_error

THANK YOU